INVESTING
IN DEMOCRACY

INVESTING IN DEMOCRACY

Engaging Citizens in Collaborative Governance

CARMEN SIRIANNI

BROOKINGS INSTITUTION PRESS
Washington, D.C.

Copyright © 2009
THE BROOKINGS INSTITUTION
1775 Massachusetts Avenue, N.W., Washington, D.C. 20036
www.brookings.edu

Library of Congress Cataloging-in-Publication data

Sirianni, Carmen.
  Investing in democracy : engaging citizens in collaborative governance / Carmen Sirianni.
    p.   cm.
  Includes bibliographical references and index.
  Summary: "Discusses how government can serve as a partner and catalyst for collaborative problem solving. Details three success stories and explains what measures were taken and why they succeeded. Distills eight core design principles that characterize effective collaborative governance and concludes with concrete recommendations for federal policy"— Provided by publisher.
  ISBN 978-0-8157-0313-6 (cloth : alk. paper) —
  ISBN 978-0-8157-0312-9 (pbk. : alk. paper)
  1. Citizenship—United States. 2. Civil society—United States. 3. Civics. 4. Political participation—United States. I. Title.
  JK1759.S59 2009
  323'.0420973—dc22   2009002994

1 3 5 7 9 8 6 4 2

The paper used in this publication meets minimum requirements of the American National Standard for Information Sciences—Permanence of Paper for Printed Library Materials: ANSI Z39.48-1992.

Typeset in Adobe Garamond

Composition by R. Lynn Rivenbark
Macon, Georgia

Printed by R. R. Donnelley
Harrisonburg, Virginia

Contents

Preface

As this book goes to press in November 2008, a historic presidential election has just been decided and a new administration is preparing to take office. The campaign of Senator Barack Obama was historic for many reasons, not the least of which is that he repeatedly appealed to citizens to become active agents of change and bottom-up problem solving for the long run. While all campaigns are by definition partisan and mobilizing, he also appealed to a deeper tradition in American politics in which people with diverse interests, values, and political perspectives can recognize, as he notes in *The Audacity of Hope,* that "we have a stake in one another, and that what binds us together is greater than what drives us apart, and that if enough people believe in the truth of that proposition and act on it, then we might not solve every problem, but we can get something meaningful done."

The campaign of 2008 will, we hope, help reverse the long-term decline in political participation evident in American society for decades. This is most welcome news for the vitality of our democratic institutions, especially if we can continue to meld networked communications with face-to-face organizing in creative ways. The argument of this book, however, is that we are not likely to renew our democracy for the complex challenges ahead unless we also engage citizens in shared governance between elections, especially in those innovative forms of collaborative public problem solving that have been on the rise in recent years. Government can serve as a partner and catalyst for this civic work, as I hope my empirical analyses make clear. Indeed, I argue, government ought to invest in generalizing capacities for democratic collaboration in a far more strategic and sustained manner than it currently does. Although like so many others I was an unabashed partisan in the election of 2008, the argument presented in this book is that the vitality of our democracy ultimately depends on our willingness and ability to find productive ways of working together as citizens and stakeholders of our republic, despite our many differences. For the new administration, collaborative governance presents a historic opportunity to enable the "we" in "Yes we can."

Acknowledgments

The first and most important debt I have incurred is to those several hundred individuals, both within and outside of government, who have helped me understand how collaborative governance works in their communities and through their civic associations and public agencies. They generously provided me time for interviews, shared documents from their files, invited me to planning meetings, and introduced me to colleagues and critics. Some also provided detailed feedback on drafts, to ensure that I got the facts right and understood the full range of diverse perspectives on the ground, and even agreed to let me interrogate them still further. These people are too numerous to thank individually, though many are present in the case narratives and endnotes.

The bulk of this manuscript was written while I was also busy with duties as professor and department chair and thus would not have been possible without much institutional support. Adam Jaffe, dean of arts and sciences at Brandeis University, and Marty Krauss, university provost, deserve special thanks not only for their deep commitment to nurturing a collaborative democratic culture in the university but also for personal and institutional support at critical junctures of the research and writing. The Norman Research Fund at Brandeis provided financial support for fieldwork. To Alan Melchior, Cathy Burack, Della Hughes, Andy Hahn, and Susan Curnan, of the Center for Youth and Communities at Brandeis's

Heller School for Social Policy and Management, I owe a special debt—for scholarly insight, practitioner wisdom, and a welcome home for several related projects. In the Department of Sociology at Brandeis, David Cunningham was generous with his knowledge of social movements, and Judy Hanley with just about everything else. Karen Hansen, my close colleague and dear friend for the past two decades (and now my boss), helped make it all come together. I can never thank her enough.

I have also benefited from the work of various research assistants at Brandeis, both wonderful graduate students and our university's outstanding undergraduates. I especially wish to thank Melissa Bass, Elena Bayrock, Ben Brandzel, Jennifer Girouard, Anna Jaffe-Desnick, Caitlin Nichols, Anastasia Norton, Diana Schor, Alexandra Piñeiros Shields, and Stephanie Sofer.

Several people provided detailed comments on the manuscript and helpful suggestions: Frank Fischer, Lewis Friedland, Archon Fung, Judy Karasik, Matt Leighninger, Kent Portney, Gene Sofer, and Andrea Walsh. Archon also engaged important questions in our regular lunches and teas. Lew Friedland, close collaborator for many years, also helped convene four youth civic engagement conferences in 2001–02 that informed my research in various ways. Andrea, my wife, provided close editing, above and beyond the call of duty, in addition to substantive feedback as a sociologist and cochair of our local community board. I am especially grateful for all her support.

I wish to thank David Mathews and John Dedrick of the Kettering Foundation for supporting a related project and Michael Delli Carpini, Tobi Walker, and the Pew Charitable Trusts for supporting yet another. All provided substantial insight, in addition to research funding.

I received valuable feedback in a variety of settings in which I presented earlier parts of this research and analysis: the Community Involvement Conference, the U.S. Environmental Protection Agency; the Neighborhood Planning Forum, Evans School of Public Affairs, University of Washington; the Behavioral and Social Sciences Working Group, Centers for Disease Control and Prevention; the Maxwell School's Minnowbrook III conference The Future of Public Administration, Public Management, and Public Service around the World; City Year Thought Leaders meetings and superseminar; Strengthening Public Engagement and Knowledge Sharing within and across Federal Agencies, a Champions of Participation conference sponsored by America*Speaks*; the Symposium on Democracy in the Age of Networked Governance, Virginia Tech Institute for Policy and Governance; the Aspen Institute's State of Nonprofit America project; the Civic

Engagement Research Group, Tisch College of Citizenship and Public Service, Tufts University; the Conference on Youth Politics, sponsored by the Center for Information and Research on Civic Learning and Engagement and the Carnegie Corporation of New York; and annual meetings of the American Sociological Association, the American Political Science Association, and the American Planning Association. Editors and reviewers of the *Journal of the American Planning Association, American Behavioral Scientist,* the *Brookings Review,* and the *National Civic Review* also provided valuable feedback. I especially wish to thank Dr. Stephanie Bailey, Roger Bernier, Jeffrey Berry, Gloria Rubio-Cortes, E. J. Dionne, Kayla Meltzer Drogosz, John Forrester, Bill Galston, Cynthia Gibson, Joe Goldman, Colonel Rob Gordon, Lars Hasselblad Torres, Amy Helling, Rob Hollister, Max Klau, Peter Levine, Richard Klosterman, Carolyn Lukensmeyer, Mike McGrath, Marilyn Metzler, Bobby Millstein, Andy Muñoz, Derek Okubo, Susan Ostrander, Kent Portney, Norm Rice, Charlie Rose, Joyce Rothschild, Lester Salamon, David Sawicki, Eva Sørensen, Max Stephenson, and Jim Youniss.

In the later stages of finishing this manuscript, I benefited from feedback on various proposals by a broad range of people involved in several nonpartisan policy projects focused on opportunities created by the 2008 election: Service Nation, the November 5th Coalition, and Strengthening Our Nation's Democracy. Special thanks to John Bridgeman, Stuart Comstock-Gay, Carolyn Lukensmeyer, Alan Khazei, George Mahaffy, Miles Rapaport, Pat Scully, Julie Segal Walters, and Martha McCoy.

I also benefited from discussions with those in the collaborative governance policy cluster that I coordinated within the urban policy committee of the Obama campaign and the broader network of those in the civic engagement, energy and environment policy, and government reform committees. Special thanks to Bob Weissbourd, Rachel Godsil, Harry Boyte, Paul Schmitz, Kirk Emerson, Lisa Bingham, Greg Wolff, Hank Topper, Miles Rapoport, Joe Goldman, Martha McCoy, Matt Leighninger, Jim Diers, Chris Gates, Spencer Overton, Bill Potapchuk, Rich Stolz, Beth Noveck, and the two dozen or so others who helped to generate many interesting ideas. Others contributed to an important postelection analysis of possibilities for leveraging the campaign's innovative field-organizing experience to collaborative governance and leadership development in nonelectoral and nonpartisan settings, especially Marshall Ganz, Jeremy Bird, Nicole Derse, and Dan Grandone. Thanks especially to Jody Kretzmann and John McKnight for hosting this meeting in Chicago. Harry Boyte,

xiv   *Acknowledgments*

with whom I wrote the initial framing essay for the civic engagement group, was an especially close partner throughout, as well as on a good number of related projects over the years. Needless to say, none of these individuals necessarily endorses my analysis or policy proposals.

Mary Kwak has been especially helpful in providing wise guidance on the manuscript. Katherine Kimball provided superb editing. Many thanks also to Janet Walker and others at the Brookings Institution for helping bring this project to completion.

My son, David, provided love and moral support throughout, and even learned to use democratic ideas against me, when (he thought) necessary. That's why David sometimes wins.

1 | Government as Civic Enabler

A 2005 volume entitled *Democracy at Risk* arrived at a conclusion that was as blunt as its title. Pulled together by a prestigious committee of the American Political Science Association under the guidance of Steven Macedo and his colleagues, the book notes that American democracy is at risk because of "an erosion of the activities and capacities of citizenship," which in turn tends to undermine the quality of democratic governance, the legitimacy of self-rule, and the ennobling influence self-governance can have on citizens. Despite some deep and disturbing trends in our society, however, this risk can be substantially reduced by policy design and institutional choice, which "shape the incentives, interests, identities, and capacities of citizens to participate effectively in civic life."[1]

This book attempts to extend the report's argument by examining more fully the ways government can serve as a critical enabler of productive engagement and collaborative problem solving among ordinary citizens, civic associations, and stakeholder groups—and how public policy and administration can be designed to support this involvement. I use the term *citizen* in its normative sense, not to denote a legal or membership status, since the focus here is on the productive public contributions that everyone can make. I argue that government's role as civic enabler is becoming ever more important as public problems grow increasingly complex, stakeholders become ever more diverse, and deep cultural and institutional trends continue to erode civic life. Vibrant self-governance in America today

1

requires that government—local, state, and federal—design policy and invest strategically and systematically in building civic capacity to enable the everyday public work of citizens. I elaborate this in terms of the concept of collaborative governance, theoretically (in chapter 2), empirically (chapters 3 to 5), and with proposed federal policy initiatives (chapter 6).

Democracy in America, of course, entails much more than the forms of collaborative civic problem solving upon which I focus. Democracy includes the full range of voting and campaign activities essential to representative government, even if there are clear downsides to the hyperpartisanship we see today.[2] Also essential to enriching democracy and periodically renewing its institutions have been social movements that operate outside the bounds of normal politics, often forging new identities for civic actors, reframing key public problems, inventing civic practices, and winning new rights.[3] In recent decades, many forms of organized interest group representation, including rising citizen and public interest lobbies, have become important components of a vital democratic system, even though many would call attention to the limits of a democracy dominated by national lobbies.[4] Independent and often contentious community organizing has also been critical for empowering citizens locally and leveraging this power in state and national campaigns.[5] Indeed, independent organizing of various sorts is typically a precondition for robust collaborative designs, even if the frames of advocates may shift in the process.[6] If, according to its ancient Greek derivation, *democracy* means "rule by the people," the organizational ecology of engaging and representing the *demos* has been enormously diverse and ever shifting throughout American history, and citizens and theorists alike have repeatedly contested which configurations best embody the democratic spirit and potential of the times.[7]

Why Government?

Government needs to become a much more strategic, systematic, and effective enabler of civic engagement for several reasons. First, long-term changes in civic organization and culture make it unlikely that capacities for self-government will simply bubble up from the wellsprings of civil society, and they will certainly not come about through the invisible hand of the market. Civic changes have been propelled in many cases by profound and irreversible socioeconomic shifts, such as the replacement of the highly civic-minded World War II generation, increased female participation in the labor force, and the continual spread of technologies that encourage individualized leisure. Second, to the extent that government policies and administrative practices are often implicated in disabling effective and responsible civic action, they will need to become a focus of redesign. If government has become part of the problem, then we need to examine how it can, at minimum, reduce its disabling impacts on citizens and, more ideally, become an energetic partner in renewal. For government to just "get out of people's way" and unleash market or civic forces, or both, hardly represents a serious option. Third, the costs of doing civic democracy well have continued to rise as a result of the increasing complexity of public problems, the diversity of publics and stakeholders, and heightened expectations for voice and inclusion among citizens.

While civic associations and nonprofit funders make invaluable investments in promoting innovation and building civic capacity, and should certainly be encouraged to do so more ambitiously and effectively, their contributions are unlikely to be adequate or strategic enough on their own. The costs of doing civic democracy well are substantial and rising, and government can and should rise to the occasion.

Transformations in Civic Organization and Culture

Certainly a key reason that government needs to play a more robust role as civic enabler is that long-term socioeconomic, civic organizational, and cultural trends have left the supply side seriously wanting. Over the past decade or so, social scientists have offered various explanations for this supply-side deficit. Some accounts are complementary, others are competing, but virtually none sees the problem as easily self-correcting.

In *Bowling Alone* and other writings, Harvard political scientist Robert Putnam advances what has become the most widely known and vigorously debated thesis on American civic life: that social capital—those stocks of social trust, norms, and networks that people can draw upon to solve common problems—has been steadily eroding for a half century owing to generational, technological, and other changes. Many measures of associational membership and political participation reveal clear declines. Electoral participation and political knowledge have decreased, despite overall increases in education, and younger generations lag considerably behind previous ones in this respect. Grassroots volunteering for political parties and party loyalty have declined. Participation in church-related groups and regular attendance at church services over the past twenty years are down by one-fifth—a significant development in light of the importance of churches for incubating civic skills. Union membership has steadily eroded since the 1950s, falling to less than half its peak. Membership in the Federation of Women's Clubs is down by 59 percent since 1964, and in the League of Women Voters by 42 percent since 1969. Membership in fraternal organizations such as the Elks and the Lions is also down significantly, Putnam shows. While volunteering has risen, it happens increasingly on a one-on-one basis rather than through church and community groups. Especially worrisome is the collapse of the activist membership core of civic organizations of all sorts, which witnessed a 45 percent drop from 1985 to 1994 alone—nearly half of America's civic infrastructure obliterated in a single decade.[8]

Neither self-help groups nor social movements have effectively counteracted these trends, according to Putnam. The former are not closely associated with other forms of community involvement, and the latter have generally resulted in professionalized direct-mail organizations with little or no active membership or local chapters. Even when mass membership in organizations that do not rely on face-to-face member interaction and professional associations that have increased along with rising occupational levels are factored in, total associational membership declined significantly between 1974 and 1994 within all educational categories. Other forms of associational ties, such as family and informal neighborhood socializing, have also eroded, as has generalized social trust, which is highly correlated with associational membership.

Deep social transformations underlie these trends, Putnam argues. Accounting for roughly half the decline is the slow but steady replacement of members of the "long civic generation," born between 1910 and 1940 and sharing formative public experiences, such as World War II. Neither the baby boomers nor Gen Xers have maintained similar levels of civic engagement. The technological transformation of leisure, which has led to increasingly private listening and viewing habits, accounts for another 25 percent of the decline. Indeed, the number of hours spent watching TV is, for Putnam, the single most consistent predictor of the decline of civic engagement. Suburbanization, commuting, and sprawl account for another 10 percent of the decline, as do the pressures of time and money, including the increasing movement of women into the labor force, which makes them less available for community involvement.[9]

For Theda Skocpol, the problem is less the depletion of diffuse stocks of social capital than the decline of a specific type of associational structure that provided the genius of American civic life for much of our history. Since the 1960s, a dramatic shift has occurred—away from broad, multitiered civic associations that combined local engagement with state and national advocacy and toward narrow, professionally managed advocacy organizations with few links to genuine membership participation through local chapters and little capacity to mobilize large numbers of citizens in agenda-setting campaigns. The United States became a nation of joiners and organizers, according to Skocpol's *Diminished Democracy*, not through action focused primarily upon local community but by linking to other like-minded citizens organized in multitiered associations—Moose, Elks, Woman's Christian Temperance Union, National Grange—across many states and at the national level. Indeed, the organizational impetus and agenda were typically supplied by national offices and conventions, which in turn provided local recruits with avenues of leadership development upward in the associational structure.

Multitiered associations were thus able to take advantage of the political opportunity structures provided by the federal constitutional system. These associations nurtured civic friendships and socializing, provided charity and group insurance, and fostered virtues of fidelity and honor through elaborate rituals. Through associational affiliations, elite strata interacted with working people and provided the latter with vital leadership skills, such as running meetings and debating public issues. In addition to volunteer provisioning and support campaigns during and after wars, multitiered associations engaged in national moral crusades and policy advocacy. They provided members with a sense of belonging to something bigger than themselves or their local communities. Even amid some of their worst vices of social exclusion and intolerance, these associations inculcated an American identity of republican self-governance and service to the nation.

In Skocpol's view, the decline of classic multitiered associations resulted from multiple factors. As gender and racial norms changed, the solidarities based upon associational segregation of men and women, blacks and whites, dissipated. Patriotic bonds of associational brotherhood declined in the wake of the divisive Vietnam War and professionalization of the military. Educated women, who had been key leaders in cross-class associations, have shifted their involvements increasingly to professional societies as occupational barriers have fallen. Advocacy has been professionalized, and many other professions have shifted from thinking of themselves less as trustees of the community and more as specialized experts. Elites, who have always occupied a disproportionate share of leadership roles in civic associations, no longer have to rise through the ranks or develop the leadership capacities of nonelites to influence policy. The newer advocacy groups are much more inclined than in the past to "do for," rather than "do with," their nonelite counterparts. Because the newer advocacy groups depend much less, if at all, on membership dues, they are less accountable for their actions and often rely for funding on foundations that are even less democratically accountable. Because they depend on impersonal appeals and targeted activation through efficient campaign and communication technologies, messages become increasingly narrowed and public discourse polarized.[10]

Other scholars offer different explanations for long-term civic decline or deficit in the United States, and many contest important issues of measurement, concepts, and overall trends. Sociologist Robert Wuthnow, for instance, finds a much more mixed picture on declines in association memberships, with the lion's share of losses concentrated in more marginalized segments of the population.[11] Political scientist J. Eric Oliver finds that suburban segregation demobilizes citizens and decreases civic capacity for effective metropolitan governance.[12] Economists Dora Costa and Matthew Kahn further confirm that their increased participation in the labor force has made it more difficult for women to maintain previous levels of civic involvement, and they see rising socioeconomic inequality, ethnic heterogeneity, and immigration in some metropolitan areas as the biggest factors in the erosion of social capital.[13] Putnam's more recent analysis from the Social Capital Community Benchmark Survey similarly finds that higher ethnic diversity lowers social capital on a variety of measures, such as trust and expectations that people will cooperate to solve common problems. More surprisingly, these negative impacts, at least in the short to medium term, apply to both bonding (within-group) and bridging (across-group) social capital.[14] For political scientists Wendy Rahn and John Transue, increasingly materialistic values among youth are eroding social trust.[15] The most ambitious study of generational shifts in participation in the United States, conducted by Cliff Zukin and his colleagues, finds an increasing split between declining political engagement among youth and their rising volunteer and community service activity.[16]

It is not my purpose here to adjudicate this lively and rich debate. Indeed, this overview merely scratches the surface of the empirical and analytical issues involved.[17] It is critical to recognize, however, that the socioeconomic and cultural factors implicated, in one way or another, in these and other accounts are not ones that can easily be reversed in the short to medium term, if at all. The civic-minded generation from World War II is disappearing, as are the gender and racial solidarities underlying the old multitiered associations. The technological transformation of leisure is, if anything, becoming more deeply embedded with the spread of the iPod and similar devices. The participation of women in the labor market is unlikely to be reversed significantly, though we certainly should be able to design working-time options that better accommodate and encourage civic participation.[18] Ethnic heterogeneity is not likely to diminish anytime soon, even if immigration were suddenly closed off, since immigrant communities already here tend to have higher birthrates than other groups. Although rising inequality could and should be addressed more vigorously through social and economic policy, its reduction will undoubtedly be a long and difficult process. Even if some forms of fluid, informal, and "loose connections" may have increased in recent decades, there is good reason to doubt that these are as conducive to the pursuit of collective goals and public problem solving as the organizational forms that they have been replacing both in the United States and in other countries.[19]

The Internet, of course, offers some genuine possibilities for enhancement of civic voice, especially when combined with face-to-face organizing, as the 2008 presidential campaign of Senator Barack Obama clearly demonstrates. The Internet also can serve as an important tool for collaborative planning and democratic problem solving, as is demonstrated in the case study chapters that follow. On the other hand, as Cass Sunstein argues, it can also promote the kind of "information cocoons" and "cybercascades" that further exacerbate group polarization.[20] We will not automatically be rescued by technology; rather, we will have to design and use technology to support collaborative democratic governance.

To be sure, even in the face of some forms of decline, civic innovation has proceeded on a number of important fronts in recent decades, as Lewis Friedland and I demonstrate in *Civic Innovation in America* (2001) and as Robert Putnam and Lewis Feldstein, among others, have also subsequently shown.[21] The growth in young people's volunteering and community problem solving may also provide a more solid foundation for new forms of collaborative governance if policy and institutional design can establish more effective links between service and the democratic polity, especially with the most recent increase in youth voting. As Zukin and his colleagues note, however, this will require a "conscious, collective, and systematic effort to provide young Americans with the motivation, skills, and opportunities to participate in politics."[22] If government can play an important role in this systematic effort, then clearly it should.

Government as Civic Disabler

A second reason to focus on the potential role of government as a civic enabler is that government too often functions to do exactly the opposite: disabling civic problem solving by putting up too many barriers, not providing the right incentives, or overinvesting in professional, technical, and bureaucratic tools. Instead of being part of the problem, government needs to become a much more vigorous part of the solution. To paraphrase the old mantra, if government is not part of the solution, then it is part of the problem.

Scholars have examined a variety of ways in which government can undermine capacities and proclivities for productive civic action. Welfare state policy and administrative structure often construct citizens as passive and processed clients dependent on street-level bureaucrats, subject to the norms of clinical reasoning and authority imposed by credentialed professionals, and denied opportunities to use their own local knowledge, mobilize community assets, or formulate collective voice. This is especially true for poor and disadvantaged communities, which are often viewed as bundles of deficits and are provided services in ways that are profoundly stigmatizing and controlling.[23] Command and control methods of the regulatory state, while often indispensable, can also disable civic and business actors from finding creative solutions to problems. Command and control too often emphasizes narrow rules and bureaucratic silos that hinder holistic strategies—although the threat of regulatory hammers, under the right circumstances and with appropriate policy design, can trigger collaborative civic action.[24]

In recent decades, many forms of direct delivery of services or enforcement of rules by government bureaucrats have given way to what Lester Salamon of Johns Hopkins University characterizes as "an elaborate system of *third-party government* in which crucial elements of public authority are shared with a host of nongovernmental or other-government actors, frequently in complex collaborative systems." This "new governance" is exercised through a "dense mosaic of policy tools," including grants and contracts, loans and loan guarantees, vouchers and tax incentives, and much more. Rather than hierarchical agencies exercising command and control, the new governance emphasizes organizational networks, partnership between public and private sectors, and negotiation and persuasion.[25]

Various tools of the new governance are central to the policy design principles and case analyses that follow. But it is important to recognize up front that many of the new tools also have costs and risks from the perspective of a robust citizenship and democratic accountability and thus need to be addressed more fully in policy design and administrative practice. Government, in short, can still be very much part of the problem in the new governance. Government-financed services provided through nonprofit agencies, for instance, are also liable to treat citizens as passive clients rather than empowered community members capable of mobilizing assets and networks to solve problems. Indeed, even those nonprofits that use substantial numbers of volunteers can do this, while the old street-level bureaucrats turn into the "new street-level bureaucrats," in the apt phrase of Steven Rathgeb Smith and Michael Lipsky.[26] The dense, complex mosaic of tools and providers can lessen visibility and accountability as well as fragment constituencies in ways that make collective voice even more difficult. Professional dominance is no less a risk when licensed experts, disconnected from communities, ply their trade through nonprofit or for-profit agencies, unless policy design and organizational culture encourage otherwise. Market-based tools can turn citizens into customers and undermine the sense of obligation and public spirit.[27]

That government can be a civic disabler is not directly connected to the overall size of the welfare state. In fact, considerable evidence shows that some welfare states proportionally larger than the American one also have higher levels of associational life and civic engagement. As political scientist Bo Rothstein points out, "The two countries with the most extensive welfare policies, the Netherlands and Sweden, also have the highest scores in the volume of unpaid work in voluntary associations." The Swedish state, for instance, provides financial support for the widespread study circle movement, and universal social insurance benefits seem less likely to have negative impacts on civil society and trust than means-tested ones. It is much more the design than the size of welfare state institutions that is critical.[28]

The Rising Costs of Doing Democracy Well

A third reason government needs to play a more ambitious role as enabler is that the costs of effective civic engagement and robust self-government are substantial and rising. Relative to national income or investments that society makes in other forms of problem solving (professional, bureaucratic, market), civic investment has most likely declined, though this is nearly impossible to calculate with any degree of confidence. Relative to contemporary public challenges, however, local civic

groups are unable to generate sufficient resources, and private foundations, while often helping to spur innovation, cannot be counted on for
sustained and substantial civic investing. Without commensurate and
strategic investments by government, the nation will fall considerably,
even dangerously, short of revitalizing our civic infrastructure and problem-solving capacities.[29]

Stephen Holmes and Cass Sunstein, political and legal theorists, address
some of the costs of democracy in their complementary arguments in *The
Cost of Rights: Why Liberty Depends on Taxes*. According to Holmes and
Sunstein, rights are secured by government, as clearly recognized in our
Declaration of Independence and Constitution, but "rights cannot be protected or enforced without public funding and support. . . . All rights make
claims on the public treasury." Enforcing rights requires, for instance, adequately funded courts of law and legal training. Rights to public safety
require us to fund police departments, and protecting the rights of suspects
and detainees is enhanced by investments in police training. The right to a
jury trial has added costs—by one 1989 estimate, an average of $13,000 a
trial. The constitutional right to due process, such as the private right to
bring an action in contract or tort, presupposes that "at the taxpayers'
expense, the state maintains and makes accessible complex and relatively
transparent legal institutions within which the cumbersome formalities of
fair, public, and understandable adjudication occur." Private property, mis-
leadingly counterposed to government by some conservative theorists, is
itself a complex bundle of rights that are quite costly to enforce.[30]

If we are to enjoy rights to safe products, we must fund such federal
agencies as the Consumer Product Safety Commission and the U.S. Food
and Drug Administration. Rights to collective bargaining are secured
through the National Labor Relations Board. The right to vote, of course,
requires government to provide polling stations and voting machines, as
well as training and oversight of poll workers. To be sure, many forms of
private investment and voluntary action—from public interest lobbies to
volunteer poll workers and grassroots rights advocates—enable us to secure
rights effectively. But as Holmes and Sunstein conclude, "The amount a
community chooses to expend decisively affects the extent to which the
fundamental rights of Americans are protected and enforced."[31]

Self-governance by engaged, informed, and skilled citizens also requires
public investments. To illustrate this, I add community policing to the argument of Holmes and Sunstein about rights to public safety and take a
brief look at Chicago.

In the early 1990s, the mayor and police chief of Chicago, responding to citizens mobilized for more effective and responsive approaches to crime, established the Chicago Alternative Policing Strategy, which has become the premier big-city program of its kind in the nation. Under the widely publicized slogan "Safe Neighborhoods Are Everybody's Business," the reform recognized public safety as a complex public good that police officers alone, acting according to narrow professional norms and bureaucratic procedures, could not produce effectively. Police would have to learn to collaborate with ordinary citizens, as well as with a variety of stakeholders (landlords, clergy, shopkeepers, senior citizen groups) and other city agencies (buildings, transportation, forestry, health, streets and sanitation) to develop integrative, holistic strategies to "coproduce" public safety. Enhancing safety on a particular street, for instance, might require paying special attention to problem tenants, trimming trees for better lighting, altering a bus route, and fixing various "broken windows," such as removing abandoned cars or cleaning up a vacant lot. Citizens themselves would need to share their local knowledge of crime patterns and players with police and collaborate in developing strategies tailored to specific neighborhoods, blocks, business establishments, and other institutions. They would also need to act directly in ways that complement the plans developed collaboratively with police.[32]

Thus in Chicago, citizens organize parent patrols to enhance school safety and "walking school buses" as convoys for children to and from school. They march to "take back the night" to protect women and girls from predators, and they hold prayer vigils and barbeque "smoke outs" in the midst of street drug markets to drive them from the neighborhood. They organize "stand ups" in front of businesses that generate problematic street behavior. Citizens also clean up graffiti and gang markings, picket the homes of landlords whose buildings are sites of crime and violence, and organize court advocacy to monitor judges as they mete out sentences. To help neighbors secure their homes and report crime rapidly to the police, residents develop safety education initiatives. To fix broken windows that signify social disorder, they organize "clean and green" efforts, with implements and trash bags provided by the city. Citizens volunteer in mediation and cooperative truancy reduction programs with schools. They work with young people and court officials to develop teen courts (or "peer juries"), which typically hear cases of first-time offenders, fourteen to sixteen years of age, in crimes such as shoplifting, vandalism, minor assault, disorderly conduct, and drug and alcohol use. Youth themselves, with assistance from pro bono lawyers and retired judges, volunteer for teen court service to help ensure restorative justice and a sense of responsible engagement in community life.

To facilitate such collaborative work, the police department has been decentralized into twenty-five districts and 279 beats. These beats convene regularly scheduled (typically monthly) meetings at which local residents and officers together analyze patterns of complaints and statistically generated neighborhood crime data, develop beat plans for problem solving, review past progress, and revise strategies. For community policing in Chicago to work effectively, however, has required not just organizational decentralization and civic opportunity but also substantial investment of public monies, some provided by federal and state agencies. While some local civic groups had developed relevant organizing skills before the reform, the city has had to invest in training to generalize problem-solving skills across all neighborhoods. In 1995–97, when the program transitioned from its prototype stage to citywide application, the police department contracted with the Chicago Alliance for Neighborhood Safety, the lead citizens group on crime, to help provide joint community-police training to 11,700 citizens through 1,065 training events. The cost of the contract was $2.9 million, not including direct costs to the department for police trainers or the previous training during the prototype stage. Since the citywide rollout, the department has continued to offer periodic training to citizen beat facilitators and beat officers, as well as to middle and upper management to transform the organizational culture in lasting ways. It has also recruited dozens of community organizers into permanent staff positions.

To encourage broad participation in beat meetings, attended monthly by about 6,300 to 7,500 residents across the city, the department also invests in widespread advertising and outreach. In 2003 the public safety program spent $950,000 on television advertising alone, and its core civic message eliciting engagement and coproduction appears everywhere—on buses and subways, in church bulletins and utility bills, local stores and restaurants, schools and libraries, and in city employee paycheck envelopes. In 2003 the department also offered a landlord training course on screening and managing problem tenants, attended by eight hundred landlords with more than ten thousand rental units. Some landlords were required to attend as part of settlements with the Drug and Gang House Enforcement Section of the city's Department of Law. In the Chicago Alternative Policing Strategy, the skill set of private landlords as both stakeholders and citizens complements the civic problem-solving skills of ordinary residents and beat officers and thus represents a worthy public investment in the democratic coproduction of public safety. While it is impossible to estimate the exact dollar amount of public funds devoted to developing the relevant professional and civic skills, ensuring broad outreach for diverse participation across the city, and building organizational capacities for collaborative problem solving, the investment of the Chicago Alternative Policing Strategy in civic capacities has clearly been substantial—several million dollars or more a year averaged over the life of the program to date.[33]

The Rising Costs of Self-Governance

As indicated by this example and much other research, various general factors drive the cost side of civic problem solving and collaborative governance. Among the most important are the increasing complexity of public problems, the growing diversity of publics, and the rising expectations of citizens for voice and inclusion.

Increasing Complexity of Public Problems

In Chicago, public officials and organized citizens opted for community policing partly because, in line with a large body of emerging research, they recognized that public safety in the contemporary city cannot be effectively addressed by the usual segmented, bureaucratic, and rapid-response methods that had become the norm over several generations of police professionalization.[34] This new environment required police to think more systematically about a broad range of interrelated problems, from housing, land use, and transportation to social services, schools, and race and gender dynamics. After years of devaluing local knowledge and neighborhood networks, officers had to find ways of realigning these with their own professional skills. Community policing also required that citizens be able to analyze complex, geographic crime data, combine them with their own local knowledge of neighborhood patterns, and deliberate and plan effectively, instead of just complaining and protesting or, worse, retreating behind closed doors and shaded windows.

The well-being of our water supply is another example. To protect and restore ecosystems, scientists, river movement leaders, and government officials at all levels of the federal system have come to broad agreement that virtually all discrete problems of water—quality, supply, fisheries, flood control, habitat preservation, biodiversity—need to be understood as part of hydrologically defined drainage basins known as watersheds, which have at least as many components as crime in the big city. A National Research Council report published in 1999 summarized the emergent consensus: watersheds require integrative management linking all components (rivers, wetlands, ground water, atmosphere, flood plains, upland areas), and effective management needs to integrate biophysical and social sciences, as well as lay and professional knowledge.[35] Reaching the pollution reduction goals of the Chesapeake Bay Program, notes a 2007 report from the National Academy of Public Administration, will require joint efforts by 6 states, the District of Columbia, 3,169 local governments, and 23 federal agencies; 678 watershed associations, a large number of citizen-run "riverkeeper" organizations, 2 interstate river basin commissions, 30 regional councils, 36 state-created tributary strategy teams; eighty-seven thousand farm owners and 5 million to 6 million homeowners; hundreds of lawn care companies, an uncounted number of land developers, homebuilders, construction companies, agribusinesses, and other companies that pollute the bay; and a large number of other civic and nonprofit organizations.[36]

The watershed approach presents an enormous challenge in civic capacity building: creating and sustaining watershed associations and kindred organizations for some two thousand major watersheds and still more numerous subwatersheds; developing these associations' ability to do scientifically sound volunteer monitoring to gather usable place-based data; generating their staff capacity for complex watershed planning rooted in broad public education and deliberation; mobilizing volunteers for hands-on restoration projects; and enhancing the training capacities of state, regional, and national intermediary organizations, such as the Colorado Watershed Assembly, the Southeast Watershed Forum, and River Network. Climate change, which barely figured into early analyses, now further compounds the complexity of the public management and civic capacity–building challenges for effective watershed work.[37]

When we consider these challenges in light of the decline of multitiered civic associations, at least two things stand out. First, no existing multitiered associations in the first half of the twentieth century had cognitive frames capable of addressing this level of complexity, and few if any demonstrated any propensity to develop such frames thereafter. Second, in such a diverse organizational ecology comprising so many different types of civic and other stakeholders, branded local chapters of national multitiered associations become structurally less privileged as civic aggregators at the local level and thereby in the system as a whole. This structural deficit emerged gradually, independent of and in addition to the sociopolitical causes that Skocpol analyzes. Government investments in civic capacity at multiple levels of the federal system become increasingly necessary because social and policy complexity disrupt the civic value chain of the classic multitiered association.

Scholars in many other policy arenas—from community health and family services to education reform and urban and regional planning—demonstrate that the increasing complexity of public problems has elicited new challenges and thereby raised the bar for the types of civic skills and organizational capacity required to address them effectively.[38] As Clarence Stone and his colleagues argue in *Building Civic Capacity: The Politics of Reforming Urban Schools,* sustained reform of urban education systems requires far more than the latest pedagogical techniques and management practices. Urban school systems are what the authors call "high reverberation subsystems . . . characterized by frequent reshuffling of mobilized stakeholders, multiple and strongly felt competing value and belief systems, deeply held stakes by both educators (the professional providers of education) and parents (the consumers), and ambiguous boundaries." Existing stocks of social capital, even if substantial, will not help much unless civic mobilization occurs in ways that engage business elites, community groups, educational professionals, and political leaders in forging a shared definition of the problem and frame of action and also support parents through training and other means to become skilled and committed players in a sustainable coalition.[39]

Growing Diversity of Publics

As the American public becomes more diverse and the organized stakeholders that might constitute the relevant "publics" for any given problem or policy arena become increasingly variegated, the challenges of forging workable consensus and ongoing collaboration rise commensurately. The most obvious form of diversity, of course, is demographic. Our communities are becoming increasingly diverse in terms of race, ethnicity, and immigrant status, as well as other social and cultural identities. In addition, the norms of fair representation and deliberation have become much more inclusive than in earlier periods of our democratic development. Not only are various types of formal exclusion now illegal, but it is also much less acceptable to sanction official public forums and decisionmaking processes that draw primarily from the "usual suspects," even if the process meets formal requirements of openness.

Chicago, for instance, has spent millions of dollars for public outreach and skilled beat-meeting facilitation to ensure that participation in community policing reaches not only white but also African American and Latino communities, not only homeowners but also renters, not only middle- and upper-class residents but also those residents from less economically advantaged neighborhoods. The Department of Neighborhoods in Seattle invests in relational organizing among new immigrant and refugee communities to include them more quickly and thoroughly in the civic life of the city and to generate bridging social capital across communities. Demographic diversity, of course, is not only a statistical census category but also one deeply imbued with distinct cultures, identities, and styles of public communication, which further add to the challenges of facilitating democratic deliberation and building civic relationships that can enable common public work.[40]

Publics are also becoming ever more diverse as a result of increasing institutional differentiation, pluralization of interests, and proliferation of stakeholder groups.[41] Such diversity raises the costs of negotiating interests, aligning perspectives, and building ongoing relationships of civic trust. In more and more communities and policy arenas, it has become clear that the hyperpluralism of fragmented interest representation too often leads to unacceptable levels of conflict, stalemate, and suboptimal policies. To counter such tendencies, various innovations in community visioning, consensus building, and civic partnership have emerged. These often include dozens of stakeholders—100 or more in some cases—involved in what Indiana University public management theorist Robert Agranoff calls "complex value creation networks."[42] An ecosystem partnership in the West, for instance, might include a dozen watershed, conservation, and recreation groups; an equal number of farmer, rancher, timber, irrigator, and other local business groups; various federal, state, and local agencies operating with diverse legal mandates and organizational cultures; local foundations and land trusts; schools, universities, and research institutes; and elected local officials from multiple jurisdictions.[43] To take another case, a multistakeholder partnership for comprehensive community revitalization in a minority and poor neighborhood of Portland, Oregon, during the 1990s included forty-one different civic and nonprofit groups and an equal number of government agencies, schools, universities, and business groups that collaborated in developing and implementing the plan through 140 public meetings over a three-year period.[44]

For broad community visioning, complex participatory planning, and sustainable multi-stakeholder partnerships to work well typically requires various kinds of investments. These might include trained facilitators to ensure effective and fair deliberative processes as well as association and government staff that can play ongoing bridging and trust-building roles. Investments might also be needed for broad outreach and public education to ensure engagement and participation by ordinary citizens and associational memberships as well as planning support systems capable of generating usable place-based data.[45] The City of Seattle provided $4.5 million directly to independent neighborhood planning groups—which typically included representatives from diverse community councils, neighborhood business associations, and other civic and nonprofit groups—to develop inclusive participation, broad consensus, and technically sound proposals. In addition, the neighborhood planning office hired ten project managers to assist the neighborhood planning groups, help build trust among various stakeholders through ongoing relational work, vet the emerging plans with a dozen or so city departments in a continuous iterative process over several years of planning and the first years of implementation, and coordinate the entire process with the city council's neighborhoods committee to ensure democratic accountability at the city level. Without these public investments in collaborative governance, it is very likely that comprehensive planning in many areas of the city would have stalled and—as a result of delay, disruption, and legal action—imposed comparably higher costs on city departments, business investors, homeowners, and renters.

Rising Public Expectations for Voice and Inclusion

A third factor driving the costs of civic problem solving and self-governance is citizens' own rising expectations that government consult them and provide them with opportunities to contribute productively, as well as the proliferation of citizen veto opportunities to obstruct government action. This was the case in Seattle, where the 1985 downtown plan was sabotaged by a successful initiative campaign for a Citizens Alternative Plan. Such heightened expectations are no surprise to public officials who have to manage clamorous public claims for voice or veto, nor to scholars of participation, who attribute such heightened expectations to increases in education, postindustrial job skills, and democratization of information as well as various value shifts favoring self-expression and inclusion.[46]

In Hampton, Virginia, an innovative citywide system for youth civic engagement emerged in the early 1990s when young people themselves, convened as part of a collaborative community planning process, made it clear that they wanted to be treated not as problems but as problem solvers and contributors to the community at large. But if they were to be given new opportunities to participate, they wanted to be sure to have the requisite skills and leadership development so as not "to be set up for failure," as one seventeen-year-old leader said. In response, the city began to institutionalize a system of youth civic engagement with a variety of complementary components: a youth commission made up of two dozen students from the city's seven public and private high schools, part-time teenage youth planners (housed in the Hampton Planning Department), a superintendent's advisory group for students in all public high schools and principal's advisory groups in each high school (later expanded to middle schools), and youth representation in neighborhood associations and on the citywide neighborhood youth advisory board, as well as on advisory boards and programs of various other city departments, commissions, and public-private partnerships.

To provide leadership development to youth, and to help catalyze culture change among adults in city agencies and nonprofits, the city council invests some $400,000 a year in staffing the Coalition for Youth (a small city department) and enabling it to provide training contracts to a local youth development nonprofit. The public schools also contribute $70,000 annually to similar training and facilitation, not including their recent introduction of service learning across the high school curriculum.

Investment in Civic Capacity

In short, the costs of doing civic democracy well in contemporary America are substantial and rising. The growing complexity of problems, increased diversity of publics, and heightened expectations of citizens for voice and inclusion all contribute to the enhanced civic skill sets and organizational capacities needed for effective problem solving and democratic self-government. Rising costs are hardly peculiar to forms of engagement sponsored or supported in some way by government.

Congregation-based (or faith-based) organizing—arguably the most effective and steadily growing form of independent community organizing today—now recognizes clearly that sustained investments in leadership development must be made if ordinary citizens are to acquire the capacity to grapple with complex issues in their communities, build bridges across denominational and ethnic-racial boundaries, and establish sustainable institutional and policy partnerships, such as job training or education reform. Indeed, professional organizers from the major national networks, such as the Industrial Areas Foundation, the Pacific Institute for Community Organization, and the Gamaliel Foundation, agree to work with a community only on condition that the coalition of congregational leaders sign a contract promising to provide sufficient resources for developing the kind of citizen-leaders that can build "relational power" for the long run. True, faith-based organizing can draw upon stocks of social capital and civic skills already existing in congregations, as well as within other member organizations that one might find in a coalition. But substantial up-front investment, as well as much more systematic attention to leadership and partnership development than was typical in earlier community organizing, is requisite to realize genuine value added in building inclusive, accountable, relational power capable of sustained achievements.[47]

Not all investments by government, to be sure, are wise, even in some of our best cases. Programs thus need to be continually evaluated for effectiveness, often revamped, and sometimes discontinued. Some up-front investments, such as those for citizen and professional training during the initial citywide rollout of a program, can be reduced considerably during later phases, as more skilled participants train and socialize newcomers in a variety of informal ways and as civic problem solving becomes more embedded in organizational and professional cultures. There is no one model for providing training. Often it makes sense for a government agency to contract with an independent citizens group or intermediary association or institute, sometimes to provide some or even most of the training itself. Community policing in Chicago began with one model and later switched to another. In any case, citizens invariably mix civic skills from many sources—families, schools, churches, and jobs—as well as organizing or advocacy quite different from those that are the focus of this book.[48] Some of these skills will derive, at least partly, from government investment, as with civic education and service learning in public schools or national service through AmeriCorps.[49] Others reflect the continued vitality of some independent associations and community groups, large and small. Government neither is nor ever should or could be the prime mover or sole provider.

Not all citizens, of course, need to develop higher-order civic skills, such as those one might use to facilitate a beat meeting in a big city, organize study circles on contentious and complex issues, lead a community-based research project on cumulative toxic risk, or cochair a multistakeholder ecosystem partnership. For some, it will be enough that they can build relationships with neighbors and get them to help out regularly with a parent patrol at the school, deliberate in a study circle for several sessions over a three-month period, monitor air quality periodically at a busy intersection in their neighborhood, or help plant trees in the springtime to restore the riparian buffer of a local stream. A vibrant civic democracy can undoubtedly thrive with many citizens who are only occasionally involved and have fairly circumscribed civic skills and with some who are not involved much at all— although a good polity might certainly wish to aim for some minimum of civic virtues and skills for all citizens.

Nor do all professional staff partners in a government agency need to have well-developed enabling skills for a civic partnership to work well, as long as enough of them do and as long as the broader organizational culture and administrative practices of the agency do not undermine civic modes of problem solving. Capacity building, both on the civic side and the agency side, is never a question of every citizen, professional, or organizational partner having the perfect skill set but rather requires a rich enough mix available through the relevant networks to enable effective democratic work, determined through a pragmatic process of testing and mutual learning.

Shared Responsibility for Civic Investment

If the costs of doing civic democracy well are rising, some might nonetheless also ask why government should become a major, strategic investor. Indeed, why should it play any role at all? Is not this the proper role of civil society? Are there not dangers that government will discourage or distort investments by citizens, civic associations, and nonprofit funders or that it will co-opt and undermine independent civic action? Chapter 2, on elements of policy design for democracy, addresses some of these concerns, and later chapters provide case analyses that take them up in more detail. Let me here make only a few basic points.

First, democratic government has a fundamental and fully legitimate interest in its citizens' having the requisite civic skills, networks, and deliberative forums needed to sustain a self-governing republic—at least if, to paraphrase Benjamin Franklin upon exiting the Constitutional Convention in 1787, we wish to keep it. We may test—and contest—what a self-governing republic means for a complex polity in a globalizing world of the twenty-first century and how direct civic engagement can and should be properly interwoven with democratic representation, bureaucratic administration, and other tools of governance. Some would undoubtedly contest government investment in a citywide neighborhood association system on grounds that it might compete with independent, faith-based community organizing. Others would prefer a social movement with an us-versus-them frame over a collaborative one or national advocacy for command and control over local multistakeholder partnerships. Indeed, in Holmes and Sunstein's parallel argument, Americans are always contesting the boundaries and forms of various rights and hence the types of investments we might make to secure them effectively.[50]

Some conservative thinkers have vigorously contested the role of the federal government in funding national service and service-learning programs through the Corporation for National and Community Service, established in 1993, as well as earlier national service programs. Nonetheless, the core normative debate has largely been resolved in favor of a government role, and national service has found many conservative enthusiasts and leaders.[51] Justifying a democratic government's fundamental interest in helping to ensure adequate civic skills and capacities and backing up its interest with the investment of public resources of various sorts (funding, tools, staff support) are not problems of a different order from justifying investments in civic education or national service. This is especially true if one recognizes, as Putnam argues, that "like all public goods, social capital tends to be undervalued and undersupplied by private agents."[52] A democratic polity needs capable and connected citizens and should do what it can to enable them to develop as such.

Second, democratic government has an interest in investing in some types of civic capacity building over others and, indeed, of not investing in some types at all. Government funding of trial by jury, voting machinery, and training of poll workers, as already noted, is clearly fundamental to protecting democratic rights and securing democratic representation. We all accept this as unproblematic, even if we might battle over the types of poll machines to use or the trustworthiness of specific vendors to ensure fairness and accuracy. My argument takes this one step further: democratic government has a fully legitimate interest in investing in the kinds of civic capacity building that enables it to solve public problems effectively and to enlist diverse citizens and stakeholders to collaborate in doing so. Government, in other words, ought to invest in collaborative governance to help ensure that its partners have capacities for fair and informed deliberation and shared work, especially those forms that engage citizens in productive and value-adding roles. Evidence of effective performance and value added contributions, of course, is critical to building and maintaining public support for such investments, an issue I examine in this book on the local level but one that also begs discussion for national policy.

However, democratic government has no business investing in certain electoral partisans or advocacy groups over others. It is also not the role of government to sponsor protest movements. The right to protest, of course, is vital to a democracy, and many contentious movements have made enormous contributions to expanding democracy and participation and to changing how government works—indeed, even to supplying civic activists for collaborative problem solving along the way.[53] But resource mobilization for protest clearly remains a task for independent organizing that stays largely clear of government financing. In practice, of course, it is not always easy to draw clear boundaries, especially when policy feedback loops can tend to encourage some forms of civic mobilization over others.[54] However, as long as government protects rights to independent citizen action and makes adequate investments (through civic education, open public information, courts) to ensure that citizens understand and are capable of exercising their rights to protest, its investment in collaborative forms of governance is not fundamentally problematic, though there are important issues at stake, to be sure.

Third, government investment is critical because investments from the independent civic and nonprofit sector, as essential as they have been, tend to fall short for a variety of reasons. On the positive side, it would be difficult to imagine some of the important civic innovations and sustained capacity building of the past several decades without the leadership and resources of private foundations, large and small. The Kellogg Foundation, for instance, has made strategic field-building investments in service learning that have paid substantial dividends.[55] The Kendall Foundation funded a series of watershed innovators workshops in the mid-1990s that enabled critical learning for state watershed networks and agency programs that have become essential to the watershed approach.[56] A number of important foundation leaders, from the Kettering, Surdna, and Boston foundations and the Walter and Elise Haas Fund, among others, formed a "civil investing group" to help educate the larger foundation world about the critical need for investments in civic infrastructure and practice. The Grantmakers Forum on Community and National Service changed its name to Philanthropy for Active Civic Engagement as it began to recognize a much broader mission that included community problem solving, civic education, and leadership training.[57]

However, such foundation leaders and program officers are generally the first to admit that private foundation investments in civic infrastructure are hardly adequate relative to existing and future needs or comparable to those investments that government can make. As critical as Kellogg's investment in service learning has been, for instance, Learn and Serve America, a program of the Corporation for National and Community Service, has made strategic field-building investments several times the magnitude of those of Kellogg and other leading foundations. And still further investments in service learning and the broader civic mission of schools are sorely needed.[58] Similarly, the Kendall Foundation's investments in developing the watershed approach and building the civic capacity of the field, while formative, have been dwarfed by those of the U.S. Environmental Protection Agency (EPA), the National Oceanic and Atmospheric Administration, and many state environmental agencies—and again, the unmet need is still substantial.

Foundations, of course, also go through faddish innovation cycles and often fail to sustain their civic capacity–building work. Many also tend to be hooked on categorical programs and issue-specific niche funding, as well as professionalized therapeutic interventions for clients rather than problem solving by citizens. Although much room exists for private foundations to increase investment in building capacity for robust civic problem solving, and various public policy designs should elicit further increases through matching grant requirements and the like, there is little sign that private foundation investments will be adequate any time soon. In addition, there are some forms of investment, such as police training and staff time for collaborative problem solving with citizens, for which reliance on private foundation funding would clearly be inappropriate.

Finally, of course, government is accountable to the general public, however complex and challenging a task such accountability has become, whereas private foundations are accountable first and foremost to their boards. If a foundation board chooses to invest in programs that treat people as recipients of charitable services and as communities defined by their deficits, we may complain and criticize and try to induce changes in practice. When our government fails to invest in the tools we need to be effective citizens and to enable our collaborative public work, or even worse to impede it, we have every right and responsibility to hold such a government accountable.

Indeed, we have the right and responsibility to hold one another accountable. As citizens, we are accountable for our collective willingness to invest in our civic capacities. Yet we can only begin to properly hold one another accountable if we understand clearly that a vibrant civic democracy is not a free good. Civic capacities do not simply bubble up from the well-springs of community life, supplied by the bountiful aquifers of grand republican traditions, at least not in the complex and transformed world in which we currently live. It is relatively easy for us to appreciate the need for capital investment if business is to grow, and as taxpayers we agree to various tax incentives to make this happen. Those who are homeowners know that maintenance and renovation have long-term payoffs, and we expect our financial institutions to support us in such work, even when we put up the studs and sheetrock or new clapboards ourselves. In fact, we also grant tax deductions for interest on home equity loans and recognize multiplier effects to ourselves as well as our neighbors—the value of their homes increases when we make certain kinds of improvements to our own.

We have become far more aware as a society than we were a half century ago that human capital investments have multiplier effects of many sorts—for employers, employees, and the nation's productivity as a whole. Management theorists now recognize that investing in leadership has multiplier effects in attracting, retaining, and optimally engaging human capital. But we have not yet developed a sound understanding of the nature or importance of investments in civic leadership, collaborative tools, and organizational and network infrastructure, especially those kinds of investments that government itself can and should make. Investments in civic problem-solving capacities and governance do not typically show up on our public balance sheets, even in a city like Seattle, where there is clear recognition that investments in neighborhood planning have not only reduced costs owing to delay and obstruction but have also helped yield, many times over, a positive return on investment in the form of highly visible public improvements.[59]

The following chapters begin to explore public investment in civic capacity, especially through specific components of policy design and administration. Investing, of course, takes many forms: funding to help build associations and networks that can tackle public problems effectively; training and leadership development for both citizens and agency staff and staff time devoted to collaborative problem solving; matching grants designed to leverage additional resources and volunteer labor from other institutions and communities themselves; information systems to enable citizens to generate, share, and productively use knowledge.

Like other types of investment, whether private or public, civic investing raises a range of questions that will typically be contested and will challenge elected leaders, agency officials, advocacy groups, nonprofit service organizations, and foundations to account for the rationality of choices: visible versus less tangible impacts, direct costs as well as opportunity costs, long-term and short-term payoffs, problem-solving capacities versus immediate service deliverables. Will investing in community policing have greater impact on public safety than putting a hundred more cops in cruisers, and what will be the relative impact of each choice on race relations in the city? Will extended deliberation to bring regional stakeholders to a working consensus take too much time in the face of urgent problems that might be amenable to a regulatory or market solution? When budgets are tight, do we cut money from the city's direct service or leadership development programs, the latter already only a tiny fraction of the former? How do we measure return on investment and develop plausible accounts that generate support for elected leaders willing to invest in democracy?[60]

Although real dollars matter enormously, investment should not be construed too narrowly. In many areas of our lives, we often ask ourselves and one another whether we are sufficiently "invested"—in our friendships, our marriages, our children's future, our work projects, our spiritual well-being. These are questions not of money but of meaning, metaphor, and motivation. Being invested entails commitment, time, attention, not taking for granted. Underlying the issues of policy design, administrative innovation, and public monies thus lurks the larger question that we can ask and answer only as citizens: Are we really invested in making our democracy work?

Research Methods and Plan of the Book

In this section, I discuss some methodological strategies employed in this book to understand how government can be a civic enabler and strategic investor. Those not wishing to be burdened by such issues at this point might jump ahead to chapter 2, which presents my conceptual approach, and then to the case study chapters, or even start with the case study narratives and later return to method and theory.

The research design of this book represents a hybrid of three elements: normatively grounded and empirically generated typological theory of collaborative governance, especially as this relates to questions of policy design and administrative practice; case study research on three relatively robust cases (also known as building-block studies) at different levels of the federal system in the United States that can throw light on the rich mix of potential components and configurations of collaborative governance, as well as the processes of policy learning through which these emerged and for which case research is especially well suited; and policy proposals at the federal level that are informed by the theory and cases, as well as additional empirical research of my own and other colleagues concerned with similar questions. There are thus several modes of democratic inquiry at work here. The main policy proposals in the concluding chapter are oriented to working carefully within the limits of current knowledge and to enable energetic learning while doing, thereby helping generate positive movement forward amid genuine scholarly, as well as political, uncertainty.

Chapter 2 outlines core principles of policy design that can enhance civic capacities for self-government. I call the overall mix a typological theory of collaborative governance. My use of this term stresses collaboration among engaged and empowered citizens, not just organizational or interagency collaboration, though the latter are also essential. Others would use the closely related term *democratic network governance*. Since there is a growing literature in this field, and because a good number of the key actors from my case narratives are highly reflective practitioners who draw explicitly on various of these principles, I put the typological theory up front.[61]

I make no pretense to have discovered these all from my own empirical research but stand on the shoulders of other policy analysts, democratic theorists, social scientists, and civic practitioners in sketching certain fundamentals that have emerged in the relevant literature. Of course, I have selected and configured these principles in a way that I find most coherent and useful for empirical analysis and "policy design for democracy."[62] As I make clear, I do not see all policy in a vibrant civic democracy as requiring all of the core principles; rather, I encourage a pragmatic mix appropriate to specific kinds of policy problems and contexts while also attending to overall cumulative impacts of those tools of governance that do not directly enable civic engagement or, worse, may marginalize it. It is the mix that matters, not any one specific configuration or application on its own.

For the sake of a broad public and policy audience, I do not engage all the nuances one finds in the lively theoretical debates on these design principles, such as deliberative democracy, reciprocal accountability, or democratic network governance. Instead, I direct the reader to key bodies of literature, tease some issues out further in the case studies, and, in the concluding chapter, provide a policy design proposal that would productively lodge such debates in the heart of federal agency learning.

Case Studies

Chapters 3 to 5 examine three extended case studies of relatively robust policy and program designs and sets of public administration practices, to which I have alluded already. The two city-based cases, Seattle's neighborhood system and Hampton's youth civic engagement system, are widely recognized as among the best in their fields, and both have been winners of Innovations in American Government Awards, bestowed by Harvard University's Ash Institute for Democratic Governance and Innovation, in collaboration with the Council for Excellence in Government. Both models competed with the broadest range of types of government innovations. Both have various institutional and programmatic components and thus provide—a bit like Russian dolls—the opportunity to examine cases within cases, which is especially useful in case study research. Both have also benefited from federal programs and provide a window onto how various federal agencies might provide further support, especially for cities less favorably situated to innovate on their own. Both cities have also proved capable of sustaining their innovations and extending their reach over the years.

I have chosen the Environmental Protection Agency to explore how a major federal agency with strong command and control origins could, through successive changes in national administration, introduce increasingly coherent community-based program innovations and help build civic capacity through state and local agencies as well as various civic networks. My previous work in the 1990s with several other federal agencies, as well as more recent scans of their community-based work, convinced me that the EPA was probably the most robust case to study at this point, other than the one agency with an explicit civic mission, the Corporation for National and Community Service, to which I turn briefly in the last chapter. The Environmental Protection Agency, of course, has not been a prime mover. Rather, the agency has been responsive in various ways to local groups, state and local agency innovators, national intermediaries, and social movement leaders, though, as one might expect, it has often taken much pressure to elicit responsiveness. It will no doubt take more.

Within the EPA, I have selected three program areas and two cross-agency initiatives. I have chosen the three program areas (watersheds, Superfund, and environmental justice) not only because they have been important innovators on community engagement but also because they have had important differences among themselves (statutory basis, levels of funding, degrees of contentiousness at the community and movement levels). In addition to these three program areas within the EPA, I examine the two major cross-program culture change initiatives within the agency to understand how deeper agency culture change and broader civic and policy learning take place and how networks in the larger field of civic environmentalism have been part of this process. The first initiative, Community Based Environmental Protection (CBEP), began in 1994. Although its organizational home, the Office of Sustainable Ecosystems and Communities, disbanded in 1999, CBEP networks across headquarters and regional EPA offices, state programs, and civic associations, as well as CBEP's cognitive framing, have continued to reverberate ever since.

The second initiative, currently ongoing, is the Community Action for a Renewed Environment (CARE) program, which grew directly out of CBEP networks but has been designed to avoid problems faced by the Office of Sustainable Ecosystems and Communities as well as to integrate other programmatic staff (and their various tools) into its network. In addition, CARE has partnered with the Centers for Disease Control and Prevention and the Agency for Toxic Substances and Disease Registry; this promises fruitful interagency collaboration on building capacities for disease prevention and community health promotion. Staff from CBEP and CARE have also been leaders within broader federal networks.

As political scientists Alexander George and Andrew Bennett argue in *Case Studies and Theory Development in the Social Sciences,* and as other methodologists also show, case study research has a variety of advantages but also clear limits. Among the strengths of case study research is its ability to generate high levels of conceptual validity, especially on core concepts such as "democracy, power, political culture . . . [that] are notoriously difficult to measure."[63] When adding, as in the present context, *network* to "democracy," *relational* to "power," and *collaborative* to "political culture," the need for rich case study analysis only increases.[64] Similarly, process tracing in case study research permits a nuanced understanding of complex causal relationships and causal chains—or multiple conjunctural causation, in University of Arizona sociologist Charles Ragin's terminology—as well as insight into policy learning and diffusion, which are central to my analysis.[65]

In Seattle, collaborative approaches emerged over two decades from the complex interplay of local neighborhood activism and environmentally sustainable city planning, mandated by state law (chapter 3), which find important complements through the design of the Puget Sound National

Estuary Program and various collaborative salmon, shellfish, and other restoration projects and networks. These, in turn, helped shape the design of a new state office with a broad civic structure and strategy (chapter 5). I am interested in each piece of this causal puzzle, and exploring them expands the range of cases and "causal lumpiness" along the way. "The constitution of [case] populations is a theory-laden, concept-intensive process," as Ragin notes.[66] Case study research is well suited to the diversity and complexity of social life, with multiple interaction effects, as many researchers and methodologists recognize. It is especially suited to studying those forms of civic policy design and governance that emerge in direct response to increasing complexity and diversity.

Case study research also addresses the issue of "equifinality," or identifying different causal paths that lead to a similar outcome in different cases. Diana Schor and I have addressed this specifically in our more strictly comparative case study analysis of the youth civic engagement systems in Hampton and San Francisco, where city agency culture change, enabling more robust engagement and collaborative problem solving among youth and adults, emerged through two distinct pathways—reinventing government and social movement, respectively—reflecting the very different political cultures of the two cities.[67] Equifinality is an especially important issue for federal policy design, as I take up in chapter 6, if policy would seek to enable actors located in diverse communities, networks, agencies, and policy arenas to move along paths that might strengthen their capacities for collaborative governance and problem solving. This does not entail "multiple convergence" at an exactly similar point, to be sure, but within a range of appropriate possibilities that are complementary and mutually reinforcing for the nation's overall capacities for democratic self-government—a theory-laden issue if there ever was one.

Because case study research has various limits, especially when not strictly comparing cases (and even then), it is important to draw upon other kinds of research whenever possible. Jeffrey Berry, Kent Portney, and Ken Thomson's now classic study, *The Rebirth of Urban Democracy* (1993), uses quantitative and comparative data across many cities (and then a smaller subsample of five) to demonstrate the relatively more robust democratic impacts of citywide and city-supported systems of neighborhood participation, in comparison with those cities with more selective or different modes of engaging residents.[68] Their work has inspired my own in specific ways, though neither I nor other researchers have since developed a large-N sample of this sort for city models today. Chapter 5 draws upon the National River Restoration Science Synthesis, which provides a very large-*N* sample of watershed restoration projects. Its findings clearly support civic engagement in watershed projects as the most important factor in generating accountability for results, but its central focus is the natural science side of evaluating ecological impacts.[69] Paul Sabatier, Will Focht, Mark Lubell, and their colleagues bring what they call second-generation methodological tools to studying collaborative watershed management in a relatively large sample of cases, and I draw upon their important findings, when relevant.[70] Other studies that I use, such as those of AmeriCorps and Learn and Serve, employ quantitative analysis and control groups to measure biographical and institutional impacts.

While case study research is certainly limited, the policy design proposed in the concluding chapter provides much room—indeed, I argue, the necessity—for the use of many different methods of analysis and evaluation to refine and advance workable, appropriate, and diverse forms of collaborative governance and network capacities. Two other methodological strategies immediately come to mind here. The first entails using "fuzzy set" tools that combine qualitative and quantitative assessment linked to set-theoretic relationships, especially as developed by Ragin. Building upon a configurational approach to complex relationships and causal pathways, "this approach searches for heterogeneity within 'given' or preconstituted [case] populations and conceives of 'difference' in terms of kinds and types of cases, replacing the conventional view of difference as variation (i.e. as deviation from the mean)."[71] Since fuzzy sets allow degrees of membership in types of cases (for example, collaborative watershed governance, neighborhood planning, community policing), they can be especially useful to policymakers and administrators, who invariably face a diversity of possible configurations of civic design and must make choices on whether to promote some over others and under what specific enabling and constraining conditions. Analytic types and degrees of membership reflect multiple and conjunctural causality, rooted in such factors as local political and agency culture, preexisting civic capacities and partnerships, demographic size and geographic scope, and specific policy challenges. Administrators must also make judgments based on expectations of probable pathways of development and relative likelihood of success and evaluate programs in a policy universe of relatively large numbers.

The second methodological strategy would combine typically qualitative (policy network analysis) with typically quantitative and formal (social network analysis) methods of specific policy fields and subfields, along with the rich mix of qualitative, quantitative, and cultural methods that have become increasingly common in recent social movement network analysis. As I note in chapter 5, for instance, elaborating a watershed policy frame to guide collaborative governance and field building has been a highly interactive process among grassroots movement networks, agency officials, academic scientists, policy analysts, legal theorists, and others. Indeed, this cognitive framing has been essential to constituting the broader watershed movement as a network of meanings that run the gamut from the economic value of ecosystem functions to the cultural symbolism of "totem salmon," which has been so powerful in motivating civic action in the Northwest and beyond.[72] Combining these methodological approaches and moving beyond previous "analytical cliquishness" in network analysis would facilitate building fields more strategically, a core principle of collaborative governance that I discuss in the following chapter and return to in the policy proposals of chapter 6.[73]

Interviews with Agency Staff and Partners

I have used a variety of data collection methods for the case studies, especially formal interviews, field observations, and documentary sources. First, I conducted semistructured (or focused) interviews, in person and by telephone, with 271 public administrators, staff from local, state, regional, and national intermediaries who partnered with government for training and other forms of capacity building, and local citizens and youth leaders engaged in civic action. Most interviews lasted approximately one hour, though some were as long as three hours, and interviews with youth leaders tended to be less than a full hour. In some cases, I interviewed individuals multiple times and over a period of years during the course of my field research (2000–08), though I have drawn upon a few interviews from an earlier research project as well.

Multiple interviews with some key informants and their successors (for example, successive agency directors, chairs of city council land-use committees, youth planners) have permitted me to follow developments over several phases, to interrogate some further on the basis of diverse perspectives elicited from interviews with others, and to explore unanticipated consequences and unforeseen opportunities or constraints that emerged. My interviewees included some who have played roles in successive iterations of a program and others who performed what, in retrospect, one might see as a string of complementary roles in various government agencies and civic organizations over the course of one or more decades, sometimes shifting the main focus of their work from one sector to another or from one level of government to another.

My interviews ranged across various topics, depending on the interviewee, including the development of programs, tools, funding, frames, trust, and networks; opportunities and obstacles to policy and network learning and agency culture change; and relevant political context, such as changes in elected leaders and appointed administrators, conflicts between city council and mayor, and grassroots community and social movement mobilization. The titles of those interviewed, as well as the ages of youth leaders, are those at the time of the interview, unless otherwise stated. Interviewees were provided the opportunity to speak off the record at any point in the interview or to request anonymity. One agency office preferred that no staff be cited by name (probably because of a delicate change in leadership at the time). Otherwise, real people appear in the case narratives of policy learning and program development in the hope that readers will recognize that government staff, and not just community activists or movement leaders, can act as flesh-and-blood agents of civic change and partnership building to enhance democracy. I have yet to encounter a faceless bureaucrat in my research, even among those with serious reservations about various aspects of civic policy design.[74]

The great majority of those interviewed, both within and outside of government, were quite free with criticisms and shortfalls they perceived in design and practice. One state agency official, for instance, noted more than halfway through the interview that "your question makes me nervous," at which point I expected him to close down; instead, he indicated that the following remarks were off the record and added that he still was not sure whether the new policy design was "just rhetoric." He had already been surprisingly blunt on the record and had been referred by someone who also was initially quite hesitant, agreeing to a fairly limited amount of time but then prompting me to ask far more, well beyond the agreed-upon forty minutes.

Before, during, and after my interviews, I used similar snowballing techniques to solicit other potential interviewees, both those who could corroborate, refine, or expand on evidence or perspective and those who might have divergent and more critical views. When seeking lists of potential interviewees from key informants, I was explicit about seeking diverse views, including those that were quite critical, at least of some parts of programs or implementation. Indeed, I factored key informants' willingness to suggest the names, e-mail addresses, and phone numbers of critics—in some cases, even before I asked for them and including critics of their own actions—into my overall judgment of the balance and reliability of the information and perspectives they offered. While I certainly did not survey the full universe of potential types of critics in any given city, program, or agency, I did get a fairly broad range of critical views and triangulated these through documentary evidence and secondary studies whenever possible.[75]

I took extensive, sometimes near-verbatim, notes during my formal interviews and recorded most of my informal conversations shortly after they occurred. I did not tape-record the interviews, having been taught a subtle lesson some years earlier, during a tape-recorded interview with relational organizer par excellence Ernie Cortes, of the Industrial Areas Foundation, that if one wishes to learn about organizing while building trust, one does not turn on a tape recorder. At least that is the lesson I drew when, midway in the interview, Cortes walked to the opposite side of the large room so that his responses could no longer be picked up clearly by the recorder. I hit the off button, and the interview continued productively.

Field and Participant Observation

Second, to collect further data I conducted direct field observation as well as participant observation as an engaged scholar.[76] I conducted, or was accompanied on, a variety of tours of neighborhoods, government agency and civic association offices, and physical projects accomplished by a variety of initiatives. In some cases, I got drawn into spontaneous conversations among those present, such as during an evening barbecue among neighborhood leaders after a hard day's work at one of Seattle's community gardens. I took extensive field notes of various training and strategy conferences, staff meetings, and public as well as closed meetings of civic activists and stakeholders.

As academic adviser to the CARE program at the EPA, I participated in on-site and teleconference trainings of the CARE staff, on-site national CARE grantee trainings, staff-only strategy and planning meetings, and annual EPA agency-wide community involvement conferences. Another EPA team that developed the new train-the-trainer collaboration curriculum for middle managers included me in the feedback process before piloting the program in May 2008. I also had the opportunity to present and discuss a paper on the civic mission of federal agencies at a conference of officials from various federal agencies in 2006 and to continue discussions through conference calls over the next year. The paper, later published in the *National Civic Review,* was circulated through CARE networks agency-wide, and I received much useful feedback.[77]

In Hampton, I observed an array of meetings of the youth commission, youth planners, the school superintendent's advisory group, and the neighborhood youth advisory group as well as meetings with adult agency staff and the city's major youth leadership intermediary, Alternatives Inc. In addition, I participated in the four-day national conference and related activities, organized jointly by the City of Hampton and Alternatives, with teams of innovators from ten other cities designed to facilitate network and policy learning and diffusion. I followed up with telephone interviews for a comparative analysis of youth commissions and other citywide strategies for youth civic engagement as well as for a potential federal policy design that might help build the capacity of various intermediaries and networks within the field. This conference, funded by Hampton's Innovations in American Government Award, also included representatives of several national youth engagement and development intermediaries. On an earlier occasion, I observed a conference in Hampton of the BEST (Building Exemplary Systems of Training for Youth Workers) Initiative, a national training program to upgrade the professional skills of youth workers, including their capacities to facilitate youth participation. The program is housed at the Academy for Educational Development in Washington, D.C., and Hampton innovators serve as core partners at the local, regional, and national level.

I convened four three-day national strategy and research conferences on youth civic engagement, at which I took extensive field notes, and had access to all audiotapes of session presentations and discussions. Each conference was preceded and followed by personal and telephone interviews. These conferences included adult and youth innovators across a variety of youth civic engagement fields and projects, including city-sponsored and independently organized citywide projects and partnerships, university-based ones, and national youth engagement organizations and intermediaries. One of my undergraduate research assistants served as co-organizer (with Campus Compact staff) of the National Student Summit at the Wingspread Conference Center in September 2002, at which I also took extensive field notes. In addition, I conducted field observations and interviews among several major grantees of the Corporation for National and Community Service (City Year, Corps Network, YouthBuild USA, Campus Compact, American Association of State Colleges and Universities,

Portland State University, National Network for Youth) and served as a "thought leader" for City Year during the planning and rollout of its civic leadership curriculum. I also took field notes at a conference sponsored by the U.S. Department of Housing and Urban Development for the grantees of its Community Outreach Partnership Centers program.

These various trainings, meetings, and conferences provided much opportunity for formal dialogue, as well as numerous hours of informal conversation, and enabled qualitative insight into various civic engagement networks, including their partners in local, state, and federal agencies. As anyone who has done this kind of research knows, the informal conversations and ongoing follow-up dialogue by e-mail and phone often provide some of the most important information and insight, especially with government agency staff, funded intermediaries, and local partners, who are understandably concerned with issues of trust in their own networks, as well as with researchers who would study them. Such informal exchanges are too numerous to cite in the footnotes and in some cases, even when not explicitly off the record, deserve to remain confidential.

In Seattle, my research was enriched by the public dialogue that occurred around the draft of my article on neighborhood planning for the *Journal of the American Planning Association* in 2007. The draft circulated among various department offices, city council, the mayor's office, and neighborhood activists, especially those serving on the city neighborhood council, at a point when the city was in the midst of redesigning the process of neighborhood plan updates and implementation. A good deal of disagreement had emerged around the mayor's proposed approach, on display especially at the neighborhood council's meetings and city council committee hearings. The city council commissioned the Office of the City Auditor to do a formal audit of plan implementation, to which I was asked to contribute extensive written comments and a telephone interview after conducting a further round of my own interviews and viewing live hearings and webcasts.

When the revised *Journal of the American Planning Association* article appeared in print, it was posted on the website of city councilor Sally Clark, head of the Planning, Land Use, and Neighborhoods Committee, as well as the website of the city neighborhood council. As the city attempted to design a way to bridge differences, I was then asked by former mayor Norm Rice, under whom neighborhood planning had been initiated in 1994 and who had been informally charged with trying to bring various parties together, to keynote the citywide forum on neighborhood planning in March 2008. At this forum, I had the chance to further observe and understand different perspectives, as well as the process by which the city was attempting to move toward consensus.

While I also helped frame the debate in terms of broad lessons, I assumed a multiperspectival presentation style, so that (for instance) neighborhood leaders would make the effort to understand the perspectives and constraints of the planning department and its professionals and city councilors (including the chair of the budget committee) would make the effort to understand neighborhood leaders' perspectives on the relative importance of continuing to invest in civic capacity. This rhetorical strategy removed me substantially, though probably not fully, from the underlying political debate and internal administration tug-of-war over new policy design. This forum also led to a further series of interviews, informal conversations, and detailed minutes of all the break-out sessions. Although at times I felt caught in a maelstrom of competing views and proposals, or as if I were trying to catch a moving train, while being sent a steady barrage of e-mails and agency documents—some records of internal discussions wrenched from city departments through Freedom of Information Act efforts by local activists—my engagement with this process in 2007–08 provided me with new and diverse sources of data and perspectives. I was most impressed by the integrity of the key actors I dealt with in this process and their efforts to recognize my role as a scholar seeking to understand all perspectives of what is most certainly a complex set of issues in planning and governing a dynamic and diverse world-class city, while engaging its citizens in consequential ways.[78]

Indeed, were I to admit revelation, or at least revelatory moments, in the research process, I would have to say that I learned some of the deepest truths about collaborative governance culture by the way in which various parties in Seattle, often in the midst of intense disagreement and representing different roles and histories of engagement, talked about one another both on and off the record in my interviews. My own research ethos and implicit ground rules undoubtedly elicited some of the mutual respect and willingness to entertain other perspectives. But much of the profoundly democratic, communicative ethos of the conversations that emerged, not just in Seattle but in my other cases, was the product of interview subjects themselves, acting as highly sophisticated and reflective civic agents and civil servants with multiple perspectives engaged in a research process that was more than simply academic to them.

Documentary Sources

Third, I gathered data from a wide variety of documentary sources for each case. For data on program design, funding, implementation, and evaluation, I examined agency strategic planning and framework documents; mission statements and visioning reports; neighborhood plans and updates; internal and external evaluations; reports of EPA's Office of Inspector General and the U.S. Government Accountability Office; reports of National Academy of Public Administration and National Research Council panels; federal advisory committee and local planning commission reports; official program reports and participant surveys; annual program guidance documents and budgets; webcasts of trainings, meetings, and hearings; regional and national EPA program newsletters; city and neighborhood news coverage; unpublished memos, timelines, and lists of coordinators; and official minutes and summaries of meetings.

For documentary data on intermediary organizations, networks, and local civic groups, I examined membership and partner lists; sponsor and participant lists and affiliations from conferences and trainings; annual reports, budgets, and financial audits; project evaluations; and conference proceedings and reports. I also reviewed various tools (neighborhood planning, youth commission, volunteer watershed monitoring, community organizing and visioning manuals; environmental education and service-learning curriculums; online data, geographic information systems, and planning toolkits, templates, and portals) developed by intermediaries and field-tested with local groups, typically with funding from agencies or, when developed by agencies themselves, with collaboration from intermediaries and local groups. My interviews gave me added insight into the network processes through which such tools were developed, including the negotiated back-and-forth among agency professionals and civic activists, representing different mixes of professional expertise and local knowledge.

In addition to getting feedback on various presentations and articles along the way, I shared drafts of the case study chapters with several key informants in each. In some instances, they read the entire manuscript. They helped refine and correct specific details and set me along still other paths of inquiry, interview, or interpretation. Only one individual asked me to omit a short sentence from a quotation, not because it was inaccurate but because it might convey an overly flippant response that was not intended and that some citizens might misinterpret. Reflecting on the importance of the civic trust at stake in the city, I agreed to the request, without altering the substance of what had been said.

In the concluding chapter 6, I reprise my findings and present a set of major proposals for the federal government, if it is to act more vigorously as a civic enabler and strategic investor. I draw upon further interviews and documents beyond my case study chapters, especially from several other federal agencies, national service programs, and White House offices.[79] Of course, state and local governments, and many other independent civic actors, need to join in this work—indeed, to take the lead in many areas. But the federal government is in a position to play an especially strategic and catalytic role among state and local partners—hence the focus of the last chapter. Developing a policy agenda can hardly be based upon three extended case studies, to be sure. But these cases, and much scholarly literature on other cases, fields, and levels of government, are suggestive of what we might do at the federal level.

My proposals are designed to proceed within the limits of what we know reasonably well and to build capacity for learning while doing—iterative, reflexive learning and self-correction. Unlike some of the big and provocative proposals that have been offered in recent years to revitalize American democracy,[80] the ones I develop do not rely upon deliberation among randomly selected groups of citizens but remain rooted in the everyday public work, relationship building, embedded deliberation, and network learning among citizens, organized associations, and public agency staff. Such work, of course, must find more creative ways to inform policy deliberation and agenda setting among elected officials and advocacy coalitions.

The agenda I propose is far from a complete one. Others have pointed to democratic deficits that would not be directly addressed by the forms of collaborative and network governance that are the focus here. But the proposals in chapter 6 are intended to provide a handle for energetic, yet careful and incremental, federal action, should we get the kind of elected leadership that recognizes the challenges of a democracy at risk as well as the opportunities available for finding ways to engage citizens productively and collaboratively.

2 Collaborative Governance and Policy Design: Core Principles

"To consider a particular policy in civic terms," argues Boston College political scientist Marc Landy in a formative 1993 Brookings Institution volume, *Public Policy for Democracy,* "it is useful to abandon a purely instrumental conception of it as a machine designed to spew out specific outputs and to think of it instead as a constitution." Constitutions establish broad ends, define powers, and prescribe specific institutional arrangements. They determine who is to be included as a member and thereby define publics, the tools available to them, and the lessons they are likely to learn about the polity and their role in it. Policies, in effect, construct citizens in specific ways, encourage and discourage certain kinds of civic virtues and behaviors, and provide ongoing civic education—or miseducation. It is thus critical that policies be designed to encourage and enable self-governing citizenship and that public administrators, including senior bureaucrats, view themselves fundamentally as civic educators.[1]

In collaborative governance, policy design aims to "empower, enlighten, and engage citizens in the process of self-government."[2] This chapter draws upon a burgeoning theoretical literature and recent empirical analyses of civic engagement and collaborative governance, as well as from design components in the case studies that follow, to extract eight core principles of collaborative governance. Each principle is worthy of a much more extended and nuanced discussion, to be sure, and later chapters complicate them in various ways. My purpose here is to highlight these principles, not to probe all their theoretical implications and attendant debates.

Not all specific policies or broad policy problems, of course, could or should embody all eight principles or configure them similarly. Indeed, some policies, offices, or agencies clearly need not embody many because of the nature of the public goods they produce, the relative effectiveness and cost of other available governance tools for producing them, and the limited externalities and disabling effects of some tools. If identifiable point sources of pollution clearly cause a particular environmental harm, for instance, then command and control regulation or an emissions-trading scheme may be much more relevant than investment in a complex ecosystem partnership—though the latter may nonetheless be needed for related problems, and the cumulative impact on community capacity of using too many noncivic tools needs to be part of one's overall judgment of good policy options. Thus in addition to core principles of collaborative governance and policy design, policymakers and administrators need some potential axioms for choosing when and how to employ them.

These principles have import not just for policy design but also for the education and ethics of policy analysts and public administrators. Terry Cooper, professor of policy and planning at the University of Southern California and author of the widely used textbook *The Responsible Administrator,* makes a compelling case for the indispensable administrative role of nurturing engaged and informed citizens. If we are to keep our self-governing republic, Cooper argues, the public administrator should be held "ethically responsible" for encouraging participation of the citizenry in the process of planning and providing public goods and services, and schools of public administration should offer tools to enable them to carry out this responsibility. Indeed, such schools should foster the professional identity of public servants as civic enablers. No less than civic associations in Tocqueville's classic *Democracy in America,* schools of public administration and planning should become "schools of democracy."[3]

William Ruckelshaus, first administrator of the EPA in the early 1970s, who returned to rescue the agency from political crisis in 1983 and enabled several important civic innovations in agency practice, put the general challenge thus in his 1996 Webb Lecture at the National Academy of Public Administration:

Thomas Jefferson once pointed out that if the people appeared not enlightened enough to exercise their control of government, the solution was not to take away the control but to "inform their discretion by education." The cooperative processes that are springing up around the country are doing just that, giving to large numbers of citizens a new comprehension of the complexity involved in government decisions, out of which has got to come a heightened appreciation of, and tolerance for, the necessary work of government. If these processes work, if they spread, if they become an indispensable part of government at all levels, we may take it as a sign that we, as a people, have moved up a grade in democracy's school. It holds out the hope that, eventually, the United States will be ready for self-government.[4]

No head of a federal agency, to my knowledge, has ever put it better.

Designing for Collaborative Governance

The eight principles of policy design presented in this chapter are broad and integrative but are not intended to be all inclusive, or all-or-nothing. Some theorists and practitioners might configure them differently, place them under various other rubrics, or employ terminologies that they see as either more rigorous theoretically or more resonant among citizens and practitioners—two criteria that inevitably generate some creative tension. The principles, all of which address shared power in one form or another, represent a selective menu whose various combinations might be relevant for some governance and policy problems but not for others. Certain public goods might warrant vigorous public deliberation but do not lend themselves well to coproduction—and vice versa—and some might well include both. How we configure the specific processes of sharing expertise with citizens and using their own local knowledge will vary considerably from one policy arena to another or from one level of problem solving to another. Employing certain design principles within specific structures of power and inequality might generate unintended consequences for other public values, such as fair process and just outcomes, for which neither a theory of democracy nor a theory of justice can provide foolproof guidance. There are always relative costs, trade-offs, and unintended consequences to which civic policy analysts and practitioners will have to attend.

A pragmatic approach to questions of policy design, complex governance, and democratic theory is thus critical, as Archon Fung, professor of public policy at Harvard's Kennedy School of Government, argues.[5] One key proposal for federal policy design presented in chapter 6 attempts to

Table 2-1. *Eight Core Principles of Collaborative Governance and Policy Design*

Core principal	Policy design
Coproduce public goods	Policy should enable the work of citizens themselves in coproducing public goods.
Mobilize community assets	Policy should enable communities to mobilize their own assets for problem solving and development.
Share professional expertise	Policy should mobilize expert knowledge to enlighten and empower everyday citizens and to use citizens' own local knowledge.
Enable public deliberation	Policy should enable and expect citizens to engage in the public reasoning upon which good policy choices, democratic legitimacy, and effective implementation depend.
Promote sustainable partnerships	Policy should promote collaborative work and partnerships among citizens, organized stakeholders, and public agencies.
Build fields and governance networks strategically	Policy should mobilize field-building assets strategically to enable citizens, civic associations, and broader governance networks to work effectively together.
Transform institutional cultures	Policy should catalyze public and nonprofit agencies to become learning organizations for community empowerment and civic problem solving and draw market actors into civic partnerships and culture change as well.
Ensure reciprocal accountability	Policy should promote mutual accountability for collaborative work among the broad range of democratic actors and partners.

build reflexivity and pragmatic self-correction into the civic policy-learning process, and various existing models have already done this relatively well at the local level. Yet we should not lose sight of the forest for the trees— the cumulative and interactive effects of choosing some cluster of designs and tools over others and how our choices impact our policy-specific, as well as our overall, capacities to act effectively as self-governing citizens. Table 2-1 provides a schematic overview of the eight principles.

Coproduce Public Goods

This first principle of design holds that policy should recognize and encourage robust roles for ordinary citizens in coproducing public goods. Because public goods are complex and often cannot be effectively produced and delivered by some direct tool of government, policy should be crafted in ways that enable and encourage ordinary citizens, collaborating with public servants and other professionals, to contribute to producing them. Citizens should have roles that go well beyond simply advocating for public goods, paying for them through taxes, and then consuming them as services and benefits. Not only should policy expect citizens to coproduce public goods, but it should also help provide the tools and templates to enable them to become skilled, responsible, effective producers.

While some theorists of coproduction have had a decidedly narrow view of it as designed primarily to reduce agency costs by using volunteers or to involve only direct consumers or clients of public services, others have developed a relatively expansive version of citizens as essential public producers with a wide range of potential roles.[6] Harry Boyte, of the University of Minnesota, has written extensively on the citizen as producer engaged in visible public work throughout American history.[7]

Policy design can enable citizens to become coproducers in myriad ways. As discussed in chapter 1, the defining mission of the Chicago Alternative Policing Strategy has been "Safe Neighborhoods Are Everybody's Business." This mission is designed to encourage a major shift in mindset among police and residents alike: ordinary citizens have many roles to play in ensuring a safer city, and their work represents an essential part of the ongoing production of public safety. Residents can enhance school safety, reclaim the streets from predators and drug dealers, and fix the literal and figurative broken windows that signify social disorder. Many stakeholders, from the faith community to landlords, have their work to do as well. Everybody has work to do.[8]

Public health is a public good also amenable to coproduction. An Institute of Medicine report, summarizing a great deal of research, defines health as a state of well-being and a set of functional capabilities enabled by many factors outside the formal health care system, such as cultural norms, nutrition and exercise, environmental conditions, safe and adequate housing, and social support systems. The importance of community health improvement is articulated in the first principle of the report: "Communities should base a health improvement process on a broad definition of health and a comprehensive conceptual model of how health is produced within the community." This includes identifying the full "range of actors that can affect community health . . . and mak[ing] a constructive contribution to the health of the community."[9] An effective community health strategy would thus mobilize productive contributions from many kinds of actors beyond formal health care providers, including faith and family networks, youth peer groups, environmental justice activists, and community development groups, to name just a few.

Healthy Boston, for instance, organized by the city's Department of Health and Hospitals in the 1990s, supported the work of community coalitions in peer education to reduce asthma, domestic violence, smoking, teen pregnancy, breast cancer, substance abuse, obesity, and HIV/AIDS. Some of their efforts were directly coordinated with the city's community policing strategies, thus demonstrating the close linkage for communities of various kinds of public goods requiring coordinated coproduction across agencies. Healthy communities projects across the country, many sponsored by city, county, and state agencies, have also recognized coproduction as an essential component of their work.[10]

Another policy arena in which coproduction has become an indispensable component of the policy frame is ecosystem health and sustainability. Since the 1980s, it is no longer possible for policymakers or local activists to imagine that regulators or scientific professionals, acting on their own, can protect and restore complex ecosystems, as one prestigious report after another of the nation's top scientists and environmental policymakers has come to recognize.[11] Citizens coproduce essential data without which regulators and planners could not do their jobs effectively. Boating associations and anglers clubs monitor illegal dumping and communicate and enforce moral standards, while homeowner associations and scout troops replace riparian buffers on streams and remove invasive species. Community college students provide essential aerial photography and replant oysters to replenish the bay. Indeed, the list of what individual citizens, families, schools, and associations now do to protect and restore ecosystems is too long to catalogue briefly. Many approach their work not just as episodic volunteerism, a good deed here and there, but also within a larger strategic governance framework and even, at times, with the grand vision of "restoring creation," performing "a sacred task," "building cathedrals," and expending "blood, sweat, and tears," often with a rich lore of work stories to motivate continued civic action.[12]

Perhaps the foremost message of civic policy design, its chief teaching, is that ordinary citizens must come to view themselves as vital coproducers of public goods and that their full dignity as citizens entails becoming ever more responsible, skilled, and effective as producers of those goods. Public policy and administration can and ought to provide them with many kinds of tools and opportunities to enable their productive public work. Citizens are not just bearers of rights or informed deliberators. They are public craftspeople, men and women—and, increasingly, girls and boys—with the ability to produce a democratic commonwealth.[13]

Mobilize Community Assets

The second, and closely related, principle of design is that policy should encourage communities to mobilize their own assets for problem solving. In the famous formulation of John McKnight and Jody Kretzmann, all communities—even some of the poorest and most marginalized—have assets that can be mapped and mobilized for productive work and visible improvement if civic actors can shift their mindset away from deficits and dependence. "Clients have deficiencies and needs. Citizens have capacities and gifts."[14] Communities possess many kinds of underused assets—local knowledge, hidden skills, vacant land, small businesses, everyday purchases, religious congregations, public buildings, private institutions, civic associations, friendship networks—that can be mobilized in fresh ways and with new synergies. Public policy, and the practices of public agencies and nonprofit contractors, as well as business partners, can employ an assets frame to elicit coproduction and help transform clients into citizens by shifting their cognitive frame from deficits to assets—a shift that can hardly be overemphasized in recent community practice.

The asset-based community development frame has been diffused widely since the early 1990s, both in grassroots community development efforts and initiatives sponsored by foundations, United Way chapters, and public agencies in youth development, public health, disabilities, aging, and social services as well as in urban planning, community forestry, and ecosystem sustainability. In the latter, as one prominent policy analyst notes, asset-based development has "become a key concept of sustainability science."[15] Under the earlier direction of Dr. Stephanie Bailey, now chief of public health practice at the Centers for Disease Control and Prevention, the National Association of County and City Health Officials developed an environmental health assessment protocol that also uses asset-based principles.[16]

As part of their federally mandated mission under the Developmental Disabilities Assistance and Bill of Rights Act of 2000 to catalyze advocacy, capacity building, and systems change, state councils on developmental disabilities have also been incorporating asset-based training into their work. Connecticut, for example, began such training more than a decade earlier. Chicago's community policing program has recently contracted for training more than ten thousand local resident leaders in asset-based principles and practices. In the past five years, administrative capacities of cities to assist in local asset-based community development have been growing notably. Kretzmann and McKnight's *Building Communities from the Inside Out,* initially published in 1993, has sold more than one hundred thousand copies, and another twenty-five thousand have been given away to various community groups and larger initiatives. Its attendant asset-mapping tools have been used by a wide array of public agencies and nonprofits, with the Asset-Based Community Development Institute at Northwestern University serving as the hub of a national network of trainers.[17]

In Rochester, New York, asset mapping is a core activity of the Department of Community Development's innovative Neighbors Building Neighborhoods program, a system of neighborhood planning that since 1994 has been integrated into the comprehensive plan. Citizen planners in each of ten newly consolidated sectors were charged with mapping land, buildings, and other familiar assets and cataloguing nonprofit, school, church, and business partners who might become coproducers for some part of the improvement strategy. The Neighbors Building Neighborhoods Institute helped with training, and a neighborhood empowerment team provided city staff support in each sector. In Sector 10, a predominantly African American and Latino area encompassing Upper Falls, South Marketview Heights, and North Marketview Heights, the NorthEast Neighborhood Alliance formed as a response to the sector structure and asset-based development strategy of Neighbors Building Neighborhoods. It brought together representatives from more than forty local associations and agencies, from tenant, youth, and ethnic organizing groups and churches to women's, independent living, and neighborhood resource centers.

Through a succession of rounds of Neighbors Building Neighborhoods planning, the alliance took the lead in a broad array of initiatives for housing, public safety, urban agriculture, and local business development, in collaboration with various public agency and private partners. Its organic urban agriculture project, Greater Rochester Urban Bounty, for instance, employs neighborhood teens during the summer. Since youth are responsible for all aspects of the business, from nurturing seedlings and harvesting produce to local marketing to restaurant owners and chefs, they receive training in agricultural methods as well as leadership, communication, and entrepreneurship. A grant from Learn and Serve America at the Corporation for National and Community Service enabled the Rochester Institute of Technology to develop a robust partnership with the NorthEast Neighborhood Alliance across a broad range of projects, thereby engaging students and faculty in helping develop geographic information system tools, small business plans, marketing assistance, interior design, and sustainable development strategies. As Sydney Cresswell, Jordan Wishy, and Terrence Maxwell at the Nelson Rockefeller College of Public Affairs and Policy argue, the asset-based process of the Neighbors Building Neighborhoods program enabled the alliance and citizen planning groups in other sectors to leverage considerable funding from private foundations, such as the Kellogg and Enterprise foundations, as well as from banks and other private sectors firms. The city's civic investments, in short, had a substantial multiplier effect.[18]

Share Professional Expertise

The third principle of design calls for public administrators and other professionals, enlisted through policy to solve public problems, to use their expertise in ways that empower citizens as problem solvers. Professional expertise becomes a shared resource, especially valuable when organized transparently and presented in formats that ordinary citizens and communities can employ in practical ways and always open to question as well as enrichment by citizens' own local knowledge.

Local knowledge, according to Charles Lindblom and David Cohen's touchstone 1979 policy study, *Usable Knowledge: Social Science and Social Problem Solving,* is "knowledge that does not owe its origin, testing, degree of verification, truth, status, or currency to distinctive . . . professional techniques, but rather to common sense, causal empiricism, or thoughtful speculation and analysis."[19] Neighborhood residents might generate local knowledge of crime, for instance, when they observe suspicious patterns of coming and going at a home or business, or traffic at an intersection, during certain hours of the day. Parents talking together at the playground may suspect an unusual incidence of cancer near a manufacturing facility or landfill. A local fisherman might notice curious fish kills in a favorite stream and suspect that increased water temperature owing to upstream discharges might be responsible and, indeed, might also be having a larger impact on the entire watershed. Local knowledge testifies to the capacity of everyday citizens to be observant, vigilant, practical, and imaginative.

Of course, none of this guarantees truth or automatically produces wise and effective solutions. Local residents can be horribly prejudiced and wildly misplaced in their suspicions of criminal behavior, and caring parents can let chemical superstitions get the best of them. Even an experienced fisherman might simply have spent too much time in the sun! But citizens are capable of more systematic observation and testing. At the local

beat meeting, they can try to match their observations with those of officers on the beat and with statistical crime data from precincts and headquarters. Mothers can collaborate with medical professionals to conduct a
convincing "popular epidemiology" of unusual cancer patterns in a community.[20] The fisherman can get others in his local watershed association to
use sophisticated temperature probes to produce stream temperature data
recognized as valid by professionals in the state department of environmental protection. The department can even supply the probes, provide
quality assurance guidelines and oversight, help convene watershed associations across the state to improve their volunteer monitoring techniques,
and even use their findings to modify its own TMDL (total maximum
daily load) measures, required by the federal Clean Water Act, as well as
alter the water discharge policies of a major city. Indeed, all this happened
in New Jersey when trout fisherman Ross Kushner and his fellow citizens
insisted that their local knowledge of the Pequannock River become part of
the professional and regulatory mix.[21]

The key term here is "mix." As planning professor Jason Corburn, of
the University of California at Berkeley, shows in *Street Science,* his rich
study of environmental health action in the Greenpoint-Williamsburg
section of Brooklyn, local citizens challenged city and state agency professionals, as well as the EPA and the dominant paradigm of risk assessment, on a host of issues. They brought to the table various forms of
locally generated knowledge about ethnic dietary habits, subsistence fishing, the incidence of asthma, and home remedies through a variety of
methods: door-to-door community surveys, focus groups, and trained
community health promoters (*promotoras de salud*). They also used personal stories, public murals, and community maps of the numerous toxic
facilities in the neighborhood. In one project, neighborhood residents and
students were trained to analyze data with the epidemiological software
package Epi Info. Truth was not guaranteed by local knowledge itself or
by the very act of resistance to inadequate professional paradigms but by
the extent to which the various actors in the scientific, regulatory, public
health, and community sectors learned to generate trust through mutual
interrogation and negotiation of their various methodologies and came to
view themselves and one another as genuine "co-producers of expertise."[22]
In the end, professionals in these and many similar cases recognize their
own professionalism as enhanced, not diminished, by such collaboration
across diverse ways of knowing, and community actors often revise their

own understandings of likely causes and potential solutions by exposure to professional points of view.

For expertise to become a shared resource often requires investments in data systems that are sophisticated yet usable by the public. Planning theorists, such as Richard Brail and Richard Klosterman, refer to these as planning support systems that integrate multiple types of information and are flexible and user friendly. Ideally, these systems permit everyday citizens and professional partners to select appropriate analysis and forecasting tools from an intelligent digital toolbox that helps users identify the most appropriate methodologies and tools for particular problems; link the analytic and projection tools to appropriate local, regional, or national stored data systems; run appropriate models to determine the implications of alternative policy choices and different assumptions about present and future; and instantaneously view the results graphically in the form of charts, maps, and audio-video displays that can enhance citizen understanding. Such planning support systems facilitate a genuine process of collective design based on rich democratic social interaction.[23]

There now exists a wide array of such tools, often based on interactive maps and geographic information systems, that support open group decisionmaking and networks of citizens and multistakeholder collaboratives generating, interpreting, and using such data to build trust—including trust in data from multiple and self-interested sources—and to reach workable consensus to guide common action. For instance, CommunityViz, a decision support system for community planning and design applications based on ArcView's geographic information system, is especially suited to rural communities grappling with issues of development, environment, and economic sustainability and uses photo-realistic three-dimensional visualizations, scenario constructions, and policy simulations, including tax, land-use, and capital-budgeting choices. Community workshops making use of this tool enrich the potential of public choice based on sound knowledge and community values, and individual citizens can access the system from many different starting points (and virtually any personal computer) to become engaged and informed participants.[24] Archon Fung, Mary Graham, and David Weil make a more general case for the emergence of a third generation of public information tools, which they call "collaborative transparency." Such tools, equipped with user interfaces that "become much more interactive and customized" and thus can be revised at a much faster pace, will "empower information users themselves to provide and pool much of the essential data." To further policy purposes, government will most likely play a key role as convener and facilitator.[25]

Enable Public Deliberation

The fourth principle is that policy should promote robust public deliberation among citizens themselves. Policy design should enable citizens to engage in reasoned dialogue, evaluate evidence, weigh options, and consider costs, benefits, and possible trade-offs. Rather than simply ratify expressed preferences and preexisting perspectives in some aggregative formula intended to yield the greatest good for the greatest number, policy design should encourage citizens to reflect upon their own self-interests in a mutual search for common interests, shared values, and pragmatic solutions—though there is no guarantee that these will emerge. Forms of citizen deliberation should be designed in ways that are appropriately inclusive, given the nature and scope of the problem and the relevant publics. They should not preempt or displace the deliberation of legislatures, expert commissions, or administrative bodies but should be devised in ways that yield what I have called "deliberative democratic complementarities," that is, plural forms of public reasoning that enrich and challenge one another in an iterative and corrective process.[26]

In the large body of deliberative democratic theory of recent years, several arguments tend to be prominent. First, public deliberation can produce better policy outcomes by generating sources of evidence and insight that might otherwise be unavailable to elected representatives or public administrators deliberating on their own, even using extensive poll data. Second, by directly engaging citizens in public reasoning with one another, and perhaps with various organized stakeholders and agency officials, they are more likely to appreciate varied interests and perspectives, as well as hard choices about costs and trade-offs, and thereby to attribute higher levels of legitimacy to decisions, even when their own preferences are not met as fully as they might wish. Enhanced legitimacy increases the likelihood of more-effective policy implementation by reducing potential obstruction and eliciting coproduction and community asset mobilization. Third, engaging citizens in active deliberation signals civic respect and mutuality as well as the recognition of citizens as autonomous agents rather than mere objects of legislation and administration. This expressive function can enhance public spiritedness and generate trust that carries over to other forms of civic collaboration.[27]

To be sure, deliberative democratic theorists do not assume that these benefits are automatic or always achievable or that citizen deliberation should be emphasized to the exclusion of other forms of civic action or tools of governance. The key, as with shared expertise and street science, is finding the appropriate mix, as well as designing forms of citizen deliberation most suitable to specific problems and publics. These forms of engagement should also control for a variety of participatory hazards, such as biases toward citizens with more education or groups with greater power resources to bring to the deliberative table. Such hazards, however, are hardly limited to deliberative forms of engagement but indeed have been found to arise in egalitarian social movements, public interest lobbying, community and labor organizing, peasant revolutions, and many other forms of civic action. As there are no perfect tools of governance, so there are no ideal forms of democratic engagement or public deliberation.

Since certain forms of structured dialogue seem to elicit more-productive listening, self-reflective reasoning, and civil argumentation than others, and because the potential of deliberation appears "highly context dependent and rife with opportunities for going awry,"[28] deliberative democracy theorists and practitioners are continually experimenting and evaluating which design might best fit specific kinds of issues, disputes, and communities. Over the past several decades, practice has proceeded on many fronts. One of the most familiar is community visioning, generally an open and inclusive process involving ordinary citizens and organized stakeholders who meet periodically over a period of months to forge a common vision of a desired future.

Community visioning is designed to guide and motivate specific initiatives, some of which might be taken by civic and business actors, others by government, though often in partnerships of one form or another. Participants consider alternative scenarios, assess the civic infrastructure (often using tools such as the National Civic League's *Civic Index*), and map various other community assets that might be mobilized for action. In some cases, elected public officials or agency staff initiate, guide, and even officially authorize the visioning and deliberative planning process through legislation. In others, public officials participate as stakeholders on an equal footing with civic and business actors or simply lend support though research, facilitation, or meeting space. For instance, the visioning and deliberative design of the Henry's Fork Watershed Council, a multistakeholder forum with more than a decade of experience, has been officially sanctioned by the Idaho legislature, whereas the community visioning that guided sustainable development in Chattanooga, Tennessee, was sponsored by a nonprofit but included elected officials and public agencies as participants and partners.[29]

Study circles, another growing form of citizen dialogue, are small, diverse groups of eight to twelve participants who meet over a period of weeks or months to deliberate about some critical public issue (crime, race, schools, budgets). Community-wide study circle designs might engage hundreds of or even several thousand citizens. In this and several other related deliberative models (national issues forums, deliberative polls), nonpartisan issue booklets representing various issue-framing options and choice scenarios might be used as a resource for discussion, and trained discussion facilitators remain neutral on the issues. Some designs, such as the 21st Century Town Meeting pioneered by America*Speaks,* combine small group dialogue, networked computers, electronic keypads, and video screens to enable large groups of citizens to develop compelling recommendations on public policy, such as the District of Columbia's budget priorities over a multiyear cycle of citizen summits. Still other designs provide for collaborative forms of "wiki-democracy," as Beth Noveck, of New York University School of Law, demonstrates in *Wiki Government: How Technology Can Make Government Better, Democracy Stronger, and Citizens More Powerful.*[30]

There are still many other variants of deliberative design intended to address policy issues of specific kind and scope and local political or agency cultures or to better grapple with full democratic inclusion, shared power, or consequential public action. Consistent with the theoretical formulations of political theorists Amy Gutmann and Dennis Thompson, among others, the deliberative democracy movement has been experimental and self-reflective, combining various types and levels of public reasoning among citizens and public officials in a manner designed to produce critical learning and self-correction in the interests of practical public action.[31] Deliberative practitioners also frequently cluster various components of collaborative governance with formal deliberation as such.

The crafting of the Oregon Health Plan presents a rich policy example of deliberative and other civic complementarities and multilevel learning over an extended period, though the debate surrounding it has often tried to squeeze its lessons into overly narrow boxes. Formal citizen deliberations occurred through some forty-seven community meetings across the state in 1990, designed to clarify guiding public values, and served as a complement to deliberation through the legislature and an appointed health services commission and also as a corrective to some of the priority health service rankings of an expert panel. These deliberations were preceded by years of extensive and embedded dialogues convened in churches and ministerial associations, senior and community centers, chambers of commerce and Rotary clubs, and medical and nursing school classrooms as well as in hospital settings and in two statewide "healthcare parliaments."

The civic bioethics group that coordinated these meetings, Oregon Health Decisions, catalyzed a far-reaching network of health professionals (nurses, doctors, technicians, physical therapists, billing staff, and others) committed to inclusive coverage, especially of poor women and children. The organization's networks also extended to organized stakeholder and advocacy groups, such as the Black Health Coalition, United Seniors, the Human Services Coalition, the Human Rights Coalition, Oregon Fair Share, and the Northwest Foundation for Children. Within these diverse community and institutional settings and across these stakeholder networks, leaders of Oregon Health Decisions built civic and political trust for more than a decade, allowing fruitful collaboration despite an admittedly imperfect deliberative community process at its inception. John Kitzhaber, president of the Oregon State Senate (and later governor) and a physician embedded in these same networks, was thus able to leverage this trust in negotiations on various delicate trade-offs and reform sequences, enabling him to become the critical policy entrepreneur that could make reform happen in a fiscal context quite unfavorable to expanded Medicaid coverage and innovative services. He could thus respond creatively to practical questions of equity and social justice while also recognizing the strongly articulated public value of living within limits, which allowed him to achieve overwhelming bipartisan support in the legislature.[32]

While increased citizen deliberation might be relatively unproblematic in helping to set the terms of public discourse and thus to inform proper legislative deliberations, many would question why deliberative processes should be further interlaced into administration. Simply put, bringing citizen deliberation into the administrative process is increasingly necessary because the standard mechanism of democratic representation—legislative deliberation combined with instrumental delegation to administrators acting within strictly defined parameters—performs suboptimally for a host of well-known reasons. Legislatures are often simply incapable of fine-tuned deliberation on the many aspects of the many policies with which they must deal and for various technical and political reasons are prone to pass vague laws, which require administrative agencies to become policy-makers through their exercise of discretion. Such discretion can easily become a form of bureaucratic domination, unless agencies themselves facilitate citizen deliberation as part of the ongoing process "whereby we make up our minds about what we ought to do," as political theorist Henry Richardson, of Georgetown University, argues.[33] Furthermore, the usual mechanisms of public opinion polling provide crude and often highly self-interested ways for elected representatives to determine what the public, especially a reasoning public, might want.[34] However, even if there were more robust forms of public deliberation in policymaking and agenda-setting processes, the problem of implementation would remain and hence also the challenge of bringing deliberative and other civic tools into the everyday work of public bureaucracies.

Promote Sustainable Partnerships

The fifth principle of collaborative governance and design is that policy should encourage collaboration between citizens and stakeholders, including those who may have histories of conflict, wherever this might strengthen civic infrastructure and lead to better policy outcomes. Public life often becomes quite contentious for reasons familiar to political theory: different interests, scarce resources, unequal power, divergent values, excluded identities. Compared with other forms of government, pluralist democracies have developed mechanisms for organizing and representing differences and managing conflict in reasonably effective and legitimate ways. But these mechanisms prove inadequate in many policy arenas, as citizens and organized stakeholders fail to discover a larger public good or common enterprise amid their divergences, leading often to policy stale-mate and suboptimal outcomes. Policy design and administrative practice should thus explore and facilitate productive, ongoing collaboration among stakeholders and across various boundaries of interest, identity, and institution. There is no singular common interest, to be sure. Not all politics can or should be collaborative. But much policy and public problem solving can and should explore how to elicit collaboration.

Democratic collaboration, of course, reprises many other principles of civic policy design by promoting ongoing deliberation among participants, mobilizing assets of various stakeholder networks, sharing expertise and information across institutional and professional boundaries, and eliciting value added coproduction from a broad range of civic, business, institutional, and agency partners. But collaboration also adds a distinctive focus on building relationships, producing trust through ongoing work together and, to some extent, reconceiving power itself as relational—"power with" rather than "power over," in the famous distinction first developed by Mary Parker Follett and later elaborated in various organizing, management, and institutional change models. Here, too, a large scholarly literature has emerged, along with much innovative practice.[35]

In many cases, collaboration does not reach deeply into organizational memberships or associational networks and thus can hardly be characterized as civic democracy. However, in other cases, partnership provides the framework for extensive engagement by ordinary citizens and diverse associations. For instance, Project QUEST, winner of a 1995 Innovations in American Government Award and a 2003 Enterprise Foundation and J. P. Morgan Chase Foundation Award for Excellence in Workforce Development, emerged as an innovative job-training partnership in San Antonio, and then spread to several other cities in Texas, because congregation-based community organizing built "relational power" across denominational, ethnic, and racial lines and then leveraged this power to bring employers and a local community college into a sustained partnership with the community. Citizens deliberated intensively in house meetings to understand existing job-training failures, based upon their own experiences, and to help devise the new program. They conducted research one-on-one meetings with various academic experts—another form of citizen science—to ensure state-of-the-art design, and with employers to ensure that the program would also meet their legitimate self-interests for well-trained and motivated employees. The congregations have also provided extensive outreach, prescreening, and moral encouragement to make the program succeed, as well as vigorous grassroots advocacy for government funding. State and city agencies—not without various battles, to be sure—have provided a range of important financial and programmatic supports, as has the U.S. Department of Labor.[36]

The City of Seattle designed the staff role of neighborhood planning project manager, and then its successor during the initial years of implementation, neighborhood development manager, in a way that would facilitate ongoing relationship and trust building among a wide array of actors. These included diverse civic groups within a larger neighborhood often characterized by various lines of potential division based on geographical location and proximity to nuisances, home ownership or rental status, racial-ethnic and immigrant identity, and type of organization (resident-led community council, staff-led nonprofit, neighborhood business association). In addition, planning staff were tasked with building relationships among civic groups and relevant street-level and middle-management staff from a dozen or so city departments, who were challenged by the holistic visioning and planning process to work across bureaucratic boundaries so that all pieces—from land use and transportation to housing and parks—would fit together and generate high degrees of public and professional legitimacy. The neighborhood planning process included a good deal of democratic deliberation in public settings, but these meetings could not begin to ensure the necessary types and levels of collaboration for effective planning, implementation, and legitimacy. Legitimacy tends to erode as time elapses between the deliberative event and the actual work entailed, because people have selective memories, unforeseen obstacles arise, and the "public" itself undergoes change in leadership and demographics.

The role of the neighborhood planning manager thus built in high expectations of communicative ethics and trust building during the work itself: gathering and vetting information, understanding the interests and perspectives of diverse parties, facilitating one-on-one communication, developing workable plans, and then generating credible commitments for ongoing collaborative work among various public actors, not just government staff, to bring projects to completion.[37] Indeed, as democratic planning stretched into the implementation phase, these planning managers also played an important role in interpreting, with citizens and other city staff, the meaning of the different temporal layers of deliberation, relationship building, and mutual commitments. After all, no item in a formal plan listed in an approval matrix could capture the richness of the public process that went into putting the item into the needed bureaucratic form or elicit adequate trust as further adjustments were needed once the rubber hit the road. Here is a case where using one principle (deliberation) without another (collaboration), and indeed a cluster of still other principles, would probably not have been especially effective. Much complex democratic problem solving is of this sort: less a menu of optional items, more a choice of clustered components, among which relationship building becomes typically central. For much, if not most, democratic problem solving, deliberative democracy needs to become progressively embedded in ongoing relational work to ensure efficacy and sustained legitimacy.[38]

Build Fields and Governance Networks Strategically

The sixth principle of collaborative governance and policy design holds that government should help build fields strategically to ensure that the full range of civic components needed to solve complex public problems can be brought to bear in a relatively coherent, effective, and sustainable manner. Building civic capacity is not just about providing broad civic education or episodic grants to help community projects get off the ground and then hoping for the best. It is about systematically attempting to ensure that the overall configuration of appropriate governance components in any given field—community development, watershed protection, or community health—is present and remains dynamic, indeed generating synergies across field boundaries where needed.[39]

Field building, to be sure, can be approached only with considerable experimentation. There is much uncertainty about how various components might best complement one another and also unavoidable disagreement about what might constitute the "democratic" in democratic network governance. Building civic capacity across entire fields is a strategic challenge on a par with developing the range of other institutional capacities needed for public problem solving, as well as reflecting on the democratic norms entailed by field-building design choices.

Government, of course, should not assume the full burden, nor should it necessarily do the bulk of the heavy lifting. But it needs to be a major strategic player in many, if not most, arenas, the critical "civic switchboard," in the felicitous phrase of Steven Goldsmith and William Eggers.[40] Other players in the civic and nonprofit sectors generally lack the public mandate, financial resources, or strategic position to sustain capacity building adequately across entire fields, whether these are citywide systems of neighborhood planning or national networks for watershed protection.[41]

Strategic field-building choices and challenges run a wide gamut. Take the issue of a federal agency, such as the EPA, that helps build network capacity among civic organizations in a field as broad as watersheds. How should an agency choose among an array of sometimes collaborating, sometimes competing, national and regional capacity-building intermediaries and also achieve the optimal degree of complementarity and division of labor among them? What types and distribution of federal grants and training for local capacity building and coproduction should be provided through national and regional intermediaries, state programs, local governments, or directly to local watershed associations and partnerships? What are the best mechanisms (matching grants, state and national endowments and trusts) for leveraging funding and other resources from local and state governments, foundations, businesses, universities, and civic groups themselves, and what mix of diverse funding sources best ensures independent citizen power? What kinds of online and other information tools are needed for stakeholders to generate, share, and use knowledge effectively for local problem solving and broader network development? How can federal agencies with overlapping responsibilities best align their strategies for civic capacity building and induce states to do likewise, and which agencies should take the lead? What are the most appropriate ways of supporting genuine learning networks and communities of practice across the full range of civic and institutional partners, lay and professional actors, so that best practices in collaborative management and planning and in volunteer monitoring and restoration are diffused widely?

As network forms of governance become increasingly common, governments must address their own role in regulating them according to principles consistent with core democratic ideals, as a growing body of political theory has come to recognize. Is there sufficient power balancing and equitable distribution of capacities within networks and sufficient "democratic anchorage" in a range of participatory groups and affected citizens? Are the forms of representation that networks embody well aligned with core institutions of representative government?[42] These are no small challenges. But regulating networks should not let us lose focus on government's role in systematically enabling them and helping build the requisite civic capacities to make them more democratic. Government needs to invest strategically and systematically to build network capacities for democratic work and self-governance in an increasingly complex world.

Transform Institutional Cultures

The seventh principle is to transform the cultures of government institutions and nonprofit contracting organizations in ways that can support citizen coproduction, shared expertise, and other collaborative practices. No policy aimed at encouraging citizens to become engaged coproducers or persuading professionals to use their expertise to empower communities can be expected to have substantial and sustained impact if the organizations charged with implementing it do not reorient some of their most fundamental organizational practices and mindsets.

Transforming organizational cultures to enable civic problem solving and coproduction typically requires a mix of strategies. First and foremost is changing the language the organization uses to characterize the public. The term *client,* while appropriate in some ways, often signals dependence and deference to professional norms and bureaucratic routines. Clients get diagnosed, then served and saved; they generally are not expected to act as empowered members of communities mobilizing their assets and making substantial contributions. Efforts to reinvent government, however, have too often simply substituted *customer* for *client*. But as public service scholar Paul Light, of the Brookings Institution, argues from his studies of innovative public sector and nonprofit organizations, "customer is not the right word for creating collaboration. . . . Customers are entities to be persuaded, cajoled, even manipulated, but they are not always persons to be consulted or given a role in design. . . . However important customers may be to an organization, they are rarely coproducers, partners, or stakeholders. . . . I recommend *partner* as an alternative, though *citizen* is not bad either."[43]

Closely related to the language agencies use in describing the public is having a civic mission to enable overall mission management for dynamic learning organizations. The civic mission can be explicitly formulated as a core part of an agency's statutory mandate or emerge from its own practice and internal process of discovery and reinvention. As chapter 4 discusses in fuller detail, the City of Hampton, Virginia, having gone through a multi-stakeholder collaborative planning process in the early 1990s, developed an explicit mission to empower its youth and provide systematic opportunities for them to contribute at all levels of city life—public policy, city planning, community service, institutional governance, and advisory roles in schools and other public institutions. While an office at city hall was designated as the government catalyst for this mission, the major youth development non-profit agency contracting with the city similarly committed to transforming itself into a learning organization guided by a mission to actively engage youth and develop their leadership potential, rather than simply trying to fix them according to the latest deficit models and treatment regimens. The alignment of government and nonprofit civic missions gave license and legitimacy for a wide array of initiatives enabling young people and adults to work in partnership based on principles of asset-based community development, coproduction, and public deliberation.

Similarly, university and community stakeholders promoted the explicit democratic mission of Portland State University in Oregon as "Let Knowledge Serve the City," now emblazoned in bold gold lettering on the skywalk over Broadway. As a result, networks within the academy, nonprofits, neighborhood and civic associations, city and county agencies, and local businesses became especially energetic in finding ways to link academic learning with civic engagement and to build an array of sustainable partnerships. Aligning its mission with that of the city's bureau of environmental services, for instance, the university's community watershed stewardship program has engaged more than seven hundred students through class projects, leveraging significant expertise of faculty and advanced graduate students, who in turn have helped mobilize twenty-seven thousand community volunteers engaged in a quarter million hours of hands-on work to restore fifty acres of watershed, including planting eighty thousand new plants. The locally generated civic mission of Portland State has been supported with critical capacity-building grants from Learn and Serve America at the Corporation for National and Community Service, whose own civic mission is central to its authorizing statute, and from the U.S. Department of Housing and Urban Development's Office of University Partnerships. Portland State's leaders have also been generative actors in the national movement to renew the civic mission of higher education, reaching across a thousand or so campuses and a good number of national associations within the higher education field.[44]

Transforming institutional cultures presents many other challenges, to be sure, depending on the type of public good, regulatory or service problems, or other factors in the larger organizational environment.[45] Regulatory agencies, for instance, have to figure out ways of aligning core programs with holistic, community-based ones and getting staff to collaborate across disciplinary cultures, such as technical, legal, and ecological cultures. In some cases, this may require statutory changes. In other cases, an innovation office or leadership team can carve out room for network learning across organizational silos. Several innovative programs and cross-agency network strategies at the EPA have laid the foundation for such culture change, and the agency's Innovation Action Council and National Advisory Council for Environmental Policy and Technology have recently issued several detailed reports on how redefining the agency's mission around stewardship and collaboration is necessary for making continued progress to protect the environment.[46]

Culture change to support civic capacity building depends critically on developing strategies for recruiting staff with the relevant skills and rewarding and promoting them as first-class organizational citizens rather than as second-class staff who possess the less essential or "soft" skills, as has too often happened in the past. Lester Salamon refers to the needed shift from bureaucratic management skills to *"enablement* skills, the skills required to engage partners arrayed horizontally in networks, to bring multiple stakeholders together for a common end in a situation of interdependence."[47] Such enablement skills include activating problem-solving networks, orchestrating collaboration, convening adversaries, brokering relationships, facilitating sustained dialogue, and developing the kinds of planning and data tools that citizens need to become effective problem solvers. To be sure, recruiting and retaining such staff represents part of a much larger challenge of developing a "new public service," as a "quiet crisis" in the old one has now become visible and pressing.[48]

In many cases, change in institutional culture requires considerable identity work that reconfigures various aspects of the professional identities of government and nonprofit staff. In Chicago's community policing reform, for instance, culture change required addressing officers' core professional identity issues and their fears of being set up for failure as social workers rather than crime fighters; in other cities these challenges have been infused with questions about the gendered nature of community policing, which may be seen as more suitable to female than male officers.[49] In Hampton, those youth service providers who could not shift from therapeutic fixers to civic enablers left the nonprofit agency. Similar challenges exist for professionals in many fields, from planning, architecture, and medicine to teaching, social work, and family therapy, and signal the need to develop more robust models of civic or democratic professionalism as key to institutional culture change.[50] Transforming institutional cultures, and indeed managing democratic governance networks, thus entails a reciprocal process of forming identities of both citizens and their partners among agency staff and related professionals with whom they interact.[51]

Ensure Reciprocal Accountability

The eighth principle of collaborative governance and policy design is to enable reciprocal accountability among a complex array of democratic actors, from ordinary citizens and organized stakeholders to elected officials and public administrators. In an age of partnerships and networks, policy design should strive to develop workable forms of collaborative accountability, under which the accountability environment is not so neatly divided between those who hold others accountable and those held accountable—the holders and holdees, so to speak. In his important book *Rethinking Democratic Accountability,* Robert Behn of the Kennedy School of Government refers to this challenge with the apt metaphor of "360-degree accountability": the wheel continues to spin full circle, and we must find appropriate ways of enabling all to account responsibly for their actions and performance to all other relevant actors.[52]

As Behn, along with Donald Kettl and others, argues, the classic forms of bureaucratic accountability in public administration, which have a long pedigree from Woodrow Wilson, Max Weber, and Frederick Taylor a century ago to inspectors general and special prosecutors today, cannot adequately address the complex challenges of democratic governance that we face.[53] Bureaucracies cannot purge discretion nor guarantee efficiency. Policy and politics cannot be neatly separated from implementation. Increasing accountability for finances and fairness often comes at the expense of accountability for performance. Nor does adding new forms of professional, legal, and political accountability to old forms of bureaucratic accountability lend greater coherence to our system of democratic accountability. The "new public management," which stresses enhancing performance through various flexible, competitive, and frontline empowerment practices, too often skirts the question of accountability to citizens with broad public purposes in favor of narrow responsiveness to customers making market choices.

But this also needs to be looked at from the other direction. As James March and Johan Olsen argue in their fertile discussion of developing political accounts, "A prolonged combination of citizen power with citizen exemption from accountability introduces intolerable elements of irresponsibility into a democratic polity."[54] Many of the populist accountability scripts one finds in everyday politics and administration, and especially in election-year mobilizing and media framing, confirm this and reveal some deeper sources of the erosion of democratic governance and legitimacy. When network anchor Lou Dobbs asks every night on CNN News, "Doesn't anyone deserve a government that works?" he not only fails to challenge citizens themselves to be accountable but also defaults on his own responsibility as a journalist for framing the complexity of the accountability problem in a democratic society.

Two concepts are especially important for moving us forward on democratic accountability in a world of empowered citizens engaged as coproducers in complex partnerships and through extended networks. The first is the idea of accountable autonomy, developed by Fung, especially in his study of citywide programs of citizen participation in Chicago; the second is multiple, simultaneous accountability, articulated by Edward Weber of Washington State University in his studies of grassroots ecosystem management partnerships in the western United States.

Accountable autonomy, for Fung, entails a bargain at the heart of policy design for community policing and local school councils in Chicago. In return for substantial autonomy, through which communities are empowered to become effective civic problem solvers collaborating with professionals in the police and school departments, citizens agree to be accountable for the quality of their own work. Citizens are accountable, not just empowered, for several simple reasons. First, elected city officials, answerable to all citizens and not just those in specific neighborhoods, bear responsibility for the overall performance of these systems. Citizens empowered by the policy design must agree to respect this framework if they are to be granted enhanced autonomy in specific beats and schools.

Second, while citizens have compelling claims to be involved in how these systems run, citizen participation comes with hazards that need to be limited as much as possible. Citizens, for instance, often make parochial claims that favor their own neighborhoods or children at the expense of others and use participatory structures to mobilize for conflict along these lines. Citizens may speak with great passion but with limited expertise. Some get caught up in groupthink and are not well skilled in critical deliberation. In many settings, the most educated or articulate dominate discussions, while others remain intimidated or silenced or indeed do not return to such forums, further skewing their representativeness. In addition, race, gender, and immigrant or home ownership status may distort deliberations, leaving a deficit of legitimacy for public action. These issues, all too familiar to democracy theorists as well as public administrators, are the basis for continued skepticism about participatory reform.[55]

To help residents and parents enhance their capacities for effective and fair deliberation and problem solving and thus reduce the hazards that can accompany grassroots engagement, the policy design of community policing and local school councils in Chicago provides resources and support in the form of training, feedback, troubleshooting, networking on best practices with others across the city, and templates for iterative problem solving and for developing beat plans and school improvement plans. But the local beat meetings and school councils are required to report on their performance and are often informed of corrective action that ought to, or in some cases must, be taken if the grant of autonomy is to continue. Local school councils can, for instance, be placed on probation for persistent failure to correct problems with their deliberative processes; the Illinois legislature has mandated three days of training as a condition for serving on the local school councils.

The purpose of such oversight is improvement, not punishment—in Fung's words, to restore wherever possible "the integrity of deliberative mechanisms."[56] But residents are clearly accountable for the quality of their deliberation and planning and for meeting specific performance measures (crime rates, test scores) that they have helped establish. If the collaboration of other city departments—such as housing and sanitation with the police department—is required for the model to work, then accountability for interdepartmental responsiveness must become an essential component of the 360-degree accountability design. Accountable autonomy, in short, makes public professionals more directly accountable to the citizens with whom they collaborate but also entails a new level of public accountability among citizens for the quality of their own democratic work—their deliberations, planning, problem solving, everyday collaboration, and achievement of results.

Edward Weber's concept of multiple, simultaneous accountability addresses collaborative governance issues that extend across geographical and jurisdictional boundaries and levels of the federal system and involve a wide array of organized stakeholders. In recent years, hundreds of ecosystem partnerships have emerged, but scholars and environmental activists are often skeptical that new forms of collaborative governance can achieve democratic accountability because such partnerships are subject to capture by powerful local interests and because networks are inherently weaker than bureaucracy when it comes to ensuring accountability, especially where state and federal laws are concerned. As Weber demonstrates, however, collaborative partnerships at the local or regional ecosystem level can, under certain conditions, achieve multiple, simultaneous accountability, that is, a relatively high degree of accountability to individual citizens and diverse community stakeholders, including those with deep-seated conflicts of interest, while at the same time conforming to state and federal laws, even expanding their scope and effectiveness. Weber examines in depth several cases of grassroots ecosystem management that employ some combination of open collaborative design and consensus-based decision-making, promote strong participant norms that "enculturate" virtue (honesty, civility, inclusiveness), practice holistic management with a broad knowledge base derived from science and local knowledge, and focus on measurable results that stakeholders agree represent genuine indicators of ecosystem and community improvement.[57]

Many other scholars and practitioners have struggled with issues of democratic accountability as collaborative and networked forms of governance spread. The challenges are quite complex: how to create robust linkages between community indicator projects and government performance measures, how to ensure that equity is appropriately built into performance measures, how to apportion responsibility under conditions of highly complex and interdependent causality and chains of value creation, and how to link network forms of representative accountability to our other forms of representative government and accountability.[58] Public policy design must continue to experiment and expand the boundaries, even amid inevitable imperfections and disappointments, because we are far beyond imagining that we can take secure refuge in some new and improved form of bureaucratic or market-mimicking accountability.

Conclusion

These principles of collaborative governance and policy design find a variety of configurations in the case studies that follow, but they also encounter a range of challenges. None of the cases offers the perfect mix, since there is no such thing, and no single model can simply be transplanted to other settings. None of the principles, it should also be strongly emphasized, can replace political judgment and leadership on how and when to employ various combinations and in what sequences. Leaders require not only civic imagination but also political realism as they attempt to generate new opportunities for collaborative governance. They invariably run up against obstacles of various sorts and must attend to broad questions of coalition building, compromise, and availability of resources. In some cases, as in Seattle, the judgment of key elected officials and administrators is informed by their own experience in civic collaboration before coming to office—a pathway that appears increasingly common and that ought to be further encouraged.

What is especially noteworthy about these cases is that they employ a fairly wide array of core principles and specific tools of collaborative governance. Innovators from government and other sectors, including ordinary citizens, have brought a substantial degree of pragmatic democratic wisdom to their work. They have negotiated a "logic of appropriateness" that was not always clear when they began their efforts.[59] Moreover, they have engaged in a sustained process of learning, often through conflict and shortfalls along the way, indeed often prompted by spirited battles from the very beginning.

Neighborhood Empowerment and Planning: Seattle, Washington

The city of Seattle, with a population, according to the 2000 census, of five hundred and sixty-three thousand in a metropolitan area of 2.4 million, took its first steps in creating a system of formal neighborhood representation in 1987–88 when it established twelve district councils to represent independently organized "community councils," the preferred term for neighborhood associations in the city. In addition, an Office of Neighborhoods was established to provide city staff support for the district councils. A city neighborhood council, consisting of elected members of the district councils, was also created, designed to provide an independent citizen voice on neighborhood issues at the citywide level. This system, which would evolve considerably in subsequent years, emerged as the product of innovation in the face of intense conflict, on the one hand, and intentional learning from other cities, on the other.

Seattle has a long tradition of community councils and neighborhood activism as well as other forms of civic and labor movement engagement. The city is famous for its General Strike of 1919, for instance, and during the 1960s, houseboaters in the Floating Homes Association engaged their fellow members in the needed work of welding the pipes, hooking up the sewer lines, and building the public relationships needed to protect Lake Union as a working lake and public environmental treasure for all. However, Seattle's urban regime was dominated by a rather narrow and predominantly corporate old-boys network well into the 1960s. Under pressure for much more inclusive participation by the 1960s movements, progressive reformers were then able to transform the city into what Margaret Gordon and her colleagues at the University of Washington have called a "strong-mayor, strong-council, watchful citizens network."[1]

However, the city largely ignored the neighborhood plans that citizens helped develop in the 1970s, and the following decade Seattle witnessed rising activism and outright resistance to unchecked development and top-down, zone-by-zone planning. The neighborhood reinvestment movement, strengthened by the federal Community Reinvestment Act of 1978, sought to ensure that the redevelopment of Pike's Place Market would protect elder and low-income housing, especially for the retired merchant marines living in the area. Indeed, a citizens' alternative plan, approved in a ballot initiative by a wide margin in 1989, obstructed implementation of the 1985 downtown plan. Homeowners in other neighborhoods were described, even by their supporters, as having gone "berserk" over planning, transportation, increased housing density, and other city initiatives on which they had not been consulted. Disputes typically resulted in raucous public hearings and then worked their way through the courts.[2]

In this context, city councilor Jim Street, elected in 1984 and head of the council's land-use committee for the next twelve years as well as a supporter of the citizens' alternative plan, met with neighborhood activists to see whether there was a better way to deal with neighborhood issues. The Seattle Planning Commission, with support and funding from the city council, held public hearings, conducted surveys, and hired consultants to visit cities that had instituted neighborhood representation systems over the previous decade. High on the list were Portland, Oregon, and St. Paul, Minnesota. George Latimer, the innovative "reinventing government" mayor of St. Paul, was invited to Seattle to meet with city leaders. The planning commission then prepared a series of recommendations on neighborhood planning and assistance, which Street brought as a resolution to the city council. Charles Royer, Seattle's popular third-term mayor (and an opponent of the citizens' alternative plan), at first resisted, arguing (in Street's retelling) that "citizens don't care about empowerment. . . . They care about whether their services are delivered efficiently." The coalition of minority executive directors in human services, and their supporters on the city council, also objected; they favored more money for traditional social services instead and feared that neighborhood participation would mostly empower white middle-class homeowners. But Street was able to get a veto-proof majority on the council and proceeded with a vision for energetic outreach and organizing in minority communities as well as more broadly.[3]

Over the next two decades, Seattle would expand its neighborhood system considerably and innovate further. The city developed the ambitious Neighborhood Matching Fund program, which received an early Innovations in American Government Award from Harvard's Kennedy School of Government; the model has since been borrowed by other municipalities and various government agencies in Washington State and beyond. The city brought its neighborhood service centers into a consolidated Department of Neighborhoods and provided their directors and other department staff with considerable training; these staff, in turn, have provided leadership development to neighborhood groups, both existing ones and those newly forming. The P-Patch and Cultivating Communities gardening programs, also brought into the department, have helped generate much civic energy in neighborhoods across Seattle, including among new immigrants and public housing residents. In response to the state's growth management act in 1990, Seattle instituted a systematic process of neighborhood planning that has engaged citizens, planners, and professional staff of multiple city departments in community visioning and collaborative implementation and aligned their local visions and detailed plans with successful citywide bond and levy referendums to provide the resources needed to support their work. While Seattle's system has not been without problems, as has been clear in recent lively debates on the policy design for neighborhood plan updates, it has managed to engage citizens in neighborhoods in a way that productively complements both representative democracy at city hall and administrative responsibility in city departments.

Department of Neighborhoods

The Department of Neighborhoods proved to be a catalyst for civic initiative. Jim Diers was hired in 1988 to direct the department, and for the next thirteen years he oversaw its growth as a consolidated department. Trained in Alinsky-style organizing by the Gamaliel Foundation, Diers worked as an activist in the distressed Seattle neighborhood of Rainier Valley in the late 1970s. Through his national ties to faith-based community-organizing networks, he closely followed their subsequent shift to relationship building as both philosophy and method.[4] In his next job, with the Group Health Cooperative of Puget Sound in the early 1980s, Diers developed what some prominent health policy analysts regard as one of the most innovative designs for deliberative citizen councils in any large health maintenance organization or other health care system in the nation.[5] This early career, combined with his great sensitivity to what citizens in Seattle wanted to achieve productively through their engagement, enabled Diers to shape Department of Neighborhoods programs around several of the core design principles discussed in chapter 2: building relationships and partnerships, citizen coproduction of public goods, deliberative democracy, and asset-based community development, for which he became a national (and now international) trainer through the Asset-Based Community Development Institute's network.

Of course, Diers did not do this alone. He hired some good staff and worked tirelessly with city councilors, three mayors, the planning commission, and the staff of various city departments who shared his passion for and vision of local democracy. He also maintained relationships with independent organizing groups across the city, some neighborhood based, others not. Because he and his staff did this work as city employees, not as independent organizers, they added some distinctive twists in weaving together the various strands of innovative community organizing and development. The neighborhood matching fund, the community gardens programs, and the system of district councils represent key components of Seattle's democratic design for neighborhood empowerment.[6]

Neighborhood Matching Fund

Created in 1989 with a modest $150,000, the neighborhood matching fund quickly grew to $1.5 million in 1990, $3 million in 1998, and then to $4.5 million in 2001 before difficult budgetary times forced cutbacks of roughly 15 to 30 percent, depending on the specific fiscal year. Almost all of the investment has been drawn from the city's general fund, though a small portion has come from federal community development block grant monies ($220,000 out of $4.5 million in 2001) and occasional other grants. The core idea of the fund is simple: the city awards grants for neighborhood-generated projects that commit to matching these funds with their own in-kind contributions, cash, and labor. Neighbors might raise cash through bake sales, fund-raising appeals, or grants from private foundations. Local businesses and households might donate equipment and materials, such as lumber and sand for a playground, seed and plants for a community garden, or computers and desks for a community learning center. Citizens usually do a substantial part of the work to make a project happen, from the general tasks of hauling and planting to the more skilled tasks of architectural design and carpentry. All volunteer labor is currently valued at $15 an hour, though higher-end skills were previously calculated at market value. Local groups can seek outside partners, but at least 25 percent of the match must come from the community that benefits from the project.

To qualify, projects must be neighborhood based, and groups applying must have open membership and actively seek the involvement of area residents and businesses. Initially, groups also had to be neighborhood based, but to counteract the underrepresentation of immigrants and communities of color in many neighborhood organizations, eligibility was extended in 1990 to ethnic associations and similar groups—though not without initial resistance from some traditional community councils. Organizations and informal groups with a broad range of interests are thus eligible, from arts, education, and history to environment, public safety, and recreation. Projects must be time delimited, with distinct phases that can be broken down into separate components. Ongoing programs are not eligible, nor can funds cover operating costs such as rent or staff salaries. Proposals can be presented to the Small and Simple Projects Fund, with a limit of $15,000, or to the Large Projects Fund, with a current cap of $100,000. Large projects can take up to a year to complete.

There is also a Small Sparks Fund of up to $250 to enable virtually any new group with a creative idea to get started. In addition, several other categories have been added along the way. For instance, through the Tree Fund groups of neighbors work with the city arborist to choose varieties. In return for the city's donation of the trees, residents must receive proper training, organize the fall planting, provide necessary tools, and take responsibility for watering and maintenance. While it also improves neighborhood aesthetics and reduces noise pollution, the Tree Fund aims to absorb carbon dioxide and filter air pollution, provide shade to cool streets in warm weather, and serve as habitat for birds and wildlife. The neighborhood matching fund's new climate protection category, funded in collaboration with the Office for Environment and Sustainability, is designed to support a broad range of civic projects, from sharing neighborhood assets such as lawnmowers and tools to weatherizing buildings and conducting workshops on home energy efficiency.

The citywide review team of the city neighborhood council, composed of neighborhood representatives from each of the (now thirteen) district councils into which neighborhoods have been clustered, reviews proposals four times a year on a competitive basis according to criteria of quality and feasibility as well as a stated set of core values shared by citizens and the city: civic participation, diversity, self-help, collaboration, and sustainability of the project. It is the intent of the matching fund not only to yield products of visible public value but also to build civic capacities that will continue to bear fruit in other ways. The fund design, to be sure, was not invented out of whole cloth by the Department of Neighborhoods but evolved over time with considerable input and criticism from neighborhood groups and the city neighborhood council. Key to the matching fund's policy design and incentive structure is that citizens coproduce public goods and mobilize community assets.

One cannot walk through a Seattle neighborhood today without seeing substantial evidence of the collaborative work of its citizens as a result of the matching funds. In its first fifteen years, more than twenty-five hundred projects had been completed. Citizens have built or renovated more than 150 playgrounds, many celebrating the unique history and identity of their neighborhoods; they also help maintain them as prideful public work. Citizens have restored streams and wetlands, reforested hillsides and ravines, and designed nature centers to make environmental sustainability a central part of everyday civic education. Indeed, the product and process of many of the matching grants are designed for continual education in civic and public values; they are far more than bricks and mortar, lumber and bolts. Several hundred projects have engaged parents, teachers, students, and neighbors in partnerships between community and schools that might include landscaping and gardening, classrooms open for intergenerational learning, or homework centers and art and music lessons offered to students by local residents. Out of these partnerships, Powerful Schools has spun off as a nonprofit working with a cluster of schools and community groups in Rainier Valley. A special Youth Fund, later folded into the neighborhood matching fund, sponsored such groups as the Multicultural Youth Action Council, B'nai B'rith Youth Organization, and the Seattle Young People's Project in a range of cultural and educational projects and community-organizing workshops.

Citizens have painted beautiful murals to honor favorite heroes and causes and to signify the rebirth of economically distressed neighborhoods. They have constructed major works of sculpture, such as the Freemont Troll, that have become famous to tourists from around the world. To affirm their distinct identities as part of a common civic culture celebrating everyone's contributions, immigrant and refugee groups and ethnic associations have used the matching funds to build community centers and gardens. A technology matching fund has helped the Lao Highland Association and similar groups establish community computing centers. For every dollar of city money invested through the matching fund, citizens have leveraged another $1.60, on average.[7]

The fund's projects have elicited active involvement from several tens of thousands of citizens. Groups can also apply to the Outreach Fund for up to $750 to help expand and diversify their membership through special newsletters, community picnics, and the like. Many existing organizations have seen an increase in membership, and a good number of new civic groups have been created through an ad hoc effort first enabled by a matching grant. "Playgrounds, for instance, are a revolutionary idea," said Rebecca Sadinsky, head of the Neighborhood Matching Fund program for its first twelve years and a former housing organizer. Asserted with self-conscious exaggeration, but to make an emphatic point, Sadinsky explained, "People come together on the design. Then they do the work and have a community space where they can regularly gather. Then they say, 'Now that we have built this playground, what else can we do together?'" To enable next steps, the Department of Neighborhoods has organized the matching fund in such a way that citizens can continually learn from one another as part of a citywide network. The annual Ideas Fair originally featured twenty or so model projects from which other groups could learn, and the criterion of cross-neighborhood learning has now become part of the application process. Workshops throughout the year are organized by peer trainers, who may be "just five steps ahead of the others. . . . But peer learning is key. It is seen by the neighborhoods as the most helpful."[8]

With prize money from its Innovations in American Government Award, the matching fund produced and widely disseminated a series of six *Help Yourself!* booklets on environmental projects, cultural heritage, children's play areas, public art, neighborhood organizing, and public school partnerships. These booklets provided not only program guidelines and model project profiles but also an extensive set of resources and contacts among local, state, and national civic associations, nonprofits, government agencies, and funders who might assist local citizens in their work. In the 1993 environmental projects booklet, for example, the community and environmental division of the Seattle Metrocenter YMCA—whose director, Richard Conlin, would soon become the neighborhoods champion on the city council and currently serves as council president—was listed as a key contact. Neighborhoods and schools were encouraged to connect with the Y's Earth Service Corps, an environmental service–learning program, which also had its national offices at Metrocenter, with significant staffing from AmeriCorps. As an important network node, the Metrocenter YMCA also housed Sustainable Seattle, which developed sustainability indicators that became important for comprehensive planning as well as an international model of such indicator projects developed by citizen networks. The state's community and urban forestry program, also linked to ambitious training efforts supported by the U.S. Forest Service, was another among more than one hundred resources listed from the emerging field of civic environmentalism.

The Department of Neighborhoods, in effect, helped Seattle citizens map networks and assets on a much wider scale than they might do on their own—indeed, it helped provide a cognitive frame for thinking in terms of civic networks as problem-solving assets. Recognizing its innovative work, the Urban Resources Partnership, initiated by the U.S. Department of Agriculture in cooperation with six other federal agencies, provided $450,000 additional funding in 1995–96 through Seattle's matching fund for environmental projects that empower traditionally disadvantaged communities, thereby leveraging civic engagement for social justice.[9]

Achieving greater diversity and equity in the civic life of the city was a goal of the matching fund from the beginning. Minorities were becoming an increasing proportion of Seattle's population, growing from 8 percent in 1960 to 20 percent by 1980 and 25 percent a decade later. By 2000 a full 27 percent of the city's population was minority; the number of recent immigrants increased by 40 percent over the 1990s.[10] Children in Seattle's public schools today speak some 102 languages. As Sadinsky recalled, "In the first month, I expanded [the neighborhood matching fund] to [include] people of color and immigrants. I told city and neighborhood leaders that the program can't just be for people who vote. These other communities had to come to the table. . . . And Jim [Diers], of course, knew them from his organizing days." Indeed, Diers had served as director of the Southeast Seattle Community Organization, which, along with other independent organizing groups, helped to build and maintain a diverse and highly integrated community in southeast Seattle, even down to the block level.[11]

In a city famous for process—some even say paralyzed by process—the matching fund's focus on project and product has had several advantages in regard to diversity. For Bernie Matsuno, director of the community-building division of the Department of Neighborhoods and one of the original staff of the matching fund, "building relationships and maintaining relationships truly happens when people work and do things side by side. . . . In neighborhoods, the way you build strong relationships and break down race and other barriers is to get them to work side by side, often on a physical project." For new immigrant and refugee groups, who are often quite averse to public meetings, deeply suspicious of government, and divided among themselves, matching fund projects also provide the opportunity for Department of Neighborhoods staff to do "lots of one-on-ones" to build trust and establish respect. Indeed, as Matsuno noted, "in some cases, we would need to work six to eight months doing one-on-ones. . . . And we often served as the go-between for different factions in the Somali community."[12]

Others have noted similar dynamics within the Cambodian community, some residents of which were former Khmer Rouge and others were victims of the Khmer Rouge, or among various other Southeast Asian immigrant groups. Anne Takekawa, who works to expand the kinds of matching fund "inclusive citizen engagement" projects emphasized by the city's Race and Social Justice Initiative, described her role thus: "When I do outreach, I am 'reaching in' to a whole culture. . . . It takes longer, but you can't shortcut it. You can't turn down tea."[13]

The matching fund also prepared the basis for systematic neighborhood planning begun in 1995. The fund enabled the city to develop and refine project contracts with civic groups or their nonprofit fiscal agents (if they were not themselves incorporated). These contracts, which included citizen commitments to ongoing maintenance once projects were completed, would became a critical model for later contracts made directly with the city, under which neighborhood planning groups would be held accountable for substantial work and inclusive representation. The matching fund also provided the basis for building relationships with staff in city agencies, who seemed initially resistant to many projects and indeed had legitimate concerns with liability, technical design, and potential opposition from other citizens. "We were not the favorite staff among city agencies at first," Sadinsky noted. "But we found agency staff to work with, and the fund paid for some of their salaries. . . . We would sit down in a coffee shop and network an idea [from the community] with them, test the idea. . . . And then we would go back to a group of, say, ten neighborhood activists and tell them, 'I'll broker a meeting with you and city engineers.'"[14] Brokering relationships among staff in multiple city agencies and various community groups, often based initially on one-on-ones, would become a critical part of the role of planning staff in the far more complex process of the comprehensive plan.

P-Patch Community Gardens

In the early 1970s a truck farm owned by the Italian Picardo family became the site of the first organic community garden in Seattle's municipally managed program, now one of the largest in the country. P-Patch was absorbed into the Department of Neighborhoods in 1997, and local groups have used the neighborhood matching fund, as well as sources such as the U.S. Department of Agriculture's Urban Resources Partnership grants, in their extensive efforts to design and build dozens of gardens in every type of neighborhood across the city and in partnership with community groups, senior centers, schools, and public housing. Seattle's program, though part of a long U.S. tradition of government support for community gardening going back to the early twentieth century, incorporates civic design principles throughout.[15] Indeed, back in the 1970s the *P* in P-Patch, formally acknowledging the founding Picardos, informally stood for "passionate people producing peas in public."

First, P-Patches are more than gardens for individuals to grow vegetables and flowers on more than two thousand separate plots. They are also community gathering places, often with benches, picnic tables, play areas for kids and teens, public art, and classrooms. Gardeners gather to socialize during the day, hold birthday and anniversary parties, celebrate the Fourth of July and New Year's Eve. A concert or Halloween festival may bring out several hundred people. Raised garden beds accommodate older people and those with mobility impairments. Despite a strong sense of ownership by the neighborhood, all gardens are completely open to the public and experience virtually no vandalism, and the P-Patch website posts maps and bus routes to encourage visiting.

Second, the gardens are clearly the product of the community's democratic work together. Every P-Patch has been designed and built by the gardeners themselves or other residents contributing their specific skills. They haul the dirt, secure the wooden tiers, and set the stones and cement for the walls, often in spirited work parties. They coordinate all the work themselves through volunteer site coordinators. Local artists, who often are gardeners themselves, design and build distinctive structures, such as the breathtaking ceramic-tiled public restroom at Bradner Gardens Park, made from fragments of neighbors' old dishes—a striking public symbol of what can be done with underused community assets and an act of meaning making that enriches the civic culture. In addition to an annual membership fee of $24–58, gardeners contribute at least eight hours a year on common maintenance and organizational tasks.

Third, P-Patches become nodes in broader civic networks. They might provide connections to local block watches, district-wide and citywide park alliances, Kings County Extension master gardeners groups, the Food Security Coalition, and Seattle Tilth. In addition, Friends of P-Patch and the P-Patch Trust, formed to protect P-Patch through difficult city budget times, continue to advocate and raise private funds for additional land purchases. The University of Washington's Design/Build program in the College of Architecture and Urban Planning engages students and faculty in P-Patch and similar community service–learning initiatives. School groups, the United Way, and Starbucks employees might also contribute to the work; Starbucks partnered with the Department of Neighborhoods and the Department of Parks and Recreation to develop its own neighborhood park grants program to help communities with their match. Lettuce Link, established by Friends of P-Patch, facilitates a network of gardeners across the P-Patches to contribute some seven to ten tons of organic produce to food banks each year.

Fourth, in addition to mobilizing the assets, especially the skills, of local residents to design, build, and maintain the gardens, P-Patches can themselves become an asset in community revitalization. One neighborhood of non-English-speaking renters, with a street right-of-way that served as a drug bazaar, was transformed when a new resident, a construction supervisor by trade, moved in and mobilized his neighbors to construct a P-Patch on the property. Reclaiming this public space became a catalyst for broader efforts. In other neighborhoods, homeless and at-risk youth grow produce for their own use and for sale in the local farmers' markets, as is the case with Marra Farms and the Seattle Youth Garden Works. A dozen or so human service agencies also have garden plots maintained by their clients.[16]

As with the neighborhood matching fund, the P-Patch program aims to reach out across income and ethnic barriers. Some 15 percent of gardeners have incomes below the federal poverty level, and many are people of color, recent immigrants, and refugees. Friends of P-Patch has partnered with the Seattle Housing Authority to develop seventeen organic community gardens in public housing projects and to eliminate the use of leaded soil for these gardens. For many, the gardens serve as places to grow native produce and use traditional methods. With support from Department of Neighborhoods staff, some communities, especially Southeast Asians, have become "very self-organizing . . . and have developed extensive networks to sell their produce to stores in the International District," according to Martha Goodlett, director of Cultivating Communities, the Department of Neighborhoods program established within P-Patch in 1995 to focus on public housing. The gardens can also "bridge ethnic and racial differences [and] tensions—of which there are plenty in the community—by working side by side, sharing produce, showing each other techniques." To get things done, the linguistically diverse gardeners "have to speak English to each other." Residents with diverse language skills serve as paid organizers and outreach workers, and AmeriCorps volunteers work in developing the program for elementary school students. Cultivating Communities, financed by the Seattle Housing Authority, the matching fund, and several foundations, was recognized by the U.S. Department of Housing and Urban Development with a Best of the Best Award in 2000.[17]

Although most P-Patch development now occurs relatively smoothly and has become part of Seattle's comprehensive plan, citizens have often had to mobilize to lay public claim to the scarce resource of valuable land. A coalition of four local groups fought city hall for two years to get the original P-Patch at Bradner Gardens in southeast Seattle expanded to include a basketball court, more growing area, and a classroom for education in organic gardening and sustainability practices. The contested land, covered with asphalt and an old school building, was owned by the parks department; powerful people, including a former mayor living in the neighborhood, wanted the land developed for eighteen market-rate units of housing. The dispute was finally resolved when citizens presented the city council with a long list of signatures of support.

Through this and other projects, the parks department has come to realize that P-Patch can work to its own agency interests. Its staff now meets monthly with the Southeast Park Alliance and sends other citizens to Bradner to see what can be accomplished by community action. The department accepted the community's plan for protecting the old-growth forest in Seward Park, at a savings to the department of $90,000 that would have gone unnecessarily to logging hazard trees in the extremely unlikely probability, modeled statistically by citizens themselves, that a tree would fall on someone. In the words of Joyce Moty, Bradner activist and now citywide leader for community gardens, green space, and the arts, "We've gone from city hall pariah to city hall darling."[18]

Neighborhood Service Centers, District Councils, and Leadership Development

Two key components of Seattle's system of neighborhood democracy are the neighborhood service centers, part of the Department of Neighborhoods, and the district councils, representing independent community councils and other civic groups within each of the city's thirteen districts but with formal city recognition and staff support provided by the department. The neighborhood service centers, previously known as "little city halls" when first created in 1973 under the Model Cities program in six distressed neighborhoods, were extended citywide and became part of the Department of Neighborhoods in 1990. The centers have two broad functions: individual service and civic convening and organizing. The service function of the department, as in many cities, might entail the payment of utility bills and parking and traffic tickets; applications for pet licenses, passports, voter registration, and business licenses; human service referrals; and magistrate hearings for minor infractions. The neighborhood service centers also provide applications for neighborhood matching funds, P-Patch, and summer youth employment, as well as information on numerous other services and programs offered by city and nonprofit agencies. Free public access to the Internet is also available. Since a substantial number of people pay their utility bills through these centers, especially poorer people and those faced with shutoffs, the public utilities fund the service staff. Some centers also house, or are housed with, other local city offices, such as police, library, housing, senior citizens, and civil rights, as well as neighborhood business associations and community development corporations, thereby making them a hub of daily activity.

The second function of the neighborhood service centers, civic convening and relationship building, is designed to add democratic capacity to the overall system in Seattle. The thirteen service center coordinators, or district coordinators, are organizers in the broadest sense of that term. They serve as staff for the district councils and their elected leadership. The coordinators seek to facilitate collaborative work among community councils and other civic groups, a permanent challenge given the contentious quality of much neighborhood politics in most, if not all, cities.[19] As Rob Mattson, the coordinator of the Ballard district whom many call "the mayor of Ballard" for his incessant activity as a community problem solver, described his role:

> I am a convener. I get people to park different sets of boots under the same table. I am a mediator. I facilitate group dialogue. . . . I find

people who are frustrated and are not plugged into the process and are just throwing rocks, and I meet with them and help them understand how they can work with their neighbors, or meet with the new principal to build a relationship with the school. . . . My goal is to build relationships and a system of problem solving around these. . . . But I'm not the architect, just the convener.[20]

Gary Johnson, former service center coordinator for downtown, recounts that he attended numerous meetings of the separate civic groups to build relationships of trust with them as a city employee. He also brokered one-on-one meetings among the leaders of various groups. When a potential conflict emerged in the International District–Chinatown, for instance, over the Chong Wa Benevolent Association's proposal to build Chinese ceremonial gates at both ends of King Street, Johnson intervened. The proposal required permission from nearby property owners, including Uwajimaya, a large Japanese grocery. Aware of a history of bad blood from a previous and costly legal suit against Uwajimaya on another street—a case that went all the way to the state supreme court—Johnson

> suggested to Tomio Moriguchi [Uwajimaya's CEO] and Tak Eng [head of the benevolent association] that we get together over tea. . . . Both were willing to come to tea because I asked them. After Tak briefed Tomio on the gates project and reminisced about how his family used to grow sprouts for Tomio's family store decades ago, they began to reach out and build a relationship. . . . In the end, Tomio not only came to support the gates project but also donated money to it.[21]

While everyone recognizes that the independent civic associations provide the core of leadership in the neighborhoods, the district coordinators also see their job as helping to develop such leadership. They build relationships that might not otherwise emerge because of geographic boundaries, ethnic and income differences, focus on specific issues, or long-standing tensions among the various groups in the districts. Neighborhood service center coordinators teach neighborhood association leaders and activists how to map and mobilize the assets in their neighborhoods and the district as a whole. They are also repositories of a great deal of local knowledge: Who can get things done? Who is easy to work with? What are the obstacles one is likely to run into? What expertise is one likely to need, and where can one get it? What local institutions have resources that might be helpful? Service center coordinators also advise city departments about the distinctiveness of local neighborhoods and how best to communicate with their leaders. As Diers so aptly put it, these coordinators are "double agents," serving the city and citizen groups, brokering relationships from each direction, interpreting interests from multiple perspectives.[22]

That these double agents sometimes prove unable to "walk a fine line in a complex situation," as Gary Johnson insists is so necessary, should not surprise us. When Department of Neighborhoods staff seem to side with neighborhood activists against the city, the mayor can become riled. When neighborhoods perceive the district coordinator as a spy for the city, activists can feel betrayed. Appearing to line up with one neighborhood, ethnic, or business group against another can destroy the trust a coordinator has built up. Despite the trickiness and ambiguity of their role, however, and the inevitability that some civic groups whom district coordinators may have helped get organized will at times berate the city and even the coordinators personally, district coordinators have contributed considerably to civic problem-solving capacities and can draw upon a wellspring of trust that generally carries them to higher ground in difficult situations.

Johnson recalled having crossed the line in an incident in Pioneer Square but being rescued by accumulated trust. When he perceived one group of stakeholders "being particularly Machiavellian in manipulating [a committee] election . . . I called them on it publicly." Almost immediately, he recognized this as going beyond the formal definition of his role. One is reminded here of a core insight of political theorist Jane Mansbridge when studying the town meeting process in Vermont. As Mansbridge argues in *Beyond Adversary Democracy,* when people in a community have to live and work together over many years, and thus depend on one another's respect and cooperation beyond any given issue or town election, they often prefer less public ways of expressing criticism to protect personal reputations. As Johnson recalled, with a favorable twist, "I was then called to meet with the head of the development association. To my surprise, instead of chewing me out, he said that his employees had acted wrongly and that it would never happen again."[23]

The district councils, as noted above, represent the community councils and business associations in their area, ranging from about a dozen in the smaller or less well organized districts to three dozen or so in the larger or better organized ones. District councils, particularly important in a city with at-large city council elections, are essentially forums for discussing issues and budgetary matters that cut across various neighborhoods within the district and for developing collaborative projects and strategies. Most meet monthly, and many have subcommittees to work on specific issues, such as transportation, open space, arts, or public safety. Some have also been active in neighborhood planning and implementation. Each district council has a committee responsible for rating matching fund projects within the district, and at least one member sits on the city neighborhood council review team, which makes final recommendations to the mayor and city council. District councils cannot themselves apply for such funds; only civic groups can, whether members of the district council or not. District councils, of course, experience their fair share of conflict as well as collaboration.

The Delridge District Council, for instance, was created as the thirteenth council only after a "little civil war, akin to the recognition of Palestine," according to Delridge coordinator, Ron Angeles, who grew up in public housing in the area "before we even knew there was a Delridge." The key issue was that the have-nots of West Seattle felt their voice was being overshadowed by the haves. Despite much skepticism and resistance, activists in Delridge, led by the tireless Vivian McLean, organized enough new community councils, block watches, and other groups to finally be recognized as a separate district council.[24]

Membership and by-laws are determined by each district council itself, though there have been continual efforts to broaden the councils' membership in recent years and reduce the kinds of "participation biases" prevalent in neighborhood representation systems.[25] Thus in addition to the typical community councils, a district council expansion plan might include parent-teacher associations, churches, business associations, youth groups, ethnic associations, environmental groups, human service agencies, and senior and disabled groups.

In 2004, for instance, the Queen Anne–Magnolia District Council approved an expansion plan by first identifying seventy organizations as potential members. John Leonard, coordinator at the time, proceeded to reach out to these groups and encourage them to join. In the first nine months, membership increased from nine civic associations to twenty-six. The new ones included such groups as the Michaelson Manor senior housing resident council, part of the Seattle Housing Authority; the Queen Anne Helpline, a community social service and referral agency founded by several churches; and Heron Habitat Helpers, a creek restoration and wildlife habitat protection group in the Kiwanis Ravine.

On the basis of successful experiences in Queen Anne–Magnolia and several other districts, the Department of Neighborhoods coordinators met in a series of retreats to develop further strategies for inclusiveness, which have begun to show substantial payoff. But resistance to expanding district council membership, especially in South Seattle (particularly Southeast Seattle) with many more nonprofits serving poorer populations, raises more issues for those community councils who resent having to compromise the principle of representation for democratically governed civic organizations, rather than ones run by paid staff serving clients.[26]

The Neighborhood Leadership Program, under the Department of Neighborhoods, was a critical component in enabling the neighborhood system to become largely one of proactive and inclusive problem solving, though budget cuts have progressively whittled the program down to such an extent that, at least as of early 2008, it no longer functions. The leadership program provided classes, workshops, formal consultations, and informal mentoring to help citizens develop skills needed to form organizations, run them democratically, and navigate the city's agencies, programs, and regulations. This has been especially important in drawing new leaders into civic life and broadening the circle of the usual voices heard in neighborhoods, according to Brent Crook, former head of the department's community-building and leadership development programs and former independent public housing organizer: "We have a good history of community involvement in the city, but we needed broader ownership."[27] The city recognizes its stake in more diverse participation among new immigrants, who may not have prior experience in democratic participation and often have no clue about how the city works, and among poorer people, who may feel marginalized by the middle-class homeowners in their neighborhoods.

In many cases, people want to contribute but cannot stomach an endless round of meetings, especially ones that may become noisy and contentious. By helping develop skills that broaden the range of participants, the city has sought to achieve greater legitimacy for decisions taken and to reduce chances for relatively small minorities to hold agencies and other civic groups hostage through opposition that does not have to be put to the test of collaboration. The Department of Neighborhoods also provided specific training in asset-based community development for its own staff and for neighborhood leaders and nonprofit agencies. Prominent national trainers, such as Jody Kretzmann of the Asset-Based Community Development Institute, worked with staff and citizens, separately and conjointly. The department also offered this training to Seattle Housing Authority resident councils. For many department staff, neighborhood leaders, human service professionals, and Alinsky-style organizers in Seattle, asset-based training has been a genuine eye-opener that has helped generate civic energy and new ways of working together and in collaboration with other city departments.[28]

Planning at the Neighborhood Level

In the early 1990s the neighborhood matching fund helped generate civic energy that could not be contained when the city began its comprehensive planning to meet the requirements of the state's new Growth Management Act (1990). This legislation was a response to civic initiative, environmental mobilization, and regional visioning in previous years, as well as to a widely discussed "Peirce Report" in the *Seattle Times* calling for smart growth, open space, and new urban villages.[29] The act required King County, in which the city is located, to establish a growth boundary to protect rural areas and assign urban population growth targets. Planning, of course, is a highly complex process with innumerable points of possible contention based on divergent interests, asymmetrical distribution of costs and benefits, and the clash of professional and local perspectives. Jim Street, champion of the Department of Neighborhoods and chair of the city council land-use committee from the mid-1980s through the mid-1990s, was clearly committed to neighborhood participation but felt it could be productive only after the basic plan was readied. Antigrowth NIMBYism (*NIMBY*: not in my back yard) in the city might threaten the whole enterprise if citizens were involved on the front end, before key parameters were established and explained.[30]

The Growth Management Act required localities to plan for four types of "urban villages," following the famous terminology of urbanist and activist Jane Jacobs. Staff in the Seattle planning department developed the 1994 comprehensive plan, Toward a Sustainable Seattle, with considerable sensitivity to widely held popular values of sustainability. *Urban center villages* have the densest land use and projected housing and employment growth and are envisioned as the backbone of the regional rapid transit system. Of the twenty-one such urban centers designated throughout the state, five are in Seattle. *Residential urban villages* have low- to moderate-density residential development and the lowest projected employment growth. *Hub urban villages* contain a balance of housing and employment and provide a focus for goods and services for communities not close to urban centers. *Manufacturing and industrial centers* are the home of the region's industry. Alongside the official comprehensive planning effort, the nonprofit Sustainable Seattle, which referred to itself as a "volunteer network and civic forum," conducted extensive community forums and convened a "civic panel" to help develop sustainability indicators and lend democratic legitimacy to the process.[31]

Despite such efforts, activists rose up in arms to wage a neighborhood rights campaign to ensure greater participation and, in some cases, to contest their specific designation. Many distrusted the city, of course, because of earlier struggles over downtown planning, elimination a few years earlier of citizens' right to appeal a development project on environmental grounds, and the presence of other loopholes in earlier planning regulations. However, before the release of the plan, Mayor Norm Rice laid important groundwork for what was to follow. He convened his staff to think deeply about what neighborhoods really meant to people. As he put it, "They asked me questions, such as 'what did you like about your neighborhood when growing up?'" Rice, the first African American mayor in the city's history, was among the city councilors skeptical of creating the original Office of Neighborhoods but had since been "comforted" by the management style of Jim Diers. During his staff conversations, as he recalled, he had also become convinced of the vision put forth by Gary Lawrence, director of planning, for linking sustainability to neighborhood planning. So when public furor erupted, Rice responded with a major speech agreeing to neighborhood engagement in planning, on condition that citizens agree to meet core planning goals, such as equity and opportunity. He turned to the Department of Neighborhoods, which invited local leaders to a neighborhood planning conference to develop a different way of proceeding.[32]

Some two hundred and fifty to three hundred people came to the workshops and general sessions at the University of Washington to express core concerns and potential alternatives; the group then designated eleven representatives to begin designing a multistage collaborative process that would ensure acceptance and participation by a broad range of citizens within each of the thirty-seven neighborhoods targeted for growth. The eleven were commonly referred to by its members and others alike as the Gang of Eleven, a term of irony intended to evoke both the Gang of Four in China and the Big Ten of businessmen who effectively ruled Seattle in the decades preceding the 1960s. Unlike either group, however, the Gang of Eleven operated as the hub of a learning network of citizen activists, city staff, and independent professionals. Public forums and hearings helped further refine the process, and the city council then created the Neighborhood Planning Office in late 1994 to "enable the City and the community to work in partnership" to build community and improve life within the neighborhoods while meeting citywide goals. These goals included conforming to the core values of community, social equity, environmental stewardship, economic opportunity, and security established by the framework policies of the comprehensive plan and addressing the growth predictions for new jobs and housing in the urban village strategy.[33]

All plans, of course, had to conform to existing laws and environmental regulations. The Strategic Planning Office committed itself to developing a "neighborhood planning toolbox" to "demystify the art and science of planning for citizen planners," and the city council approved $4.5 million to support the civic process, as well as $4.8 million to staff the Neighborhood Planning Office over two years, later extended to four, with a further budget increment.[34] Five key components of neighborhood planning proved especially important to its democratic design, though some specific features emerged only from a process of learning along the way: the structure and philosophy of the newly established Neighborhood Planning Office; the inclusive visioning process required in each participating neighborhood; the tools provided to help neighborhood groups do good planning work; formal review of plans by city government; and the role of planning office project managers as relational organizers building trust and reciprocal accountability.

Neighborhood Planning Office

The new Neighborhood Planning Office, which reported directly to the mayor, oversaw the process that emerged over the next several years and was deliberately designed for learning and trust building. This process was quite complex and clever, balancing various concerns for citizen participation and accountability. Underlying all components, however, was a core philosophy, established most clearly by Karma Ruder, the newly hired Neighborhood Planning Office director who had previously overseen the district coordinators at the Department of Neighborhoods. In Ruder's view, planning as a complex system could work only to the extent that the city developed "self-organizing models" with heavy investments in building relationships and trust. "It's all about relationships and building a very elaborate web of trust"—trust among neighborhood groups that may have been battling one another for decades, among businesses and local activists, among all these and the staff of various city departments, who, as public administration scholar Kaifeng Yang demonstrates, typically have many good reasons to distrust citizen participation.[35] No rational and equitable plans, from above or below, validated by professional expertise or large turnout and deliberative discussion at neighborhood meetings, could ever substitute for the ongoing work of nurturing relationships and building trust. In the context of planning, Ruder reflected, this would inevitably be "very messy, organic, unpredictable, and nerve wracking"—not terms for a formal job description, to be sure.[36]

In early 1995 Ruder hired a team of ten project managers to work with the neighborhoods. She aimed for a mix of professional skills—land use, housing, communications, finance, community organizing—as well as diversity in gender, age, and ethnicity. In selecting staff, she insisted on one common denominator for everyone: "All had to believe that the community had wisdom and . . . be willing to trust and believe in it." Ruder coached the team in such a way that project managers would be able to learn continually from one another and from the community to ensure that the program was "cocreated."[37] As John Eskelin, project manager with a degree in planning who had previously worked on the comprehensive plan, recalled, "The first six months we spent just on training. Karma did some herself. She brought in people from the Department of Neighborhoods, from independent local groups, and from around the country. This prepared us well to provide training to the neighborhood groups themselves."[38]

A University of Washington report on the Neighborhood Planning Office's first twenty months found a substantial impact of training on the level of skills that citizens were able to bring to the neighborhood planning process and the formation of a range of new community associations, community development corporations, business associations, and neighborhood coalitions as a result of training and the overall program design. Training partners included not only those specializing in civic leadership development but also members of the University of Washington School of Business, the Neighborhood Business Council, the Seattle–King County Council on Aging Housing Task Force, and various city departments. The formation of new groups and partnerships, as well as the unevenness of local civic capacity and project manager skill and the relative scarcity of available planning consultants for a simultaneous citywide effort, led the city to extend the initially projected process from two years to four.[39]

In a further elaboration of the initial Gang of Eleven network learning design, the Neighborhood Planning Office was guided by an advisory committee of citizen representatives from the district councils, the citywide neighborhood council, and the new planning groups, along with

members of the city council, key city departments, and the planning commission. This ensured continuous—though sometimes painfully contentious—feedback through a deliberative process involving a broad spectrum of civic, political, administrative, professional, and business leaders
and enabled citizens and staff alike to draw upon a storehouse of lessons
from previous decades of planning.

Tom Veith, a citizen representative from Wallingford who served on the
executive group of the advisory committee, noted several of its contributions. First, the advisory committee determined that each neighborhood
planning group should, within certain broad parameters, design its own
process. "Monoculture," as he put it, would never suit the diversity of
neighborhoods in the city. Second, though representatives of various city
departments served as nonvoting members on the advisory committee—to
the dismay of some activists—these staff generally supported the core concerns of citizens, at the same time anticipating questions that the departments would inevitably raise down the line. Although such staff did not
vote, the consensus norm in advisory committee discussions helped to
ensure that the neighborhood planning process would not systematically
generate the kinds of plans that professional staff would later reject or sub-
vert. Third, the advisory committee came to realize that the neighborhood
planning groups would have to set priorities among their recommendations. Some planning groups had already begun to do this, but the mandate came rather late and thus angered other groups that felt rushed in
developing priorities or that their results did not adequately reflect neighborhood consensus.

This late learning, so to speak, came about because the city as yet had no
budget for funding plan recommendations and because, as Veith put it,
city officials "didn't realize how rich the process would be."[40] The planning
design invited citizens to envision neighborhoods holistically, in terms of
all aspects, not just capital and land-use projects but aesthetic, ecological,
and social ones as well. The civic imagination of Seattle residents, though
eventually generating the political will and tax revenues to support many
projects, needed to be complemented by their civic responsibility to set
priorities and agree to live within budgetary limits.

Inclusive Visioning

Neighborhoods were given a choice: to participate in developing a local
plan or to defer to the comprehensive plan, that set out in *Toward a Sustainable Seattle.* All thirty-seven neighborhoods targeted for growth chose

to participate, and a thirty-eighth group emerged from subsequent recon-figuring. The neighborhoods were free to identify their own scope of work—housing, open space, transportation, local commercial revitaliza-tion, arts, human services—and to proceed holistically rather than tailor their recommendations to each city department separately. During the first phase, which planning groups initiated at various points in 1995 and well into 1996, neighborhoods were eligible for $10,000 to help define a neigh-borhood vision and involve the broad community and all major stake-holders through public meetings and surveys.[41]

To mitigate the common problem of domination of the process by well-organized, middle-class, and typically white homeowners, each neighbor-hood was accountable to the Neighborhood Planning Office for developing a detailed stakeholder analysis and outreach plan to engage the full diversity of its residents. Were minorities and recent immigrants represented? People with disabilities? Youth? Renters? Were affected businesses and other insti-tutions at the table? The planning office also supplied an outreach toolkit with ideas and resources (for example, extra funds for language translation) for use in engaging those who might normally fall under the radar. In Del-ridge, for instance, thirty-five distinct languages are spoken, and the plan-ning group translated its neighborhood survey and other materials into three primary ones, Spanish, Cambodian, and Vietnamese. In China-town–International District, the neighborhood planning process has had to negotiate a fundamental tension between a modern Pan-Asian activist network, which coincided relatively well with the geographic planning boundaries, and more traditional enclaves committed to protecting ethnic interest and identity.[42]

A range of well-known factors tend to skew participation in neighbor-hood associations. Homeowners have a financial investment in their homes and tend to have longer ties to the neighborhood, whereas younger people are more mobile and tend to have fewer children in the schools. Educated people attend more often and speak more confidently at community meet-ings, and recent immigrants, especially those with limited English language skills, often feel intimidated and unwelcome or are deeply distrustful of the state as a result of their own homeland experiences or current immigration status—or both. The Neighborhood Planning Office did not imagine that all these factors could be undone. Nor did it see the solution as simply packing meetings with those typically marginalized. The strategy was not quantitative but qualitative, according to Ruder. Each neighborhood was challenged to understand what those who were not at the table might want and to devise a way of finding out. If small business did not show up at meetings, then perhaps the neighborhood associations should design a survey just for small businesses. If homeless people did not come to officially sponsored events, then perhaps people should be interviewed at food banks. This "conceptual flip," as Ruder characterized it, challenged each neighborhood to internalize the problem of imagining and discovering the diversity of stakeholder interests as a more or less permanent mindset.[43]

The relational work conducted by the Department of Neighborhoods with recent immigrants and communities of color in the matching fund, P-Patch, and other programs also provided a foundation for making the democratic deliberation of planning more sensitive to the problems of difference. Ruder's approach might be considered a version of what political theorists Amy Gutmann and Dennis Thompson refer to as discovering the "moral constituents" that need to be at the deliberative table, exploring whether there is an effective way to get them there physically or in proper proportions. In Norm Rice's more prosaic formulation, "Karma drank the Kool-Aid and kept the values intact."[44]

The challenge to make a conceptual flip was combined with a warning and a threat to each neighborhood planning group. The warning: your plan will unravel later if factions to whom you have not reached out arise to oppose it. For instance, the Downtown Seattle Association, representing the most influential corporations (finance, construction, real estate, retail, hotels, sports) as well as media and cultural institutions, was told by the Neighborhood Planning Office project manager that unless it was willing to share power with local residents, nonprofits, artists, and small shopkeepers, the resulting plan would meet the fate of the 1985 downtown plan, which was blocked by mobilized residents. Kate Joncas, the association's president, was a planner by background and a trust builder by style, and she responded well to the collaborative philosophy and design of the program. In the downtown, which included five separate neighborhood planning committees (Commercial Core, Chinatown–International District, Pioneer Square, Belltown, and Denny Triangle), there was a further challenge: only to the extent that each neighborhood could demonstrate that its process was inclusive would it have legitimacy when sitting at the table in the Downtown Urban Center Planning Group to negotiate the overall downtown plan.[45]

A threat accompanied the warning: if your planning group excludes any major stakeholders who clearly need to be at the table, your planning dollars, which would be more substantial in the next phase, could be withheld. This happened, for instance, in the Queen Anne neighborhood when residents at the top of the hill, represented by the Queen Anne Community Council, tried to dominate the visioning process at the expense of those at the bottom, who faced greater problems, were less organized, and lived in neighborhoods that already had greater housing density. The Neighborhood Planning Office informed the neighborhood planning group in no uncertain terms that the city's planning dollars belonged to everyone. The ensuing battle was fierce, but the planning office's approach proved nonetheless educative, as the planning group developed a more inclusive process and a plan that reflected broader interests. Today, several common board memberships help bridge the Queen Anne Community Council and the Uptown Alliance, which had formed to claim its seat at the planning table and get the uptown recognized as a distinct neighborhood (though still within the neighborhood planning group).[46]

Tools for Empowering Citizens

The third component of empowered neighborhood planning was the set of tools (financial, data, programmatic, process) that the city provided. Accountable autonomy, in other words, was matched with resources to enable citizens to do good deliberative work. Once the city was assured that the initial outreach was broadly democratic and that the scope of proposed planning made sense, each neighborhood became eligible for $60,000 to $100,000 (with additional funds set aside for urban centers and distressed areas) to conduct the second phase of actual planning, which occurred variously between 1996 and 1999. Using ArcView software, the Strategic Planning Office developed a geographical information system mapping and database tool called the Data Viewer, which enabled citizen planners to access neighborhood-specific information on demographics, land use, transportation flow, system capacity, and environmental constraints and to print maps and aerial photographs for reports and public presentations. Under a separate but complementary program, design review boards, with neighborhood representatives included alongside design, development, and business professionals, began to oversee the design features of larger residential and commercial projects beginning in 1994. When combined with the intensive relational and trust-building work of project managers, this planning support system exemplifies what planning theorist Richard Klosterman refers to as "collective design," facilitating information sharing, mutual learning, and community debate—though not, to be sure, with the far more sophisticated tools available today.[47]

City departments, from housing and police to transportation and utilities, produced citizen toolkits to help residents understand their options within existing programs and regulations. The neighborhood planning toolbox in the downtown neighborhood service center, for instance, consisted of a crate (approximately 24 × 12 × 12 inches) full of guidebooks and five additional thick binders of materials that could not fit in the crate. These covered a broad range of issues: outreach, housing, land use, environmentally critical areas, historic preservation, block watches, open space, public school partnerships, human services, and pedestrian facilities. Another downtown office in Pioneer Square posted ongoing designs on the walls to keep citizens, businesses, and various subcommittees up to date. Other neighborhoods used *The Urban Forest Tool: Preserving, Protecting, and Enhancing Your Neighborhood Forest.*

Some tools were unfocused and produced too late in the process, and not all planning groups made effective use of them. Many activists also knew much more than the new Neighborhood Planning Office staff hired to assist them, and thus training occurred in both directions, recalled Chris Leman, chair of the city neighborhood council planning committee at the time. Most planning groups mastered the relevant skills and regulations well enough to develop workable proposals. Critical to the civic design, as downtown project manager Eskelin emphasized, was that the very process of developing toolkits, whatever their limits, compelled city departments to "begin thinking more like citizens."[48]

Neighborhoods chose to focus on various mixes of housing, open space, transportation, public safety, arts, human services, and business district revitalization, with fifty to two hundred specific recommendations in each plan. In addition to working closely with the project managers from the Neighborhood Planning Office, the local planning committees hired their own consultants with the money allotted. Each committee presented options, often in visually rich and well-documented formats, at an Alternatives Fair to which the entire neighborhood was invited. Such validation events, as they were called, elicited fresh ideas and modifications—sometimes major ones that were the product of serious neighborhood disagreements—and drew in additional people to help plan and do further outreach. When a draft plan was finally ready, it was sent in a "validation mailer" to all households in the neighborhood, as well as to businesses and property owners, who cast their votes on the enclosed ballot or at an open meeting. Further revisions were then possible.[49]

For instance, the Crown Hill–Ballard Neighborhood Planning Association, a nonprofit formed from various local groups to facilitate collaboration in planning the Crown Hill residential urban village and the Ballard hub urban village, led the process in these two contiguous neighborhoods. (Ballard–Interbay Northend developed a separate plan for its manufacturing and industrial center.) The Crown Hill–Ballard group hired Green-Woods Associates to help design a visioning process, which included Saturday morning "topical seminars." Between twenty and fifty participants turned out for each forum. There were six topical areas in all, each with an ongoing committee. As Jody Grage Haug, a longtime community and environmental activist who oversaw the process, recalled, "We feared that special interest folks would come out and dominate [each forum]. But except for one meeting, this didn't happen." The visioning process challenged participants to think of how all the parts would fit together. A steering committee met monthly, and informal weekly breakfast meetings facilitated the exchange of information across committees and built trust in the quality of this information—a key ingredient in successful collaboration.[50]

The residential development committee, for instance, engaged renters in its leadership. After the initial visioning was complete, the committee worked on a draft plan for multifamily and affordable housing. It then conducted a survey and held a community-wide town meeting of two hundred participants. In addition to developing specific proposals for public arts, the arts and culture committee formed Arts Ballard to link the efforts of various organizations on an ongoing basis. The human services committee helped develop a network among forty providers who met monthly and also helped bring to fruition the Ballard Family Center that had been launched in 1995 with a small matching fund grant.

Each of these efforts represents field building within a specific neighborhood. The economic development committee anchored various components in the design of a new Ballard municipal center and elicited collaboration between the Ballard Chamber of Commerce and the Ballard Merchants Association, which had not spoken to each other in years. The open space and recreation committee developed an integrated set of proposals for specific parcels around the idea of "green links" connecting them. In April 1998 the *Ballard News Tribune*—which, along with the Crown Hill–Ballard Neighborhood Planning Association newsletter, kept citizens informed of the planning process throughout—mailed a validation issue to all households, businesses, and property owners in the area. Two public validation meetings followed, and after reviewing all comments, the Crown Hill–Ballard board made revisions and sent the plan to the city council, all within the timeline generally followed by most neighborhoods (see table 3-1). Some eight hundred citizens in Ballard and Crown Hill actively engaged in the planning process.[51]

Formal Review and Citizen Accountability

The fourth component of Seattle's neighborhood planning was the formal review process. All final plans were sent to the Strategic Planning Office, which coordinated a review and response team of representatives from relevant city departments. Was the neighborhood plan consistent with the comprehensive plan and the urban villages rubric? Did it comply with all laws, including environmental ones? Did the neighborhood set priorities among its proposals and document its participation process adequately? The review and response team enabled agencies to advise the city council, whose neighborhoods committee further reviewed each plan and then held a formal public hearing to determine whether the community had, in fact, achieved general consensus on the proposals—a standard that citizen activists themselves strongly insisted on.[52] Accompanied by department staff and often the mayor, the committee also conducted tours of each neighborhood to learn about issues. Although estimates are inexact, somewhere between fourteen thousand and thirty thousand residents participated at one time or another in the various public meetings, land-use walks, planning workshops, door-knocking campaigns, surveys, and other events.

As a result of the iterative process based on broad outreach and continual revision, most plans yielded consensus among all stakeholders. According to Richard Conlin, a member, and later chair, of the city council neighborhoods committee, the council had to "mediate two or three plans. In another four or five cases, there was pretty strong dissent." But narrow interest groups or neighborhood factions had not generally hijacked the process. All neighborhoods produced plans that accommodated growth as envisioned by state law but under terms they felt they could control. Some plans were much more elaborate and well documented than others, and some neighborhood planning groups could undoubtedly have used additional staff support or more time to review their official plan summaries, known as approval and adoption matrixes, before presenting the plan to the city council for final approval. Nonetheless, the city council's investment of money and time in neighborhood planning, which included designating every member a "council steward" for several neighborhoods, had generally paid off.[53]

Table 3-1. Seattle Neighborhood Planning Timeline, 1994–2007

Comprehensive plan (1994)	Neighborhood visioning (1995–96)[a]	Draft plan components (1996–97)[a]	Validation and approval (1997–99)[a]	Implementation and update (1999–2007)
City council approval	Establish neighborhood planning groups	Topical committees	Alternatives Fair	Bonds, levies
Neighborhood protest	Train Neighborhood Planning Office project managers and neighborhood planning groups	Public forums	Validation mailer	Departmental decentralization
Neighborhood planning program approved by city council		Surveys	Validation meeting(s)	Interdepartmental sector teams
	Neighborhood planning advisory committee established	Consultants facilitate planning	Neighborhood tours	Stewardship groups
	Stakeholder analyses	Components integrated	City council and department review and response	Neighborhood development managers, budget cuts in 2002 and 2003; duties shifted to district coordinators
	Topical dialogues (land use, housing, open space, and so forth)		Adoption and approval matrixes	
	Consultants facilitate visioning			

a. Varies by neighborhood.

The approval and adoption matrix summarizes plan details, showing each recommendation accompanied by priority ranking, time frame, and proposed implementers, including public agencies, civic groups, institutions, community development corporations, businesses, developers, and property owners. City departments also indicate on the matrix whether the project is feasible, whether resources are available for it, and where other resources might be found. While there are certainly many traditional items for improvement requiring the attention of a single agency, the matrixes are not primarily a set of citizen demands requiring agency action and are certainly not the typical spreadsheets found in top-down agency planning. Rather, the matrixes are summaries of proposals refined through extensive public deliberation and one-on-one communication tapping numerous sources of citizen and agency expertise and trust—all within a broad neighborhood vision that various stakeholders commit publicly to work on together. The approval and adoption matrixes are what I would call coproduction spreadsheets.

The Department of Neighborhoods has posted all narrative plans and matrixes on its website, with an account of each local democratic process and periodic updates on setting priorities and implementation of projects, thus adding a further degree of transparency within and across all neighborhoods. More than a dozen departments use the neighborhood priority reports to assign appropriate administrative responsibility and develop their own overall agency plans. The expectation to list projected nongovernmental partners in the approval and adoption matrixes was taken seriously in most neighborhoods across the city, even if not all plan items were amenable to this. A surprising 18 percent of plan recommendations listed a community organization as the lead agency for implementation; only the Seattle Department of Transportation was more frequently listed as lead agency.

Equally important to policy design as a democratic teaching of self-government was the process of engaging neighborhoods in thinking about the costs of each proposal, though these were not included in the final matrixes. Key for Sally Clark—who first managed the approval and adoption process for the city council, then served as a neighborhood development manager in the southeast sector and is currently city councilor and head of the neighborhoods committee—was the process of engaging neighborhoods in thinking about the costs of each proposal. "The neighborhoods were often surprised at the costs. But this [matrix process] was very educative for them. It gave them a sense of how much it costs to run a city! . . . This gets us closer to honestly governing ourselves."[54]

Project Managers as Relational Organizers

An essential fifth component of the planning process was the Neighborhood Planning Office's project manager, who could operate as relational organizer to help weave that "very elaborate web of trust" envisioned by the office's director, Karma Ruder. Helping build relationships among the wide array of actors in neighborhood associations, city departments, local chambers of commerce, and the city council itself became an indispensable function of the project manager's job, though clearly one designed to leverage the ongoing relational organizing of many neighborhood activists themselves. Reflecting on her position as neighborhood development manager at the implementation stage, Clark listed various responsibilities. Then, as if stepping back suddenly to view the job from the distance of several years outside of government, Clark said that building relationships was "pretty much all of it."[55]

Project managers engaged in relational organizing in several ways. First and foremost, they brokered one-on-ones between individuals with various perspectives on a given issue. They targeted those with strong and often divergent views, expressed in private or at public meetings, and asked them to get together, often in one of the hundreds of coffee shops that pepper Seattle. The meetings could be simple getting-to-know-you meetings, sharing some initial perspectives or common values and establishing the basis for further independent contact, or they could focus on a tough issue and explore possible solutions and how to bring others into future conversations. In some cases, the meetings first had to clear the air of past conflicts or heal old battle wounds. If, as has been said, "all organizing is reorganizing," the project manager often proved important in getting competing neighborhood associations and leaders to reorganize around a broader neighborhood vision and planning projects that crossed antiquated boundaries or put to rest ancient skeletons.

The project manager also served as translator between the vernacular understanding of neighborhood problems and solutions, on the one hand, and agency cultures, with strong bureaucratic and professional norms that reflected their own understandings of equity, efficiency, technical elegance, regulatory mandate, and common good, on the other. The project manager might even convene a veritable "on-the-spot one-on-one," for instance, while residents confronted a transportation engineer during station area planning and try to get each party to understand the other's point of view. Indeed, helping each party see the perspective of the other, including values, interests, constraints, and accountability, was a central part of the project manager's job and allowed individuals and groups she met with separately to trust her as an honest broker and a reliable conduit of information. In short, project managers acted officially, systematically, and strategically on behalf of citizens and the city alike as "intermediaries of trust," in political scientist Russell Hardin's felicitous phrase, and as the relational pivot of what public policy analyst Robert Behn calls "360-degree reciprocal accountability."[56]

Project managers communicated and negotiated regularly with city councilors and their staffs to resolve problems and conflicts. Mayor Rice encouraged the Neighborhood Planning Office director to help his agency officials understand how to build on relational self-organizing principles down the line. He also visited with all department heads and with middle managers to generate understanding and a sense of ownership. To help his cabinet grapple with how this approach could promote their departmental interests, he even devoted one of his regularly scheduled and facilitated annual retreats and formed a cabinet-level neighborhood planning work group. Rice later recalled, "I used a lot of my inspirational political capital on this, though I never thought of it as risky, once I found the value proposition. It's not that risky once you yourself believe it."[57] Although the notion of relational self-organizing "drove agency staff crazy at first," in Ruder's words, some agency heads got it quickly, and all, "trying hard," got it to some degree.[58] Support from the top further helped neighborhood planning project managers identify and build relationships with a selected number of mid- and street-level staff, who could be counted on to work creatively with citizens on the ground, preparing the way for even deeper collaboration when interdepartmental teams were established for implementation.

Relationship building did not always go smoothly. Despite repeated attempts, some in the various neighborhood associations within a planning area could not manage to work together. In some cases, the project manager would suggest another area of productive activity for one of them (for example, a move to a different subcommittee), but this did not always prove successful. Activists and business people did not always achieve agreement or even agree to a one-on-one meeting. As director Ruder noted, sometimes a neighborhood planning committee representative would "storm into my office and say, 'if we don't get a new project manager, we all quit!' . . . And some project managers came in and said, 'if I don't get a new community, I quit!'" Committee-manager divorces—the exit option within an overall design for voice, in economist Albert Hirschman's famous phraseology—were thus arranged for various reasons, including some committees' having become too dependent on a specific project manager.[59]

What prevented the neighborhood planning process from becoming just another complex bureaucratic maze of technical details, participatory process requirements, and multilevel accountability mechanisms were the relational civic skills and philosophy underlying the project manager's role. What might have appeared as straight lines on an organizational chart became, in reality, circles of continuous relational exchanges of information, perspectives, and validation designed to produce trust—or, rather, complex webs of exchanges within clear overall parameters of authority and accountability. For downtown project manager Eskelin, who later served as neighborhood development manager during implementation, "validation was not just the formal neighborhood event or publishing the proposed plan in the local newspaper for feedback. We did validation from day one, with continual check-ins with all kinds of folks every day."[60] In this sense, the project manager's role was to enable ongoing, pragmatic, democratic discourse among diverse actors according to a communicative ideal with optimal degrees of comprehensibility, sincerity, legitimacy, and truth, factors planning theorists John Forester and Judith Innes view as critical for contemporary planning.[61] Project managers performed this role in a way designed to achieve multilayered and reciprocal accountability among citizens and stakeholders (participatory democracy), the city council and mayor (representative democracy), and city departments (public administration) (for a graphic presentation, see table 3-2).

Implementing the Plans

When Seattle's new mayor, Paul Schell, took office in 1998, just as many neighborhood plans were nearing completion, issues of funding and implementation stared him starkly in the face. Only a small fund ($1.5 million, or $50,000 per planning neighborhood) had been designated by the city council for early implementation, primarily to keep civic energy flowing, something far from assured in a long, complex process with no guaranteed outcomes.[62] Indeed, one reason that building up a fund of trust was so important in the planning process was that it might help leverage a fund of actual dollars down the line. Schell, originally a businessman and developer, had become deeply committed to neighborhood planning while director of the Department of Community Development. He had defeated

Table 3-2. *Multilayered and Reciprocal Accountability Mechanisms in Seattle Neighborhood Planning*

Democratic actor	Accountability mechanisms
Neighborhood planning group[a]	Stakeholder analysis (representativeness)
	Committee reports, presentations, updates
	One-on-one meetings, informal group meetings
	Neighborhood newspapers (reports, debates)
	Validation mailer (to all residents, property owners, businesses)
	Validation meetings (open, public)
Neighborhood project manager[b]	Check-ins, one-on-one meetings; communicative generation of trust, comprehensibility, legitimacy, and truth among all stakeholders, including departments; relational pivot for 360-degree accountability
City council and mayor	Check-ins (council stewards and planning groups)
	Neighborhood walking tours
	Public hearings
	City council adoption and approval; mediation
	Mayoral oversight of Neighborhood Planning Office
City departments	Review and response team (advises city council's neighborhoods committee)
	One-on-one meetings with stakeholders, project managers
	Mayoral oversight

a. Stakeholders: community councils, district council, individual citizens, nonprofits, businesses, landlords, open space coalition, watershed association, ethnic associations, community development corporation.

b. Under the Neighborhood Planning Office.

the candidate backed by voters in the neighborhoods opposed to the growth mandates of the comprehensive plan—a victory helped along by the many public validation events that happened to occur during the election season. This was yet another sign that well-designed participatory democracy could contain NIMBYism. The mayor, working closely with Conlin on the city council, decided to proceed to implementation of the neighborhood plans on several fronts.

Dollars for Implementation

First, Schell and Conlin committed to expanding the neighborhood matching fund from $1.5 million annually to $4.5 million to enable neighborhood groups to begin to carry out projects envisioned in the plans.

Since this was still far from enough money to implement the more than forty-two hundred recommendations in the plans (with a twenty-year target completion date for the comprehensive plan of 2014), the mayor placed on the ballot a series of bond and levy measures that represented common plan items. At first, many thought he was crazy to go to the taxpayers with large requests. But in 1998 citizens passed a nearly $200 million library bond measure (called Libraries for All) to fund new building, expansion, and renovation for twenty-seven branch libraries, including Seattle's most underserved areas, as well as a new downtown library. The following year they approved a similar measure to fund community centers, and the year after that one for parks and open space, with an overall total of $430 million, much of which could be targeted for specific recommendations in the neighborhood plans. Citizens also voted to renew the low-income housing levy, which would raise $86 million in 2002 under the next mayor.

Advocacy groups, of course, also worked for these measures and in some cases had involved themselves in the neighborhood planning process. However, the democratic breadth of planning, as well as improved economic times, enabled them to convince voters who had been skeptical or had actually rejected similar bond proposals only a few years earlier, as in the case of libraries. Since the city had been willing to invest in democracy during the planning process, citizens were willing to invest their tax money in turning neighborhood visions into reality.[63]

Decentralizing Departments

Mayor Schell also decentralized various city departments into six sectors (overlapping police precincts and most district council boundaries) so that local departmental units could work collaboratively with the neighborhood planning stewardship groups that succeeded the planning committees in each area. Stewardship groups reside mostly in existing community councils and district councils, though some originated as independent organizations out of the planning process itself, and most have ongoing relationships with a broad range of other civic groups. Nonprofit community development corporations, working closely with district councils, have assumed the stewardship role in some instances. The mayor also urged departments to align their existing budgets with neighborhood plan priorities. An interdepartmental team coordinated the work of the departments in each sector to respond to the integrative and holistic quality of the neighborhood visions and plans.[64]

As the Neighborhood Planning Office was dismantled with the final approval of all plans in 1999, the Department of Neighborhoods became responsible for providing staff support for citizens in the stewardship groups and for coordinating their work with the interdepartmental teams. This role was performed primarily by six neighborhood development managers, often referred to as sector managers, three of whom were carried over from their project manager positions and one of whom (Clark) had managed the approval process for the city council. The stewardship groups could continue to clarify the vision, reprioritize recommendations in the light of perceived constraints and new opportunities, and hold the city accountable for following through. They could also continue to map and mobilize community resources in ways that built upon asset-based community development strategies. Together, the stewardship group and the interdepartmental team could ensure that multiple plan components, available resources, and agency regulations were well aligned; if zoning and other changes were needed, proposals would be brought to the city council.

The neighborhood development managers became the lynchpin for the city, performing perhaps the most complex role of broker in the entire civic policy design.[65] They had the best overall view of each plan in their sector, the way all the components fit together, and how the process had evolved, including many complex temporal layers of public deliberation and one-on-one relational work to produce trust and working consensus. Some of the development managers had already established good working relationships with neighborhood leaders and committee chairs during the planning phase, and the new hires energetically set out to do the same. In the words of Jody Grage Haug, who chaired the Ballard district council stewardship committee, the neighborhood development managers worked "very effectively with us and got us the information we needed. There was not much hierarchy here. We were all just part of a network."[66] The managers were responsible for convening the interdepartmental teams and pushed hard for the departments to work together. Although often expected (in their words) to "kick ass" in the city bureaucracies to keep them responsive to stewardship groups, the development managers focused especially on "nurturing relationships" and "catalyzing networks" with departmental staff so that, over time, "shepherds" and "champions" of the neighborhood plans would voluntarily carry the work forward within each city department.[67]

Such champions emerged especially among project managers within departments; they often received official license to help align agencies' own ten-year plans with neighborhood ones and help transform agency practices more broadly. They educated senior staff who would later be charged with working together in the next mayor's subcabinet to ensure that long-term city planning and policymaking in a dynamic environment could remain responsive to neighborhood visions, as well as shifting priorities and new opportunities. Neighborhood development managers met with the mayor four times a year to report on progress and offer advice on how to maintain momentum within each department. Finally, an important part of the development managers' role was to leverage and pool resources from a variety of sources to help implement plan recommendations. In addition to the bonds and levies, such resources could come from private foundations, developers, the arts commission, mitigation funds, utility companies, state programs, and, of course, the neighborhood matching fund. When combined with relational organizing and asset-based community development practices, this leveraging role was a powerfully integrative one that no individual department or neighborhood stewardship group could perform on its own. For Brent Crook, whose views were echoed by neighborhood leaders and staff in various city agencies (including some well-placed initial skeptics) and confirmed in a formal survey of stewardships groups and by a subsequent city auditor's report on plan implementation, the neighborhood development managers were "an amazing catalyst" in the whole system of planning.[68]

Culture Change within City Departments

For decentralization to be meaningful over the long run would require genuine culture change in the departments to enable them to work collaboratively with neighborhoods. That so many other city planning efforts, from the comprehensive drainage plan (2005) and environmental action agenda (2005) to the urban forest management plan (2007) and Center City Seattle (2007), continued to mention the neighborhood plans testifies to the important public norm established by neighborhood planning. Professional planners across the city felt obligated to take into account the planning work done by citizens. In fact, the city auditor's 2007 report notes that virtually all major planning efforts in Seattle since 1999—nearly forty of which it examined carefully—included local neighborhood plans in one way or another and that "coordination across organizational boundaries increased markedly," especially owing to the work of the neighborhood development managers. In addition, consulting neighborhood plans has become a legal requirement or departmental procedure for some departments, such as the planning department (City Environmental Policies and

Procedures and Design Review Guidelines) and the Department of Transportation (Right-of-Way Improvement Manual).[69]

City departments, of course, have been responsive to varying degrees. Some have been resistant, others have hired staff away from the Department of Neighborhoods to help them transform practice. The head of the parks department, for instance, quickly accepted the principles underlying neighborhood planning, as did many younger and more idealistic staff, though I found complaints of foot-dragging on the part of others. The recreation center advisory councils across the city, on which some four hundred citizens were already serving, also provided a basis for collaboration. Passage of the parks levy in 2000 helped enormously by providing substantial new funds for work with neighborhoods, and the parks department was listed as the lead agency for 8 percent of all neighborhood plan recommendations. Library officials and staff—who also had a levy to work with—have been enthusiastic supporters, and their collaboration with communities can be seen in the design of the new branch libraries, some of which have community-oriented programs, affordable housing, neighborhood service centers, and even community development corporations clustered in and around their buildings, as in the Delridge neighborhood. During the planning phase, librarians held community forums and met with neighborhood planning groups; they strongly reiterated their own civic professional mission within "the most democratic of all institutions [that is, libraries] helping citizens engage in self-governance."[70]

During the planning phase, the head of the Department of Transportation also became an early enthusiast, as did some line staff. But when he left, progress slowed. As various planners, neighborhood activists, and other officials recounted, transportation staff encountered greater technical constraints than other departments, had fewer built-in win-win options available within any particular neighborhood, and seemed to fall back to the defensive stance that because some people in the neighborhoods are going to beat up on them no matter what they do, they might as well just employ their best professional technique and judgment and take what comes. Even within transportation, however, some sectors were better than others. Midlevel transportation project managers in the downtown often worked collaboratively with the neighborhoods and the development manager; and the Department of Planning and Development brought Gary Johnson, who had much experience working with citizens as a neighborhood service center coordinator and public housing organizer, into the agency as its center-city strategy coordinator. One long-time citizen activist noted that the Department of Transportation worked collaboratively with the neighborhood stewardship group in Wallingford to redesign several major corridors (45th Street, 50th Street, and Stone Way) and that some engineers came to understand that their job was not just to "facilitate flow" but also to preserve the integrity of real places inhabited by real people.[71]

The Department of Transportation also hired Pamela Green, the district coordinator for Southeast Seattle, as its light-rail community liaison. A former community organizer and current member of the board of the King County National Association for the Advancement of Colored People (NAACP), Green had a particularly delicate task in Rainier Valley. Although the community was involved in station design and had its share of battles with the city over station location, once construction began a whole host of new problems arose because contaminated soil was found on forty-five sites—relocated dry cleaners, gas stations, homes with leaking oil tanks—within a four-and-one-half mile stretch. She thus had to work closely with environmental justice activists and with the 240 remaining businesses, many of which were run by new immigrants, when the originally planned disruption of access on any given block stretched from a promised two-week maximum to several months.

Such delay and disruption appeared to have broken the trust previously established—trust that can "absolutely be destroyed quickly in these kinds of projects," Green noted. She also served on the interdepartmental team to help transform culture across departments working in the sector and now serves as the mayor's citywide director of community outreach on his senior policy team. Fortunately, the community organization Save Our Valley had persuaded the city to create a $50 million community development fund after the citizens group lost an earlier battle over putting the tracks underground, and the fund has become available for the Department of Transportation to cushion the blow to nearby businesses and to provide for a second phase of economic development.[72]

According to Conlin, former chair of the neighborhoods committee, the more an agency tended to identify itself as expert rather than as generalist or manager, the more resistant it was to working with citizens.[73] But even here some notable changes occurred. Seattle Public Utilities—with responsibility over sewers, drainage, and solid waste—initially reacted as the experts with all the answers. But more recently, especially as new environmental engineers have joined the staff, the agency has been able to recognize the many good ideas coming from citizens and has become far more responsive.

For instance, various watershed groups, active for a decade or more, had been out in front of Seattle Public Utilities on innovative ways to restore the urban streams of Seattle, and various neighborhood plans contained proposals for restoration. In 1998, in response to Mayor Schell's Millennium Challenge to spur innovative projects, Denise Andrews, a young policy analyst at Seattle Public Utilities, decided to join citizens' local knowledge with emerging professional models in storm water engineering and management. Storm water runoff, of course, constitutes a major source of pollution and, if not managed more effectively, would continue to undermine efforts at restoring streams and salmon in and around Seattle, regardless of the hands-on work of local watershed groups. Andrews led a team including a civil engineer and landscape architect, among others, in developing a pilot to demonstrate that low-impact natural drainage systems could limit pollution runoff from impervious surfaces (streets, rooftops, parking lots) into streams, lakes, and Puget Sound. In addition, natural drainage systems could manage flooding in neighborhoods, improve the appearance and function of street right-of-ways, and significantly reduce the costs of drainage and mitigation infrastructure. The system redesigns residential streets using open, vegetated swales, storm water cascades, and small wetland ponds to mimic the functions of nature lost to urbanization. Central to such projects are the plants and trees and the deep, healthy soils that support them, which form a living infrastructure that, unlike pipes and vaults, increase in functional value over time.

The team recruited the pilot neighborhood voluntarily and then enlisted citizens to become local ambassadors to other neighborhoods selected by Seattle Public Utilities on the basis of technical criteria, which included mitigating flooding in the basements of a significant proportion of homeowners in the area. According to Jim Johnson, a project manager, the team held "lots of meetings, one-on-ones, small groups, stakeholder meetings . . . a lot of one-on-one work. . . . We built trusting relationships with these people." Staff in the Department of Transportation, coordinating with Seattle Public Utilities, did likewise, though the mayor had to intervene to get the fire department to become more flexible on appropriate street design.[74]

Despite the benefits to others in the neighborhood and to the city as a whole, however, some residents resisted, especially those who had become accustomed to parking large recreational vehicles—or "their eighth car," as Andrews facetiously put it—in the city's rights-of-way. But the team stood firm on its technical criteria and the city's property rights, while offering neighbors various options on walkway materials and plants. They helped organize stewardship days to enlist neighbors to maintain the newly—and beautifully—landscaped Street Edge Alternative, which now almost all neighbors do, many saying this was the first time they actually met some of the neighbors on the block. Younger neighbors assist older ones, and peer pressure has brought around most of the initial resisters. Those who understand the true environmental significance of the design—roughly a fifth, according to Andrews—have become a source of networked civic education for others in the immediate neighborhood and beyond. In 2004 the natural drainage systems won an Innovations in American Government Award from the Kennedy School's Ash Institute for Democratic Governance and Innovation, another "Oscar in government" for the City of Seattle.[75]

Policy Design Challenges in a Dynamic Environment

Seattle's neighborhood system of district councils, matching funds, community gardens, and neighborhood planning embodies the core principles of civic policy design discussed in chapter 2 (see table 3-3 for a partial summary). The Neighborhood Matching Fund program, for instance, has coproduction as its core principle and mobilizes community assets of various sorts, from the hands-on and heads-in work of local residents to contributions of cash, materials, and equipment. P-Patch and Cultivating Communities similarly mobilize the skills of local gardeners, help build civic relationships across ethnic and racial lines, and link local neighborhoods to city and county networks for community-supported agriculture. District councils enable ongoing public deliberation among community councils and other civic organizations and facilitate partnership building among civic and business groups, local institutions, and city departments. Neighborhood planning has incorporated inclusive visioning, democratic deliberation, ongoing relational organizing, and reciprocal accountability. In addition, it aims to transform institutional cultures so that civic collaboration becomes both norm and practice within large city bureaucracies. These core policy design principles, of course, emerged piecemeal, often through conflict, and certainly remain imperfect in application.

Although the neighborhood system has demonstrated a capacity for institutional growth and learning over two decades and several mayoral administrations, it also faces important challenges if it is to remain robust in a dynamic economic, demographic, and political environment. There

Table 3-3. *Eight Core Principles of Civic Policy Design in Seattle's Neighborhood Planning Programs*

Core principle	Programs, activities
Coproduce public goods	Neighborhood matching fund (design, construction, maintenance of public space, civic education, ecosystem restoration, public art)
	P-Patch, Cultivating Communities (design, construction, maintenance of public space, planting, harvesting, distribution)
	Neighborhood planning (identification and engagement of civic and nonprofit organizations as lead agencies and partners for implementation)
Mobilize community assets	Neighborhood matching fund (skills, land, tools, materials, money, leadership, peer learning)
	P-Patch, Cultivating Communities (skills, land, tools, materials, money, leadership, peer learning)
	District councils (asset-based community development training and and practices)
	Neighborhood planning (Neighborhood Planning Office project managers and neighborhood development managers facilitate asset-based community development approaches)
Share professional expertise	Neighborhood matching fund (civil servants, University of Washington Design/Build students and faculty, citizen professionals, such as planners, carpenters, teachers, artists, business managers)
	P-Patch, Cultivating Communities (civil servants, cooperative extension master gardeners)
	Neighborhood planning (DataViewer, toolboxes, city staff and paid consultants, citizen-experts, training and network learning)
Enable public deliberation	District councils (public discourse among community councils, other civic organizations; communication with wider community through forums, newspapers)
	Neighborhood planning (inclusive visioning, public forums, Alternatives Fairs, committees; one-on-one meetings among citizens, stakeholders, and city staff; consideration of priorities and costs)
Promote sustainable partnerships	Neighborhood matching fund (one-on-one meetings, project collaboration among neighborhood and ethnic groups, city departments, schools, environmental and extralocal networks)
	P-Patch, Cultivating Communities (Seattle Tilth, Food Security Coalition, Lettuce Link)

(continued)

Table 3-3. *Eight Core Principles of Civic Policy Design in Seattle's Neighborhood Planning Programs* (continued)

Core principle	Programs, activities
	District councils (one-on-one meetings, collaboration among community councils, local businesses, and other neighborhood stakeholders or extralocal organizations and institutions)
	Neighborhood planning (enablement of community-wide initiatives and coalitions; fostering of long-term relationshhips between stewardship groups and departmental staff)
Build fields strategically	Neighborhood matching fund (all neighborhoods, multiple city departments, linked to neighborhood planning and P-Patch)
	P-Patch, Cultivating Communities (part of neighborhood and comprehensive planning; networks to extralocal community-supported agriculture movement)
	District councils (help forming new community councils and bringing in other types of organizations, such as land trusts, senior resident councils, human service nonprofits, ethnic associations)
	Neighborhood planning (planning groups in all areas designated for growth; systematic and strategic trust building among all relevant stakeholders)
Transform institutional cultures	Neighborhood matching fund (building relationships between neighborhoods and departments)
	P-Patch, Cultivating Communities (building relationships with parks department, Seattle Housing Authority)
	Neighborhood planning (mayoral retreat with department heads, neighborhood development managers work with interdepartmental sector teams and other departmental staff; departmental hiring of Department of Neighborhoods staff and independent community organizers; laws and regulations requiring some departments to consult neighborhood plans; public norm emerges among other planners to incorporate neighborhood plans)
Ensure reciprocal accountability	Neighborhood matching fund (citizens contractually accountable for work performed and assets used in match)
	City neighborhood council (screens proposals; one-on-one meetings)
	Neighborhood planning (stakeholder analysis, continual check-ins, validation events and mailers, review and response, neighborhood tours by city councilors and mayor, transparency of approved plans and updates, oversight of implementation by stewardship groups)

has been some slippage in the institutional infrastructure supporting collaborative engagement over the past five years or so, as well as unresolved design problems inherited from the past. Elected officials, department staff, and neighborhood leaders engaged in a lively public debate in 2007–08 on how to regain lost momentum and move forward in ways that enrich democracy while enhancing complex collaborative problem-solving capacities among a wide range of public actors. To remain a strategic investor in democracy, the City of Seattle will have to address several major challenges.

The first is to reverse the tendency to disinvest in some of the critical civic infrastructure that followed the initial years of neighborhood plan implementation. Modest cuts began under Mayor Schell, primarily as a temporary response to the dot.com bust that hurt the city's tax revenues at the turn of the century. Cuts then accelerated under Mayor Greg Nickels, whose centralizing style of leadership failed to appreciate adequately the importance of the support of Department of Neighborhoods staff for empowered community problem solving and neighborhood planning, even when budgetary pressures eased. As I have argued in the *Journal of the American Planning Association,* and as the city auditor's report on neighborhood plan implementation further confirms, cutting the number of neighborhood development managers, first from six to three staff positions, in 2002, and then eliminating them entirely in 2003, represented an important loss in system capacity.[76] Without neighborhood development managers as the relational pivots of reciprocal accountability among departments and local citizens and stakeholders, it was much more difficult to convene interdepartmental sector teams, build trust with potential champions among departmental staff, and check departmental tendencies to revert to bureaucratic silos and technical mindsets. That so many of the other city planning efforts continued to mention the neighborhood plans is testimony to the important public norm established by neighborhood planning. Planners across many agencies feel obligated to take account of the planning work done by citizens.

But norms can erode in the absence of appropriate organizational design and civic infrastructure support. Indeed, as the staff in various departments took up other duties, new staff seldom received appropriate training for collaborative work with neighborhoods, and the mayor demonstrated little leadership in this regard. Without neighborhood development managers (and, of course, the project managers in the Neighborhood Planning Office who preceded them), the trust often painstakingly built with neighborhood planning groups and then implementation stewardship groups began to erode as well. Many neighborhood leaders began to complain that they could not identify who in the various departments has any "ownership" over the plans. The responsibilities of neighborhood development managers shifted to the Department of Neighborhoods district coordinators (technically becoming 20 percent of their job responsibilities), but district coordinators do not have the same authority and coordinative clout as the developments managers and were already overloaded with other tasks.[77] The jobs of other city staff charged with plan implementation (the division director in the Department of Neighborhoods, the database manager, geographic representatives in the Department of Transportation, instructing managers in the parks department) were also eliminated or periodically left vacant, significantly reducing total neighborhood plan implementation staffing by roughly two-thirds, from 10.7 full-time employees in 1999 to 3.61 in 2007 (see table 3-4).

In addition to these reductions in support staff for neighborhood plan implementation, the new stewardship groups were not provided the kind of contract funding that enabled their predecessor planning groups to work effectively and independently. Indeed, they received no funding at all. Furthermore, the leadership development program in the Department of Neighborhoods was also cut. As a result of these added civic disinvestments, some of the energy of the stewardship groups dissipated. The normal attrition one might expect among neighborhood leaders who had worked on planning for a good while and were ready for new civic challenges—or a well-deserved rest—was compounded by disenchantment among other experienced leaders and a decline in recruitment and training of newcomers, even though 83 percent of the more than eight hundred citizens in the auditor's (nonrandom) Zoomerang survey expressed a willingness to participate in planning updates.

The weakening of the support infrastructure also meant that stewardship groups were less able to integrate newcomers, that is, orienting them to the complex layers of democratic deliberation and trust building that underlay the plans as approved while also being open to the new ideas and interests they might bring to the table. Furthermore, staff cuts made it that much more difficult to post plan updates, maintain an accurate database of items at various stages of implementation, and keep stewardship contact information current—all of which presented information barriers to ongoing citizen engagement.[78] In a dynamic environment presenting new opportunities, unforeseen constraints, and continual challenges of adjustment in the midst of so many other planning and development efforts occurring across the city and region, the decline in capacity to integrate newcomers into the stewardship groups and keep everyone abreast of ongoing developments could easily breed new conflicts within neighborhoods and diminish democratic legitimacy, inclusivity, and trust.

A second, related challenge of Seattle's neighborhood system is to bring greater diversity to the district councils and neighborhood planning. A large scholarly literature points to the participatory biases in neighborhood systems, as indeed in many other systems of citizen engagement.[79] Some of these biases can be addressed, as were Chicago's police beat meetings discussed in chapter 1, by well-funded, energetic outreach and by investing in training and oversight to improve the chances for fair and inclusive deliberation.[80] But in a multifunctional neighborhood participation system, which can encompass a broad range of related issues—land use, transportation, housing, the environment, arts, human services, school and community partnerships, and safety, to name just a few—it becomes necessary to continually rethink which civic organizations should have a seat at the district council table or in the neighborhood planning group. Such rethinking, as well as periodic reconfigurations likely to ensue, represents a version of the famous question raised by democracy theorist Robert Dahl many years ago. If democracy means "rule by the *demos,*" or rule by the people, participatory democrats must always answer the question, "which *demos?*"[81]

In the context of a neighborhood system such as Seattle's, this question is not just one of openness to all individual residents of a district or even of more effective outreach and inclusive deliberation; rather, the question is whether and how to grant representation to organizations that are not the typical community councils. Some district councils are actively recruiting other kinds of organizations (senior housing residence council, social service referral agency, ethnic-based church, creek restoration group), and the official position of the Department of Neighborhoods is that inclusive democracy requires such a strategy. Citywide, the number of community-based organizations represented in the district councils has been on the increase. But some on the community councils see this change as compromising a core democratic principle, especially in the case of staff-based organizations that do not choose their leadership democratically, as community councils do—that is, with all residents having a formal right to vote.

In addition, admitting a second or third organization from one particular neighborhood could be—and has been—perceived in some districts as

Table 3-4. *City Staffing Dedicated to Neighborhood Plan Implementation, Seattle, by Fiscal Year, 1999–2007*

City staff[a]	1999	2000	2001	2002	2003	2004	2005	2006	2007
Neighborhood development managers	6.0	6.0	6.0	6.0	3.0	0.0	0.0	0.0	0.0
Division director	0.7	0.7	0.7	0.7	0.7	0.01	0.01	0.01	0.01
Database administrator[b]	1.0	1.0	1.0	1.0	1.0	1.0	1.0	1.0	1.0
Department of Transportation geographic representatives	3.0	3.0	3.0	3.0	0.0	0.0	0.0	0.0	0.0
Department of Parks and Recreation staff	0.0	0.0	some	some	some	0.0	0.0	0.0	0.0
District coordinators	0.0	0.0	0.0	0.0	2.75	2.6	2.6	2.6	2.6
Total	10.7	10.7	10.7	10.7	7.3	3.61	3.61	3.61	3.61

Source: Data from City of Seattle, *Neighborhood Plan Implementation* (Seattle, Wash.: Office of the City Auditor, September 20, 2007), p. 18, table 2.

a. Full-time equivalent.

b. The position of database administrator was vacant during some of the time between 2004 and 2007.

unfairly tilting the balance within the district council as a whole. In districts with proportionally greater numbers of nonprofits serving disadvantaged populations, as in Southeast Seattle, this issue can become the basis of fierce disagreement about the relationship of democratic participation and social justice. Systems of neighborhood representation, while seemingly neat because of size and geographic boundaries, generate their own special dilemmas in defining the *demos* in a complex, postmodern democracy with many kinds of community organizations and potential stakeholders—compounded, of course, by the relatively small percentages of residents who cast formal votes in traditional neighborhood association elections. This democratic dilemma admits to no theoretical solution, only pragmatic ones.[82]

Perhaps one way of expanding the diversity of organizations represented in the district councils while attenuating concerns of their democratic representativeness is to create further incentives and expectations for staff-based nonprofits to engage in asset-based community development. This might enable traditional community councils to better recognize the broad contributions of human service nonprofits in their districts and (even better) their efforts to engage their "clients" as "citizens," as John McKnight has so famously challenged them to do.[83] More clients acting as citizens in asset-based community development could lessen the concern of some community councils about expanding representation in the district councils, since nonprofit staff could then point to ordinary citizens who are engaged and contributing and not just to themselves as "representing clients" or simply representing their own interests as paid staff, a not infrequent accusation.

However, this strategy would require additional Department of Neighborhoods staff for continuous outreach, relationship building across ethnic, income, and organizational boundaries, and leadership training in asset-based community development. Diverse democracy in a dynamic and complex polity cannot be purchased on the cheap. In the most recent round of rethinking the process of neighborhood planning, in 2007–08 the Department of Neighborhoods, under the leadership of Stella Chao, and the Department of Planning and Development, under the leadership of Diane Sugimura, conducted some fifty community meetings with groups across the city that tend to be underrepresented. The two departments built upon trusted networks, such as those with leaders of ethnic-language communities and staff of community-based organizations, to expand the boundaries of an inclusive democracy. As Chao and Sugimura clearly recognize, however, effective inclusion will most likely require increased investment in staffing, a reversal of the disinvestment that occurred in previous years.

This represents a most promising development, though further budgetary pressures as a result of recession limit room for maneuver. The danger, it seems, is that redesigning a process of neighborhood planning by developing separate tracks of trusted relationships between the department staff and leaders of diverse groups could lessen the potential of horizontal relationships among these groups and existing community and district councils and perhaps foster resentment over privileged lines of access. Militating against this is the culture of collaboration and common visioning that the Department of Neighborhoods has brought to its work from the beginning, as well as its commitment to overriding values (sustainability, equity, inclusion) that rarely get framed in terms of balkanized identity politics.[84]

The third challenge in moving the neighborhood system forward in the coming years is to strike a new balance between accountability and autonomy in neighborhood planning. On the one hand, neighborhood leaders and the broader circles of engaged residents drawn into the process during the first major round of planning and implementation accomplished a great deal, both in the design of the planning process and in the results achieved in many neighborhoods. Much was emergent, the result of creativity and new synergies, and could never have been predicted. This first serious effort at engaging citizens in major city planning efforts, designed in the wake of much distrust, without an implementation budget, and with imperfect information tools by today's standards, has left a positive legacy that bespeaks the need for further bottom-up engagement. At the March 2008 citywide forum to consider alternative perspectives on the upcoming round of neighborhood planning, one developer even noted that "neighborhood planning is fabulous. . . . It is so helpful for a developer to work with a neighborhood council that has a vision."[85]

Neighborhood leaders thus have legitimate concerns with the civic disinvestment that has occurred, as well as with Mayor Nickels's centralizing style, which he demonstrated immediately upon taking office, not only in his administration's dealing with neighborhoods but also with the neighborhoods committee of the city council and the Seattle Planning Commission. The latter two had played important roles in the design of neighborhood planning but were largely sidestepped in the initial design of the updating process. Trust has visibly eroded in some circles. As one neighborhood leader put it at the same forum, when Jim Diers was fired by the mayor and then the neighborhood development managers were cut, "we felt deserted by the city." Such views are fairly widespread in neighborhood leadership circles. Indeed, the city council quickly countered the firing by unanimously proclaiming Jim Diers Day in Seattle. There is still a ways to go to reestablish trust among various parties who will need to work together during the upcoming round of neighborhood planning, but that trust is likely to come about only if power is genuinely shared. The city neighborhood council, as citywide representative of neighborhood groups, has pushed back hard.[86]

On the other hand, the neighborhoods and planning departments have reasonable concerns on a range of issues that neighborhood leaders need to address, of which enhancing diversity in participation is only one. For instance, the quality of neighborhood plans is uneven, as many neighborhood leaders also recognize. The planning department understandably feels that such unevenness needs to be rectified and that certain components of planning (land use, transportation, open space, capital facilities, and utilities) should be mandated in the new template, while still permitting room for a range of optional items (public safety, social services, arts and culture, urban design, and economic development). The planning department, whose leadership is genuinely committed to civic engagement in planning, is also concerned that its new planning tools, best practices from other cities, and limited staff time be optimized. This is difficult to do when all neighborhoods are planning simultaneously, in contrast to some managed form of sequencing that targets neighborhoods most in need because of such factors as the rate of demographic change, transportation challenges, and an overarching strategy of making Seattle environmentally sustainable. Needless to say, the department also feels responsible for integrating neighborhood plans with the full array of other types of planning in the city and region, as well as being responsive to civic associations that are not based in a particular neighborhood. In September 2008 the city reached what appears to be a workable compromise, and in her announcement councilor Clark specifically referenced the March forum, "where neighborhood participants seized on the concept of mutual accountability."[87]

Despite these challenges, many components of civic governance that have emerged in Seattle and its surrounding region suggest the burgeoning of what planning theorist Patsy Healey refers to as not just "episodes" and "processes" of collaboration but a "collaborative governance culture."[88] Such a culture is now evident across boundaries of diverse community councils, business associations, nonprofits, and public agencies. It is also manifest in various watershed associations and the state's new Puget Sound Partnership, which emerged out of the EPA's National Estuary Program and various other initiatives, such as the region's Shared Salmon Strategy and Northwest Straits Marine Conservation Initiative. Mayor Nickels's Restore Our Waters Strategy has highlighted additional civic environmental initiatives as essential, including a citizens' science program for training and monitoring (with the Seattle Aquarium), an aquatic resources master stewardship program, community "water watchers" education, a storm water mitigation partnership program, and a habitat restoration grant and technical assistance program to be added to the neighborhood matching fund.

The Seattle Climate Action Now Initiative, an effort led by the City of Seattle, involves various kinds of partnerships between city agencies, civic and religious groups, environmental organizations and businesses, the Downtown Seattle Association, and all kinds of museums, theaters, schools, and universities. It also provides tools for individual and family action to reduce their carbon imprint. Sustainable Seattle, critical to shaping the comprehensive plan of 1994, has progressively integrated its work with neighborhoods. Its 2005 Indicators of Sustainable Community Steering Committee included chairs of the city neighborhood council and the city council's neighborhoods committee. Its Sustainable Urban Neighborhoods Initiative, with a four-year grant from the Alfred P. Sloan Foundation, has worked with various community councils and other organizations, supported by a Department of Neighborhoods matching fund grant for asset-based community development training. Seattle neighborhoods and surrounding cities and towns now link their sustainability initiatives, such as Sustainable Ballard, Sustainable South Seattle, and Sustainable Bainbridge, in an area-wide learning network—Sustainable Communities ALL Over Puget Sound (SCALLOPS). Totem scallops.[89]

The issues facing the city, of course, share much with the big questions confronting many urban regimes. How much more should the city grow beyond what the neighborhood plans have agreed to accommodate, and should Seattle become a world-class megacity? How powerful will certain kinds of developers be in the urban regime, and will everyday zoning and development decisions relentlessly erode neighborhood planning? Where do the city's various forms of civic engagement fit within the dynamics of metropolitan governance and globalization?[90]

4 | Youth Civic Engagement: Systems Change and Culture Change in Hampton, Virginia

The city of Hampton lies in the Hampton Roads area of the Virginia coast that includes Norfolk, Newport News, Virginia Beach, Chesapeake, and Portsmouth. A mostly blue-collar city of one hundred and forty-six thousand with a modest income base, Hampton has a population that is approximately 50 percent white and 45 percent African American, with a school population that is 66 percent African American. In the early 1990s, political and civic leaders began collaborative planning to make youth a central part of their reinventing government and economic development efforts and, in the process, began to shift fundamentally the way they viewed youth. They committed the city to a vision of youth empowerment and, in the years since, have continued to broaden and deepen Hampton's strategy to build what its innovators describe as a "youth civic engagement system" seeking deep "culture change" in the way institutions value the public contributions of young people.[1] In 2005 its efforts were recognized by an Innovations in American Government Award, as noted in chapter 1.

Over the past fifteen or so years, the city government and its partners have built key institutional components into the effort to engage youth, including the Hampton Youth Commission, youth planners, and principal's and superintendent's youth advisory groups in the school system. Other youth advisory groups and strategies have been designed to help transform the culture and practices of city departments and their partners among neighborhood associations and local nonprofits. Nonetheless, Hampton still faces some persistent challenges.

Innovating with Youth and Adult Stakeholders

Four critical ingredients in the early process set Hampton on the path to sustained innovation: a set of vigorous reinventing government initiatives that then broadened to include youth; a federal grant that enabled the city to support a multiyear, collaborative planning process on youth; a dynamic youth services nonprofit that reinvented itself to help support leadership development among young people and their adult partners; and a well-designed, multistakeholder planning process that resulted in a robust mission to empower youth to contribute to the betterment of the city and generated broad commitment to develop a comprehensive strategy to realize this goal.

Dynamic Leadership at the Top

The stage for innovation was set in the mid-1980s by local "reinventing government" initiatives, themselves a response to serious problems of economic development and local revenues in an old city landlocked by surrounding cities and the Chesapeake Bay and replete with wetlands. With no opportunities to annex surrounding areas and little chance of regional consolidation, Hampton could remain resigned to limited growth and severe local government cutbacks, or it could try to reinvent itself. Led by Mayor James Eason, who served from 1983 to 1997, and city manager Robert J. O'Neill Jr., who brought with him 1960s ideas of citizen and community engagement and quickly became a national leader in the re-invention movement, the city began to flatten its own hierarchy and de-volve initiative downward. It expanded employee participation, nurtured an entrepreneurial culture, and encouraged collaboration across agencies. Hundreds of employees joined with the city council in crafting a new vision and mission statement on the purpose and role of city government: to "bring together the resources of business, neighborhoods, community groups, and government" to make Hampton "the most livable city in Virginia." Government should not just be a provider of services and regulations, the statement continues, but should also broker resources from all sectors of the community. As various innovators at the time recall, city manager Bob O'Neill would continually tell them, "don't bring me more programs; change systems."[2]

The process worked so well, said assistant city manger Mike Montieth, who served on the original Coalition for Youth, that the city decided to extend these principles to the community. The city's leaders, in fact, came to the realization that the old way of doing business simply expended too much adversarial energy. As Terry O'Neill, the current planning director and younger brother of Bob O'Neill, remembers, someone asked a simple question at one meeting: "What about the old idea of citizens taking some responsibility?" Montieth consulted a community problem–solving specialist, but when the city council refused to pay for an outsider's services, Montieth trained planners in the new methods himself. Collaborating with the community represented a "radical shift internally" for the Hampton Planning Department, though one that "came up with the best plan ever," at a time when there was a great deal of contention over a proposed new road network cutting through the city.[3]

These developments were fundamental to bringing youth into the planning process down the road. According to Cindy Carlson, the director of the Hampton Coalition for Youth, "If you can't value the voice of citizens generally, you won't value the voice of youth."[4]

Federal Dollars to Support Local Collaborative Planning

In October 1990 the federal government provided a second key ingredient for the reform process: a three-year, $320,000 community partnership grant from the Center for Substance Abuse Prevention at the U.S. Department of Health and Human Services. This grant was targeted to collaborative community planning for youth at risk. Carlson, then on staff at Alternatives Inc., the leading youth services agency in the city and the local nonprofit for youth substance abuse prevention, helped write the grant; she then directed the planning group, initially called the Families and Youth at Risk Initiating Committee and later the Hampton Coalition for Youth. The grant did not require any programmatic work, though most other grantees around the country used it to fund programs, and some in Hampton fought fiercely for this as well.

To demonstrate its commitment to planning for systems change, the Coalition for Youth returned $100,000 earmarked by the city council to support the planning process (which had begun already in early 1990), should the grant not come through, rather than use it to fund extra services. Even though Carlson and Richard Goll, the founding director of Alternatives Inc., had been supportive of efforts to expand childcare programs in the city, they resisted the demand by the head of the city's social services department to redirect the funding. According to Goll, "Had we said yes to that request, we would not be sitting at this table today talking about youth civic engagement in the city of Hampton . . . and we would never have gotten the public support needed to fund many of the [early childhood] programs we have today."[5]

A Youth Services Organization Reinventing Itself

A third key ingredient in the reform process was that Alternatives Inc. was willing to reinvent itself as a youth leadership development agency. Founded in the early 1970s, Alternatives had become nationally recognized for its work. Its local political strategy had been to cultivate long-term relationships to shape the use of power in the city. As Goll notes, "Our bottom line is relationships, relationships, relationships." While they were not community organizers, and had no prior awareness of the emerging forms of faith-based and relational organizing, the leaders of Alternatives had, in effect, done intentional relational organizing for years, which positioned them to take advantage of the reinventing government efforts in the late 1980s. They thus had the legitimacy to convene a broad group of community stakeholders to address youth services in new ways.[6]

Alternatives was also active in national youth development networks that had begun to question the dominant frame of youth services, which viewed young people as bundles of deficits in need of fixing by outside professional and clinical intervention supported by separate silos of categorical funding (substance abuse, runaways, teenage pregnancy). William Lofquist, the editor of the journal *New Designs for Youth Development* and a member of the community youth development guide team in the National Network for Youth—an umbrella group with some eight hundred local youth agencies as organizational members—was particularly influential in helping Goll, Linda Hansen, and other staff at Alternatives to recognize that youth had to be viewed as resources and directly engaged in community life and that Alternatives itself had to become a "learning organization."

Alternatives thus created a learning team, which read selections from Peter Senge's *The Fifth Discipline* and related works and considered how they might reinvent their agency. With the Center for Substance Abuse Prevention dollars, they also hired a group of twenty young people as consultants to develop a report and recommendations to the board. These youth consultants were told that they would be doing a job for the city of Hampton. The diverse youth group was identified through networks of guidance counselors and others. Although Alternatives felt it was "at the top of its game" as a substance abuse agency, these young people said that it was not really doing what young people needed. Youth, it was argued, did not want to be viewed as broken and in constant need of fixing. They wanted to be challenged and provided opportunities to make real contributions to the community. They viewed as most successful those programs of Alternatives that had involved them in problem solving, such as youth-to-youth programs.[7]

Some staff at Alternatives had a hard time not seeing themselves as therapeutic "fixers." But the board accepted virtually all recommendations proposed by the young people. To signal a radical change in approach, the agency officially closed its doors on June 30, 1992, and then reopened the next day with staff who were committed to working with youth in a fundamentally new way. Eight decided to leave the agency rather than reorient their practice. From "treating" several hundred young people, Alternatives began "engaging" several thousand. It dropped the drug treatment language, since young people and their parents felt stigmatized by it, and several years later dropped the drug treatment program entirely. (The agency maintained a partnership, however, with the Hampton–Newport News Community Services Board, which does provide substance abuse services.) As Goll recalls, after the board accepted the youth recommendations and Alternatives reopened with a new mission, "we never looked back." Similar to innovative nonprofits and public agencies profiled in Paul Light's *Sustaining Innovation,* Alternatives used its organizational and networked learning to move away from a "clientelized" view of the public to one that engages youth in doing public work themselves as "partners, coproducers, or stakeholders."[8]

As the system of youth civic engagement in Hampton began to add a variety of components in subsequent years, Alternatives' role in training and mentoring both youth and their adult partners and in reframing their relationships became ever more ambitious. Kathryn Johnson, who succeeded Goll as director in 2001, expanded its range of activities and helped lead its staff in further enriching the language describing its mission and explicitly linking it to democracy. As Johnson noted at the four-day network learning conference convened in Hampton with teams from ten cities in April 2007, "We are engaged in intentional relationship building for the purposes of community building . . . and [thereby] building social capital. . . . Building relationships is critical to everything we do. . . . If we are truly interested in our own democracy, this is what we need."[9]

Collaborative Planning:
Generating a Youth Empowerment Mission and Strategy

The fourth ingredient critical to reform in Hampton was the collaborative planning process itself. The twenty adult members of the initial Coalition for Youth's planning committee represented civic organizations, nonprofits, and city agencies and included the superintendent of schools, the police chief who had pioneered community policing, and assistant city manager Montieth. Carlson challenged them to reach out broadly among their constituencies: "The answer to our questions does not lie only in this room." Despite some resistance to opening up the process further, Janice "Jay" Johnson was hired to coordinate a broad outreach strategy through five task forces (youth, parents, community groups, business, and youth workers and advocates). Facilitators within each group were provided considerable training to implement the strategy. More than seventy-five task force members volunteered to participate in the training and other task force activities. As many as five thousand people sent in comments or participated in forums, one-on-one conversations, luncheons, and house meetings. These activities were organized by constituency.

At the meetings, participants were asked to describe where the city is now and to articulate their vision for where they would like it to be in terms of relationships with youth and families. They also generated many suggestions for how to get there. Each group could also request research it needed. Although unintended, one result of having each constituency meet separately was that it leveled the power of the groups to set the agenda.

In late summer of 1992, the twenty adult planning committee members, forty additional adult stakeholders from the task forces and meetings, and the twenty youth that Alternatives had convened separately as the Youth Council met in a two-day retreat. Participants broke up into small, multistakeholder groups and generated recommendations for a specific topic that had emerged as a priority theme in the previous meetings, such as safety or diversity. Trained facilitators again led the groups. The result was a striking degree of consensus on principles of positive youth development. No one simply argued for more cops to reduce youth violence. Youth made a strong case that their voice was an essential part of any solutions. At one point Superintendent of Schools William Canady came, literally, nose to nose with one teenager whose father was in jail for murder and who spoke only in rap—to the great annoyance of almost everyone who dealt with him. It was a transformative experience for the superintendent, one that convinced him he could build trusting relationships with empowered, even in-your-face young people.

A turning point was reached when stakeholder groups reported to the mayor and city councilors and presented their suggestions. Young people were seated up on a riser. Parents performed a skit. And no one bashed the city. There was a profound sense of collaborative work needed by many different groups. The meeting marked a milestone in relations between citizens and city government.

The city council was surprised at the vision document the coalition presented in its January 1993 report, "2 Commit 2 the Future 4 Youth." Mayor Eason, who, with city manager Bob O'Neill, was a strong supporter of reinventing government, had expected point-by-point proposals but admitted that "the more I read it, the more I like it." Carlson suggested, in a friendly but pointed fashion, "well, then I suggest you go home and read it a little bit more!"[10]

The report contained eleven recommendations (Healthy Start and Healthy Families programs and Neighborhood Initiative among them), but it was first and foremost a vision and mission statement.

> *Our Mission:* Hampton will create an environment in which youth contribute to the community in a manner that positively impacts the quality of life. We will empower our youth to meet their full potential. . . . To empower someone means to give them both authority and responsibility. . . .
>
> *Partnership in the Community:* All young people in Hampton are entitled to be seen, heard, and respected as citizens of the community. They deserve to be prepared, active participants—based on their level of maturity—in community service, government, public policy, or other decision making which affects their lives and their well-being.[11]

Other cornerstones of the vision included the importance of families, a commitment to the whole child, an emphasis on strengths and assets brought by families and neighborhoods, respect for diversity of every kind, and lifelong learning in and out of school. Collaboration was highlighted as essential in an era when "no longer can we look to single programs and fragmented approaches to solve problems." The report insisted, however, that "strong public policy" could lead the way by outlining the kind of community to which all children are entitled. But over and over again, the document returned to empowering youth as the most fundamental mission. To implement this, the report called for "*a comprehensive system of opportunities for youth to be involved in the life of the community.*"[12]

Building a System of Youth Civic Engagement

In elaborating this system in a strategic, if incremental, manner over the next fifteen years, Hampton innovators have built upon several core premises: develop structured pathways for progressively more challenging civic roles for youth; invest in training to enrich needed civic skill sets; catalyze culture change among adult partners in government agencies and other organizations; and cultivate a dynamic, shared language weaving components from various democratic and youth development frames.

First, Hampton's system is premised on the idea that youth need a wide array of opportunities to contribute actively to the community, from the relatively simple and episodic, such as tutoring a younger child after school or cleaning up a river on the weekend, to the increasingly complex, which might involve long-term planning, policy development, and sustained problem solving in partnership with other youth and adults. The simple tasks can elicit contributions from virtually everyone; they serve as a portal to community engagement and the development of a broad civic ethic. The more complex tasks can be intentionally designed as pathways to develop progressively higher civic skill sets needed to carry out more ambitious projects and to represent the interests of large numbers of youth, whether in a neighborhood, high school, or in the city as a whole.

In my interviews with them over a period of six years, many of Hampton's youth leaders noted that when they first got involved they were well aware of the structured pathways from tasks to consultation to shared leadership. Opportunities for progressively more ambitious leadership, they said, were part of their initial motivation to become involved. But others became aware of such pathways only along the way. Some, urged by school counselors or teachers to get involved in community service, even began relatively unmotivated; they described themselves as shy, even depressed and disengaged, and later rose to some of the most demanding youth leadership positions in the city.[13]

A second emergent principle of the Hampton system is that development of civic skills among youth requires that the city invest seriously in training and continuous leadership mentoring by adult professionals. The city should not simply create opportunities for engagement. It should provide the kind of training that increases the likelihood of their success when young people take on challenging civic roles. By investing in training and leadership mentoring, the city enables youth to add genuine public value today (safer neighborhoods and schools, better city planning) as well as to provide an expanded pool of dynamic civic and political leaders for tomorrow's Hampton—and, indeed, for other communities in which they might later settle. Kathryn Price, a seventeen-year-old youth planner and, before that, a youth commissioner, stressed the importance of training at our February 2002 national strategy conference on youth development and civic engagement: "We have a lot to share, but we don't want to be set up for failure."[14]

A third core belief is that productive youth engagement in city affairs is not just a task for young people; it represents an ongoing challenge for the adults who run and staff municipal agencies and contracting nonprofits. Effective engagement requires significant culture change within agencies so that adult staff come to view young people as potential resources and partners rather than as passive clients who must be served or problems that must be controlled. Such culture change also requires investments in training and intentional relationship building.[15]

Tying these all together is what has become the fourth core feature of the Hampton system: a common language of youth civic engagement that dynamically interweaves themes from various frames: youth as community assets, an understanding that derives from the positive youth development frame that emerged as a critique of much research and practice on youth as problems and deficits; training in developmental assets, an effort that has been spread by the Search Institute in Minneapolis and stresses forty assets that young people need to become healthy and responsible; a focus on creativity, which views the capacity for serious play and artistic creation as closely tied to leadership competency and problem solving; and a view of relationship building as democratic community building, which emphasizes trust, collaboration, partnership, and dialogue for the purpose of empowering youth and citizens generally. In her comparative study of community-based youth organizations in the San Francisco Bay area, Jennifer O'Donaghue of Stanford University demonstrates that having a "public language" is important to the empowerment of youth.[16]

In Hampton, adult leaders in the youth civic engagement system, as well as a good number of the youth leaders, employ a common public vocabulary in their work, though with distinct emphases in different settings, that anchors their persistent efforts to transform organizational cultures. When I questioned fourteen-year-old Michael Bock, a member of the Youth Commission in 2007 and, before that, of his middle school principal's youth advisory group, on how he became involved in these various activities, he began by naming specific individuals who nurtured his leadership capacity but finally blurted out, "it's just in the water here!"[17]

Institutional Scaffolding for Engaged Youth

Several important institutional components of the youth engagement system in Hampton are the Youth Commission, youth planners, a principal's advisory group in each of the four public high schools, and the school superintendent's youth advisory group. In addition, an independent youth action coalition has emerged that provides an organizational base outside official city venues, while linking to them in various ways.

Youth Commission

The Hampton Youth Commission, composed of twenty-four students from four public and three private high schools serving the city, was established in 1997 on the recommendation of teenagers Patrick Johnson and Sheena Patrick, who had been hired by the city to work as part-time youth planners in the Planning Department.[18] In many ways, however, the Youth Commission emerged as an outgrowth of the task force of twenty youths who had helped guide the collaborative planning process several years earlier. A Mayor's Youth Council dating back to the 1970s was viewed by youth as neither effective nor sufficiently powerful. The term *commission* was chosen to parallel other official commissions in the city, and the Youth Commission was given authority to report directly to the city council.

Commissioners, who serve two-year staggered terms, are recruited through broad outreach to schools, community centers, youth organizations, and public meetings. In the spring of 2007, there were forty-seven applications for twelve available slots. Students apply and are selected by existing commissioners and adult training partners who may have mentored them in various other leadership capacities, such as the principal's and superintendent's advisory groups or other neighborhood and faith-based groups, with increasing avenues from middle-school leadership programs as well. This ensures structured pathways of leadership development based on experience, trust, and performance, though all applicants must go through a rigorous set of interviews and group exercises before being chosen.

The Youth Commission is intended to represent a broad spectrum of Hampton's young people and is explicitly not designed to draw exclusively from an elite group of students with high grade point averages. At meetings with youth commissioners between 2002 and 2007, I could usually not tell the difference, in terms of public speaking and small- and large-group facilitation skills, between students from professional families and students from poorer or working-class families. For instance, as I later found out, the mother of one skilled commissioner in an April 2007 meeting with adult innovators from ten other cities, including mayors, aldermen, and planning directors, was a crack addict who just recently had accidentally burned their house down. Certainly, there is no apparent difference, based on traditional hierarchies of race or gender, in civic skill levels or leadership roles among the youth commissioners. If anything, some commissioners have joked, "African American girls run the city!"[19]

During the school year, the commission meets twice monthly, once in an open work session of the entire commission, half of which is devoted to the specific subcommittee projects on which the commission has chosen to work that year. There are three standing subcommittees, each with responsibility for working on two of the six general goals contained in the youth component of the city's official community plan. Each committee organizes a large public forum annually on one issue within its purview, and the commission as a whole organizes one other. Commissioners thus attend general and committee meetings from three to six times a month, sometimes more frequently, depending on the issue, the deliberative public process selected, and their level of commitment. Most larger forums are convened in city council chambers, where commissioners sit in the councilors' seats. Twice annually, the Youth Commission presents formally to the city council, which is televised, and to the Planning Commission.

Commissioners commit to active outreach to involve a broad range of young people in commission deliberations, and efforts extend to school groups, teachers, and friendship networks. An outreach video, DVD, and website help in recruitment and publicity. The Youth Commission has also published a detailed manual on how to start and improve youth commissions and advisory groups to empower young people. As youth commissioner Gregory Harrison, an eighteen-year-old senior at Bethel High School, put it, "Besides putting up fliers everywhere, especially in high schools . . . I drag all my friends to come to public meetings"—a method similar to the way some of the best congregation-based community organizing coalitions around the country reach out beyond their leadership core for larger public events.[20]

Youth commissioners develop a progressively more expansive civic skill set through formal training and various kinds of formal and informal mentoring by a well-coordinated network of adults and youth within and outside of city government. Newly selected commissioners receive training by Alternatives and more-experienced youth leaders during the summer before they assume their positions. They typically refer to this as boot camp, signaling the discipline and seriousness of their work, though these and other youth events are almost always intermixed with a good dose of creative fun. In addition, the Coalition for Youth, the city office under whose jurisdiction the Youth Commission falls, provides continual mentoring and help with coordination, logistics, and transportation.

Quelonda Bruer serves as the pivotal city staffer for the Youth Commission and all youth events and is assisted by a part-time youth secretary of the commission. But the network of mentors in April 2007—all of whom had highly developed civic skills and mindsets for working with youth and citizens generally—extended to the director of planning (Terry O'Neill), a senior and junior planner (Donald Whipple and Remington Ham, respectively), the superintendent of parks and recreation (Art Thatcher), the director of In-SYNC Partnerships between schools and neighborhoods (Michael Canty), the director of secondary education (Donna Woods), two youth planners (Will Bane and Ivey Hawkins), and two individuals who have been critical to building the network of mentors from the beginning, Cindy Carlson, director of the Coalition for Youth, and Allyson Graul, director of the Youth Civic Engagement Center at Alternatives. Several of these mentors attend the Youth Commission executive meeting every Tuesday afternoon at four o'clock, assisting commission and subcommittee chairs in developing agendas and debriefing their various meetings, workgroups, and public events.[21]

Graul, who oversees Youth Commission and high school leadership training, notes that Hampton follows a philosophy of relationship building and close mentoring and coaching of youth commissioners, with continual feedback to enable them to refine their leadership skills. As she notes, "We help them through a process of personal-level learning. But we don't directly worry about their personal development. We tell them: 'You have a job to do, a public role.' And they generally step up to the task." Tamara Whitaker, a seventeen-year-old youth commissioner in 2002 and a member of the school superintendent's youth advisory board, concurred: "Relationship building is essential. . . . People keep coming back because of the relationships."[22]

When the commission meets in open session on an important issue, the city council chambers are often packed to capacity. In September 2002, for example, 240 people convened to discuss "the rights of youth," with five lawyers volunteering to help clarify legal issues. In March 2004 the commission hosted a candidates' forum for the city council and mayoral election to another packed chamber, using a *Wheel-of-Fortune* game-show format that other civic groups, such as the League of Women Voters, then borrowed for their own election forums. Youth Commission forums typically combine general discussion with lively break-out sessions. These discussions involve serious, often nuanced deliberation facilitated by commissioners in a strikingly professional manner. Indeed, in observing these and other meetings with the school superintendent, high school principals, and other community partners, I was struck immediately with the poise and skill that youth display as they led large- and small-group discussions, brainstormed ideas on flip charts, developed strategies, consulted with authorities, planned outreach to parents, teachers, and other youth, and held each other accountable for the work commitments they made to see a project through to completion.

At an April 2002 Youth Commission meeting to develop joint strategies with the Citizens Unity Commission on supporting diversity in Hampton, for instance, Kathryn Price, then a high school senior and youth planner, coordinated break-out sessions with perfect poise among the 157 youth present, whose racial composition roughly matched that of the city's youth as a whole. The break-out groups, led by commissioners, deliberated thoughtfully on some difficult issues in the schools: the insensitivity of teachers and other adults to changing norms of race, the need for students to have a say in teacher hiring, the use of principal's advisory groups to report on negative racial dynamics in classes, the merits of neighborhood schools over racial redistricting, and the possible benefits and drawbacks of mandating racial sensitivity workshops. Each group came up with a priority ranking of action items from lists generated at an earlier citywide youth summit. Despite the seriousness of the comments, there was a spirit of ease, laughter, and spontaneous high fives among black and white students in the break-out groups, little sign of stereotypical positions based on race, and not the least bit of racial polarizing.[23]

The Citizens Unity Commission is composed of twenty citizens appointed for four-year terms, including six high school students. It had sponsored the youth summit the previous year and has looked to new African American leadership in the youth culture to help move Hampton along at a much faster pace on racial issues. After the April 2002 meeting, the Youth Commission worked with the Citizens Unity Commission in planning Hampton Unite, facilitated by the Study Circles Resource Center (now called Everyday Democracy), a nationally known center with much experience in community dialogue on race and other issues. However, youth chose to proceed with their own model of study circles combined with other education and action projects. They helped establish a "diversity college" and have trained young people to serve as trainers and "diversity champions" throughout the city. Ninth- and tenth-graders, for instance, have developed a five-session curriculum for after-school workers to use among sixth-graders; other youth serve as cotrainers with adults to develop more productive ways for generations with widely diverse cultural experiences to collaborate in the workplace.[24]

The mayor and other city officials also bring ideas to the Youth Commission to consider before making formal policy proposals. In January 2007, for instance, the mayor suggested building a second trade school in the city to the commission. He made a half-hour presentation, and youth commissioners questioned him for another fifteen minutes. In follow-up discussions, the Youth Commission determined that the new trade school plan was not a compelling idea, at least in its present form. The existing trade school was currently underenrolled, and the proposal did not address the main reasons behind high school dropout rates. Furthermore, the cost was substantial, and existing high school buildings could use the funding instead for much needed repairs. As a commission, they felt that they had responsibility to take into account the limited resources available to the city. But how do you turn down the mayor? As Jaron Scott, sixteen-year-old commissioner, put it, "We didn't want to stand him down, so we wrote him a letter and said that the dialogue was still open." The letter, signed by commission chair Gregory Harrison, was phrased diplomatically and noted that the commission would consider this or another proposal if it addressed a list of specific concerns. The mayor wrote back, thanking the commission, and the proposal was put on hold. As both the planning director and the superintendent of schools told me, the youth commissioners had zeroed in exactly on the core problems with the trade school idea.[25]

The Youth Commission, though focused primarily on policy, supports the work of other groups in the city through its youth grants, which amount to $40,000 a year, allocated to the commission from general funds. There are two basic grant categories: service and initiatives. Service grants are small, generally several hundred dollars, designed to help a group, such as a youth ministry at a church, with a short service project. These kinds of service projects have always been important to the Youth Commission. Indeed, for the first two years of its existence there was an internal debate on whether the commission should primarily act as a service organization, and several commissioners resigned when it was finally resolved that service was not its core mission. Initiatives grants are larger, ranging sometimes as high as $15,000, and are generally tied to the core policy goals of the subcommittees and the community plan.

Those groups receiving grants are held accountable for their work by the Youth Commission. Commissioners often negotiate with groups over proposals before giving their final approval and are encouraged to make site visits, thus also building relationships across many types of youth groups in the city. Contracts for the larger initiatives grants, which can run as long as one to two years, require two site visits. Commissioners examine the product, such as the quality and distribution of a youth action magazine they have funded, and give feedback on the leadership quality of the group, in one recent case holding back on further funding until the leadership was reorganized. In 2006–07 the commission gave out twenty-three grants, the largest an initiative grant of $7,500. In years when commissioners feel they do not have enough high-quality proposals, they return money to the city, the first commission ever to do this, which earned it enormous credibility.[26]

Youth Planners

The Planning Department hired two youth planners beginning in 1996 after Terry O'Neill, the director of planning, had an eye-opening experience facilitating a local planning meeting in the Aberdeen neighborhood. "A light bulb came on for me. The room was filled with thirty-somethings and retirees. Where were the young people?" So he decided to convene another dialogue with youth. "Quite frankly, they participated at a better level than the adults." Youth were then invited to join with adults in neighborhood planning. In fact, O'Neill noted on another occasion, the youth came up with a much better plan for the proposed recreation area that saved the city tens of thousands of dollars. "I realized that it was in my self-interest to involve youth. . . . I don't like making bad planning decisions and spending money I don't need to."[27]

Creative youth involvement helped the Aberdeen neighborhood be named a finalist for the Neighborhood of the Year award given by Neighborhoods USA. Since then, according to Shellae Blackwell, senior facilitator in the Hampton Neighborhood Office and a member of the original youth coalition in the early 1990s, "the community does not do anything without first involving youth."[28]

Youth planners work, on average, fifteen hours a week all year round and serve two-year staggered terms, so that a senior youth planner is available to help break in a junior one, typically a rising junior in high school. The senior planner received $8.65 an hour in 2007 and the junior one $8.09 an hour. In any given year, there might be six to twelve applicants for the one open slot, and those chosen have already proved themselves in a range of other leadership roles, on the Youth Commission or various of the youth advisory groups. They thus start with a good set of skills for running meetings and focus groups, making public presentations, and conducting one-on-one meetings with other relevant staff and stakeholders. The adult staff of the Planning Department are available to help the youth planners learn a range of other skills and to mentor them through phases of any given project that they might undertake at the behest of the Youth Commission, for which they formally serve as staff.

Youth planners can also conduct research and projects for other youth advisory groups and city departments, such as neighborhoods, schools, and parks and recreation. Because they have the full cooperation of the school system, they can administer surveys through the schools and thereby move relatively quickly from collecting data to writing reports (for example, on neighborhood youth safety or youth spending power), then to deliberation in the Youth Commission, and finally to action. Youth planners learn how to conduct and analyze statistically valid surveys, do field observation, analyze census data, and present findings using Excel spread sheets and PowerPoint. They use basic geographic information systems and plot mapping tools and conduct *charrettes,* collaborative planning meetings used in urban planning, architecture, and other areas of industrial, interior, and graphic design. Though not generally involved in land-use and rezoning activities, youth planners have accompanied professional staff to study transportation layout in other cities to help youth determine options for their own bikeways and for bus routes that serve the needs of young people. They provide reports to the city's Planning Commission for ten minutes at the beginning of its monthly meetings.

Like other staff in the Planning Department, youth planners work as a self-managing team, generally seeking assistance from a half dozen or so other planners, though they have access to all planning staff, should they need it, and meet with the network of adult mentors for a half hour every week before the Tuesday Youth Commission executive meeting. Youth planners are treated as full members, not interns, and attend all staff retreats and similar events. Their office is next to the director's, and they have access to City Hall and the Planning Department should they wish to come in on weekends or evenings. While their pay is capped for any two-week period, they often put in more than thirty hours because they find the work so interesting, important, and at times urgent. I know of at least one mother who pleaded with city staff to get her daughter to limit her hours so as to spend more time on her homework; Kathryn Price found ways to sabotage this nonetheless by bringing her work to other city offices and still was accepted to prestigious Ivy League colleges and state universities. Last I heard, she was on her way to medical school.[29]

The youth of Hampton are soon to see one of their bigger planning ideas come to fruition: a teen center codesigned by young people working with professionals. The idea for the center emerged from focus groups and speak-outs as well as a formal survey of 1,099 teens conducted by the youth planners. Youth who participated in the original planning process, in 1998–99, expressed a strong desire for youth-driven programming and a mixture of activities, including sports, dance, computer clinics, a media center, the arts, an arcade, meeting rooms, and a recording studio. The center is also expected to provide teenagers with a strong sense of membership and ownership and encourage youth participation in governance of the space itself. Youth recognize the need for a safe space with supervision by adults, such as nonuniformed security personnel, but in an unobtrusive way. "Youth want to have independence without adult dictation. . . . Young people do not want to be constantly watched and criticized by adults but want to be themselves."[30]

When a private health and fitness center became available for purchase, the Youth Commission had to compromise on some of its original goals, such as location; and when the existing center was delayed in moving to a new space, the project lost some momentum. But the youth planners returned to the project once the city announced a date. Seventeen-year-old senior youth planner Will Bane coordinated a design *charrette* in the fall of 2006 with four architects hired from a design firm. Some eighty-five young people attended, and youth commissioners facilitated eight groups in brainstorming and priority setting. They drew floor plans and placed ideas on stick-it notes. They discussed with the architects the safety features of alternative designs. They also designated those elements of the design that were nonnegotiable, in case the budget would not support everything they wanted. Four groups then carried the work forward: a youth board to determine the details of programming; a multistakeholder steering committee, including youth planners and commissioners but also representatives from business, police, schools, and the neighboring golf course; a project team to oversee the construction phase, with representatives from the Hampton Coalition for Youth as well as planning, engineering, and parks departments; and the "Move" subcommittee of the Youth Commission to help plan transportation to and from the center. The teen center was scheduled to open by the end of 2008.[31]

Youth planners in Hampton have also helped in developing a *Youth-Friendly Guidebook* and certification program to rate businesses and service organizations and to enable them to learn what it means to become "youth friendly," if they are not already so. The planners held focus groups throughout the city to determine the criteria that young people felt constituted a welcoming environment. As Alicia Tundidor, a youth planner involved at this earlier stage, explained, the focus groups came up with some seventy-five characteristics, which the planners grouped into three categories with a total of twenty-one questions for the initial survey of 240 businesses (to be followed later by nonprofits, community centers, and libraries). The questions asked about such issues as cleanliness, respect for youth, safety, youth hiring, and whether youth were followed while on the premises. Youth evaluators, paid through a Youth Commission grant, conducted the site visits. Those businesses that passed got a youth-friendly window sticker to display in their establishment and a letter of certification, and they were honored at an awards breakfast in council chambers attended by the mayor.[32]

Needless to say, those who did not make the grade were often quite upset. But the planners and youth commissioners have offered assistance, through the guidebook and personal consultation, on how to improve to attract more young people and win certification. Another round of site surveys is planned. Bradford Knight, a youth commissioner, explained the evaluation process as "realizing the power of youth as consumers," in a vein similar to what the political scientist Cliff Zukin and his colleagues see as the increasingly common practice of youth being engaged through boycotting and "buycotting." But youth planners and commissioners view the site visits and consultations as an opportunity to build relationships with business owners and supervisors—a relational, community-building variant of the larger phenomenon. As Tundidor noted, "The Youth Commission and planners were trying to help [the business owners] pass." In this, as with the other activities in which she engaged, "the most important thing in the whole process was the relationship building."[33]

Since the creation of the Youth Commission, youth have played a formal role in the development of Hampton's comprehensive plan, which has now been combined with its strategic plan into an overall community plan. The teen center proposal was the key recommendation on youth space emerging from the research, focus groups, and public meetings conducted by the youth commissioners and planners for the 1999 *Youth Component of the 2010 Comprehensive Plan,* but youth also focused on issues of transportation, employment, and community interaction. After this initial document was developed, the Youth Commission's comprehensive plan committee continued to conduct surveys and public forums on the plan, worked successfully to implement several of its recommendations, and reported regularly to the Planning Commission and the city council. When the new community planning process was set in motion, youth claimed a role as one of the eight main "vision and goals" groups and also provided feedback to the seven other groups, such as healthy business climate, healthy neighborhoods, and diverse community. As senior planner Donald Whipple noted, these groups provided a "youth filter" for the work of all the groups.[34]

To refine their own goals, youth planners and commissioners conducted a new round of surveys and focus groups. As youth planner Tundidor recalls, "We did tons, millions . . . at least fifty focus groups" in high schools and neighborhoods across the city. "We did ice breakers, . . . had stations around the room, posters, to keep them moving, and divided them into teams to compete for good suggestions." Youth commissioners and planners then organized the results of this public process into six categories of goals: caring relationships; youth sharing leadership; essential life skills; career preparation for all youth; places to go and things to do; and getting around. Under each goal, they listed specific objectives, backed up by their reasoning and research. This new *Youth Component of the Community Plan,* forty-seven single-spaced pages in all, was officially adopted by the city council on February 8, 2006, along with the overall plan. To maintain momentum on implementation, the Youth Commission then established three subcommittees, each to take continuous responsibility for two sets of goals and objectives. At the commission's summer retreat, commissioners and planners now decide on the key focus of each subcommittee for that school year to establish momentum early in the fall, when the new commission formally convenes.[35]

According to planning director Terry O'Neill, youth planning has been successful and has enabled a whole series of policy changes that the planning office and adults acting alone would otherwise never have come up with. Youth planning has also given young people a sense of ownership, but of the kind that comes with the responsibility to learn how to navigate and negotiate the interests of others who might be affected (for example, bus commuters who might fear increased youth ridership). O'Neill says he could easily employ more youth planners were it not for budgetary restrictions and would thereby be able to move things forward at a much faster pace. Youth planners in Hampton have received a Virginia Planning Award from the American Planning Association's Virginia chapter and honorable mention for the youth component in the 2010 plan, where it was competing against adult professional planners as well.[36]

Principal's Advisory Groups

Each public high school has a principal's advisory group. Members meet with the principal on a regular basis and often run the meetings themselves, though with training by Alternatives staff. Like the Youth Commission meetings, they plan and brainstorm in a very deliberative fashion and have rigorous standards of accountability for follow-through on commitments. Some schools sponsor more ambitious projects with more extensive participation than others, of course, but most deal with a range of issues such as youth-to-youth mentoring, school safety, and inclusion of students who feel left out due to teasing and bullying. Most now have projects aimed at transforming attitudes and behavior on sexual harassment and dating violence. The advisory groups plan events such as student-teacher breakfasts. Some also tackle academic improvement issues, as well as staff hiring, which, in at least one case, included the search for the principal.[37]

At Kecoughtan High School, with some nineteen hundred students, the Principal's Advisory and Consulting Team meets monthly with the principal in an evening session, and various committees meet during the week. Participation has varied over the years, from a core group of twenty active students to as many as sixty working on various projects. Principal Arnold Baker has become a believer in youth as resources at a deep level over the years. He began with a dialogue group when he was a sixth-grade teacher and then developed an advisory group when he became a middle school principal. As principal of Kecoughtan, Baker initially used this dialogue-and-gripe session model; but when the city received some grant money to train youth, he says, "we shifted to partnerships. . . . We became project oriented in order to improve the school." As a result, the number of involved students increased substantially. He also set strict rules that the consulting teams' meetings not be used as a venue for complaints against specific teachers—"No names," he tells students. Most teachers have come along, he adds. "Teachers often don't want to give up power to kids. But we are not equals, we are partners."[38]

The Safe School subcommittee works on keeping violence out of the school and conducts a safety survey and focus groups each year. Together with the principal and a core group of supportive teachers, students developed a *Safe Schools Handbook* that has become a resource for other schools. When a fight occurred at a dance, Baker challenged students to own the problem and come up with their own plan before he would schedule another one. As Leah Dixon, who served for her last two years of high school on the principal's consulting team, noted, "Instead of him making rules himself, he discussed [the incident] in an informal forum." Students then studied the problem and proposed a new set of rules (no tickets sales at the door, required dressing up, ten chaperones and two police officers present); since then there has not been another fight at a school dance. Noticing the number of disciplinary actions among ninth-graders, the team later did a survey of fights in the halls, interviewed teachers and the principal, and developed a set of recommendations, such as youth mentors during freshman orientation.[39]

Students participate in a variety of other ways to help transform school culture. They interview job candidates, including teachers, guidance counselors, and coaches, and organize a tour of the school for them. In one instance, students strongly supported one candidate for guidance counselor over another who was favored by adults on the hiring committee. The principal ultimately accepted the students' rationale and hired their preferred choice. Confronted with what Baker admits are the "terrible physical facilities" in Hampton schools, students at Kecoughtan organized a group of youth and adults to paint the interior of the school themselves (though some teachers, not surprisingly, complained about the choice of colors). When students recognized the academic disservice often done to school athletes, they mobilized their own assets to help tutor them to achieve the grade point average required to play. The Principal's Advisory and Consulting Team has also developed a "caring poster campaign" with hundreds of poster-sized, digitally enlarged, laminated photos of students throughout the school. These photos lay claim to ownership of the public space by students and aim to enhance the norm of individual caring and knowing everyone by name. As Mary Patterson, youth and community development director at Alternatives who oversees training for Kecoughtan's consulting team, puts it, through activities like these, students "create and interpret a culture."[40]

With a core group of teachers and administrators supporting their civic problem-solving work in the school, the Improving Student Achievement Committee at Kecoughtan High initiated a project in 2001 to make classrooms more stimulating. Keisha Ashe, vice chair of the committee, noted that "teachers felt very restricted by [Virginia's standards of learning], so we decided to get more creative ideas . . . and to create stronger bonds with teachers." Students interviewed other students, as well as teachers they especially respected, and then classified effective teacher practices and attitudes into categories, such as teacher ability to build relationships, manage the classroom, create high expectations, manage time, and engage students as resources in learning. The Principal's Advisory and Consulting Team then published the *Kecoughtan High School Idea Book* filled with innovative learning techniques, photos of teachers and students working together, quotations from famous educators and leaders, and small tips to help teachers create a caring and learning environment. They distributed it to all teachers. Baker, much impressed with the product, agreed to use the booklet in new teacher orientation at the beginning of the next school year and to have team leaders serve as cofacilitators of training.

Several years later, the students decided to develop a second, more substantial edition of the *Idea Book,* using the developmental assets framework more systematically but weaving their own heartfelt experience and field research around the eight assets they chose as relevant for school, such as commitment to learning, boundaries and expectations, social competencies, and constructive use of time. They convened forums between youths and adults to get further ideas and examples and then held a roundtable editing session, paying careful attention to language adults would find convincing. Instead of waiting for fall orientation of new teachers, they presented the revised product at faculty meetings on May 7 and 8, 2007, and engaged the teachers in a "scavenger hunt" as a reflective learning exercise. While there are certainly skeptics among the faculty—one teacher was overheard saying, "I feel welcome; can I go now?"—the school deeply respects the everyday practical knowledge of students as a democratic resource and uses it to inform the professional practice of teachers in their school community.[41]

The principal's advisory groups have systematically taken on issues of sexual harassment and violence, as well as related issues such as verbal and physical bullying. With funding from the Center for Injury and Violence Prevention at the Virginia Department of Health, Alternatives, along with youth leaders from the advisory groups, developed a peer trainer's manual based on national research and participatory pedagogy. It then began to provide rigorous two-day trainings for classroom peer education in ninth-grade health classes. The RELATE Project (Relationship Education Leading Adolescents Toward Empowerment) aims to enhance students' understanding of sexual and peer violence and to engage them in developing competencies for recognizing and resisting it, while building healthy relations based on respect. Working in pairs, in classes that range in size from twelve to thirty students and using creative skits and role-playing, peer trainers lead a week-long module, generally with the health teacher or another staff member present but not playing any direct role in the instruction. Twins Shauna and Imani Adams, who served as RELATE trainers at Phoebus High School through their tenth, eleventh, and twelfth grades, became trainers as an extension of their other work on the principal's advisory group and because, as Imani noted, "we see harassment every day." Lydia Huey, a trainer at Bethel High School, added that "I really wanted my younger brother and his friends to get what was happening, to change the way they act."[42]

The RELATE project at Phoebus, with twelve peer trainers in 2006–07, encompassed the entire ninth-grade class, more than four hundred students in all. As part of the hundred-member school band, Shauna and Imani Adams were able to recruit other trainers through its networks and to leverage its prestige in getting students to take their work seriously— including a prominent football player who laughed off the training in his freshman year but later came around as a strong supporter. Their approach is not just to teach a discrete set of classes and hope for behavioral changes but also to help establish and nurture lasting networks of support among students, as well as between students and teachers, throughout the school year. In one case, the mother of a student in the class could barely wait for the module to be over so that she could have the curricular materials for her own learning and use. While the pretest and posttest surveys of attitudes that accompany each RELATE module show a positive impact, the student trainers stress the change they see in behavior—less visible harassment, greater use of assertive language and boundary setting. To the extent that sexual and other forms of harassment and peer violence limit youth—especially girls—from becoming full citizens in the public square, as various feminist political theorists have argued, Hampton's young leaders have been hard at work trying to ensure that no one feels excluded from the school polity as a result of being physically and emotionally intimidated.[43]

Michael Cromartie, principal of Phoebus who was hired with the involvement of students, engaged his advisory group in 2006–07 to conduct focus groups to help articulate the language that they wanted as part of the school's official vision. The advisory group began with the captains of teams, presidents of clubs, Junior Reserve Officer Training Corps, and psychology classes. Cromartie made a commitment to use their visioning sessions to frame the fall 2007 student orientation. As he put it, "They are being the great interpreters at this moment." Creators and interpreters of a democratic public culture.[44]

Superintendent's Youth Advisory Group

The superintendent's youth advisory group comprises student representatives from all public high schools in the city. Some two dozen student members generally attend two evening meetings every month, facilitated by Andrea Sealey of Alternatives. One monthly meeting is devoted to planning and work groups for various policy issues on the advisory group's agenda, which they set during a one-day retreat at the beginning of the school year though revise as needed during the year. At these meetings, Sealey also works to build the civic skill set of the commissioners: making public presentations, having one-on-one conversations with public officials and other adult stakeholders, facilitating workshops and focus groups, doing research to help refine issues, and developing policy agendas over a multiyear period. Dinner with the superintendent and the director of secondary schools starts off the other monthly meeting, followed by a playful community-building exercise, such as circular rhythm sticks, where all (including school officials) tap complex rhythms with those around them. Discussion then turns to serious matters of district policy. School officials display no sign of "professionals know best" but listen carefully and work collaboratively toward mutually acceptable solutions in an atmosphere that is at once thoughtfully deliberative and playfully energizing.[45]

During an April 2002 meeting on state standards of learning and early school-day release in senior year, for instance, students discussed course sequences, SATs (Scholastic Assessment Tests) and PSATs (Preliminary SATs), practical training, and apprenticeships. They offered thoughtful suggestions based on detailed knowledge; almost every student participated in the general discussion. They spoke confidently and deliberatively and with sensitivity to students intending to go to four-year colleges, as well as those more likely headed for community colleges, the armed services, or apprenticeships (for example, auto mechanics). The discussion was student driven throughout, though the superintendent and secondary schools director made a formal report on a student survey and provided critical insight into state mandates. Tamara Whitaker, a seventeen-year-old senior, facilitated the general meeting—though now Sealey herself facilitates so that all students can fully engage in the substantive conversation. Other students facilitated four break-out groups, which developed detailed suggestions for a broad student and parent outreach strategy.[46]

During the 2005–06 school year, the superintendent's youth advisory group took up the issue of guidance counseling in the high schools, about which students citywide had voiced serious discontent. To get a better sense of how students viewed the problems, youth advisers began with one-on-one meetings with their peers, including members of the principal's youth advisories, with whom they often consult. They continued their conferences with guidance counselors and other key stakeholders. Their conclusion from these meetings was that guidance counselors often just did not have enough time to do adequate and timely counseling because they had become loaded down with responsibilities related to testing and the requirements of Virginia's standards of learning. The youth advisory board then developed a proposal for the superintendent that included two options: hire a testing coordinator in each high school to unburden the guidance counselors or reassign staff to try to achieve the same result, so that guidance counselors could focus primarily on high-quality and timely guidance. In response, the superintendent created a new testing coordinator position in each school, largely by redesigning the registrar's role, thereby enabling the school system to meet the students' policy proposals without spending nearly as much money as creating four new positions would require.[47]

The superintendent's advisory group addressed the issue of service and service learning policy in the high schools during the 2006–07 school year, though the group had begun planning even earlier. Service learning has developed at a slower pace in Hampton than in many other cities, and certainly more slowly than anticipated in the original 1993 report and vision statement to the city council. Alternatives began in the late 1990s by offering a three-semester course enrolling students from all four high schools. The first semester, organized during the summer, focuses on personal leadership and functions as a "learning community" of twenty-five to thirty individuals, in the words of Graul, who has coordinated the course from the beginning. In the second semester, offered in the fall, students do their work through distance learning and periodic group meetings. The third semester, in the spring, requires field placement in a leadership position in a community or school group or in a city agency (for example, youth planner, youth advisory board).[48]

The next systematic effort to bring service learning into the schools aimed at the eighth-grade civics course, since there was a state standard of learning for civics in middle schools and the curriculum leader for social studies, Beth Leatherwood, strongly supported the idea. With funding from a State Farm grant, as well as from Alternative's Youth Innovation Fund grant from the Kellogg Foundation, Hampton piloted a course based on Project Citizen, a curriculum developed by the national Center for Civic Education, with earmarked dollars from Congress. A public policy-based form of service learning, Project Citizen requires students to decide collectively on a policy issue in their school, neighborhood, or city, define the problem, and then develop a proposal for policy change and implementation. During the first year of the pilot, a project from one Hampton class won the state competition and went on to the national one. Rollout of the eighth-grade curriculum was delayed for a year because of staff turnover, but the new social studies curriculum leader then signed on, and the course has been offered across all middle schools beginning in the 2007–08 school year.[49]

The superintendent's youth advisory group made community service and service learning an agenda priority for high schools when the superintendent asked the group to take up the specific question of mandatory service hours as a graduation requirement. The youth advisers' initial deliberations revealed strong resistance to any mandates, so they decided to do a survey that might yield deeper insight into the patterns of and preferences for volunteering among high school students. The survey showed a strong desire for greater opportunities to volunteer and a strong preference to become engaged through school and with their friends. After further deliberation, the advisory group endorsed the idea of service learning, as well as a graduation seal noting the number of hours of community service performed. Since this did not match up with his initial agenda, superintendent Patrick Russo decided to bring the issue to a top administrative staff meeting at the end of the 2005–06 school year. To his surprise, he got only two questions from his staff: "Have you surveyed students in the International Baccalaureate Program?" and "Have you considered service learning for elementary schools?" As no further questions were forthcoming, Russo responded, "So, can I take your silence as a 'yes' for service learning?" The entire staff nodded quietly in approval, as if to signal that it was a no-brainer.[50]

However, this was only the beginning of a year-long process in which the policy design was researched and refined and then finally approved by the school board in May 2007. The youth advisers did some preliminary research over the summer of 2006 and then, in October, brought the issue to the school board, which requested that a full policy proposal be presented by the end of the school year. The director of secondary education, Donna Woods, asked the youth advisers a fundamental question: "How much do you want to own this policy, or do you want to turn it over to the school system?" The advisers were clear in their response: "No, we want to own it."

So they began much more systematic research on service learning around the country. They looked at models in the cities of Philadelphia and Chicago and in the states of Michigan, New Hampshire, and Vermont. They examined studies on mandated requirements and impacts on student achievement. According to Woods, who attended the advisory group meetings, the work groups did meticulous research on different aspects of service learning, and the general meetings engaged in "a very deep discourse." They also met with principals, teachers, and other students in Hampton to better understand the opportunities and constraints. Youth advisers Eliott Clark, Yana Kupke, and Carmen Hills, along with Sealey and Leatherwood, visited with experts in Washington, D.C., including Nelda Brown, director of the National Service-Learning Partnership, and Kenny Holdsman, deputy director of the Campaign for the Civic Mission of Schools. This traveling team of three youths and two adults also made a side trip to Stafford County, which had the most well known service learning model in Virginia, though one quite different from the one the Hampton advisory group eventually developed.[51]

The group's design called for a multiyear rollout, beginning in the second year with the twelfth-grade government classes, which were not subject to state learning standards, followed by world geography (ninth grade), world history (tenth grade), and finally by U.S. history (eleventh grade). By the end of the five-year rollout period, students in every grade in high school would have at least one service learning opportunity each year, and teachers in these subjects would be required to offer at least one opportunity in one of their courses every year. Teams of teachers would work across these and other disciplines to develop their service learning curriculums.

During the first year of the rollout (2007–08), a planning coalition of students, parents, teachers, administrators, and community groups would work on the details of implementation.

In addition to doing Internet and field research, building relationships through research one-on-one meetings with teachers and principals, deliberating among themselves and with top school officials in the advisory group's monthly meetings, and developing a policy proposal, the youth advisers had hoped to have individual meetings with school board members before the board's upcoming meeting. But as Eliott Clark, a seventeen-year-old senior from Kecoughtan High School and member of the traveling research team, told me, "The timelines were a roadblock," especially given the advisers' other commitments to school, work, and other activist projects. Nonetheless, nearly the entire advisory group attended the school board meeting of May 1, 2007, and several presented the results of their research and their proposed plan. What most impressed the school board, according to Ann Bane, the director of community and legislative relations, Hampton City Schools, was not just the thoroughness of the students' research and their polished presentation but also that "they just came back so passionate" from their trip to Washington and that when questioned by the school board on topics for which they had not prepared, "to the school board's amazement . . . they were so good thinking on their feet." The board passed the proposal unanimously.[52]

The superintendent's youth advisory group has become increasingly robust as a forum for policy deliberation through the tenure of four superintendents. The first, William Canady, who had that transformative nose-to-nose experience with one of the young people during the original collaborative planning process, became a big supporter. When later appointed as Virginia's superintendent of schools, he added a student representative to the state board of education. The next superintendent, Allen Davis III, who inherited the youth advisory, also became a supporter; in April 2002 he told me, "I am an equal at these [advisory group] meetings and they treat me as such. . . . If I were to run into a roadblock on any of their recommendations, I would bring it back to them. But so far I haven't turned any down." After Davis retired, he was succeeded by Kathleen Brown as interim superintendent for one year, but she never demonstrated much enthusiasm for the advisory group.

Russo, with a history of support for youth civic engagement in several other schools systems he previously headed, has certainly become an enthusiastic supporter. Though a few of Hampton's youth civic engagement leaders wondered in the beginning whether he would really "walk the walk, and not just talk the talk," they now recognize him as a genuine leader in this regard. In addition to his productive collaboration with the youth advisory group on a whole range of other policy issues, Russo has been hands on in regularly bringing his leadership team into each school to discuss various issues with teachers, including budgets, and in meeting every year with all students in each school's fifth- and eighth-grade classes. Despite some parental skepticism owing to notorious school shootings in other cities, students themselves devised restrictions on cell phones, which were to be kept in lockers or cars during school hours, with a graduated set of penalties for violations. When the new cell phone policy was passed, Russo decided to model it himself and says, "I never take my cell phone out in the hallway of a school."[53]

Facing relentless fiscal and demographic pressures, with an aging white population becoming increasingly disconnected from the majority school-age African American population, Russo and his administrative team also decided to launch an annual Community Priorities Workshop that builds upon the city's early designs for collaborative planning for youth, as well as his own experiences with the youth advisory group. The first three-hour workshop, conducted on February 25, 2005, with 140 participants, developed a set of six goals. Participants represented a wide range of stakeholder groups for students, parents, administrators, teachers, elected officials (city council, school board, constitutional officers), city personnel, higher education, neighborhoods, civic organizations, realtors, military, business, and faith communities. Each stakeholder group was chosen so as to include broad representation based on age, race, gender, and geography. Stakeholder groups met separately and then in mixed groups to refine the goals, which the school board then adopted as division-wide community priority goals.

The superintendent assigned each central administrative department and individual school the task of developing three to five simple, quantifiable, written objectives, resulting in some two hundred tools to implement the six overall goals. As a result of continued collaboration among stakeholders during the following year, teachers were given a substantial raise, and the board agreed to finance significant new school construction. In addition, seven new school-church partnerships were created, the first preschool for three- and four-year olds was started, and students' adequate yearly progress scores rose by more than 20 percent. Critical for democratic legitimacy in this demographically asymmetrical community, 95.9 percent of the community surveyed said they now understood the school division's mission and vision. After its second year, the school system's community priorities workshop won a prestigious award from Virginia Tech University's School of Education.[54]

Building an Independent Base for Organizing and Advocacy

Compared with many other cities, Hampton has had relatively little independent youth advocacy and organizing.[55] This began to change in 2004, when the interim superintendent placed the Alternatives' contract for leadership development in the schools on the budgetary chopping block. Such cuts would have affected the superintendent's and principal's advisory groups, as well as RELATE trainings and the year-long leadership course that enlists students from all four high schools. Fortunately, Alternatives had received a Youth Innovations Fund grant the previous year from the Kellogg Foundation, which included independent youth organizing as one of its models, and had hired Kim Borton from the Milwaukee YMCA to help develop this missing piece in Hampton's youth engagement culture. Borton began recruiting students, and when the funding crisis hit, the students mobilized. At a rally involving perhaps as many as a hundred youth at the school board meeting, which was televised, fifteen students spoke out, presenting data on the number of students who had benefited from Alternatives' leadership training and its cost effectiveness in terms of their contributions to the schools and the city as a whole. They were particularly adamant that the schools themselves should not provide the training. The funds were restored the next day.[56]

The youth coalition that mobilized against the cuts has since become Youth Achieving Change Together (UthACT) and has been working on a variety of issues. One is a campaign to achieve youth representation on the school board itself. Another is an effort to get more-balanced coverage and accountability in stories about youth in the city's media. Members of the "Voice" committee conducted a year-long content analysis during 2006–07 of reporting on youth in the *Hampton Daily Press,* the city's main newspaper, and presented their report to the editors in a meeting in June 2007. The Voice committee also produces *Word!*—a magazine that calls itself "the voice of youth inspiring action"—as well as video and web-based projects. Zachary Ferguson, a seventeen-year-old senior headed for a community college in the fall of 2007, became a member of UthACT in its early days. Describing himself as an introvert, "not really out of my shell until my second year," he was drawn to media work after Borton took him and others to a set of workshops in New York City on youth media and activism. The experience "made me want to do much more and made me on fire for providing change for the community."[57]

Transforming Agency Culture

A core principle of Hampton's approach is that youth civic engagement can realize its potential only if there is corresponding culture change in institutions, including administrative agencies of city government. It is not enough that youths volunteer and have a voice; adults must also change their behavior at a deep level. Administrators and professionals must encourage productive public work by young people. They must share expert knowledge, recognize youth as resources for problem solving, and value their special insights. They must accommodate the daily rhythms and pressures of young people's lives, provide developmentally appropriate tasks, and offer public challenges of consequence to the life of the city, not just to youth as an interest group. Institutional culture change such as this takes many years, Hampton's innovators have long recognized. It goes against the grain of the way most professionals and administrators have been trained—and how they are evaluated and rewarded. It requires continuous relationship building and mutual accountability at many levels.[58]

Coalition for Youth

The Hampton Coalition for Youth, which became an office of city government after the completion of the collaborative planning initiative in 1993, plays the key role in a coordinated, citywide strategy of institutional culture change. As assistant city manager Montieth explained in a 2002 interview, the coalition's role is to "catalyze best practices" and "establish a learning community throughout city government, not to run programs." The coalition serves as a clearinghouse for youth development and capacity-building practices for agencies and other organizations. It coordinates the city's strategies of seeing youth as resources and developmental assets. The coalition's budget (approximately $400,000) funds a small staff and contracts for training and facilitation services by Alternatives (beyond the nonprofit's contract with the school system). The coalition also helps raise money from national foundations to help the city continue to innovate.[59]

Carlson, director of the coalition since its inception, plays a pivotal role in the entire system. She has built long-term relationships with many key players in city government, community groups, nonprofit agencies, and the schools, where she once coordinated substance abuse prevention and intervention services as staff for Alternatives. Carlson oversees the Youth Commission and has close mentoring relationships with a good number of youth leaders. In effect, she has functioned as a relational organizer among youth and adults within city government and the community. Other staff work on the developmental assets strategy, broad outreach, and the Youth Commission. Carlson reports directly to the city manager and the mayor.

Neighborhood Office

The Planning Department and the school system have made youth engagement a core component of how they conduct their business. The Hampton Neighborhood Office has also helped engage young people in neighborhood projects and planning. A product of the same collaborative planning that led to the creation of the Coalition for Youth as a city agency, the Neighborhood Office and local volunteers set about helping neighborhood associations in the fifty-six neighborhoods consolidate around ten planning districts. It also lent assistance to form and strengthen associations in neighborhoods where they were underdeveloped. Joan Kennedy, former director of planning, who others remember as having made the breakthrough comment back in the late 1980s about "the old idea of citizens' taking some responsibility," became director of the new office in 1993 and worked directly with Montieth and Carlson on overall institutional design. Since her retirement in 2006, the Neighborhood Office has been placed directly under Terry O'Neill in planning.

The office operates on principles of asset-based community development and provides small matching grants and larger neighborhood improvement funds for local projects. Working with the school system, the Neighborhood Office's Innovations for Schools, Youth, Neighborhoods, and Communities (In-SYNC) partnerships operate through a network of some forty organizations and their youth and adult volunteers— Girls Inc., Boys and Girls Club, Foster Grandparents, United Way, Hampton University Leadership Program, city agencies—to provide afterschool and community-based education programs and was recognized with a National Civic Star Award by the American Association of School Administrators. Neighborhood College, also sponsored by the office, provides courses in local government, as well as neighborhood leadership development. While the courses, enrolling more than three hundred in the first decade, began with an emphasis on how government works, the college has shifted in recent years to building partnerships with government, including partnerships between youths and adults. The Hampton Neighborhood Commission, with representatives from all ten districts along with faith and school communities, other institutions, and city government, includes two youth members. Youth also serve on a citywide Neighborhood Youth Advisory Board.[60]

In April 2007 the advisory board cosponsored a public meeting with the Youth Commission at the Northampton community center to focus on public safety in the neighborhoods. Though not as well attended as many city hall meetings, youth from each district met in break-out groups to brainstorm assets in their neighborhoods as well as the key problems they faced, such as domestic violence, drugs, gangs, sexual harassment, theft, and a dearth of social and artistic activities. Planning director O'Neill floated on the edge of the small discussions, taking in what young people said without intervening or trying to steer them in any particular direction. Some district groups were quite systematic, while others floundered. Kiara Joseph-Majors, the board's chair, facilitated the report-back session with the two youth planners. While disappointed in the turnout, even more pronounced in a large gymnasium with bad acoustics, the facilitators skillfully refocused the energy of the general meeting to deliberate about likely causes and potential solutions of the problems identified. After the rocky start, this represented an "astounding" recovery, as one of the Innovations in American Government team members from the mayor's office in Denver put it during a reflection session the next day, to the general agreement of the visiting group.[61]

To be sure, not all neighborhood associations or planning districts are as inclusive of youth as they might be. Neighborhood associations tend to be dominated by older homeowners, many of whom see young people as threats to area safety, appearance, and quietude. This has been changing as younger families move into many neighborhoods and as the Neighborhood Office has focused more attention on engaging youth. To become a "registered neighborhood," associations are now required to do a self-assessment every two years, which includes how they have been involving young people as assets. Associations receive assistance from the capacity committee of the Neighborhood Office to help them figure out how to do this more effectively. Shellae Blackwell, a senior neighborhood development specialist, reflected in 2007 on the long learning process involved: "Fourteen years ago, when we started this, youth were viewed as problems. But with the help of the capacity committee [in the registering and assessment process], more neighborhoods are identifying youth engagement as important, especially in the last six years or so. It has become more a part of the culture."[62]

Parks and Recreation

The Hampton Parks and Recreation Department includes two youths on its nine-person advisory board. Superintendent Art Thatcher, who has a deep appreciation of the range of pathways for engaging youth, noted that in a resource-poor city, it becomes even more important to find ways to get young people to contribute. "We have little money, so we involve as many people as possible." The former superintendent, Laurine Press, deeply committed to youth participation for many years, believes that the more voice young people have, the more they will use the facilities and programs. "They are my customers, just as if they were adult customers," she noted in a 2002 interview. But they are not just "customers," she cautioned; they are also "citizens" with responsibility to engage directly in constructive dialogue and problem solving with local residents who may fear a skateboard park in their neighborhood or are upset at late-night basketball or profanity on the court in the presence of young children.

To develop the ethos and skill at the street level for youth participation and co-ownership, the department has provided staff with three-day trainings through Alternatives and has also been energetic in getting them to participate in the BEST Initiative training sessions, designed to upgrade the professional skills of people working with youth, including their capacities to facilitate youth participation. Youth on the parks and recreation advisory board have provided input to ensure that more recreation suits the needs of young people. However, they are instructed that they sit on the board to represent the needs of the entire community, not just youth, and are explicitly challenged to imagine the kinds of recreation they would like to see for their children when they become parents. They do not approve of programs just because they are directed at youth and can be very rigorous in evaluating, and sometimes rejecting, proposals for youth recreation.[63]

Challenges Ahead

Hampton has been quite successful over a sustained period of time in developing its youth civic engagement system, which embodies various of the eight core principles of civic governance outlined in chapter 2 (see table 4-1), and undoubtedly deserves its reputation as a model for city government innovators who would empower young people through city-led

Table 4-1. *Eight Core Principles of Civic Policy Design in Hampton's Youth Civic Engagement System*

Core principle	Programs, activities
Coproduce public goods	Community improvement (schools, parks and recreation, public and school safety) is everyone's business
	Youth not framed as interest group but as contributing citizens and responsible members of community
	Civic engagement training for youth to become skilled contributors, producers of knowledge and visible public goods
Mobilize community assets	Youth as assets in all youth civic engagement venues
	Principles and practices of asset-based community development, especially in neighborhoods and community development, school-neighborhood partnerships
	Diversity as an asset
Share professional expertise	Planners (planning tools, research reports, surveys)
	School principals, school superintendent, director of secondary education, teacher-mentors on youth civic engagement activities
	Alternatives staff (RELATE and service learning curricular development, Idea Book)
	Private architectural firm (for teen center)
Enable public deliberation	Initial collaborative planning on youth by stakeholders in community
	Youth Commission (public issue forums at city hall, in community; candidate forums during election years)
	Youth planning (public forums, focus groups, design charrettes), part of community planning process
	Principal's and superintendent's youth advisory meetings
	Citizens Unity Commission (study circles, youth facilitators)
Promote sustainable partnerships	Youth-adult partnerships in all youth civic engagement venues
	Relationship building as central to all work and youth civic engagement training
	Youth-friendly businesses as project and process
Build fields strategically	Building a system for youth civic engagement as explicit charge emerging from initial collaborative planning
	Development of new components to complement existing ones, beginning with youth planners and Youth Commission; catalytic role of Hampton Coalition for Youth across institutions
	Development of structured pathways of leadership development
	Networks of youth across and within institutions, intentionally linked to network of adult mentors in various public agencies, institutions, and through Alternatives Inc.

(continued)

Table 4-1. *Eight Core Principles of Civic Policy Design in Hampton's Youth Civic Engagement System* (continued)

Core principle	Programs, activities
Transform institutional cultures	Reinvention of Alternatives Inc. (from social service and therapeutic provider to youth civic engagement enabler)
	Change in mindset and behavior among adults as well as youth; youth as culture makers and interpreters
	Culture of schools (mutual respect, shared ownership of public space, shared problem solving, reduction in physical and sexual intimidation that excludes some from full participation in polity)
	Departments of planning, neighborhoods, parks and recreation; police department (but backsliding)
	BEST training for youth workers in public agencies, nonprofits, and schools
	Common vocabulary (youth as assets, youth civic engagement as community building and democracy enhancing)
Ensure reciprocal accountability	Strong norms of accountability in all youth projects (youth and adults provide reasons, account for results, address shortcomings and possible improvements)
	Formal reporting of Youth Commission and youth planners to city council and planning department
	Site visits and oversight by Youth Commission of youth grant recipients (dollars spent, projects undertaken, projects accomplished)
	Registered neighborhood self-assessment on youth involvement

initiatives. Even for those cities that have taken other paths to youth commissions, such as San Francisco through its youth movement mobilization and referendum campaign, Hampton holds important lessons for establishing so many complementary institutional components and structured pathways for youth leadership. Its emphasis on relationship building has enabled it to form and sustain youth/adult partnerships of various kinds, as well as catalyze culture change within a range of city departments and nonprofit agencies.

Hampton's adult innovators went into this work with eyes wide open and fully expected that agency culture change would be long and difficult work. They would also be the first to admit that this process has been uneven and incomplete, and in some cases reversed. Some agency cultures are more difficult to transform, and various factors, such as budget shortfalls and leadership turnover, either have put some efforts on hold or required new forms of mobilization to maintain gains. Hampton weathered the threat during the interim school superintendent's tenure several years ago, and has even moved significantly forward with the development of service learning on a school-wide basis. But gaining a solid foothold in some other agencies that could be expected to better enable, as well as benefit from, youth civic engagement has not been as successful as in the ones discussed above. And in some there has been slippage.

The police department, for instance, began auspiciously in the 1990s by including youth within its larger community policing strategy in what is known as Y-COPE (Youth Community-Oriented Policing). A school resource officer program places officers in schools, where they perform traditional policing duties, but also build relationships and trust, provide mentoring, and teach law modules in classes. The department has sponsored a Citizens Police Academy, as well as a Youth Citizens Police Academy, which met regularly for two weeks every summer. Youth and police have also co-written a curriculum for the police academy that embodies the principles and practices of "youth as resources" and "police as servants of youth," which aims to move beyond programs to deeper culture change. Officers meet to develop strategies with neighborhood associations, local youth groups, and representatives from the Neighborhood Youth Advisory Board. Several neighborhoods initially targeted for Y-COPE reduced juvenile crime by half and received the Governor's Excellence in Safety Award. As detective Tony Perkins noted of the collaborative Y-COPE work at a 2002 community meeting, "In our group [in Newtown], we vote. My vote counts only as one. If I am outvoted by youth, that's OK."

Youth leaders, such as Alvin Hunter, president of the Newtown Leadership Group at the time and a member of the Neighborhood Youth Advisory Board, received training to educate the community about domestic violence and to organize "speak outs" among previously incarcerated residents. Officers have been recognized and rewarded for their work with youth and communities. In 2002, for example, officers Perkins and William Davis were named among six "exemplary assets builders" in the city, and Davis was named "detective of the year" and promoted to captain, with special recognition for his youth work. However, such exemplary work, which requires labor-intensive relational organizing, has been hard to maintain in the face of budget shortfalls, the call-up of a good number of officers to the state's National Guard to serve in Iraq—including some in the forefront of community work—and new leadership that has not been as convinced of the value of Y-COPE and youth civic engagement in general as previous police chiefs.[64]

Resource issues and leadership turnover, even outright resistance, have also seemed to obstruct progress on youth civic engagement in some agencies and nonprofits. The Department of Public Works does engage youth in its Hampton Watershed Restoration Project, various Adopt-a-Stream clean-ups, and efforts to mark storm drains. However, youth seem considerably less engaged in environmental and conservation activities than one might expect, given the EPA's Chesapeake Bay Program and various civic partnership approaches existing in the region through city and state agencies, as well as watershed and school groups. Perhaps this will change as service learning gains a greater foothold in Hampton's schools, since watershed monitoring and ecosystem restoration activities have tended to be relatively high on the preferred list of service learning work in many other communities.

If Hampton's system of youth civic engagement remains vulnerable, it is from relentless budget pressures in this moderate-income city that might lead some on the city council to see such investments as soft and less important than others; another factor in play is that some innovators who have been in the relatively tight leadership core from the beginning are approaching retirement age. On the other hand, many young people have now had a significant amount of leadership experience through this system, and the ethos of the city regarding its youth has changed profoundly over the course of fifteen years. Many parents, including those in city leadership positions, have not only encouraged their kids to become involved, but in some cases their children have been the family educators on democracy and civic engagement. The eldest daughter of (now retired) police major Nolan Cutler, for instance, was one of the twenty young people who helped develop the original strategy for youth engagement in the city in the early 1990s. Another daughter became active in an antidrug campaign. In 2002 his son was serving on the school superintendent's advisory group. Cutler's own kids helped turn him into a true believer with a conviction that engaged young people represent a fundamental asset to the city. And though the statistics for the 2008 presidential election are not yet available, the voting rates for Hampton youth were 18.5 percentages points higher than the national average in 2000 and 28.7 percentage points higher in 2004.[65]

5 | Can a Federal Regulator Become a Civic Enabler? The U.S. Environmental Protection Agency

The U.S. Environmental Protection Agency was set up by an executive order of President Nixon in 1970. Its structure was pieced together from more than a dozen units in several federal agencies, each operating under preexisting, media-specific statutes. These statutes, along with a spate of new laws soon to follow, established a relatively clear regulatory paradigm of command and control. Congress would outlaw certain activities, set definite deadlines for reducing specific pollutants, and mandate the use of specific technologies over others. The agency would bear responsibility for enforcing these mandates. Should polluters fail to meet requirements and deadlines, it could impose penalties. Citizens, in turn, could sue polluters and the EPA itself should the intent or letter of the law not be carried out. Of course, in practice all this proved a much more complicated affair.

Command and control emerged as the preferred strategy for several reasons. First, in reducing the most pressing pollutants from point sources, such as smokestacks and outflow pipes, the strategy was quickly, visibly, and substantially effective in the early years of the new regulatory regime. Second, there were no clear alternatives to Washington's heavy hand at that point. Environmental agencies at state and local levels were too weak and untrustworthy to act as decentralized substitutes and required federal assistance to enhance their own administrative capacities. Environmental and civic groups also lacked organizational and technical capacities in the myriad local jurisdictions. Business actors were generally unwilling to engage in meaningful self-regulation or collaboration with government and civic partners; indeed, their environmental staff capacities were built largely in response to federal command. Market approaches only slowly demonstrated their theoretical relevance for selected regulatory problems.

Third, many federal environmental statutes, as well as other changes in administrative law, mandated citizen participation in the spirit of the movements of the 1960s and other federal efforts to promote "maximum feasible participation." However, the major environmental and public interest lobbies used participatory mandates to further strengthen command and control directives from the EPA and other agencies, since this was how they could achieve the greatest leverage against powerful opponents who sought to deny, delay, or dilute the new regulations. Public support for such controls remained strong even during administrations less inclined to act as enforcers—a realistic concern during the Nixon and Ford administrations—and could be politically mobilized against too much overt deregulation, as happened early (1981–83) in Ronald Reagan's first term.[1]

However, mandated citizen participation, as blunt and unrefined as it was at first, provided a rich laboratory for network learning among local civic actors, regulators, businesses, and other institutions as they grappled with the problems of making long-term improvements to real places and complex ecosystems and as they faced the challenges of nonpoint pollution and the many conundrums and unintended consequences of command and control, medium by medium, pollutant by pollutant. Corporations, for instance, could meet federal requirements in one medium (say, air) by shifting pollution to another medium (water); environmental groups could sue to win strict enforcement only to find that the overall ecosystem had deteriorated further after a decade of legal battles and even victory. From the 1980s onward, new community-based environmental movements provided a more favorable context for participatory democracy as a potentially collaborative endeavor, and regulatory communities began to experiment with civic environmental strategies under a variety of rubrics. The learning process proved messy and often conflictual; many stakeholders had to be compelled to come to the table by grassroots protest, legal challenges, and regulatory hammers.

The EPA, though designed according to administrative rationalities that left little room for local knowledge, community culture, and social capital, proceeded nonetheless to invest piecemeal in building the capacity of civic associations as well as its own capacity to work in partnership with them. By the 1990s, civic environmentalism had become a central part of the debate about the mission—and reinvention—of the agency and was subsequently embedded in strategic planning and innovation thereafter. If political scientists Marc Landy, Marc Roberts, and Stephen Thomas could justifiably chastise the EPA for "asking the wrong questions" by playing down real places in favor of abstract risks and for failing to treat local communities as "schools of citizenship," the agency soon thereafter helped to generate a substantial civic and technical knowledge base for asking much better questions when it comes to citizen action in communities of place.[2]

This chapter examines EPA efforts to develop civic environmentalism in several programs, as well as its agency-wide culture change strategies. In the case of watersheds, collaborative, multistakeholder partnerships and citizen monitoring have become increasingly central components of agency strategy. Because of the complex work involved in protecting and restoring integrated ecosystems over the long haul, the watershed approach has been the most inherently civic framework within the core statutory programs of the agency, though it faces genuine challenges in aligning itself with regulatory programs of the Clean Water Act. Superfund, the largest agency program because of the high cost of cleaning up hazardous waste sites, has had to learn how to engage the public in more productive ways than it initially was able to do when the fear of thousands of Love Canals drove the original 1980 policy design. However, because Superfund is an emergency response program designed for targeted remedy within a delimited period of time, it does not seek to build civic capacities for the longer term or through broad networks, as with watersheds, though sometimes this occurs as a by-product. The agency's environmental justice program, while responding to some similar concerns as Superfund, has been much broader in scope in its attempts to address issues of the distributive equity of environmental risks and empowerment of affected communities. Without the distinct statutory foundation that exists for these other two programs, however, environmental justice has not been able to garner comparable resources for civic capacity building.

In each case, the EPA has had to figure out not only how to work more collaboratively with specific communities and help generate appropriate state capacities for such work but also how to engage broader citizen movements, especially the watershed, antitoxics, and environmental justice movements. Despite their differences, however, by the mid-1990s watersheds,

Superfund, environmental justice, and several other EPA programs had generated enough common appreciation of the importance of community participation to warrant a systematic, cross-media, culture change strategy within the agency. Known as community-based environmental protection, this culture change strategy has had important impacts across the agency, and its lessons have informed current efforts, such as the multimedia, cross-program Community Action for a Renewed Environment grant program, the most civic mission–driven, network-learning model yet to emerge at the EPA and perhaps at any federal agency. While its achievements as a civic enabler have been substantial, the EPA nonetheless faces serious challenges in broadening and deepening its community-based work.

Watersheds as Democratic Commonwealths

During the 1970s, citizens became engaged in water issues as never before. The federal government spurred this in several ways. Responding to the ethos of the 1960s movements, Congress passed the Clean Water Act amendments of 1972 with strong requirements for citizen participation. The act's primary goal—though relatively inchoate compared with its specific remedies and appropriated dollars for chemical pollution control—was holistic ecological restoration. As Rebecca Hanmer, who has held various senior management positions in the EPA's Office of Water, recalls, her original water pollution group at the U.S. Department of Health, Education, and Welfare in the 1960s, which then became part of the new EPA, was already thinking in terms of watersheds and basin plans and was especially inspired by civic action on water quality led by local Leagues of Women Voters. But this long-term ecosystem approach competed unfavorably with the quick and measurable results possible through water pollution control technologies and municipal construction grants, which were championed by a venerable professional association of water pollution control engineers with far more status at the time than biologists and ecologists.[3]

Nonetheless, section 208 of the 1972 act created a framework for multicounty water quality management planning. The EPA provided regional staff support, local grants, and citizen participation manuals and training workshops through groups like the Conservation Foundation. As a result, hundreds of local associations, such as Leagues of Women Voters and Sierra Club chapters, were able to develop rudimentary technical knowledge of water planning in state and local jurisdictions as well as the civic skills and relationships to work with a broad range of interests. For most, this was the first time they had come to the table with other civic groups, not to mention local businesses, utilities, farmers, and myriad regulatory agencies concerned with water. The process was messy, and most planning efforts disappointing, for a variety of reasons: limited statutory authority and local political clout, especially over land use; delayed administrative guidance and stop-and-go funding that disrupted civic and institutional capacity building; the relatively low status of participation staff and contractors owing to their "soft" rather than "hard" legal and technical skills. However, a reservoir of civic skills and relationships spilled over into subsequent efforts as citizens began to form watershed and river protection groups on a broad scale and to break out of the narrow mindset fostered by regulatory controls and infrastructure projects.[4]

Although congressional defunding of section 208 in 1981 created a programmatic hiatus, especially since section 208 was the intended nesting place of strategies for dealing with nonpoint pollution, the EPA became increasingly strategic in developing capacities for progressively more effective community-based work in watersheds. First, the agency began to reframe the problem of water in robust civic terms: not just controlling discrete pollutants through regulatory action but also protecting and restoring integrated ecosystems through sustained stewardship among diverse civic, business, and government stakeholders at all levels of the federal system. Second, the EPA began to develop collaborative management, planning, and data tools to enable communities and stakeholders to work more effectively at the watershed level. Third, the agency helped to build the capacity of national and regional civic associations capable of sharing in the work and, in turn, of aiding in developing the capacity of local groups. Fourth, it catalyzed learning networks on an extensive scale so that lay citizens, professional scientists, and regulators at all levels of the federal system could develop usable knowledge and technique together.

Watersheds as Complex Natural and Civic Systems

Beginning especially with the Chesapeake Bay Program in 1983 and the National Estuary Program (NEP) of 1987 and then progressing further with the creation of the Office of Wetlands, Oceans, and Watersheds in 1991, the EPA began to reframe the problem of water pollution and to develop a broad watershed approach with two critical components. First, most if not all the key problems pertaining to water—quality, supply, fisheries, habitat preservation, biodiversity, flood control—needed to be understood and addressed as part of hydrologically defined drainage basins known as watersheds. Because watersheds, including smaller watersheds nested in much larger ones, are systems defined by complex interactions among innumerable natural and social dynamics, only holistic, problem-solving strategies tailored to specific contexts could hope to maintain and restore them. While fragmented federal regulations, command and control techniques, and massive investments in wastewater treatment had significantly reduced point-source pollution since the Clean Water Act amendments of 1972, watersheds remained at risk owing to nonpoint pollution, primarily from farms, transportation systems, and urban runoff as well as innumerable everyday activities of ordinary citizens. The familiar regulatory tools could hardly be adequate for nonpoint pollution and ecosystem restoration.[5]

Second, unlike top-down watershed planning of the big power dam models of the mid-twentieth century, the new watershed frame is inherently civic. The Chesapeake Bay Program, the Great Lakes Program, and the National Estuary Program are founded upon the idea that long-term protection and restoration of such complex ecosystems, often extending over thousands of square miles, requires that citizens develop a sense of genuine "ownership" and a "protective civic ethic." Local knowledge, relationships, and initiative are essential to effective strategies for reducing nonpoint sources of pollution as well as to generate the political will to assume the costs of upgrading sewage treatment or altering sensitive land-use policies. Diverse stakeholders must develop a shared vision and find ways to collaborate: farmers upstream with boaters and oystermen on the bay, environmentalists with developers, scientists and regulators with lay citizens and students.

Peer education is also critical. Farmers can educate one another about best management practices through open houses, twilight meetings, and one-on-one conversations. Professional associations of architects and builders can host luncheons on smart growth and green building, and ranchers can meet over coffee to consider the benefits of conservation easements. Since the health of watersheds depends on the everyday choices of citizens (in lawn care, trash disposal, household chemical use), public education plays a central role in the watershed approach. A civic network strategy, combined with interagency collaboration, is also essential because watershed boundaries do not dovetail neatly with local political jurisdictions and watershed problems do not conform to segmented agency authority.[6]

According to the deputy assistant administrator for water at the time the Chesapeake Bay Program was established, it was Congress's authorization of the initial research grant for the Chesapeake Bay study—money not requested by the EPA itself—that truly catalyzed the network of watershed thinkers and leaders. As other EPA innovators also clearly recognized, the watershed frame revived and modernized an idea proposed a century earlier by John Wesley Powell, legendary explorer and second director of the U.S. Geological Survey, namely, that governance of our natural resources requires us to think in terms of "watershed commonwealths."[7]

Reframing was not an EPA affair alone, of course. The watershed frame was fashioned through reflective and reciprocal interplay of normative ideals (democracy, justice), scientific and technical models, and practical testing among regional and national EPA innovators and watershed movement organizations and networks, as well as academic scientists and innovators in local, state, and other federal agencies. In 1993 the Pacific Rivers Council provided a key overall framing document with its book *Entering the Watershed*. The Coalition to Restore Urban Waters developed urban and environmental justice themes in the watershed frame, and visionary urban rivers leader Ann Riley brought extensive network ties to the National Association of State Wetland Managers, the National Association of State Floodplain Managers, the National Parks Service, the Natural Resources Conservation Service, the National Academy of Sciences panels, and the Waterways Research Center in the Army Corps of Engineers.

The urban river restoration manual created by the Coalition to Restore Urban Waters became the basis for training throughout the national network of youth conservation corps, now the Corps Network, with some hundred and twenty local and state corps. Within the EPA itself, Region 1's Buzzard's Bay Project and Merrimack River Watershed Initiative, following some lessons of the Chesapeake Bay Program, inspired the formation of the Office of Wetlands, Oceans, and Watersheds at agency headquarters in 1991. Peter Lavigne, an innovator within this generative New England regional network in the 1980s, later became director of the River Network's river leadership program in the 1990s, locating, mentoring, and connecting civic leaders nationwide, as the movement defined its frame and identity as the "watershed movement" seeking to establish "watershed democracy."[8]

Collaborative Management and Place-Based Tools

In addition to helping reframe the problem, the EPA has become increasingly energetic in developing the management, planning, information, and other tools to enable effective collaboration and community-based action. These tools vary, depending on the type of watershed and specific community and state context, and are certainly still quite imperfect. But they represent significant investments in the institutional infrastructure and knowledge base for network management of water resources.

The management conference, for instance, has become the key planning and implementation design, developed by the Chesapeake Bay Program and then extended to the NEP. Once a governor or group of governors convinces the EPA to designate an estuary as having "national significance," a local management conference is established with its own budget and office housed in a state or federal agency, university, or nonprofit organization. The management conference includes a broad range of stakeholders, including public agencies, businesses, academic institutions, scientists, and environmental and community groups. It is responsible for developing a shared vision and a comprehensive conservation and management plan based on sound science, to which stakeholders commit, and then developing implementation strategies, as well as further funding from government and private sources. The Peconic Estuary Program, for instance, complemented its environmental and nonmarket values analysis with an assessment of the economic contributions of the estuary, which helped generate an additional $100 million from state, county, and local governments for conservation. On average, individual NEPs generate $16.50 for every dollar invested by the EPA.[9]

In addition to policy, technical, and scientific committees, estuary programs have a local government committee to help enlist collaboration of elected public officials—for example, on land-use planning, which is so critical to future gains but occurs largely outside the statutory authority of the EPA. Management conferences also have a citizens advisory committee, with an even broader representation of stakeholder groups. The committee takes responsibility for ongoing public participation, conducting workshops and community meetings to explain scientific findings and explore options, enlisting professional and business group support for best management practices, publishing a newsletter and guides for everyday household use, recruiting civic and school groups for hands-on monitoring and restoration, brokering new partnerships, reviewing plan development and implementation, generating political support (including for local bonds and levies), serving as watchdog, and ensuring the broad publicity necessary for democratic network accountability.

The management conference possesses no regulatory authority, since the National Estuary Program is a voluntary program. However, its comprehensive conservation and management plan and implementation strategies often include highly public recommendations for local and state regulatory action and thus exercise significant moral authority to move political leaders and public agencies. Comparative studies, such as those by Paul Sabatier, Mark Lubell, and others, show that NEPs build social capital, reduce conflict between competing advocacy coalitions such as environmentalists and business, and enhance belief in institutional capacity for solving complex, diffuse, and boundary-spanning problems typically faced in estuaries. Even where serious gaps exist in stakeholder representation or where scientific research has trumped civic action, estuary programs have enhanced the numbers and capacities of local citizen groups. The EPA's investments in these programs have been critical to reducing the transaction costs of developing governance networks in contexts where institutional undersupply is endemic.[10]

The EPA has helped build watershed management capacities in other ways as well. In 1994 the Office of Wetlands, Oceans, and Watersheds established the Watershed Academy to provide in-person and (in 1996) web-based training for federal, state, and local officials as well as nonprofit and citizen watershed practitioners. The academy offers a wide array of courses on scientific, technical, data, and planning issues and on stakeholder involvement, partnerships, and public outreach. It has collaborated with the management development centers of the U.S. Office of Personnel Management to offer two-week residential watershed partnership seminars emphasizing community-based decisionmaking for staff of federal, state, tribal, and local agencies and environmental organizations and corporations. Academy webcasts, which in tight budget times are seen as highly cost effective, can draw hundreds, as did the January 2006 webcast on using the EPA's new (draft) watershed planning handbook, which drew some five hundred and fifty participants, not counting those who subsequently used the recorded version. From 2000 to 2005, the academy awarded some eleven hundred certificates to those who had completed at least fifteen modules.[11]

The academy has worked directly with most of the states to develop model watershed projects for specific basins and comprehensive state watershed strategies, funded partially through section 319 nonpoint-source grants, authorized by the 1987 revisions of the Clean Water Act. The academy, however, does not just offer courses by EPA experts; it also mobilizes a broad network of skilled practitioners from state programs and national and state watershed groups and centers to serve as trainers, who often collaborate in course design and presentation. The Watershed Academy is designed to help leverage the knowledge and best practices of innovative states and civic watershed networks.[12]

Many resources for community-based training provided directly by the EPA, or developed through cooperative agreements with other organizations, have been quite sophisticated in quality. One such course is based on the guide *Community Culture and the Environment,* which an Office of Wetlands, Oceans, and Watersheds team developed with community watershed groups and field-tested with local chapters of the Nature Conservancy. The guide adapts to the environmental field the best practices of community visioning, asset-based community development, and other consensus organizing approaches and clearly ranks among the best of the several hundred training manuals that I reviewed for the Kettering Foundation several years ago.

The Center for Watershed Protection, with support from the EPA and other agencies (in addition to fees and foundation grants), has offered intensive watershed workshops to more than fifteen thousand practitioners since 1993 and has developed a range of high-quality watershed guides. Its 230-page *Methods to Develop Restoration Plans for Small Urban Watersheds,* just one in an eleven-volume series on subwatersheds, provides a meticulously clear yet detailed set of planning and technical tools, woven seamlessly throughout with methods of stakeholder engagement and public education. The Institute for Environmental Negotiation at the University of Virginia teamed up with the Alliance for Chesapeake Bay, with support from the EPA's bay program, to produce *Community Watershed Forums: A Planner's Guide,* based on the extensive experience of grassroots efforts and partnerships over a twenty-year period. The EPA's new *Handbook for Developing Watershed Plans to Restore and Protect Our Waters* provides a clear and comprehensive guide for collaborative and participatory work.[13]

The EPA has also been increasingly energetic in developing information and measurement systems that enable local action for accountable progress. Data developed through the main regulatory water programs at the EPA have been notoriously incomplete for decades and typically have existed in fragmentary forms that fail to provide communities the means to create a holistic picture of the overall health of a watershed or to assess when, where, and why progress occurs. Some regional EPA offices, however, have partnered with watershed associations to develop "measurement that matters," in the words of Shelley Metzenbaum, former head of the EPA's Office of Regional Operations and state-local relations. Region 1 in New England, for example, collaborated with the Charles River Watershed Association and other nonprofits to develop comprehensible, credible, frequent, and well-integrated performance information to enlighten and motivate citizens and to hold agencies accountable for reaching the substantive goal of a clean Charles River by 2005—though there is, admittedly, still some way to go.[14]

The EPA headquarters has invested in the development of increasingly sophisticated web-based and geographic information system tools to provide local actors with the layers of relevant place-based data from the broadest range of federal and state agencies, tribes, and volunteer monitoring partners. In the fall of 2006 the watershed planning team began to test its new web-based planning tool, known as the Watershed Plan Builder, which promises to enhance considerably the ability of local civic groups and partnerships to plan in a manner that is increasingly effective as well as participatory. The agency has also developed the Water Quality Exchange, designed to enable far greater ease in sharing data from their online STORET (*Sto*rage and *Ret*rieval) Warehouse. The Water Quality Exchange enables users to enter such data into their own specialized applications, including water quality modeling, data analysis, priority setting and decisionmaking and information designed for public education—further motivating civic action by enhancing the possibilities for democratic accountability at the geographical level that citizens are most likely to be able to comprehend.[15]

Designing and refining tools that citizens can use has been critical to almost every aspect of watershed work (see table 5-1) The EPA has invested strategically to ensure that citizens and civic groups have an ample toolbox appropriate to the tasks at hand, not just the regulatory hammers, so to speak, but also the civic levers and linchpins, the clamps and couplings; not just the hardware but also the software to enhance civic and professional intelligence for collaborative work. Many EPA partners have helped to design the tools, test them, and improve them—by contesting them or by developing still better ones on their own. That, too, is what makes these tools democratic tools.

As one would expect, management tools and program design evolve considerably over the course of time, testifying not only to significant policy learning but also to persistent challenges in building appropriate capacities and achieving adequate results amid increasing ecosystem threats. Consider, for example, the Puget Sound NEP, among the first created in the wake of congressional authorization in 1987. Encompassing a shoreline of two thousand miles, a land and water surface of sixteen thousand square miles, and

Table 5-1. *Select Tools for Democratic Watershed Collaboration,*
U.S. Environmental Protection Agency

Type of tool	Examples[a]
Organizing	"Watersheds" as cognitive frame for civic organizing and collaboration
	Community Culture and the Environment
	Community Watershed Forums: A Planner's Guide
Network building	Environmental Protection Agency cosponsored conferences of watershed movement (see table 5-2 below)
	National Estuary Program citizen advisory committees
	Volunteer Monitor
Management	National Estuary Program management conference
	Watershed Academy trainings, webcasts, partnership with U.S. Office of Personnel Management
Data	Water Quality Exchange
	STORET Warehouse
Planning	National Estuary Program comprehensive conservation and management plan
	Handbook for Developing Watershed Plans to Restore and Protect Our Waters
	Watershed Plan Builder
Financing	Matching grants (National Estuary Program; Chesapeake Bay Program; National Fish and Wildlife Foundation)
	Section 319 nonpoint-source grants to states
	Targeted watershed grants
	Office of Wetlands, Oceans, and Watersheds, Watershed Financing Team
	University-based environmental finance centers
	Watershed Academy webcasts on financing watershed associations
Restoration	*Methods to Develop Restoration Plans for Small Urban Watersheds*
Deliberation	*Community Watershed Forums: A Planner's Guide*
Monitoring	*Volunteer Estuary Monitoring: A Methods Manual*
	Volunteer Monitor
Performance	Region 1, Charles River: development of "measurement that matters"
	The Volunteer Monitor's Guide to Quality Assurance Project Plans
	Valuing Ecosystem Services: Toward Better Environmental Decision-Making

a. There are overlapping and integrative uses for many of the listed tools.

more than ten thousand rivers and streams, this NEP recognized the need for a civic strategy from the beginning. In its first iteration as the Puget Sound Water Quality Authority, it developed a comprehensive conservation and management plan and launched watershed planning processes that were recognized as a model, especially in counties such as Thurston, where staff invested in relationship building in ways similar to Seattle's Department of Neighborhoods and Neighborhood Planning Office.

The water quality authority also provided critical funding to many local civic groups and tribes through its public involvement and education matching grants. Watershed groups and other restoration efforts generated extensive networks for subsequent initiatives, such as the Shared Strategy for salmon protection and the Northwest Straits Marine Conservation Initiative. Yet civic initiative and watershed planning could not guarantee that local governments would pay sufficient attention to problems or implement plans. In 1996 the Puget Sound Action Team replaced the Puget Sound Water Quality Authority. While still under the National Estuary Program involving multiple stakeholder groups, including environmental ones, the Puget Sound Action Team was designed to answer more clearly to state agencies. It continued to fund local group projects through public involvement and education grants. However, its civic capacity–building needs and other strategic challenges in an area with strong population and development pressures continued to outpace its management structure.

A 2005 review of the federal National Estuary Program by the Office of Management and Budget, while finding the program adequate overall and giving it a rating of 100 percent on program purpose and design, noted serious deficiencies in strategic planning, results, and accountability. Since the Washington State portion of funding had increased substantially over the years in relation to the federal contribution, and recently elected governor Christine Gregoire shared a strong focus on accountability and results, the Puget Sound Action Team was folded into a newly created Puget Sound Partnership, chaired by William Ruckelshaus. The new agency requires greater prioritization of problems and more strategic use of resources, including civic capacity building and funding from public involvement and education grants. During winter and spring of 2008, Puget Sound Partnership staff conducted community forums and topical workshops (water quality, human health, habitat, and land use) across the sound to help develop an "Action Agenda" aligned with newly emerging scientific research. These forums further revealed the range of independent civic groups, local foundations, sustainable city and neighborhood initiatives, and multistakeholder partnerships ready to come to the table—especially to "get things done," not just provide advice, as Betsy Peabody, former outreach director of the Puget Sound Water Quality Authority and founding director of the independent Puget Sound Restoration Fund, a key civic catalyst, said at a Bremerton workshop.

The emerging strategic priorities, accompanied by action area profiles of the distinct ecosystems within the sound, are impressively calibrated in terms of level of threat and urgency, relative impact and cost effectiveness, preventive and restorative tools, inventoried civic and local government program capacities, and interactive effects and potential unintended consequences among various strategies. But the Puget Sound Partnership will nonetheless be challenged with developing the kind of staff capacity that can leverage civic networks and local energies while also ensuring strategic focus and accountability to the state legislature and the governor under well-defined deadlines, which represents a key shift for the national program in Puget Sound.[16]

Building the Capacity of Associations and Networks

By the mid-1990s, a self-styled watershed movement espousing a vision of watershed democracy and collaborative management had emerged out of hundreds, perhaps even several thousand, disparate watershed associations and councils, friends-of-the-river and adopt-a-stream groups, and many other stewardship efforts. While clearly the product of local action, inspired in part by bioregionalist ideas and nurtured by the efforts of various regional and national associations and foundations, the movement has received critical support from the EPA. The agency has progressively aligned its watershed frame with the emergent frame of the movement— and vice versa—and the agency has furnished, funded, or facilitated the dissemination and use of management models, community planning practices, restoration tools, and data systems to enable more-effective civic engagement. In doing so, it has provided further incentives for citizens to organize and do effective public work, at the same time lowering information and other transaction costs. The EPA has also subsidized the costs of building movement networks by partially funding national, state, and regional meetings of the watershed movement (see table 5-2).[17]

Also essential has been the agency's role in providing grants to build the capacity of local watershed associations and kindred groups and the state, regional, and national intermediaries that work with them. The EPA's Chesapeake Bay Program, for instance, has funded a small watershed grants program to support watershed planning, capacity building, and restoration efforts. In contrast to the earlier years, however, when many organizations were in the rudimentary stages of formation, virtually all grants are now designed to promote multistakeholder partnerships, whether the direct recipient is a watershed association or land conservancy, sporting or fishing group, school system or environmental education center, local business or farmers group, city or county agency. These grants, generally ranging from $10,000 to $50,000 (with several annual "community legacy grants" of up to $100,000), were initially administered by the Alliance for Chesapeake Bay, a major regional group. Currently they are managed by the National Fish and Wildlife Foundation, established by Congress in 1984, which includes an array of federal agency partners and has leveraged federal dollars for community and regional projects nationwide approximately three times over.

The Chesapeake Bay Foundation, with some hundred and seventy-seven thousand members, combines organizing and advocacy with environmental education and hands-on restoration, the latter funded partially through various EPA and other agency grants. Some Chesapeake Bay partnerships have specifically aimed to introduce sustainability practices among farmers, architects, developers, and other business and professional associations. Others have aimed at transforming the behavior of individual citizens (for example, on the use of fertilizers and pesticides) and inculcating a civic ethic of environmental stewardship. These grants have also enabled national organizations and resource centers, such as the River Network, the Izaak Walton League, and the Center for Watershed Protection, to provide training and other assistance, in turn enhancing their own capacities for work with other groups nationwide. The Chesapeake Bay Restoration Act of 2000 authorizes such grants for cooperative tributary basin strategies and locally based protection and restoration programs or projects that complement these. By 2005 such grants totaled $14.3 million, supported 439 projects, and leveraged an additional $43 million through matches from other sources.[18]

The National Estuary Program, which in its twentieth-anniversary report subtitle refers to itself as a "network," has also provided significant support for local watershed groups and their partners. Management conferences on the individual estuaries have made public involvement and education important parts of their comprehensive conservation and management plans. All twenty-eight individual estuary programs have used some EPA funding for small-grants programs, and some have done so ambitiously. The Puget Sound estuary program provided more than

Table 5-2. *Select U.S. Environmental Protection Agency Cosponsored and Cofunded Watershed Network Building Conferences*

Conference	Date	Participants
First National Conference of Estuary Groups	1987	Save The Bay (Providence, R.I.) convenes emerging coalitions of estuary groups as National Estuary Program is established
National Citizen Monitoring Conferences	1988–2000	Biannual conference, one hundred to three hundred participants in conjunction with rotating civic partners (Izaak Walton League, Alliance for Chesapeake Bay); now part of National Water Quality Monitoring Council network (professional and volunteer monitors)
Watershed '93	1993	Eleven hundred participants from broad range of local, state, and national watershed and conservation groups, tribes, public agencies, cooperative extension, business and professional associations; hundreds more via satellite broadcast on final day
Restoring Urban Waters: Friends of Trashed Rivers Conference	1993	Coalition to Restore Urban Waters, with River Network, Izaak Walton League, National Association of Service and Conservation Corps (now Corps Network), and others; three hundred participants (followed by three other "trashed rivers" conferences)
Watershed '96	1996	Two thousand participants, plus several thousand others at 156 teleconference downlinks, from broad range of local, state, and national watershed and conservation groups, public agencies, university extension, K–12 schools, business and professional associations

National River Rally	1995–2008	Five hundred and twenty-four participants in peak year of 2006, convened by River Network, other river advocacy and watershed restoration groups, public agencies; recent falloff in EPA support, but still makes tools presentations
Regional Watershed Forums	1999–2001	Thirteen regional, multistakeholder, lay-professional roundtables, forty to eighty-five participants each; some continue as regular roundtables, with state and county offshoots; prepare agenda for National Watershed Forum
National Watershed Forum	2001	Four hundred and eighty participants from broad range of local, state, and national watershed and conservation groups, public agencies, cooperative extension, and professional associations
National Conferences on Coastal and Estuarine Habitat Restoration	2003–08	Eight hundred to fifteen hundred participants, broad multistakeholder group, convened by Restore America's Estuaries, with Save The Bay, The Nature Conservancy, National Oceanic and Atmospheric Administration, U.S. Fish and Wildlife Service, local and state agencies, business partners

Source: Telephone interviews with Curt Spalding, executive director of Save The Bay, December 23, 1999; Christine Olsenius, executive director of the Southeast Watershed Forum, which convened the first of the regional watershed roundtables, April 4, 2006; e-mail from Eleanor Ely, August 5, 2008; Kim Herman Goslant, "Citizen Participation and Administrative Discretion in the Cleanup of Narragansett Bay," *Harvard Environmental Law Review* 12 (1988): 521–68, p. 545, published shortly after the first estuary conference. See *Watershed '93: A National Conference on Watershed Management: Proceedings*, CD-ROM (U.S. Environmental Protection Agency, 1993); *Watershed '96: Achieving Results Community by Community: A National Satellite Video Conference* (U.S. Environmental Protection Agency, June 8–12, 1996); Meridian Institute, *Final Report of the National Watershed Forum* (Arlington, Va., 2001); Michael Houck, "Bankside Citizens," in *Rivertown: Rethinking Urban Rivers*, edited by Paul Stanton Kibel (MIT Press, 2007), pp. 179–96, 186.

$6 million in public involvement and education funding to more than three hundred projects and served as a clearinghouse for a broad range of other grants available through the National Oceanic and Atmospheric Administration, Sea Grant, the U.S. Fish and Wildlife Service, the National Fish and Wildlife Foundation, Washington State environmental agencies, and other organizations.

Some individual local programs have larger funds as well, such as the Long Island Sound Study's Futures Fund, which aggregates funding from many different sources. The EPA has also provided support for Restore America's Estuaries, a national coalition of citizen groups providing leadership for the estuary restoration movement, though the coalition's major regrant program, available to groups in all 130 estuaries, has been funded through the Restoration Center of the National Oceanic and Atmospheric Administration's National Marine Fisheries Service (authorized by the Estuary Restoration Act of 2000 and the Magnuson-Stevens Fishery Conservation and Management Reauthorization Act of 2006). Restoration through these and similar grants typically involves citizens directly in thousands of hours of hands-on public work: planting trees for riparian buffers on streams or eelgrass in the estuary, removing nonnative species, installing fish ladders or weirs, restoring beach nesting areas, raising oysters in schools and transplanting them to the bay.[19]

The Clean Water Action Plan of 1998, developed by the EPA in conjunction with seven other federal agencies and the Tennessee Valley Authority, helped broaden the agency's approach to building the capacity of watershed groups. With funding provided by this plan, the EPA selected the River Network to administer a Watershed Assistance grant program, similar in many ways to the small grants for estuaries. Established in 1988, the River Network had become the nation's premier national network of (freshwater) watershed groups, with two hundred and eighty dues-paying local partners a decade later and some seven hundred today, plus several thousand others in its far-flung network reach. It is chief sponsor of the watershed movement's annual River Rally, at once a grassroots training conference, national strategy meeting, and uplifting movement celebration. It has also developed and maintains the national directory of water conservation groups. From the mid-1990s, the River Network's strategic vision has been to help establish robust watershed organizations capable of forming effective local and state partnerships for monitoring, protection, and restoration on each of two thousand major watersheds across the country, especially through statewide organizations in every state—of which there are now several dozen nationwide. In the late 1990s, its regional watershed innovators workshops provided intensive learning from statewide networks and agency programs and helped establish the identity of the watershed movement with the civic goal of watershed democracy.[20]

The Watershed Assistance grant program further enabled the River Network to leverage this learning and expand its network further, as the applications for funding—775 in the first year alone—far outran both EPA and River Network expectations, not to mention available dollars. The grants enabled groups to develop their capacities to do watershed assessment and planning, build sustainable organizations and multistake-holder partnerships, educate the general public, and perform work that made visible improvements to watersheds. Capacity building, and not just project work, however, was the main focus. While the River Network raises dues and consulting fees from its partner organizations and grants and endowments from various private donors, the EPA and other government agencies have been indispensable sources for building the network's long-term capacities.[21]

When the Watershed Assistance grant program ended, the Targeted Watershed Initiative grants program—which funds a variety of innovative partnerships, nominated by governors (or tribal officials) in a competitive process—set aside funding for three national capacity-building intermediaries (the River Network, the Center for Watershed Protection, and the International City/County Management Association), along with two regional ones (the Southeast Watershed Forum and the University of Alaska, Anchorage), also chosen competitively. Together, they provided training during the first two years for more than two hundred watershed groups and several thousand other professionals and local officials. In 2006 this set-aside for capacity building was more than doubled on an annual basis (from $.7 million a year to $1.6 million a year over the three-year period from 2003 to 2006, though it has recently faced cuts). The River Network has continued to leverage this EPA funding to attract additional resources from foundations and state agencies to begin building an integrated national training and support system. This Watershed Support Network— with six pilot states (Colorado, New Mexico, Wisconsin, Ohio, West Virginia, and Kentucky) and a broad range of statewide watershed and related networks, institutional partners, several state agencies, and the U.S. Department of Agriculture's Cooperative State Research Education Extension Service as of 2007—promises far more comprehensive skill assessment and training for sustainable watershed work than ever before.[22]

As a result of the Clean Water Action Plan, the EPA also designated $100 million extra in section 319 grants for states to use in watershed work (with a federal-to-state match ratio of 60 to 40). Of course, only a fraction of this goes to building civic capacity, but it has helped states with watershed forum funding, participatory planning, public education, and hands-on restoration work. Recognizing that the agency's current budget constraints limit how much direct funding can go to watershed groups, the Office of Wetlands, Oceans, and Watersheds' Watershed Financing Team has begun to provide much greater assistance with tools and training to help groups become more financially sustainable. Here the experience of the local programs under the National Estuary Program has been critical, because the NEP has required programs to account for how much funding they have been able to leverage with federal dollars. In addition, the EPA's university-based network of environmental finance centers has developed webcast courses on financing for the Watershed Academy, as has the River Network, which were first aired in early 2006 to hundreds of participants.[23]

These investments in capacity building have not always come easily. As Richard Fox, founder of the Colorado Watershed Assembly and a River Network partner, noted in 2006, "We had to push very hard with EPA for training . . . not the types of training *they* think we need, but the kinds that the watershed groups themselves think we need. . . . And we have had to hammer them on how much more resources are needed. We could easily add another zero [that is, multiply by ten] to the set aside."[24]

Diane Regas, a former director of the Office of Wetlands, Oceans, and Watersheds, provided the critical agency leadership, according to Fox. Alert to the grassroots concerns that had emerged from the regional watershed roundtables and the National Watershed Forum in 2001, Regas was unwilling to shy away from hard truths that she thought her staff needed to hear. She thus convened two watershed dialogues, one in Washington, D.C., in January 2005 and the other at the river rally in Colorado later that spring. At the headquarters meeting, about twenty leaders from the watershed movement met with ten or so EPA watershed staff; another thirty or so Office of Wetlands, Oceans, and Watersheds staff listened on the periphery of the conference table. Staff sought feedback on the tools they had been developing, such as the web-based watershed planning tool, and on how to make the TMDL program—which calculates the total maximum daily load of a pollutant allowed under water quality standards—serve integrated watershed strategies. But as Fox put it, with dramatic flair, "Diane sicced us on them! They didn't talk at us, but really listened. From that we got a critical mass of people at Office of Wetlands, Oceans, and Watersheds behind what we were saying. And after that we got a good hearing with [assistant administrator for water] Ben Grumbles."[25]

Catalyzing Network Learning

As DeWitt John has so presciently argued, civic environmental innovation depends on the emergence of horizontal learning networks that can develop and test practical knowledge across institutional and professional boundaries.[26] One should not, however, underestimate the direct and intentional role that the EPA itself has played in nurturing such networks. While not alone among federal environmental agencies in this regard, the EPA has made critical contributions to catalyzing learning among extensive networks of watershed groups, schools and universities, professional scientists, and regulators across the federal system. Watershed movement networks for technical and organizational training, deliberative planning, and hands-on restoration work have received critical support from the EPA in multiple ways. The development of the field of volunteer water quality monitoring, essential to both regulatory programs and place-based ecosystem strategies, exemplifies how the agency has become a catalyst for network learning.

Local groups, of course, have always provided the driving force for volunteer monitoring. From the late 1960s onward, citizens who were frustrated by inadequate local data for their particular stream or lake, or who felt suspicious of information from public agencies, began to generate their own data through hands-on monitoring. National groups, such as the Izaak Walton League, provided assistance with rudimentary testing equipment and methods manuals as early as 1969. But much of this work remained technically primitive, and the league's Save Our Streams program, despite the organization's four hundred or so local chapters, was moribund when Karen Firehock took over in 1984. The young Firehock, who initially took the job because she could not afford to stay in college full time, began by answering a huge backlog of mail from local groups. She then proceeded to raise foundation money to enable the Department of Natural Resources in Ohio, which had quite a few "Ike" chapters, to hire a volunteer monitoring coordinator to respond to the requirements of the Scenic Rivers program. The state provided the biologists, who contributed significantly to the technical sophistication of the sampling of macroinvertebrates ("bugs" measures) conducted by Save Our Streams.

Firehock and the local trainers and volunteers, however, helped modify some of the biologists' own methods and added to the skill set with "local knowledge." The professionals' training, she notes, was often "too narrow. . . . Their field skills were not as good as the volunteer monitors. They were used to having all day and a scope. . . . We are always looking at the big picture, and they often missed connections and had to call in other specialists." One certified local trainer hired by Save Our Streams insisted that volunteers supplement collecting samples with "the six-pack method. You take a six pack of beer, go sit on the porch, and have a conversation." (Of course, Firehock adds, a public official is not permitted to do this!) The importance of local knowledge needed to continually be driven home. That monitoring is not just about samples was vividly demonstrated during a volunteer training several years later. As Firehock recalled,

> I was telling them to talk to the old timers. "Some have lived on these creeks their whole lives. Ask them where they dump their trash." And just then, two elderly men came out of the woods and told the group that old railroad ties with arsenic were buried over there, where they were pointing. The volunteers said I had planted these guys! But I insisted, "No!" And I really didn't![27]

What enabled Firehock and her tiny staff to bring this model from Ohio to Virginia, West Virginia, Tennessee, Louisiana, and then to many other states, however, was EPA funding and technical assistance that became available to states and estuary programs through the Clean Water Act amendments of 1987. Although volunteer monitoring was mentioned nowhere in the act, staff in the newly created National Estuary Program recognized its importance, as did those administering the nonpoint-source (section 319) grants, which have a major educational component. In 1987 the EPA's certification of the Chesapeake Bay Citizens Monitoring Program's quality assurance project plan lent official legitimacy to volunteer monitoring, and the 1989 guidelines for the biannual 305(b) state reports explicitly identified it as a potential source of data. But ideas mattered as well. As Rebecca Hanmer, the EPA's point person on Capitol Hill for the 1987 amendments, who later served as acting assistant administrator for water in 1988–89, noted, the EPA "periodically convened blue-ribbon panels on monitoring and always concluded that there was never enough money for robust [that is, professional] monitoring. But some of us in the Office of Water had a Jeffersonian model in mind. Don't forget, I was trained as a political scientist."[28]

Through EPA support, other citizen monitoring organizations entered the field or brought their work to the national level, such as the River Watch

Network in New England (now part of the River Network). The EPA, with much guidance from volunteer monitoring leaders, began developing a strategy to catalyze learning through interlocking networks at every level of the federal system. Its strategy has included a variety of components.

First, in 1988 the EPA began to sponsor biennial national citizen monitoring conferences, in conjunction with a set of rotating national and regional partners, such as the Izaak Walton League and the Alliance for Chesapeake Bay. These conferences were enormously spirited gatherings— "the Mecca for information sharing," in the words of Seba Sheavly, who previously oversaw the Ocean Conservancy's training program for volunteer monitoring. In addition, the conferences enabled citizen groups, state officials, professional scientists, and equipment vendors to build face-to-face relationships that helped them to learn from one another more directly. The EPA's regional offices sponsored similar trainings. With budget cutbacks, the national volunteer conferences became less frequent, and in 2004 the seventh conference, in Chattanooga, merged into the interagency National Water Quality Monitoring Council's biennial conferences. While the council's meetings have much less of a movement-building atmosphere, they provide even greater interaction among the volunteer and professional monitoring communities and thereby further legitimate the work of citizens.[29]

Second, to help build networks for learning, the EPA sponsored a periodic national survey and directory of volunteer monitoring groups. In addition to providing a valuable overview of the emerging field, especially in its critical first decade, the directory fostered ongoing horizontal communication among local groups across states and regions.[30]

Third, the EPA has funded the publication and distribution of the *Volunteer Monitor,* a national newsletter of volunteer watershed—originally, water quality—monitoring. Eleanor Ely, who edited the proceedings of the first two biennial conferences and developed the national directory, made a proposal to the EPA to edit a newsletter in conjunction with a rotating citizens group that had developed innovative technical methods and metrics, as well as strategies for mobilizing and training volunteers and students and for building sustainable partnerships among civic groups and public agencies. A microbiologist working in medical and research laboratories in the 1980s, Ely had switched careers to become a writer and editor for Rhode Island Sea Grant at the University of Rhode Island, home of an ambitious volunteer monitoring program. After working on the initial issue of the *Volunteer Monitor* with Adopt-a-Beach in Seattle, she began editing the newsletter from San Francisco. She assembled an editorial board drawn from leading national, state, local, and university-based monitoring groups, from state agencies, and from the EPA itself. Using lists from Save Our Streams, the River Watch Network, and other groups, as well as EPA lists of local and state government staff across the country, she quickly developed a print distribution of ten thousand, which has since grown to twice that size, in addition to the *Volunteer Monitor*'s availability on the EPA website.

For Ely, the editorial meetings served as an opportunity to build regional networks, since the editorial group for each issue was expected to convene other citizen monitors and coordinators from the area to plan the issue and contribute articles. Budget cutbacks eventually restricted Ely's travel, though she continues to view her meticulous editorial work through the lens of a civic network builder. With continued EPA support (in 2005 a mere $70,000 a year), the *Volunteer Monitor* serves as the hub of a decentralized network of citizen groups and state programs, where professional practitioners and lay citizens share best practices in a way that creatively melds laboratory science and local knowledge. With a master's degree in medical microbiology, Ely confesses, "I was incredibly ignorant when I first began. I didn't know that macroinvertebrates were bugs! I had no idea what nutrients were. I knew nothing about policy, the Clean Water Act, or regulations. But all the folks in the network, the Ph.D. scientists and policy people on the editorial board, the local groups and volunteer coordinators, and Alice Mayio [the EPA's volunteer monitoring coordinator] helped me learn." Such learning has generated what is arguably the most distributed network form of "street science" existing nationwide today.[31]

A fourth component of the EPA's learning network strategy has been its sponsorship of the development, publication, and distribution of a broad array of methods manuals by civic and watershed groups, from the Alliance for Chesapeake Bay and the Ocean Conservancy to River Watch Network and the League of Women Voters Education Fund. Volunteer water-monitoring manuals now cover the full range of estuaries, wetlands, lakes, streams, wellheads, and urban water systems.

The Ocean Conservancy's *Volunteer Estuary Monitoring* provides a good sense of the meticulous combination of technical knowledge and civic practice represented by the EPA's collaborative work with some of these organizations and their local partners. Developed in partnership, this 396-page methods manual covers all manner of project planning, organizing volunteers, managing safety, and testing the broadest spectrum of nutrients, oxygen, toxins, alkalinity, temperature, salinity, turbidity, bacteria, submerged aquatic vegetation, and other living organisms. The process for developing the manual, however, is as significant as the product. Since 1998, with EPA funding, the Ocean Conservancy had been conducting regular trainings for local networks of volunteer groups in all twenty-eight NEPs—some six hundred groups in all as of 2005. As Sheavly noted, EPA support has "enabled us to operate as a network builder where some activity already exists. We train [volunteer groups] in data collection [and] technical methods but also in fundraising, organization, and media presentations so that the data can be presented to the public in understandable formats. And the Ocean Conservancy is enriched by their work as well. These are all shared resources."

During development of the manual's second edition, the Ocean Conservancy worked with experts in each technical area of monitoring and shared the draft with all the local groups it had trained over the previous two-year period. Prominent volunteer monitoring organizations around the country contributed case studies. The final draft was reviewed by a broad array of leading practitioners from these groups, as well as from universities and extension services, local and state agencies, EPA regional and headquarters offices, and the U.S. Fish and Wildlife Service—most of whom had developed long-term relationships through EPA-sponsored activities. From local knowledge and organizing methods on one end to laboratory science and rigorous quality assurance technique on the other, this network has produced and refined a form of democratic knowledge indispensable to the stewardship of estuaries throughout the country.[32]

STATE CAPACITY BUILDING FOR VOLUNTEER MONITORING. State agencies were initially quite skeptical of volunteer monitoring, and perhaps one-third of them remain so. Hesitation and sometimes outright opposition arise from a variety of sources. First and foremost, agencies are generally prone to trust their professional staff more than lay citizens. In addition, states with few professional monitors can feel that volunteer monitoring jeopardizes their capacity to perform core regulatory functions because it adds to their management burdens and raises quality assurance problems. Some resist sharing section 319 funds with citizen groups or see a threat to their jobs should volunteer monitoring spread, and some states simply do not want citizen groups uncovering problems that could be politically contentious, as well as costly to correct. However, most states have come to embrace volunteer monitoring because they recognize it as a cost-effective way to address data requirements of the Clean Water Act. They simply cannot generate the needed quantity, type, and quality of data otherwise.

Agency grants to the states, especially from the nonpoint-source program, have been critical to building capacity, and off-the-shelf data management systems have recently begun to dramatically lower the costs of
collection, integration, reporting, and use. The volunteer monitoring office
at the EPA has rigorously addressed the issues of quality assurance with the
full collaboration of the quality assurance staff—"a bunch of sticklers, if
ever there were ones," in the words of one EPA administrator. "There is
always a struggle for dollars [for volunteer monitoring]. But no one [at
headquarters] ever resisted due to the data quality issue or because volunteer monitoring was a threat to regulatory functions." With guidance on
quality assurance from EPA headquarters and required regional office
approval of a state quality assurance project plan as a condition for receiving funds, states have become generally enthusiastic about volunteer monitoring, and some quite innovative.[33]

In New Jersey, for instance, some form of volunteer monitoring has
existed since 1992, and the state has offered training workshops in visual
and biological stream assessments to volunteer monitors since 1998. However, the state's Department of Environmental Protection was never quite
sure where such monitoring fit until it began to implement a watershed
approach. Education and outreach manager Kerry Kirk Pflugh, who as a citizen in her own community directed one of several dozen watershed associations in the state, realized that her own group's data were not being used by
the very state agency for which she worked, even though her volunteers had
followed the same protocols and had been trained by the very same professionals. She then appointed Danielle Donkersloot, one of her trainers, as the
first full-time statewide volunteer monitoring coordinator to help better
align volunteer work and agency use. Donkersloot did this by first organizing the statewide Water Watch Network, including professional monitors,
volunteer program coordinators, citizen monitors, water resource managers,
scientists, and instructors. She met with them as a group in Trenton
bimonthly and exchanged e-mails weekly as she attempted to build greater
trust between citizens and the agency.

Donkersloot also met with staff in five programs under the Department
of Environmental Protection that she identified as potential users of volunteer monitoring data (nonpoint-source grant program, section 319[h]
grants program, Watershed Assessment Team, TMDL workgroup, and
Watershed Planning Bureau). She asked them to specify the kinds of data
they could and would use from these groups, slowly building trust among
agency skeptics by responding to their concerns about data quality as well

as potential hidden agendas of citizen groups. In this sense, she served as an intermediary of trust in ways similar to the neighborhood planning project managers in Seattle.

Donkersloot drew freely from the national volunteer monitoring network and located an appropriate four-tier data model from neighboring Pennsylvania. Tiers A through D represent increasing levels of scientific rigor and quality assurance, recognizing the broad range of data and methods that ordinary citizens and students might collect and use in their own communities for various purposes. But she went further and linked specific data-collection protocols to specific responses by the state's Department of Environmental Protection. The section 319(h) grants program can use big-picture information, such as whether or not a riparian buffer is present. Visual assessment data can be used by the TMDL workgroup and the watershed planning bureau for such issues as fecal coliform and the presence of large numbers of geese. "The tiers are very appealing to the regulators," Donkersloot noted. "The fact that they can put each group's data into this or that box eases everyone's concerns."

Participants at the annual statewide volunteer monitoring summits have been enthusiastic, since the four-tiered classification system acknowledges the diversity of ways that citizens can act as vigilant monitors and responsible stewards—not all had to be equally rigorous and well trained—and because the commitment of specific state programs to use appropriate data further motivated their engagement and collaboration. Citizen ownership of the process of generating knowledge has extended even to the development of new statewide standards. As Donkersloot recalled, trout fisherman Ross Kushner of the Pequannock River Coalition "went through hell getting the department to use [coalition] data" on water temperature and trout kills before the introduction of the tiered model. Fishermen's local knowledge had never been part of the policy or regulatory process. But the group's use of sophisticated probes with downloadable data that qualified for Tier D convinced the state to introduce such monitoring on all rivers and to include temperature as a TMDL measure. It also convinced the City of Newark, which exercises water rights on the Pequannock, to alter its water release practices. As Donkersloot notes, without the initiative of the citizen group, "[the Department of Environmental Protection] wouldn't have ever known there was a problem."[34]

State programs, of course, vary considerably along many dimensions. Some are centralized, with the state agency playing the key role in funding, training, and data management for local volunteer groups. Other states use their funding and expertise to support networks of local, regional, and statewide citizen groups, often with state university and cooperative extension service partners. Some provide little or no support at all. While most states recognize the importance of volunteer monitoring to public education, only some integrate it into watershed planning, restoration activity, and regulatory functions. Some invest much more heavily than others in quality assurance, and some have far more sophisticated data management systems than others. Alabama, for instance, spends a considerably greater proportion of its volunteer monitoring funds on quality assurance than some neighboring states. Its multifunctional database, however, combines the requirements of quality assurance and quality control with direct data entry by volunteers—including real-time, multiyear data graphing—and public access to data by multiple variables. States also vary on the amount and types of training they provide or require and the types of assessment tools they support.[35]

YOUTH CAPACITY BUILDING FOR VOLUNTEER MONITORING. The EPA's environmental education division has complemented the Office of Water's volunteer monitoring program in important ways, since much environmental education in schools, nature centers, and youth organizations, such as YMCAs and 4-H clubs, involves hands-on service learning on water quality. In 1990 Congress passed the Environmental Education Act to bring greater coherence and support to building this emerging field in a strategic way. The new office provided grants to schools, universities, nonprofits, and state and local governments to develop programs and curriculums, and it established and funded several new institutional mechanisms for network learning and capacity building across the field. The National Environmental Education and Training Foundation, chartered and funded by Congress as a nonprofit, leverages additional private funds to build the field. The National Environmental Education Advisory Council, a citizen body that advises the EPA, assesses the field and reports to Congress. The Environmental Education and Training Partnership, funded through a cooperative agreement with the EPA, is a consortium of national associations of educators, innovative projects, and university centers providing training and leadership development to educators and assisting in building state associational program capacity (for example, the Environmental Education Association of Washington, an active participant in the Puget Sound Partnership). The consortium also assists with the development of professional certification, quality assurance, and program evaluation so that environmental education is scientifically accurate, pedagogically sound, and responsive to community needs.

A core partner in the Environmental Education and Training Partnership has been the North American Association for Environmental Education (NAAEE), the premier network in the field. Founded in 1971 by a group of U.S. community college educators, the NAAEE gradually expanded its individual and institutional membership base and then became trinational in 1983, extending to Canada and Mexico. Elaine Andrews, former president and executive director of the NAAEE, managed its growth in the years after the Environmental Education Act and during its five years (1995–2000) as lead partner of the Environmental Education and Training Partnership. At our Engaging Youth in Environmental Action and Restoration national strategy conference in March 2002, Andrews noted that "EPA support has been absolutely essential to building the field as a whole, as well as to NAAEE itself." As many other environmental education leaders have confirmed, grants from the EPA and the National Science Foundation enabled the NAAEE to do critical long-range planning to expand its member services in 1990, and its five-year, $9 million EPA grant to coordinate the Environmental Education and Training Partnership enabled it to develop its own training capacity and that of state environmental education associations and networks. The NAAEE's annual conference has become the premier venue for sharing best practices across state, national, and international networks.[36]

The EPA, of course, has not been alone among federal agencies in providing support for volunteer monitoring, nor has it served as a prime mover among states or citizen groups. The Cooperative Extension System, housed in the U.S. Department of Agriculture, has played an ambitious role since its 1992 national water quality initiative and especially with its Volunteer Monitoring National Facilitation Project, which seeks to build a comprehensive system of support through land-grant universities. But the EPA has played an indispensable role in catalyzing learning through the many local, state, and national associational and professional networks that have come to constitute a relatively well integrated field. Over two decades the agency has strategically deployed its assets—grants, technical assistance, quality assurance oversight, legitimacy, and convening role—to enable ordinary citizens to share in the core work of generating the usable knowledge needed for active protection and restoration of watersheds. As Sheavly of the Ocean Conservancy noted, "[the] EPA has created the chassis for the truck. The [volunteer monitoring] groups have provided the wheels."[37]

Superfund and Environmental Justice

Developing workable approaches to civic participation in the Superfund and environmental justice programs has presented particular challenges to the EPA because of the highly contentious nature of the underlying issues. Superfund was established in 1980 as a massive hazardous waste–cleanup program in the wake of the incendiary revelations of Love Canal and widely publicized threats to homes and family health across the nation. A rising antitoxics movement fueled the flames, and a flawed policy design made reasonable community deliberation on risks and remedies difficult to achieve. When rising antitoxics sentiment was reinforced by evidence of racial disparities across a wide spectrum of issues (siting of landfills and incinerators, extent and pace of remediation, differential health impacts), the mix became even more volatile. The resulting environmental justice movement of the 1990s offered an even more profound challenge to business as usual. Nonetheless, the EPA has managed to learn from these contentious challenges and has progressed significantly in building capacity for collaborative work with citizens, including many of the most militant grassroots activists.

Superfund

The Comprehensive Environmental Response, Compensation, and Liability Act of 1980, widely known as Superfund because of the large amounts of money provided for cleanup, included few provisions for formal public participation in the cleanup process. Drawing upon the experience of participatory water-planning projects of the 1970s, however, the original community relations team brought substantial practical wisdom to the task and was notably prescient about the contours of the emerging antitoxics movement.[38] Nonetheless, the rising contentiousness manifest in relations between the EPA and communities in the ensuing years would require a determined effort to reverse. Several factors contributed to the difficulties.

First, President Reagan's initial appointees at Superfund were hostile to citizen participation—indeed, to the Superfund program itself—and disrupted the community relations team in its efforts to develop workable, deliberative procedures on the ground. Second, even when good-faith efforts were made to repair the damage after Ruckelshaus returned to head the agency in 1983 and a new director was appointed to Superfund, community relations staff were ill equipped to engage communities constructively. They were subordinate to technical staff that generally expressed little interest in open dialogue. Opportunities for citizen input were delayed, discontinuous, and disconnected from actual decisions, even after the 1986 Superfund Amendments and Reauthorization Act provided for public notice and comment on cleanup plans. Thus at that time, many communities placed on the national priorities list for cleanup were given few opportunities for meaningful input until late in the cleanup process. This often bred deep distrust among local citizens who felt they were being deliberately kept in the dark.

Third, the very design of the program, especially its controversial liability schema, encouraged communities to see cleanup as a free good with no opportunity costs, thus predisposing many to uncompromising stances in favor of maximum remedies, even in cases where actual health risks were relatively low and less expensive remedies were available. The liability schema also encouraged corporate and other "potentially responsible parties" to litigate, thus leading to further delay, confusion, and conflict rather than visible progress in cleanup. If "cleaning up the mess," as one influential 1993 Brookings study put it, could be said to characterize not only the problem of hazardous waste but also the program designed to address it, finding more productive ways of engaging citizens would certainly have to be part of basic housekeeping.[39]

The agency made some clear, if slow, progress during the late 1980s and early 1990s in responding to problems of citizen participation. Even under inhospitable conditions, staff managed to learn from the field and begin to provide a fuller set of opportunities for engagement and trust building. One regional community involvement coordinator, with fourteen years of previous experience with the League of Women Voters (including two as a state legislative director), recalled that "we were just kind of inventing it as we went along. . . . It was kind of a rocky road, and there were many horribly painful public meetings."[40] Staff learned to build relationships through informal meetings with local civic leaders and activists and to understand the peculiarities of local history and context. They learned how to be more forthright and effective in communicating with citizens about comparative risks, criteria for selecting alternatives, financing options, and cleanup progress.

The Superfund Amendments and Reauthorization Act provided for technical assistance grants of $50,000 for community groups to hire their own experts to help them evaluate risks and options. Revisions in the *Community Relations Handbook* and staff training incorporated much of this learning, and the growing sophistication of risk communication theory and practice provided important resources. As Bruce Engelbert, who until his retirement in 2006 had been with Superfund from its beginning, put it, "There was a lot of contentious politics on the outside and also in the community involvement program itself. We were learning as we went along but became more focused and intentional only relatively recently."[41]

In 1995 reform of Superfund began in earnest and enabled the agency to develop a much more coherent and supportive approach to community deliberation. With the election of the Republican Congress in 1994 and the death of compromise reform legislation that had been working its way through the 103d Congress, EPA leadership under President Bill Clinton acted boldly on the administrative front to save the program. The agency began to facilitate fair-share allocations among potentially responsible parties and other measures to elicit greater corporate and small business cooperation in cleanup. In response to the critical question how clean is clean? the EPA began to permit consideration of reasonable cost of remedies, especially in view of prospective land uses that might permit "containment" rather than require "permanent" remedies. Thus if a parcel of land were likely to be redeveloped as an industrial rather than a residential or educational site, less expensive containment might be acceptable, especially if monitoring of leakage were maintained. A remedy review board contributed to the consistency and hence legitimacy of remedy selection. These and other administrative changes altered the overall context for reasoned deliberation and negotiation at the site level and enabled improved performance of the program as a whole, as Robert Nakamura and Thomas Church demonstrate in *Taming Regulation,* their tale of this surprisingly artful set of reforms.[42]

Investment in more effective participation among local citizens at Superfund sites was an essential part of these reforms. The Office of Community Involvement—previously Community Relations—was upgraded and expanded. Now called the Community Involvement and Outreach Branch, it has instituted several broad strategies to build trust, enhance the technical capacity of citizens, and develop the civic skills and management support of EPA street-level staff.

First, the EPA began to focus on forms of participation with the greatest potential to build trust. Staff had been groping toward this over a number of years, and a prominent scholarly study by Ellison Folk, published in *Ecology Law Quarterly* in 1991, clearly recommended a shift in emphasis to face-to-face relational work rather than large meetings—though, of course, public comment and open meetings remain essential at specifically defined points in the process.[43] Relationship building now takes various forms.

Community involvement coordinators, working out of EPA regional offices, are encouraged to conduct the required community interviews at
each site as early in the process as possible and to bring the remedial project manager or on-scene coordinator to some of these interviews, thus
ensuring more direct understanding of community concerns among the
top EPA management and contractor team. The range and number of
interviews vary, depending on the complexity of the site; the minimum is
generally twenty-five, but the number may run to one hundred or more.
Coordinators are expected to interview those contiguous to the site or in
the path of migration of toxics, of course, and many interviews occur in
citizens' homes.

But coordinators are also directed to interview local civic leaders, community activists, public officials, public interest groups, and even potentially responsible parties, where appropriate to ensure greater trust, shared
knowledge, cooperation, and participation. Interviews are designed to yield
local knowledge, clarify the specific cultural and demographic context of
fears, and provide an overall history of the community that might bear
upon the development of a formal community involvement plan (required
at all sites) as well as future choice of remedies. Environmental justice principles guide outreach to minority and other communities that may be marginalized from participation or bear an inordinate burden of hazards. These
community interviews represent a version of one-on-ones but with specific
guidelines (for example, strict confidentiality) to protect citizens in a context defined by administrative power—and often by fierce intracommunity
contention as well.

Independent community advisory groups, which exist at a growing
number of sites, are also designed to build trust and long-term relationships among diverse civic actors in a community, such as neighborhood
and tenant associations, environmental groups, churches and senior
groups, and professional and business associations. Community advisory
groups yield site-specific civic leadership for all phases of the cleanup
process, from problem identification to remedy, and seek to generate trust
between citizens and the EPA through continuous working relationships
and knowledge sharing rather than just periodic public meetings. While
the EPA can provide administrative support for such groups, it is not itself
a member. Whether or not a community advisory group exists, coordinators are encouraged to conduct informal one-on-ones in coffee shops, focus
groups, house meetings, and other small gatherings to facilitate open and
trustworthy communication. As one EPA regional coordinator noted, "In

earlier days, some relationships were simply beyond salvaging. . . . I can give you some examples of spectacular failures, but none recently. We seem to be finding a way to muddle through. . . . But even now, although we seek to build trust, or at least grudging acceptance [of what is ultimately an EPA decision], we say to the community, 'you don't need to trust us, just hold us accountable.'"[44]

Region 1 in New England exemplifies how management invested in building community participation and trust. Beginning in 1995 under the leadership of regional administrator John DeVillars, Region 1 energetically began to transform agency culture to support community-based, multimedia pollution prevention and other forms of innovation and collaboration, recognizing that "protecting the environment is everyone's job"—echoing the familiar coproduction motto from Chicago's community policing program. Speaking at the Quinnipiac River Symposium at Yale University in 1998, DeVillars described the goal of "culture change [as] reorienting ourselves, reinventing ourselves to be a different kind of institution . . . [and changing] our enterprise into a force for education and empowerment."[45] The Clean Charles by 2005 campaign was one example of this culture change strategy to develop performance-based, accountable civic partnerships. For Superfund, the region recruited several staff with community organizing backgrounds, and DeVillars and his deputy, Mindy Lubber, who succeeded him as regional administrator in 2000, provided them with strong, direct support.

Jim Murphy, for instance, had more than twenty years of community organizing experience—in poor black communities in the South, among senior citizen groups and energy activists in the Northeast—before coming to the EPA in 1997. Murphy is forthright in seeing his role as community involvement coordinator as "agitator, enabler, and citizen coach," at once stirring people up about key issues likely to emerge at a given Superfund site but also being "as up front and blunt as possible when citizens have unrealistic expectations." He builds relationships at each of his assigned sites—six or seven of the twenty-five are active at any given time—through tireless door knocking and one-on-one meetings, and he works to build consensus among the broad range of community actors. Over time, he has become an integral and respected member of the site teams, though not without struggle. At one point, Murphy recalled, he put it to DeVillars directly:

> "So, if the attorneys, the project manager, and the engineers are opposed to it [the plan emerging among the community], do I lose?"

And DeVillars said, "Not necessarily. You represent me." You see, [community involvement] is in the [regional administrator's] office as part of public affairs. And Mindy and John would always say, "Give me a call if there is a problem with the technical staff." They didn't just want technical staff making the decisions. And they didn't want to get surprised by the community [with a big political embarrassment].

But Murphy earns his trust within the site teams by getting the community to deliberate seriously about the hard issues: "Everyone at first wants a Cadillac. But I ask them, 'If the Cadillac will cost $40 million and we now have only $10 million budgeted, are you willing to get in line and wait ten years? Who pays the extra $30 million? Will it be you, the taxpayer?' The vast majority recognizes the reasonableness and common sense of cost-effective remedies after you have built honest relationships with them." At the Pine Street Barge Canal in Burlington, Vermont, the community advisory group rejected the EPA's proposed $50 million cleanup and, through a five-year consensus process, agreed upon a $4.3 million remedy, with potentially responsible parties committing an additional $3 million to improve the environment in the greater Burlington area. Even where, as in the case of Fort Devens, the community imposed remedy overkill as a kind of payback for such a bad history of stonewalling from the military, "there is now a very sophisticated group of citizens who see that the next phase can be more efficient. They are not asking for the Cadillac. They are capable of learning with us."[46]

To be sure, for any given site the mix of regulatory backstops, private redevelopment incentives, and public participation opportunities promoting trust through a shared information culture can vary widely and affect remediation pathways considerably. Local political and civic culture play important parts, and EPA regional offices, as well as staff within any particular regional office, bring different levels of skill and commitment to the participation process.[47]

A second broad EPA strategy has been to invest in building the technical capacity of communities listed as Superfund sites, especially through technical assistance grants and the Technical Outreach Services for Communities (TOSC) program. Technical assistance grants were authorized under the Superfund Amendments and Reauthorization Act and since 1988 have amounted to some $20 million in overall funds to enable community groups to hire independent experts to help review preliminary site assessments and technical documents, interpret public health information, and inform choices on remedy. Though now being reorganized, the TOSC program has been part of a larger set of regional university consortiums known as the Hazardous Substance Research Centers, funded by the EPA and its academic, industry, state, and federal agency partners. (There are also similar TOSC centers for Native American and brownfield communities.) Technical Outreach Services for Communities has served communities beyond those listed as Superfund sites. Community groups could apply to a TOSC center for free, though not advocate, assistance in reviewing technical documents, understanding risks, communicating with the broader public, and developing leadership for ongoing problem solving and conflict resolution.

Independent of the EPA, TOSC centers have had the mission to "empower communities with an independent understanding of the underlying technical issues associated with hazardous substance contamination so that they may participate substantively in the decision-making process." Community groups sign memorandums of agreement with the TOSC center, committing them, as partners, to contribute local knowledge and time and recognizing the center's commitment to its nonadvocacy role in providing the best available technical advice. The outreach centers have chosen to work with some communities over others (given limited resources) on the basis of various criteria, including environmental justice and health hazards, the capacity of existing community organizations, and the potential for public education. The centers, in other words, have been engaged in ways that touch upon important normative questions and contentious issues but have done so in a way designed not to involve them as stakeholder or partisan advocate.[48]

A third and critical strategy for enhancing citizen participation in Superfund has been investment in the hiring, training, recognition, and management support of the community involvement coordinators themselves. The Community Involvement and Outreach Branch has been intentional about attempting to improve the capabilities of the approximately one hundred (as of 2005) coordinators in regional offices so that they can be more skillful and effective in working with communities. Training is now organized through Community Involvement University, an ongoing set of courses on a broad range of necessary skills and topics. These include basic facilitation of meetings, trust building and resolving differences, community culture and assets, cross-cultural effectiveness, risk communication, data collection and communication on cultural and economic impacts of Superfund sites, and working with the news media, among other topics.

The outreach branch initiated the annual conference of practitioners that in 1998, under Suzanne Wells's leadership, became the agency-wide Community Involvement Conference, where best practices are analyzed intensively across the agency and with leading civic practitioners and consultants. Some regional offices specifically recruit community involvement coordinators with prior grassroots experience in community organizing, VISTA, League of Women Voters, the Peace Corps, and similar groups, and they, in turn, become resources for other staff. The agency convenes senior regional community involvement managers in monthly calls to distill lessons and promote cross-fertilization.

The Community Involvement and Outreach Branch also works with top Superfund regional managers to ensure that they set clear expectations about the importance of public involvement in site cleanup and that site managers include community involvement coordinators as integral members of site teams. Highly visible awards are given annually at the site managers conference to those site managers who have done an especially effective job involving the public. Perhaps half of the site managers in Region 1 and Region 8, for instance, have come to genuinely recognize the value of public participation. The relative status and pay of community involvement coordinators have also risen over the years. As one regional manager noted, "The vast majority of the technical people [in our region] now see the value of [public participation], but not all. And we [community involvement advisers] have to guard against becoming simply cheerleaders for the community. . . . There is a natural and healthy tension between us and the technical staff, as with the legal folks."[49]

Environmental Justice

In October 1991 the National People of Color Environmental Leadership Summit, attended by some six hundred participants from all fifty states, signaled the official birth of the environmental justice movement. Under administrator William Reilly, the EPA began to give a hearing to the movement and to respond to statistical evidence of racial and economic disparities in risk and regulatory behavior. With two strong environmental justice proponents on Clinton's environment transition team and Carol Browner as the new administrator, the agency became considerably more systematic in analyzing racial disparities and promoting environmental justice as an administrative norm and policy goal. In 1994 Clinton issued Executive Order 12898 requiring each federal agency to make environmental justice part of its mission and established the federal Interagency

Working Group on Environmental Justice, composed of representatives of eleven federal agencies and chaired by the EPA, to develop strategies and model projects. He also created the National Environmental Justice Advisory Council (NEJAC) to provide a formal voice for the movement and other stakeholders across the federal government. Browner renamed the recently established environmental equity office the Office of Environmental Justice.[50]

Since the environmental justice movement takes much of its inspiration from the civil rights movement, it is no surprise that it has sought various legal and regulatory remedies, and with important achievements, such as fairer participation of communities of color in state permitting for hazardous waste sites, greater enforcement of existing laws, expanded legal resources for communities, heightened federal administrative scrutiny, and increasing numbers of state environmental justice statutes and programs.[51] But the EPA has also focused on how to engage communities more directly and in recent years has come to promote a collaborative community problem-solving model. This results from several factors.

First, administrative and legal remedies have revealed serious limits to administrators as well as local citizen groups. For the latter, legal action can take many years, consume inordinate organizational resources, and demobilize constituents, often only to lead to disappointment. Courts have systematically refused to apply Title VI of the 1964 Civil Rights Act against polluters without direct evidence of discriminatory intent, which is notoriously difficult to prove, especially in the face of competing explanations (relative land values, housing market dynamics, agglomeration economies in industry clustering) and scientific uncertainties (differential health impacts). The EPA has had little more success with such discriminatory intent claims than have community groups and activist lawyers, and its Title VI guidance has been met with considerable skepticism by the Conference of Mayors and the Environmental Council of the States. Congress has remained deeply skeptical, if not explicitly restrictive, and the Supreme Court has ruled in ways that limit invoking disparate impact.[52]

Second, key networks of the environmental justice movement, working within the multistakeholder policy forum of NEJAC, have concluded that on key issues such as cumulative risk and pollution prevention, a place-based collaborative approach can deliver substantial payoffs for communities most vulnerable to multiple and cumulative risk factors. Two NEJAC reports represent this self-described "paradigm shift," though some movement leaders still remain skeptical of both the specific components and the framework's endorsement by government—and, from a different angle, the amount of resources the agency has been willing to put behind it. In *Ensuring Risk Reduction in Communities with Multiple Stressors: Environmental Justice and Cumulative Risks/Impacts,* the NEJAC workgroup argues that, in the presence of multiple physical, chemical, biological, social, and cultural factors, which cumulatively and in the aggregate contribute to distinct vulnerabilities for low-income and minority communities, a multimedia, place-based approach can provide the most effective way to generate a "bias for action" that engages various stakeholders in making quick and tangible improvements. Tackling immediate risks and ones broadly recognized as real problems can enable local actors and institutions, including polluters, to build trust for addressing more difficult and contentious issues down the line. Residents can directly contribute to local health diagnoses and practical solutions through participatory action research and community health education campaigns.[53]

In the other report, *Advancing Environmental Justice through Pollution Prevention,* NEJAC makes a similar set of arguments. Pollution prevention strategies have advanced significantly in recent years through a broad range of initiatives in cleaner technologies and materials, energy efficiency and green building, transportation and land-use planning, and management and work systems. The Pollution Prevention Act of 1990 and a host of voluntary programs have encouraged this effort. To get the full benefit of prevention approaches at the community level, especially for those most vulnerable, however, would require far more intentional collaboration among civic organizations, environmental groups, small and large businesses, health departments, and other local government agencies. Building the capacity of local groups for multistakeholder collaboration, as well as broad public education to make pollution prevention an everyday habit, would require serious financial, technical, and programmatic support from both public agencies and private sources.[54]

It is important to reiterate that support for a collaborative community problem-solving framework around environmental justice has been driven by various community and movement leaders, albeit in a context where the EPA and NEJAC have created a framework for genuine learning among community groups, regional movement networks, industry representatives, academic scientists, public health experts, and administrators from various local, state, and federal agencies. Charles Lee, author of the formative United Church of Christ report on race and toxics wastes and a key organizer of the first environmental justice leadership summit, chaired the

NEJAC subcommittee that conducted public dialogues on brownfields and urban revitalization in five major cities in 1995, where strong support for asset-based community development emerged. In 1999 Lee went from movement leader to Office of Environmental Justice staff, playing a key role in the NEJAC reports on cumulative risk and pollution prevention, chairing the Interagency Working Group, and recently becoming director of the office. The Interagency Working Group developed the collaborative framework for environmental justice based upon a wide scan of the community-building field and a series of demonstration projects beginning in 2000; it also paid careful attention to the forms of community collaboration that had been emerging from grassroots environmental justice action over nearly a decade.

Given its multiagency composition, the working group was especially attuned not only to the enormous complexity of environmental justice problems (housing stock, transportation patterns, industry clusters, the siting of waste treatment facilities, children's health) but also to the limits of addressing such problems through the usual programmatic and regulatory stovepipes of its separate agencies. Communities clearly needed integrative strategies that worked on the ground and involved a broad range of stakeholders, including adversaries, even as those with the least formal power and at greatest risk may still have to mobilize and protest to bring others to the table. They also needed federal, state, and local agencies to provide the institutional supports for local collaboration.[55]

Various prominent environmental justice community and movement leaders contributed to these activities: Peggy Shepard of West Harlem Environmental Action, Wilma Subra of the Louisiana Environmental Action Network, Mary Nelson of Bethel New Life in Chicago, Connie Tucker of the Southern Organizing Committee for Economic and Social Justice, Tom Goldtooth of the Indigenous Environmental Network, Tirso Moreno of the Farmworkers Association of Florida, Donele Wilkins of Detroiters Working for Environmental Justice, and Bahram Fazeli from Communities for a Better Environment in California. These leaders in environmental justice drew upon their own experiences and those of dozens of other community groups that had developed local civic problem-solving and partnership strategies. Such strategies emerged as early as 1994, with the support of various small-grant programs from the Office of Environmental Justice and funding from other offices at the EPA and several other federal agencies, such as the National Institute of Environmental Health Sciences at the National Institutes of Health. The EPA's Office of

Pollution Prevention and Toxics, for instance, provided much relevant experience through its Design for Environment program, which used civic networking strategies among trade associations in various industries with large numbers of small, often ethnic, businesses (printing, dry cleaning, and auto body repairs), as well as through its intensive research pilot program, Community Partnership for Environmental Protection in South Baltimore, and its environmental justice and pollution prevention grants program.

Some NEJAC members also took to heart the poignant criticisms of policy scholars, such as Christopher Foreman Jr., that epidemiologic and community-based approaches to improving health in poor and minority communities were far more promising than regulatory ones. Given the strong pull of the original environmental justice frame and movement ethos toward an all-encompassing radicalism, this paradigm shift to a collaborative community problem-solving approach, though certainly still selective and incomplete, has been no small feat.[56]

The various small-grants programs under the Office of Environmental Justice have proved critical to EPA learning, though they have remained relatively modest in size. Even before the grants had an explicitly collaborative focus, community groups were developing innovative ways to use local knowledge and mobilize civic networks. Community development corporations engaged neighborhood youth to clean up lots, educate local residents, and conduct participatory planning for long-term remediation. Community health center professionals collaborated with local auto body repair shops to develop alternative work methods and safe disposal practices. On childhood lead poisoning and asthma, Head Start centers and statewide associations led broad community education campaigns. To assist community groups and local government agencies in risk communication and equity planning, students in historically black colleges and universities provided research. Small grants have also been available to watershed associations and volunteer monitoring networks, to enable them to incorporate principles and practices of environmental justice into their work, and to intermediary organizations, such as the Center for Neighborhood Technology in Chicago, that work with numerous kinds of community and small-business groups. Many other kinds of civic groups have become engaged in environmental justice work through the small grants: ethnic associations, tribal communities, migrant farmworker groups, YMCAs, 4-H clubs, American Lung Association chapters, and church groups.[57]

With the launching of two rounds of Interagency Working Group demonstration projects beginning in 2000 and then the Office of Environmental Justice's Collaborative Problem Solving Cooperative Agreements in 2003, projects have typically come to involve one or more local community or advocacy groups, in partnership with several larger institutions, such as health departments, medical centers, universities, environmental agencies, and chambers of commerce. The collaborative grants, in fact, require three signed memorandums of agreement from such partners, as well as more regular consultation and reporting and a greater emphasis on environmental results and sustainability than the small-grants program.

For example, Bethel New Life, a Lutheran-affiliated community development corporation that for more than two decades has used asset-based organizing and development strategies in the low-income African American West Garfield Park neighborhood of Chicago, began its environmental justice journey as a result of two issues, the discovery of a troublesome brownfield site and the announced closing of a main transit line running through the community. After successful coalition organizing (with several suburban communities) to preserve the transit line, Bethel turned to a set of partners to help with transit-oriented development, including a commercial center designed according to green building principles, clean energy, and a walkable community with homes clustered close to the transit stop. Other green businesses will complement Bethel's job development strategy through its successful employment center. Project partners include the Center for Neighborhood Technology and Neighborhood Capital Budget Group, which provide technical and financial assistance for local projects that empower residents, the Argonne National Laboratory, and the City of Chicago's transit, environment, and planning departments. Commonwealth Edison and the Illinois Department of Commerce and Community Development provide the photovoltaic cells that power the commercial center.[58]

Getting EPA support for a collaborative environmental justice model that empowers communities and recognizes their genuine contributions to knowledge and problem solving has not always come easily. Even some leading collaboration proponents in the environmental justice movement have had to sue and protest to get a voice at the table and recognize that they may again have to do so to continue to progress. Jason Corburn shows that in the 1990s Greenpoint-Williamsburg community groups had to press the EPA, as well as local and state agencies, to get them to pay attention to the lived experiences and everyday knowledge of numerous local ethnic groups.

Despite some skepticism on the particulars, however, the EPA not only followed through on its commitment to meaningful public participation in risk assessment—a position backed by the National Research Council and the Science Advisory Board—but also used contentious community demands to enhance its own agency learning in air toxics modeling and cumulative exposure, a strategy that continues to yield benefits in other parts of the agency's work.[59]

Community-Based Environmental Protection

As collaborative watershed and other approaches became increasingly common by the early 1990s, the first ambitious culture change strategy emerged within the EPA to provide greater institutional depth and direction. This strategy received support from various reports to Congress by the National Academy of Public Administration (NAPA). Under the rubric of community-based environmental protection, the strategy was designed by senior administrators under President Clinton and implemented through a new Office of Sustainable Ecosystems and Communities (OSEC). Although the office was dismantled in 1999 after its key political champion left the agency, the strategy has helped the EPA develop important capacities and a coherent frame for ongoing work. The Community Action for a Renewed Environment (CARE) grant program, initiated several years later, builds upon its institutional legacy while avoiding some of its pitfalls. Although the strategy has by no means been as successful in transforming agency culture and practice as hoped, it offers especially important lessons for further progress.

Edgewater, NAPA, and OSEC

In March 1994 the EPA's Ecosystem Protection workgroup met in Edgewater, Maryland, to draft the "Edgewater Consensus," a document calling for an increasingly place-driven focus to engage various federal, state, and local agencies, nongovernmental organizations, and businesses in collaborative action to protect and restore ecosystems. The group was led by Robert Perciasepi, assistant administrator of the Office of Water who had previously served as Maryland's secretary of environment, and David Gardiner, assistant administrator for policy, planning, and evaluation, who had been legislative director of the Sierra Club for the preceding decade. The EPA's deputy administrator, Robert Sussman, was also a signatory. Fred Hansen, who succeeded Sussman in October, became a key champion of community-based environmental protection over the next four years. While the stage for ecosystem collaboration had already been set under administrator William Reilly (1989–92), these Clinton appointees provided a new level of senior political support for a strategy that questioned the pollutant-by-pollutant approach.[60]

The emerging community-based environmental protection frame at the EPA received considerable support from several other prestigious networks within the environmental policy community. In 1994 Congressional Quarterly published *Civic Environmentalism: Alternatives to Regulation in States and Communities,* by DeWitt John, director of the Center for Competitive Sustainable Economies at the National Academy of Public Administration (NAPA), the most authoritative organization of its kind in the country. In April 1995, under John's direction, a NAPA panel issued its report to Congress, *Setting Priorities, Getting Results: A New Direction for the EPA,* which had been commissioned the previous year when the Democrats still controlled both houses. The report (followed by several others) credited the many achievements of command and control regulation since 1970 but proposed redefining the mission and operations of the EPA so that the agency would provide a different kind of leadership. The EPA would still set national priorities and goals and would continue to enforce some standards itself while overseeing state enforcement of others. However, the agency would shift much of the weight of its operations to enable state and local governments, diverse communities, organized stakeholders, and ordinary citizens to develop their own civic capacities for determining priorities and solving problems.

The report's model of "accountable devolution" would use EPA resources—local grants, technical assistance, and state-of-the-art, place-based information—to enable communities to develop effective multimedia strategies and to measure meaningful performance by results rather than by following rules. John brought to NAPA considerable experience in community and economic development in Colorado and was active in the Denver-based National Civic League networks (notably, John Parr, league president at the time, and Scott Fosler, league board member and executive director of NAPA). The initial NAPA panel included Marc Landy, coauthor of the influential 1990 book *The Environmental Protection Agency: Asking the Wrong Questions,* which made a compelling case for the agency to become a catalyst for civic deliberation and place-based problem solving.[61]

Working alongside NAPA in similar efforts was the prestigious Enterprise for the Environment working group, chaired by William Ruckelshaus, former EPA administrator who also served on the second NAPA panel on EPA reinvention. Members of the working group included other former EPA chiefs under both Democratic and Republican administrations (Douglas Costle under Jimmy Carter, Lee Thomas during Ronald Reagan's second term, and William Reilly under George H. W. Bush) and current deputy administrator Hansen as well as several governors, members of Congress, and environmental organization and industry leaders. Enterprise for the Environment's report made similar arguments on the centrality of civic environmentalism, with the workgroup's prominent civic innovators, such as Save The Bay in Rhode Island and The Nature Conservancy, taking the lead on this section. Several other prestigious reports also highlighted the importance of place-based collaboration and civic environmentalism, including ones by the President's Council on Sustainable Development, the Progressive Policy Institute, the Aspen Institute, and the Environmental Reform: Next Generation Project at Yale University. The stars had aligned. Innovative grassroots practice, cumulative agency experience, and substantial intellectual reframing and policy learning had provided an opportunity for new ways of working with citizens and communities.[62]

The Edgewater meeting set in motion a multipronged process of learning and capacity building to "align our policy, regulatory, institutional, and administrative infrastructure to support ecosystem protection . . . [and to] reorient the Agency's culture to facilitate a place-driven approach."[63] The process included a review of the EPA's existing community-based work with citizen groups and through its regional offices and local governments and an analysis of barriers (statutory, budgetary, informational, training) that would have to be systematically addressed. Catalyzing the effort was OSEC (in the Office of Policy, Planning, and Evaluation), set up in October 1995 with forty staff redeployed from various offices and some regional staff. The Office of Sustainable Ecosystems and Communities made substantial contributions in at least three interrelated ways: promoting and publicizing community-based environmental protection practices widely; nurturing networks across various program offices and regions; and developing a coherent frame for community-based work generally and agency culture change more specifically.

First, to explore and promote best practices, OSEC worked through the regional offices with various communities more and less intensively to help them develop capacity and to test the range of roles that the EPA might play. In some, the agency was the key convener of partnerships; in others, it provided funding for a local organization to facilitate meetings among stakeholders. In some, it supplied funds to hire local residents as community organizers and educators; in others, it offered mainly technical assistance, research, and data in a form that local communities determined to be most useful. Of course, the EPA mixed and matched various roles, in some cases dedicating significant staff and monetary resources, in others helping to leverage these from other agencies and private sources.

The office clearly understood that the EPA could not and should not play a direct role in all communities but that certain niche roles could contribute to local capacity building in important ways. In addition to specific community projects supported directly through OSEC, the office engaged key innovators within and outside the agency in a broad review of existing community-based environmental protection practices and cases, legal and assessment tools, and organizational resources in the public and nonprofit sectors. It then made these available in a widely used resource book that further contributed to building the field and establishing the legitimacy of the approach. William Painter, who before joining the EPA had worked for The Nature Conservancy, which was engaged in a broad range of ecosystem partnerships of its own, brought to OSEC his extensive networks among national conservation organizations.[64]

As a relatively small office at headquarters, OSEC understood from the beginning that its success would depend on nurturing community-based environmental protection networks within the main program and media offices, as well as within the regions. This marked its second major achievement. In some cases, such as the Office of Water, these networks had already grown fairly robust as a result of civic approaches going back over a decade; indeed, OSEC was partly staffed by redeployments from the Office of Water. In other offices, important pockets of receptivity or new approaches were emerging that would soon converge with community-based environmental protection efforts, such as brownfields and environmental justice. All regional offices appointed community-based environmental protection coordinators, who networked periodically through OSEC trainings and other events. Most regions were genuinely receptive, and a few, such as Regions 1, 8, and 10, became enthusiastic supporters.

In Region 8, seven staff took on the role of community-based environmental protection coordinators. They included several relatively senior staff, who received substantial support from regional administrator Bill Yellowtail, a Clinton appointee with a clear interest in ecosystems and regional reorganization. With its main office in Denver, Region 8 encompasses Colorado, Montana, North Dakota, South Dakota, Utah, Wyoming, and twenty-seven sovereign tribal nations. Because federal land ownership in these western states tends to elicit greater collaboration between the regional EPA office and other environmental agencies than exists in many other regions, Region 8 was more open to the ecosystem management agenda that the Clinton administration was pushing across all agencies. Within the newly organized Ecosystem Protection program in the region, Karen Hamilton (now chief of its water quality unit), Ayn Schmit (chief of its resource protection and stewardship unit), and Nat Miullo (revitalization coordinator) took the lead internally in team building and culture change and externally in developing watershed initiatives and ecosystem partnerships. With solid programmatic and technical backgrounds among them, they were somewhat insulated from the charges of many regulatory staff that community decisionmaking represented an abdication of agency authority or was "just a lot of fluff." Indeed, with much good humor, even as they seriously worked to convince other staff of the results that could be achieved through voluntary programs and partnerships, Hamilton and Schmit would alternately designate each other with the honorary title "Queen of Fluff."

To be sure, these regional staff were fully aware that the threat of enforcement, for example by the TMDL staff in Hamilton's unit, might be needed to elicit a form of collaboration that produced far greater results than the TMDLs alone could do. The environmental justice and pollution prevention programs in Region 8 have also helped transform the culture, as has the recruitment of younger staff with interdisciplinary university training, though there is still a good ways to go. Programs that were at first resistant, such as the Office of Air and Radiation, have begun to dedicate staff to community-based work and are now part of the national CARE program.

To build capacity for community-based collaboration, Region 8's ecosystem program supports the work of various intermediary organizations, such as the Colorado Watershed Assembly, the Colorado River Watch Network, and similar groups in the other states. It worked with the Center for Watershed Protection to produce the eleven-volume Urban Subwatershed Restoration Manual Series to enable communities to develop their own democratic restoration plans and to implement them through technically sophisticated public work. Of eight teams in the ecosystem program, the six staff on the ecosystem stewardship team work directly with watershed groups and partnerships as coaches to develop their leadership skills. Marc Alston, for instance, has worked in drinking water, Superfund, brownfields, and watersheds and uses the terminology of both community-based environmental protection and civic environmentalism. As he put it in 2004, before he left the EPA to work directly with the Colorado Watershed Assembly, "My coaching of watershed group leaders has evolved. . . . I came to realize that the sustainability of groups is related to the strength of their leaders. Leadership of a watershed group demands technical, facilitation, organizational, fundraising, and leadership skills." As a generalist who drew upon the technical expertise of his team, Alston provided "information, advice, coordination, advocacy, and networking." He helped with financial planning and obtaining resources from a wide variety of sources. He served as liaison between the EPA laboratory and watershed groups who use it for microbiological analyses, and he aligned this work with the Clean Water Act regulatory process.

Region 8 has also collaborated with national groups, such as the River Network, American Rivers, and The Nature Conservancy. *Natural News,* the newsletter of Region 8's ecosystem program, provides a window onto local, regional, and national innovations, trainings, awards, funding opportunities, information tools, and other resources as well as movement-building events such as the national 2005 River Rally in Keystone, Colorado. Articles are written by EPA field staff, who have built long-term relationships with local groups, and by local citizens. This government publication serves, in short, as a civic forum and catalyst for a far-flung learning network.[65]

The synergy among EPA Region 8 staff, watershed groups, and state agency officials is especially evident in Colorado. Responding to EPA framing and funding incentives, the Colorado Water Quality Control Division reorganized around the watershed approach in 1997 and established four regional (within-state) watershed coordinators. As a result, independently organized watershed groups, which numbered only six in 1996, grew quickly to forty by 1998 and then established the statewide Colorado Watershed Assembly as their coalition, which in turn has spurred growth to represent some sixty groups as of 2007. The assembly sponsors training and an annual conference; in October 2007 it collaborated on the Sustaining Colorado Watersheds Conference with a broad range of other civic groups, including AWARE (Addressing Water and Natural Resource Education) Colorado, the League of Women Voters of Colorado Education Fund, the Colorado Watershed Network, the Colorado Lakes and Reservoir Management Association, and the Colorado Riparian Association. The assembly also publishes an attractive and influential annual report on the state of Colorado's watersheds and the work of its watershed groups. It has lobbied successfully in the state house and collaborated with the state water conservation board and water quality control commission to create and manage a grant program for watershed groups funded through a state income tax refund check-off program, which in turn has been used by local groups as a match source for various federal grants. The legislation creating the watershed license plate does likewise and provides each watershed group with an added incentive to reach out to the local community.

While the assembly is governed by representatives of independent citizen groups, its committees include state and federal staff working together toward collaborative solutions. "Sometimes we have to push back hard against the good old boys in some of the agencies," said Richard Fox, assembly president from 2002 to 2005 and a former U.S. Forest Service employee during the "bad old days of the 1970s," when real partnerships were few and far between. "The head of [a powerful state board], for instance, continually referred to us as 'self-appointed watershed gurus.' And I was always tempted to tell him to kiss my you-know-what. . . . But we just kept showing up and talking the language of collaboration. And they loved it when we said this could minimize lawsuits." Region 8 staff and state watershed coordinators, in particular, have been "essential" to the assembly's work, Fox continued. "I trust them. They became real mensches. . . . They responded as people looking for solutions with the watershed groups. And besides, they helped organize the picnics. . . . The Colorado Watershed Assembly believes deeply in having fun . . . and celebrating our work in restoring the watersheds. We don't let ourselves be dragged down by just fighting the good fight."[66]

In addition to promoting best practices and fostering networks across the agency and into states and communities, OSEC's third key contribution before it was disbanded was to develop the EPA's *Framework for Community-Based Environmental Protection,* which defined the approach in much greater detail than ever before and raised its legitimacy considerably within the agency. The document was the product of an extensive set of deliberations that OSEC facilitated across the agency and its regions, among state, local, tribal, and regional governments, and among civic groups, professional and business associations, think tanks, and academic institutes. The process involved facilitated discussion sessions, a formal agency-wide review and comment period involving all EPA national and regional offices, a three-month external review and comment period, and meetings with selected senior managers to resolve key issues. As Amanda Tipton Bassow, a principal coordinator and author, recalled, "The collaborative process was really drawn out. [Deputy administrator] Fred Hansen had asked us for the *Framework,* and we probably should have delivered it sooner. But we wanted to walk the walk of genuine collaboration, to go slow and get it right."[67]

The *Framework* set out core principles, goals, and relative advantages of community-based environmental protection as well as how and when it might be applied, depending upon statutory requirements, ecological and human health risks, community needs and desires, and other agencies' roles. While clearly recognizing that community-based environmental protection was more appropriate under some circumstances than others, the *Framework* called for the EPA to *"integrate* [community-based environmental protection] *principles, goals, and measures into all areas of the Agency's business."* The *Framework* clearly distinguished community-based environmental protection from some versions of community-based work that were little more than public relations or an excuse to undermine regulatory authority and standards. It also sought to assuage suspicions that community opinion could trump the best available science and emphasized instead that scientific data and information be made available to all stakeholders and decisionmakers so that choices at all levels are better informed.

Critical to future progress, the *Framework* established specific strategic goals for building agency capacity to facilitate community-based environmental protection work and provided examples of specific performance measures that might be used to track progress. The latter included staff training, hiring, career tracks and rewards, information tools, and cross-media collaboration. The *Framework* fully recognized that the success of community-based work requires serious investment in human resources at the EPA to facilitate stakeholder involvement, holistic planning and assessment, consensus decisionmaking, and systems thinking. Tying the agency's mission to its role as civic educator, the *Framework* acknowledged that effective public communication skills were required for complex ecological issues. If citizens were to become informed and empowered stewards in their communities, there was simply no way to avoid major investments in EPA staff's own civic-related skill development.[68]

While these achievements of OSEC over a four-year period were substantial, they nonetheless fell short of aspirations. A major reason for this is that senior administrators were unable to secure funds for a grant program dedicated specifically to community-based environmental protection. Deputy administrator Hansen's February 15, 1995, memorandum to all assistant, associate, and regional administrators, calling for regional offices (where nearly half of EPA staff work) to dedicate 20 percent of their 1996 and 1997 fiscal year budgets to community-based environmental protection efforts, met a combination of outright resistance and creative re-description of existing programs—"rubber suiting," as OSEC staff called it. Over a five-year period in the mid-1990s when agency budgets were basically flat—the budget for fiscal year 1997 was still slightly less than for fiscal year 1993 in actual dollars—media offices resisted shifting funds away from programs defined by statutory mandates. A special community-based environmental protection fund was created for one year, but the process of getting offices to contribute proved so painful that it was discontinued. If the deputy administrator's budget memo signaled the first "policy disaster" for community-based environmental protection, the second big mistake was not making a stronger attempt to work with legislators. While the Gingrich Congress would admittedly have been a tough sell, it is not clear that the assistant administrator for policy, whose job it was to advise Congress and who supported community-based environmental protection, made a determined effort.[69]

DeWitt John, who worked directly on these issues through NAPA until 2000, saw more fundamental problems. Few senior managers who championed community-based environmental protection had a deep understanding of civic environmentalism, according to John, and Carol Browner, the EPA administrator, whose main constituency was the national environmental lobby, was clearly wedded to command and control. When Republicans in Congress attacked the EPA as rigid and working from the top down, Browner played defense. She viewed the NAPA reports to Congress as a problem to be managed rather than an opportunity to chart new pathways. And since she had so alienated agency staff by calling the EPA a mismanaged agency during her first week in office, Browner could not have led a culture change strategy toward community-based environmental protection had she wanted to. While critical of the top leadership, John did not believe that different leaders would have ultimately made a difference during the Gingrich Congress. Ruckelshaus, head of the EPA in two Republican administrations, whose Enterprise for the Environment project was working in parallel with NAPA, also failed to make much headway in getting congressional support for civic environmentalism.[70]

Deputy administrator Hansen, a champion of community-based environmental protection, left the agency in 1998, and OSEC was dismantled the following year. With networks that had been strengthened across the agency through the office and with the *Framework* serving as a guide, however, practitioners of community-based environmental protection proceeded

with their work through the end of the Clinton administration and throughout the George W. Bush years. A good number of staff redeployed to the
Office of Water and others to policy and reinvention offices. In July 1999 the
EPA Innovations Task Force issued its report, *Aiming for Excellence,* which
made active stewardship a central principle and called for the agency to
"build leadership capacity in communities to participate in local environmental problem solving." The report pledged the agency to review participation policies, regulations, and current practices. The Office of Policy and
Reinvention then formed a workgroup to carry out the review.

The workgroup was led by Patricia Bonner, whose experience in innovative forms of community participation extended back to the earliest models of integrated regional environmental management in San Diego
County in the early 1970s, the Chesapeake Bay Program, the International
Joint Commission for the Great Lakes, and Region 10 in Seattle. The two
cochairs of the workgroup had come from OSEC: Kathleen Bailey, then at
the Office of Policy, Economics, and Innovation, and Deborah Dalton,
then at the Conflict Prevention and Resolution Center in the Office of the
General Counsel and one of the many EPA staff that linked broad conflict
resolution networks to civic engagement and collaborative governance
practices. Other members brought years of experience in community participation from their program and regional offices and from OSEC. Bonner, a history major in college with a long view of democracy's development, was determined to look thoroughly at the policy and regulations,
which had been in place since early 1981 yet left relatively invisible as they
were shunted aside by Reagan's initial appointees to the EPA. Bonner also
wanted to understand why, despite many innovative practices since then,
agency offices still had been unable to learn adequately across program
areas. In short, "Why hadn't the agency lived up to its potential as a learning organization for democracy?"[71]

The workgroup report, *Engaging the American People,* began with the
long selection from the 1996 Webb Lecture at NAPA by Ruckelshaus
quoted at the beginning of chapter 2. Bonner and her colleagues clearly
intended community-based environmental protection and related EPA
efforts as a way to help citizens move up a grade in democracy's school, as
Thomas Jefferson had long ago anticipated as a permanent challenge of our
republic, and to lay stronger foundations for self-government in a world far
more complex than he had ever imagined. This, indeed, was the emergent
civic mission of the EPA as a federal agency.[72]

Community Action for a Renewed Environment Program

While the succession of three new permanent administrators and several acting ones during the subsequent Bush administration has hardly been ideal for continuity, each provided space and legitimacy for community-based work to proceed. The participation policy workgroup's review and recommendations got a relatively favorable reception under Christine Todd Whitman. Although no major new investments were forthcoming for key recommendations, such as staff development, a revised policy and set of guidelines were issued that committed the agency to approaching "all decision making with a bias in favor of significant and meaningful public participation."[73] An extensive set of tools generated by the agency and its civic partners was made available on a new public involvement website to enable more effective learning across program offices and in communities.

The policy workgroup also called attention to Enlibra, a philosophy of collaborative environmental management endorsed by the Western Governors Association in 1998 and cowritten by Republican Utah governor Michael Leavitt and Democratic Oregon governor John Kitzhaber. The word *Enlibra* was invented to convey the notion of balance and stewardship. As Dan Kemmis, former Democratic speaker of the Montana House of Representatives and mayor of Missoula, argues in *This Sovereign Land: A New Vision for Governing the West*, Enlibra principles captured the enormous proliferation of collaborative environmental projects in the West during the 1990s that were challenging parties to work across the usual partisan divide on the environment.[74] In 2002 the White House Council on Environmental Quality sponsored, with the Western Governors Association, the Second Environmental Summit on the West (Enlibra II), and the following year Leavitt became EPA administrator.

The senior manager who took the lead in bringing the various streams together in the CARE program was Robert Brenner, who at the time wore two hats: principal deputy assistant administrator of the Office of Air and Radiation and director of its Office of Policy Analysis and Review. Brenner had a long career of accomplishments at the agency in developing both regulatory and market-based approaches and in pioneering the use of economic analysis in evaluating the effectiveness of EPA programs. He played a key role in the development, congressional passage, and implementation of the Clean Air Act amendments of 1990. Once the agency had completed its major rule writing, the 1990 act mandated that the Office of Air develop an integrated strategy for addressing urban air toxics. Building upon agency experience in the 1990s with community-based air projects, such as that in South Baltimore, and trade association network strategies, such as the Design for Environment in printing and dry cleaning, the office issued its Integrated Urban Air Toxics Strategy in 1999. It then invested in developing a model project in Cleveland, which had the strong support of both Democratic representative Dennis Kucinich and Republican senator George Voinovich, both former mayors of the city. The Cleveland Clean Air Century Campaign was coordinated by the American Lung Association of Ohio, in partnership with neighborhood associations, environmental groups, trade associations (for example, Ohio Association of Metal Finishers), the city's school district, and various state and local government agencies.[75]

Recognizing the richness of much of this work, Linda Fisher, EPA deputy administrator, authorized Brenner to develop cross-program, multimedia agency support for communities. Brenner then pulled together a CARE team, under the auspices of the Innovation Action Council, composed of deputy regional administrators and deputy assistant administrators. The council is one of the few EPA bodies with a specific mandate for innovation across program areas. Former community-based environmental protection staff, such as Bassow and Gerald Filbin (at the Office of Policy, Economics, and Innovation) and Hank Topper, from the Office of Pollution Prevention and Toxic Substances and its Baltimore Environmental Partnership and Design for Environment trade association projects, were key to program design. So was Charles Lee, at the Office of Environmental Justice, and the Interagency Working Group, whose efforts to develop the collaborative environmental justice model proved critical in getting administrators to see beyond some of their worst adversarial experiences with communities. The team that developed the *EPA Framework for Cumulative Risk,* headed by Region 6 senior scientist Michael Callahan, provided key scientific support for looking at risk from the perspective of communities, which in turn led NEJAC to call for pilot projects with a "bias for action." Regional CARE staff were recruited voluntarily through community-based environmental protection networks, as well as offices of regional environmental justice, brownfields, pollution prevention, air, environmental education, and even inspection and enforcement. Larry Weinstock, program innovation coordinator at the air office in Washington, D.C., served as the initial chair and network convener of the CARE program.[76]

Brenner himself was no easy convert, however. As he tells it, his own thinking began to shift as a result of attending NEJAC meetings, where he would regularly recount a list of accomplishments in pollution reduction and leaders in the environmental justice movement would just as predictably respond that they saw no real changes in their communities. "To put it politely, I pretty much got beat up at those meetings. . . . After getting beat up a couple of times too often, I sat down with them and began to focus on some of their specific concerns, such as the diesel retrofit program [to reduce school bus emissions]. As we worked with communities, we realized that there were other programs of interest to them." In Brenner's view, the EPA cannot keep up its progress unless it supplements its regulatory and market-based programs with robust community strategies. On the fifteenth anniversary of the Clean Air Act amendments in November 2005, just before flying back to Washington for the ceremony, Brenner announced boldly to the first national training of CARE grantees in Denver that he viewed the program as "a new way of doing business. In ten years, we hope to have hundreds of empowered communities." Although the program has admittedly begun modestly, given budget constraints, he recognized CARE as "part of a very diverse movement in communities to build partnerships, part of a much broader movement."[77]

When Jim Gulliford, assistant administrator of the Office of Pollution Prevention and Toxics, became the senior CARE administrator in 2006 (as Brenner rotated out of that role), he told EPA staff to "look for ways to be enablers." To the community teams assembled for the Second Annual National CARE Training Workshop in Seattle, he reiterated: "We are just an enabling partner for you." Region 10 administrator Elin Miller further reinforced the view of a broad communities movement and the "power of [its] ideas" in her welcome address, and Region 10 staff brought much innovative practice, and local partners, to the training sessions.[78]

A multimedia program based on collaborative stewardship, CARE provides funding for cooperative agreements to local nonprofits and government agencies working as part of a broad coalition to reduce toxics and improve health in their communities. It encourages communities to develop a comprehensive view of the sources of toxics and to choose from the broad array of voluntary solutions that best fit their needs. Local groups establish their own priorities and develop a variety of partnerships. The NEJAC principle of bias for action is designed to engage communities in real work, even amid continued scientific uncertainty, so that trust and results can motivate sustained engagement and community capacity building. Relationship building is critical, as voiced by local grantee teams and EPA staff alike at the national CARE trainings.

Groundwork Denver, for instance, serves as the sponsoring organization for Healthy Air for Northeast Denver, which represents seven low- to moderate-income neighborhoods where local residences are mixed in with small and large industrial sites and where contamination from lead, arsenic, and other chemicals is substantial. The partnership is made up of twenty-five organizations, businesses, and agencies, including neighborhood associations, the Northeast Metro Industrial Council, and the Front Range Earth Force, part of a national environmental service–learning network with school and community partnerships. According to Dennis Creamer, a now-retired oil company executive active in building a variety of environmental and community partnerships, it took five years of trust-building efforts among industry representatives alone before they agreed to sit at the table together. They then began to meet with regulators, followed by other CARE partners. The priorities of Healthy Air for Northeast Denver include reducing pollution from diesel and stationary sources, improving indoor air quality, and identifying land-use initiatives for action by the city council and other stakeholders.

On the first issue, Healthy Air for Northeast Denver did one-on-one outreach to small diesel fleets, which were more open to the partnership's tools because it was not acting as a regulator and because pro bono lawyers provided free consultation to help bring them into compliance. To develop healthy indoor air practices, especially among the Spanish-speaking population, the partnership trained health promoters to make home visits and inventories. They discussed second-hand smoke, the value of signing smoke-free pledges, and the use of household cleansers, solvents, and smoke detectors, among other issues. Upon later visits, the vast majority of households in the pilot study not only were found to be using the recommended materials and honoring the pledge but also had transferred their new knowledge through family and friendship networks, as the health education project had urged.

Armed with these data, Healthy Air for Northeast Denver convinced Denver Water to let it develop a water-wise toolkit to enable a more efficient use of household energy. To restore natural areas, it obtained the city's permission to develop vacant properties. Graduate students from the University of Colorado's school of landscape architecture and planning, under the direction of instructor Charles Chase (the Healthy Air for Northeast

Denver coordinator), work on site analyses, assessments, and design. AmeriCorps' "summer of service" volunteers do the building, city agencies provide the resources, and K–12 students and teachers in Earth Force programs serve as stewards of the restored areas. The EPA's Region 8 brings to this partnership its broad experience and organizational restructuring for community-based environmental protection, environmental justice, and other efforts over the previous decade and helps convene other city and state agency partners, when needed.[79]

The International District Housing Alliance in Seattle has developed a CARE partnership with various community, ethnic, and business associations to address a broad range of health disparities and environmental injustices owing to old housing stock, traffic infrastructure, and development patterns associated with proximity to two sports arenas. To overcome the challenges of building consensus in a neighborhood where twenty-four different languages are spoken, youth from Wilderness Inner-City Leadership Development are trained to document problems and community assets through photography (PhotoVoice), multilingual interviews and surveys among older residents, and hand-held devices equipped with computerized environmental tracking software. In this case, the EPA's Region 10 has been able to build upon the work of Seattle's neighborhood planning, neighborhood and technology matching funds, public utilities and other agency culture change strategies, and Sustainable Seattle's Sustainable Urban Neighborhoods Initiative. In fact, Stella Chao, director of Seattle's Department of Neighborhoods, had been executive director of the International District Housing Alliance before assuming her current position.[80]

While CARE builds directly upon the community-based environmental protection networks and policy learning of the 1990s, it is designed to take advantage of new opportunities and to avoid the problems experienced by OSEC. First, CARE is a grant program with its own budget line, enabling it to fund innovative community initiatives directly rather than having to bargain over limited funds with each media and program office. As the senior manager championing CARE, Brenner has been more focused and successful than his predecessors in securing congressional support up front.

Second, CARE is a program, not a separate office such as OSEC. It thus engages staff on a voluntary basis from various program offices, as a percentage of full-time equivalence and with approval of their office directors, but without removing them completely from their other tasks and relationships. This program design and network infrastructure increases the chances that CARE principles and practices will become progressively aligned with existing forms of community-based and voluntary programs in the separate offices and with regulatory and market approaches—and, indeed, that offices will step forward to have their various tools included in the CARE mix. All CARE support teams are multimedia and cross-program, a genuine breakthrough for the agency. The team that developed the risk assessment decision-tree tool for level-one (beginning) grantees, for instance, had ten people from the Offices of Air and Radiation, Water, and Solid Waste; the group had assembled in response to an air risk assessor, who was working with the Pacoima (Los Angeles) community and who knew that his expertise would fall far short of what the community coalition wanted.

The CARE program has made a deep commitment to modeling collaborative talk and practice inside the agency, as its team members elicit and expect similar collaboration in communities. Cochairs rotate on a two-year basis among major media offices, so that all offices can develop a sense of ownership and opportunity to drive collaborative work deeper into everyday operations and bring new, and often unlikely, staff on board. The Innovation Action Council continues to serve as the cross-program manager of CARE. Some staff note proudly, albeit with an ironic complaint, that they spend 50 percent of their time on their regular duties and 80 percent on CARE. But the appeal of working collaboratively across agency silos, and being at least partially liberated from protective turf reflexes that might exist in their home offices, remains a powerful motivating force among CARE staff. These are clearly federal administrators with a deeply internalized civic mission and network practice.[81]

A third feature of the program that goes beyond OSEC is that the EPA is devoting considerably more attention to providing training and technical resources to communities to enable them to work effectively and also providing training to its regional staff who will support them. In the startup year of the program, for instance, the CARE team organized four major trainings. In February 2005 some seventy staff from the regional offices and headquarters assembled for a three-day workshop in Washington, D.C. In April and May, two half-day teleconferences among all regions and headquarters included a variety of community-organizing, assets mapping, and partnership models from leading practitioners in the fields of environmental justice, community visioning, and community health. Training partners included such organizations as West Harlem Environmental Action, the National Civic League, and the National Association of City and County Health Officials, as well as local health departments with innovative community strategies. In November, teams from the twelve initial grantees gathered for a three-day national training workshop in Denver, which was followed by annual workshops in Seattle (2006), Atlanta (2007), and Chicago (2008) for a steadily expanding set of funded community partnerships.

At the national training workshops, local teams are presented with new tools and models, learn from one another's best practices and toughest challenges, and build relationships among themselves and with regional and headquarters staff to help with ongoing work. Most workshops, indeed, are conducted by the grantees themselves, and there is no sense of authority or wisdom flowing downward from headquarters to the regions and then to communities. The program design, staff ethos, and training practice are very much that of network learning. While a NAPA panel is currently conducting an evaluation of the CARE program, it is clear that the array of available tools in its online *Community Resource Guide*, combining technical sophistication, community education and mobilization, organizational and institutional collaboration, and performance assessment, has become considerably greater over the past decade, since the demise of OSEC.[82]

Finally, CARE has begun a partnership with the Centers for Disease Control and Prevention and the Agency for Toxic Substances and Disease Registry that promises to enrich and further extend work on community-based environmental health and healthy communities, especially through the broad network of public health agencies and collaborative community health partnerships and practitioners. The federal agencies have committed themselves to working together across a range of issues, including reduction of indoor air risk, environmental justice, smart growth, emergency response, land revitalization, children's environmental health, and tribal health, and to developing pilot projects and information tools for communities. They are also exploring the possibility of establishing a joint Community-Based Environmental Health Leadership Academy. Over the past several decades, practice in the community health field has evolved from many directions, and a culture change conversation has emerged at the Centers for Disease Control and Prevention on how to build upon this work strategically and perhaps articulate its own civic mission.[83]

Further Challenges Ahead

Can federal environmental regulators become civic enablers? The experience of the EPA over nearly four decades warrants a qualified yes. The provisos, however, must remain fairly substantial at this point in time. The agency

Table 5-3. *Eight Core Principles of Civic Policy Design in U.S. Environmental Protection Agency Programs*

Core principle	Programs, activities
Coproduce public goods	Civic stewardship and hands-on restoration key to watershed frame
	Tools to enable effective watershed restoration work
	Environmental justice small grants for direct improvements by civic actors
	Emergent agency mission: stewardship as "everyone's business"
Mobilize community assets	Matching grants (Chesapeake Bay Program, National Estuary Program) leverage financial resources and other assets
	National Estuary Program's community advisory committees
	Asset-mapping tools
	Land, open space as assets for community development (Superfund, brownfields)
	Environmental justice as asset-based community development through community development corporations
Share professional expertise	Watershed Academy (in-person and web-based training by and for broad array of professional and lay actors)
	Watershed Plan Builder
	Water Quality Exchange
	Volunteer Monitor as professional-lay network learning tool; volunteer monitoring conferences
	Superfund technical assistance grants
	Technical Outreach Services for Communities program
	CARE's comprehensive toolkit (civic, technical)
Enable public deliberation	Community watershed forums
	Community visioning
	Public forums on risk and remediation in Superfund

(continued)

still faces major challenges in refining its community-based and civic networking approaches, bringing them to scale and aligning them with regulatory programs, even as it reinvents environmental protection in a variety of other related ways.[84] Transforming agency culture, developing relevant staff capacity in the regions, catalyzing change at state and local government levels, and investing in building the capacity of civic associations and networks will take a great deal more strategic thinking and investment of resources. But such challenges should not blind us to the EPA's achievements, especially in terms of core design principles and program components for supporting collaborative governance (see table 5-3). If the EPA can find ways of

Table 5-3. *Eight Core Principles of Civic Policy Design in U.S. Environmental Protection Agency Programs* (continued)

Core principle	Programs, activities
Promote sustainable partnerships	National Estuary Program multistakeholder management conference
	Collaborative environmental justice problem-solving grants
	Superfund community advisory groups, relational work of community involvement staff
	CARE grants for multistakeholder partnerships
Build fields strategically	Civic watershed framing with movement organizations, state and local government actors, and academic scientists
	Reciprocal network development of broad array of watershed tools (see table 5-1)
	Network capacity building of state, regional, and national watershed intermediaries, state and local government actors, environmental education field
	Watershed, estuary, and volunteer monitoring conferences, tools, directories, networks
	State agency watershed approach eliciting statewide networks of watershed associations (for example, Region 8 and Colorado)
Transform institutional cultures	Community-based environmental protection frame and networks, regional office reinvention (for example, Regions 1, 8, 10)
	CARE cross-program and percentage of full-time equivalence teams, intra-agency network
	Superfund Community Involvement and Outreach Branch network mentoring, site teams, community involvement university
Ensure reciprocal accountability	CARE logic models for outputs and outcomes; other evaluation tools
	Charles River cleanup, development of "measurement that matters"

building upon these achievements, aligning agency culture and regulation to better support them, and investing in civic capacity-building—which, to be sure, would require consistent support from the president and Congress—a major shift in approach could become possible.

The Office of Water, for instance, has made genuine progress in reframing issues in terms of place-based watersheds and in integrating watershed principles into six core regulatory programs of the Clean Water Act reviewed by the EPA's Office of Inspector General in 2005. These include the National Pollutant Discharge Elimination System program, the TMDL program, the nonpoint-source program, the Water Quality Monitoring program, the Water Quality Standards program, and the Clean Water State Revolving Fund program. For instance, the EPA has encouraged states to develop TMDLs on a watershed basis, rather than by individual water segments, to better deal with multiple dischargers, multiple pollutants, and nonpoint sources. It has also encouraged watershed-based permitting and water quality monitoring through a rotating basin approach and use of the Clean Water State Revolving Fund for watershed-based nonpoint-source projects. Beginning in fiscal year 2003, the section 319 grants program required that $100 million annually be given to states for development and implementation of comprehensive watershed plans, and as of 2007 the EPA estimates that forty-eight hundred small watersheds are applying the watershed approach.[85]

The Chesapeake Bay Program, the National Estuary Program, and other estuary and watershed strategies have incorporated policy design principles that foreground civic ownership and partnership in visioning and problem solving. The Office of Wetlands, Oceans, and Watersheds has developed or sponsored an impressive set of organizational and data tools to help build civic capacity. These include multistakeholder management conferences, citizen advisory committees, the Watershed Academy, geographic information systems and online planning tools, volunteer monitoring protocols, and citizen planning, monitoring, and restoration manuals. The office has catalyzed and funded watershed management at the state level and facilitated learning among networks of state and civic innovators. It has funded local watershed groups through a range of matching grant programs and has made significant investment in building civic capacity through national and regional networks, associations, and training centers. It has also provided templates, incentives, and performance measures for leveraging substantial resources and demonstrating multiplier effects of watershed investments. Indeed, the office has been relatively strategic in developing the civic infrastructure of the watershed field as a whole, encouraging many types of partnerships and catalyzing learning through networks of local citizens, national associations, professional practitioners, and agency personnel at all levels of the federal system. Without the strategic support of the Office of Wetlands, Oceans, and Watersheds, the civic infrastructure and practice of watershed work would be far less robust than they are today.

Other programs have also made significant progress in helping build capacities for civic problem solving. Superfund has come a long way in building trust and capacity at the community level through its regional community involvement coordinators and through the efforts of the Community Involvement and Outreach Branch, which provides more-refined tools for communities and upgraded staff training within a larger context of overall administrative reform of the program. The Office of Environmental Justice, along with other offices, has provided financial support to local groups and developed a critically important collaborative environmental justice frame to orient sustained work in communities with multiple stressors, innumerable points of potential conflict and stalemate, and clear limits to regulatory and legal action, not to mention radical grassroots mobilization. Community-based environmental protection catalyzed the first cross-agency strategy for culture change with network learning that brought community actors, as well as state, regional, and national conservation associations, into the mix. It also developed a general frame that continues to resonate in more recent civic innovations, along with an intra-agency network of mission-driven staff capable of leveraging its lessons in new ways.

Community Action for a Renewed Environment has clearly built upon all of these, in addition to other innovative work occurring in the fields of urban air toxics, pollution prevention, brownfields redevelopment, children's health, and much more, including the new initiatives in community-based health strategies in cooperation with the Centers for Disease Control and Prevention and the Agency for Toxic Substances and Disease Registry. The CARE program has developed collaborative, cross-program networks and reflective work practices at a level never before seen in the agency and has provided a truly impressive array of enabling tools and staff support for local actors to perform complex public work to reduce risk and improve environments in ways most meaningful to communities themselves.

While the EPA has built an impressive foundation for community-based work, it faces many challenges, large and small, if it is to help institutionalize civic environmentalism on solid ground. Among the major challenges are further aligning regulatory and civic approaches, providing significantly greater resources to help build the capacity of civic associations, and developing its own staff capacities to support collaborative, place-based work and agency culture change.

First, the EPA will need to make considerably more progress integrating regulatory and collaborative problem-solving strategies. Research across a broad range of environmental agencies clearly shows that regulatory hammers, actual or anticipated, can provide critical incentives for collaborative, multistakeholder, and community-based approaches.[86] For instance, the

Endangered Species Act, with its anticipated listing of species and court action, has been a critical tool for motivating collaboration among diverse stakeholders and natural resource agencies.

But regulatory hammers can also work at cross-purposes to collaboration. While the EPA has made real progress in integrating watershed principles into core regulatory programs, for instance, it still confronts many challenges. Facing court orders and consent decrees to set total maximum daily levels for impaired waters under the Clean Water Act (which does not specify the geographic scale of TMDLs), some states are tempted to ignore EPA encouragement to develop these through multistakeholder processes on a watershed basis because this is a slower and more complex procedure. Some scholars, such as Mark Imperial and Timothy Hennessey, see TMDL regulatory requirements, entailing thousands of implementation plans, as overwhelming the capacity for collaborative watershed governance, generating further conflict, absorbing enormous resources, destroying valuable social capital, and, indeed, as being fundamentally inconsistent with a collaborative approach. Not a few state watershed program staff echo similar views. While others are more sanguine and point to clear examples of TMDLs' sparking collaboration on a watershed basis, it is clear that aligning key regulatory and collaborative watershed approaches, while building trust among state, region, and headquarters staff in the process, will not be easy, especially if budgets continue to shrink.[87]

Second, the EPA will need to provide significantly greater resources to build the capacity of civic associations if the latter are to live up to their potential for robust and sustained environmental problem solving. Of course, this is not a task for the EPA alone or only for other federal environmental agencies. Much capacity building takes place by mobilizing community assets (local skills, social capital, institutional relationships, volunteer time, individual donations) and with funding and technical assistance from local and state governments, private foundations, and, in some cases, business partners. But the EPA (and other federal) funding, and the legitimacy it brings, has been essential to leveraging local and state resources for capacity building of every kind, from the development of watershed associations and volunteer monitoring to environmental justice and cross-media community and institutional partnerships, such as those with universities.

Again, much progress has been made over the past decade. In the watershed arena, for instance, the National Science Foundation–funded National River Restoration Science Synthesis, studying the effectiveness of thirty-seven thousand river restoration projects and a subsample of section 317 projects that followed a relatively idealized process of monitoring and evaluation, found no essential differences between the two groups. "Indeed," the report notes, "the only distinction that we can draw between those projects following a 'highly effective process' and the full data set is that more than two-thirds of these projects had significant community involvement and had an advisory committee associated with the project." According to the restoration science group, this is most likely because of the increased project accountability that community involvement brings. However, despite the large role played by citizen groups overall, various capacity deficits exist, and those associated with performance monitoring and data sharing are primarily results of the lack of resources (time and money) rather than any unwillingness to evaluate projects. This nationwide academic network of scientists recommends that "mechanisms for ensuring citizen or stakeholder involvement [be included] in all restoration projects, even those undertaken by federal agencies."[88]

However, as the National River Restoration Science Synthesis and other researchers demonstrate, there remains enormous unmet capacity relative to the tasks at hand. In the watershed arena, there are now perhaps six thousand watershed associations and kindred groups, many of whom have used the EPA and other government funding to build basic organizational capacity and undertake projects. However, 40 percent of watershed groups sampled by the River Network in 2005 had no budget, 45 percent were without an annual work plan, and 74 percent lacked a fundraising strategy—a far cry from stable financing.[89] Most watersheds do not yet have robust watershed associations capable of complex analysis, planning, and monitoring of results, not to mention sustained collaboration with a broad array of state and local government partners, businesses, and other institutions. Most are not able to engage substantial numbers of ordinary citizens for ongoing restoration work. Despite the increments from section 319 funds dedicated to the development and implementation of watershed plans, states still lack adequate resources to support participatory watershed planning at the county level.

Intermediary organizations, such as the River Network, the Center for Watershed Protection, and Trees, Water, and People at the national level, and various state and regional associations, such as the Colorado Watershed Assembly and the Southeast Watershed Forum, will require substantially greater funding if they are to help build capacity effectively and broadly. While the Chesapeake Bay Watershed Assistance Network, for instance, represents an important first step in a cross-agency inventory of federal funding and technical assistance for state and local governments, private landowners, and watershed groups, it still lacks a rudimentary inventory of civic associations or an explicit strategy for investing in a sustainable civic infrastructure of watershed groups and network intermediaries needed to help restore the bay ecosystem. Indeed, as virtually all academic scholars, agency practitioners, and watershed leaders, as well as the EPA's Office of the Inspector General, recognize, building the requisite skills and organizational capacities of watershed groups across the nation remains a major challenge that will require many years and substantially greater resources than have been devoted so far. When the need for far greater proactive responses to the likely impacts of climate change on watersheds is factored in, civic capacity–building challenges increase markedly.[90]

Resource needs are substantial in other arenas as well. Local groups addressing issues of toxics, health, and environmental justice typically arise in communities with substantial barriers to resource mobilization and have generally been unable to sustain themselves without some government funding. While environmental justice grants from the EPA, including those from the Office of Environmental Justice, have been important to many local groups, this funding is far from adequate, especially as groups take on more complex challenges requiring sustained multistakeholder collaboration and technical capacity. The office itself has experienced significant downward pressure on its small-grants budget. States, especially those with comprehensive environmental justice approaches, are beginning to take up some of the slack in helping to build local civic capacity and promoting collaborative models. But environmental justice is not a statutory program at the EPA that can provide substantial funds to the states to help build such capacity, as is possible with section 319 nonpoint-source grants in the Office of Water. There may exist much legitimate analytical uncertainty about the causes and consequences of environmental disparities and risks in poor, working-class, and minority communities. However, there can hardly be much doubt that the challenge of environmental justice will take decades to address and will require civic capacity building on a fairly substantial scale, which the grassroots movement is highly unlikely to be able to generate from either indigenous resources or private foundations.[91]

Other resource shortfalls are also evident. Although it is impossible to calculate overall trends in funding environmental education, it is clear that EPA investments have declined considerably over the past decade, even as it has become increasingly imperative for young people to understand and act upon environmental challenges.[92] As an integrative office, OSEC had to struggle to get even limited grant money from the major program offices at a time in the late 1990s when new opportunities and administrative support were relatively favorable, though Congress was clearly not. Community Action for a Renewed Environment, despite its more astute strategy and design that have enabled it to increase funding during a time of serious agency cutbacks, has had to operate with considerably less than originally planned. Only the Superfund community involvement program has been relatively well funded, given the large size of the overall Superfund budget. But even here, hiring freezes have limited the ability of community involvement coordinators to facilitate timely and informed engagement and trust building, and some communities are even discouraged from seeking Superfund listing, though the sites would clearly qualify by technical standards.

Third, the EPA will have to invest considerably more in developing its own staff capacities and culture to support collaborative, place-based work. This challenge, recognized in the *Edgewater Consensus* of 1994, was elaborated in the *CBEP Framework* in 1999. As the 2007 NAPA report clearly states, the EPA needs to become a "partnering agency," to "embed partnering in its culture and to integrate partnering in its practices on an equal footing with regulation."[93] If the EPA is going to support community-based work effectively, it needs to provide further staff and management training to facilitate stakeholder involvement, holistic planning and assessment, and public communication. It must recruit new staff with these skills and provide career tracks with genuine growth and status within the agency. Job descriptions and evaluations need to incorporate such skills, rather than focusing so exclusively on legal, technical, and scientific ones.

Of course, as the agency recognizes, it cannot provide the requisite training, facilitation, and technical assistance according to a retail model but must primarily rely on wholesale delivery through intermediary associations, institutes, and local and state government programs. The White House initiative on "cooperative conservation," involving multiple federal departments, has recently provided an opportunity for EPA staff with much experience in civic approaches to help develop new forms of training and performance assessment for managers and guidelines for recruiting. In May 2008 a team led by Bonner and Dalton convened the first agency-wide train-the-trainer collaboration workshop for managers, based on its new curriculum, published as *Working Together,* and in October extended this curriculum further across the EPA, with several other federal and state agencies participating as well. Such training needs to become a core part of staff development at all levels.[94]

No one, of course, should underestimate the immensity of this challenge. As University of Florida political scientist Walter Rosenbaum has so nicely put it, "Each of the [media] offices is populated by a variety of professionals: engineers, scientists, statisticians, economists, professional planners, managers, lawyers, and mathematicians." Each comes with a special expertise and professional worldview, shaped in turn by the program's specific mission. "This tenacious media-based design appeals to Congress, environmentalists, pollution control professionals, and many other influential interests, albeit for different reasons. Each media office, in effect, has its own political and professional constituency."[95]

However imperfect and incomplete its efforts to date, and however daunting the larger challenges, the EPA has developed critical policy design components and network capacities that make it increasingly possible for citizens to step up to the plate, not just as advocates and protesters but as skilled and effective coproducers of public goods and usable knowledge. Upon this foundation, a genuine conversation has emerged on redefining the agency's mission in such a way that collaborative governance becomes critical to integrating all the tools in the EPA toolbox. Building upon an earlier Innovation Action Council report, the March 2008 report by the National Advisory Council for Environmental Policy and Technology calls upon the EPA to *"reframe its mission with stewardship as the unifying theme and ethic and strive to become the world's premier stewardship model."* Because the EPA can be "only one piece of the overall systemic solution . . . collaborative governance . . . is a key strategy" and will "require continuing EPA management attention and a long-term sustained investment." With the EPA likely playing a major new role in the Obama administration's strategy to enable climate change partnerships on a broad scale, the report's recommendations are especially timely and pertinent. The title of the report is *Everyone's Business: Working towards Sustainability through Environmental Stewardship and Collaboration.* Again, as in Chicago's community policing, everyone's business.[96]

6

Design for Democracy: Federal Policy for Collaborative Governance

The preceding chapters have analyzed three relatively robust cases of government as civic enabler and investor, each with a distinct mix of core principles of collaborative governance. The City of Seattle developed a broad-ranging system to support local civic engagement and problem solving and a process of neighborhood planning and implementation as part of the comprehensive plan process. These innovations emerged in response to contentious politics between activists and city hall and still generate some strong disagreements over the best ways to sustain citizen-driven problem solving and planning while grappling with a variety of external constraints and internal shortfalls in the enormously complex and dynamic environment faced by a world-class city. The City of Hampton has established a system for civic engagement of youth that has enabled young people to become significant contributors to their community, highly skilled deliberators and problem solvers, and respected stakeholders in a wide variety of venues, including citywide policy analysis and planning, school- and district-level policy development and implementation, and neighborhood development and agency collaboration. Hampton's model has been driven less by contentious demands from below than by reinventing government initiatives that challenged bureaucratic models, but it has also sought innovative ways to bring citizens and stakeholders to the collaborative visioning and strategic planning table. In each city, a collaborative governance culture has taken root across a range of partnerships and agencies.

The U.S. Environmental Protection Agency has developed a variety of strategies to help build capacity for community-based and collaborative environmental protection, risk reduction, and active restoration in highly complex local and regional ecosystems and institutional subsystems. It has enabled innovation in states and communities and through local and national civic intermediaries while also becoming increasingly responsive to the need for the kinds of tools that enable local users to become skilled problem solvers, collaborative planners, and effective coproducers. The EPA's dynamic of policy learning, administrative design, and agency culture change over the course of different political administrations and under diverse statutes, while certainly incomplete, provides a window into the potential for all levels of the federal system to leverage their resources and authority to enable effective collaboration among engaged citizens and stakeholders. In some cases, the design of federal legislation, such as various parts of the Clean Water Act amendments of 1987 and the Estuary Restoration Act of 2000, serves as a critical ingredient in authorizing and funding agencies to become genuine civic enablers.

Although I have not presented a freestanding state case, one can see important linkages to states through federal EPA initiatives, as in Colorado and Massachusetts watersheds and Superfund sites, the Puget Sound Partnership's transformation into a state agency from a National Estuary Program management structure and two-decade-long civic capacity–building process, and the New Jersey Department of Environmental Protection's response to federal watershed programs and local volunteer monitoring, among other state cases. The city-based cases also suggest a variety of state and federal opportunities for synergy: in Seattle, through the State's Growth Management Act, Puget Sound Partnership, U.S. Department of Agriculture's Urban Forestry program, the U.S. Department of Housing and Urban Development's Hope VI program, and the Corporation for National and Community Service's AmeriCorps; and in Hampton, through the critically important initial Center for Substance Abuse Prevention grant from the U.S. Department of Health and Human Services as well as a variety of state programs, such as the one that funded the development of the RELATE curriculum.

As noted in the methodological discussion in chapter 1, case studies such as these possess certain advantages for studying the emergence of collaborative governance as complex forms of democratic power and culture. But case studies also have clear limits. One cannot move to robust analytic conclusions or confident policy recommendations on the basis of a few case studies. However, this book hardly stands alone. It complements a growing body of research that lends support to my general argument: government can become a substantial enabler of effective civic problem solving and engagement, especially if policy design and administrative practice include some pragmatic mix of components that have become increasingly recognized in theory, practice, and empirical research. As Alexander George and Andrew Bennett argue, case study research, especially when combined with a "rich, differentiated theory," can provide not only a useful checklist for policy analysts and policymakers but can also help nurture the art of judgment that decisionmakers must inevitably employ when making real choices that entail various trade-offs, political side effects, opportunity costs, and risks.[1] There is now reasonably solid evidence from a variety of policy arenas, types of research and evaluation methods, and categories of theoretical argument not only to warrant further refinement in research and practical application but also to justify broader policy design efforts.

Design for Learning

In view of the limits of available knowledge, policy must be designed to promote robust learning among civic associations and stakeholder networks, as well as civil servants, elected lawmakers, and everyday citizens. Such learning must address a broad range of issues, from the most effective ways to build the capacities of civic intermediaries and promote reciprocal accountability for performance to how best to leverage federal dollars so that other institutional actors also are encouraged to invest strategically in civic democracy. Any robust federal design, of course, must rest on bottom-up and horizontal learning because local and network actors are often at the cutting edge of innovation. Learning must also address questions that typically arise in political and normative theory debates: fair deliberation, diverse representation, power distribution, and the impact of civic approaches on social justice. Some democratic theorists have responded relatively effectively to these general issues, but others remain understandably skeptical, and their concerns, as well as the concerns of those national public interest groups that remain wary of collaborative forms of governance, must be built into policy designs if we are to make sustainable progress and learn from practical limits and persistent normative questions along the way.[2]

Of course, a key reason that a robust learning design must remain central to policy interventions is that communities advance from diverse starting points and have varied civic and other assets with which to initiate and sustain innovation. They operate within different local political cultures and urban regimes, face varied opportunities and obstacles along the way, and are likely to traverse alternate pathways. Minneapolis, for instance, with its up-front funding for a neighborhood revitalization program in the 1990s and its sometimes intense competition for democratic legitimacy between neighborhood associations and community development corporations, is not Seattle; and Seattle is neither Los Angeles nor Indianapolis, which have developed their own distinctive systems. Seattle is not even neighboring Portland, with its own dynamic system of neighborhood associations and participatory planning, rooted in a quite different evolution of its urban regime.[3] Hampton's system of youth civic engagement emerged from reinventing-government efforts in a context quite different from San Francisco's hyperpluralist political culture and youth movement, though both have come to stress the centrality of transforming city department and nonprofit agency cultures. Other cities proceed from still other directions, though seeking to learn from both these models and others.[4] Substantial diversity exists in community policing and many other forms of collaborative governance.[5]

States also vary considerably in how they enable or mandate citizen participation in city planning, watershed partnerships, and many other areas of relevance to collaborative governance.[6] Federal environmental agencies differ on legal mandates, regulatory tools, organizational cultures, budgetary bargaining power, and the location and history of various programs for citizen participation and collaborative governance. In turn, they have different missions and challenges than many other kinds of federal agencies.[7]

Research methods, as well as policy designs, must be able to take into account complex causal relationships and alternative pathways to capacity building and diffusion, as discussed in chapter 1. There are no large-N, variable-oriented studies to instruct civic actors or policymakers on how to proceed amid complex civic and organizational relationships or under uncertain and dynamic conditions, though such studies could provide important evidence on the relative weight of specific kinds of causal factors and likely outcomes. Fuzzy-set methods and richer combinations of qualitative and quantitative network analysis hold much promise for civic research generally and in orienting policy and capacity building specifically. As there are certainly no cookie-cutter federal program models for building civic capacity and catalyzing democratic network governance, there are as yet no compelling designs for grand-scale national democratic deliberation that will yield effective and legitimate policies or spark civic engagement on a broad scale. The work ahead must be far more fine-tuned, rooted in building sustainable civic relationships and trust among many kinds of actors at multiple levels of the federal system, and designed to solve problems in measurable and accountable fashion. In this spirit, I offer some proposals that are ambitious, to be sure, but can be introduced in ways that are iterative and self-corrective, as well as politically feasible, while building support for the more substantial levels of investment needed to revitalize our democracy.

Taking the Initiative in Federal Policy

The three initiatives I propose are interrelated, though one can imagine various more and less ambitious mixes of them, depending on political opportunities and constraints. First, establish a White House Office of Collaborative Governance that would facilitate strategic learning and capacity building within and across federal agencies and, by extension, all levels of the federal governance system. Second, issue an executive order requiring federal departments and agencies to develop, within one year, specific civic mission statements to complement their substantive missions. Third, expand and align national service. This initiative would aim to strengthen national service in manageable steps, though not universalize it, while further building the capacity of its state and nonprofit networks of intermediaries and aligning the programming of the Corporation for National and Community Service more strategically with the civic missions of other federal agencies.

White House Office of Collaborative Governance

My first recommendation is to create, through executive order, a White House Office of Collaborative Governance to focus on civic engagement and governance across the range of federal agencies. A realistic strategy for a new administration burdened with other urgent matters would be to start somewhat more modestly, building upon management structures already in place and perhaps then working toward more ambitious designs.[8] One can imagine a collaborative governance office aligned in various ways with existing or redesigned offices of faith-based, community, and neighborhood partnerships and social innovation, but these details need not concern us here. The mission of the office would be to enable strategic thinking, network learning, and capacity building within and across federal agencies—and by extension, among a broad range of local and state agencies and programs.

The office would be designed to foster innovation and continuous improvement as well as to inform policymaking for democracy by legislatures and public discourse and education among citizens and the media. In doing its work, of course, the Office of Collaborative Governance would be helping federal agencies to craft, refine, and more fully implement their civic missions, my second recommendation.

The office is intended to remain lean, relative to its ambitious goals. It would aim to accomplish most of its work through various federal department and agency teams, centers, and innovation offices, such as the Innovation Action Council and the Community Action for a Renewed Environment network at the EPA. The office would also operate through networks of state and local officials, capacity-building intermediaries, professional associations, university centers, and extension services. Much of its work would, in effect, be convening appropriate agency teams and network partners to enable learning and strategic thinking. In addition to intermediaries in specific fields, such as the River Network and the Southeast Watershed Forum in watersheds or Campus Compact and the American Association of State Colleges and Universities in higher education, key national partners might include civic and professional organizations such as the International City/County Management Association, the National League of Cities, the American Planning Association, the Policy Consensus Institute, America-*Speaks,* Everyday Democracy, and the National Civic League—all of which have done important work on collaborative democratic governance.[9]

The proposed office, whose functions are summarized in table 6-1, would operate in a manner designed primarily to facilitate, not dictate. It would engage various teams and networks within agencies, understanding fully that culture change is a slow process based upon generating trust among units that may have different professional subcultures, legal mandates, budgetary constraints, deadlines, and vulnerabilities as well as varying degrees of receptivity or resistance to civic approaches. Culture change can happen only when great care is taken to align the full range of regulatory, service, and market approaches with collaborative ones, in a way that parallels how the watershed approach at the EPA has had to find ways to align with core statutory programs and regulatory tools of the agency. Culture change and appropriate alignment can be accomplished only through long-term relational work that builds trust across organizational and professional boundaries and focuses attention on appropriate performance measures, with the support of senior managers willing and able to exercise transformational leadership. In *Wiki Government,* Beth Noveck urges the

Table 6-1. *Facilitative Activities of the White House Office of Collaborative Governance*

Function	Activity, purpose, capacity
Civic mission	Develop civic mission statements for and with federal agencies
	Periodically review statements
	Align statements with substantive agency missions
Civic program	Inventory existing community-based and related programs
	Generate shared understanding of programmatic foundations, opportunities, barriers, limits, past mistakes
Agency and network capacity	Inventory agency capacities, including agency staff (training, recruitment, performance measures, collaborative culture, professional identity); usable tools for citizens and communities (data, visualization, planning, organizing, collaborative management, performance measurement, on-line policy brainstorming, social marketing); processes for developing and field-testing tools (collaboration with user communities and network intermediaries)
	Analyze network capacity, including appropriate configuration of national, state, local intermediaries and other partners; capacity for training and technical assistance; sufficient democratic anchorage in associations responsive to grassroots membership
Capacity investments	Determine how much and by what measures
	Determine short-, medium-, and long-term investment needs
	Develop strategies for leveraging federal investments (among state and local governments, foundations, businesses, universities, other institutions, citizens themselves)
	Develop appropriate measures and models for resource leveraging; diverse mixes as democratic anchorage
	Integrate into strategic planning, budget requests
Tool mix	Align civic with other governance tools in mixes appropriate to particular policy challenges, public goods
Interagency and network learning	Catalyze learning across levels of federal system (up, down, and across) and types of civic partners (civic and professional associations, nonprofits, businesses, institutions, public agencies)
	Use full range of learning tools (conferences, teams, websites, on-line manager networks, virtual training)
	Inform policy learning and policy design for democracy in Congress, other legislatures, policy networks

appointment of a chief technology officer in the White House, who would function also as a "chief democracy officer" invested in the practical knowledge and skills of citizens; the new office could help refine and widely diffuse the communication and information tools to foster collaborative culture and civic engagement.[10]

The facilitative role of the Office of Collaborative Governance entails that it studiously avoid the proliferation of new rules on public participation. Although these certainly have served a purpose over the past several decades, agencies need the flexibility to innovate. They need leadership for transforming bureaucratic cultures, not the legalistic and defensive postures that new regulations (and many existing ones) tend to elicit. One can imagine a variety of ways that annual budget requests presented to the Office of Management and Budget might require an agency report on programmatic and institutional progress and civic investment strategies. One might also imagine various budgetary incentives to encourage agencies to align collaborative and other governance tools and weave civic approaches into core programmatic areas (where appropriate). Funding increments might be tied to measures of leveraging nonfederal resources through federal investments in civic capacity. Incentives and accountability, yes, but not a new set of inflexible rules and mandates. As Lisa Blomgren Bingham, professor of public service at Indiana University, argues, a robust legal framework for collaborative governance can be developed only by authorizing further experimentation that agencies can adapt to their specific cultures and substantive mandates.[11]

Civic Mission of Federal Agencies

My second proposal is that an executive order of the president require all federal departments and agencies to develop an explicit and detailed civic mission statement that complements and enhances its substantive mission statement. Agencies would be given one year to develop this but, of course, would subsequently have opportunities to revisit, revise, and reinforce it. The Office of Collaborative Governance would provide assistance in elaborating appropriate civic missions as agencies began to develop inventories of their relevant programs, tools, and capacities.

All agencies of government have a civic mission, whether by design or default. Those that default typically treat citizens as clients to be served or objects of technocratic planning or therapeutic intervention rather than as citizens engaged productively as democratic agents with the dignity, power, and assets to shape their own worlds. In defaulting, agencies contribute to the erosion of the capacities and virtues of self-governing citizens. In many versions of the new governance, this might happen through tools other than direct bureaucratic or service delivery, as noted in chapter 1, but the policy construction of the citizen is often little different, as new street-level bureaucrats or social entrepreneurs replace old ones. Nor are citizens to be viewed primarily as market customers for whom nearly all important public goods are merely a matter of consumer choice and easy exit. If Americans are not treated by public policy and administrative practice as self-governing citizens, first and foremost, it is highly unlikely that they will be able to sustain a self-governing republic.[12]

To be sure, many agencies do better than this, with programs designed to engage citizens and stakeholders as partners and to build community and network capacity through state and local government or other intermediaries. But most agencies and their core programs either have never given serious thought to their civic mission, have ghettoized community-based work, or have discontinued programs as a result of budget cuts, staff turnover, or change of administration. In some cases, agencies have yet to recover from problematic experiences from decades past, even though models of civic engagement and collaboration have evolved considerably.[13] Authorizing statutes of Congress have also paid relatively little attention to civic mission, though they sometimes include expectations or requirements for public participation, as well as streams of funding to enable it. Hence there has been selective space within federal agencies to innovate and respond to pressures from citizens and communities for greater voice and more substantial roles in program implementation.

I have chosen the EPA as a case study because it represents an agency at the higher end of this spectrum, having sustained and deepened learning in diverse program areas over several decades and having introduced two important cross-program initiatives to make civic engagement and collaborative governance a core part of agency culture. The EPA's Innovation Action Council and National Advisory Council for Environmental Policy and Technology have also opened a discussion of reframing the agency's mission around stewardship and collaboration. A major new EPA role in catalyzing local, state, and regional climate change partnerships in the next administration could leverage this learning with a breadth and depth never before seen in the federal government and could provide one of the most effective ways of engaging citizens in collaborative governance on a major public policy issue.

Not all agencies are alike, needless to say, and the EPA, while arguably having developed an implicit or emergent civic mission, is still a good ways from having an explicit one to inform the broad array of its activities. In both Hampton and Seattle, explicit civic mission and vision statements have guided city programs and agencies, at least beginning in some and then finding ways to align with still others. In Hampton's case, the city's mission statement on empowering youth was reciprocated and reinforced by reinvention of the main youth nonprofit around its own civic mission. Of course, this is easier—though by no means easy—to do at the local level. But civic mission–driven work through local and state government can find a range of supports through federal agencies operating with an ample civic toolbox, as well as with their own emergent civic missions. Mission-driven work, as much research on government, nonprofit, and business organizations tells us, is critical to sustaining innovation and preventing organizations from slipping back into old patterns and practices. Transformative leaders at all levels have a much greater chance of succeeding when they can invoke a clearly articulated mission as beacon.[14]

Because agencies differ in so many ways, one would expect civic mission statements to vary considerably. At the baseline level, one might expect each agency to articulate its role as civic educator, as Marc Landy has argued. This entails operating in a manner that educates citizens about why and how the agency produces the public goods and services it is charged to produce and effectively informs citizens about its stewardship of public resources in doing so. Public agencies should educate the public about the true costs of public goods and services as well as the trade-offs that might be entailed in making public choices. Many of the toughest public policy and budgetary problems Americans will face for decades to come will entail more effective forms of civic education and public deliberation about real costs and tough trade-offs. No self-governing republic, indeed no self-respecting citizenry, should be led to imagine by the design of public policy or the practices of public administration that public goods are free or can be provided without trade-offs with other forms of public investment.[15]

For the effective production of many public goods and services, however, agencies must become civic enablers and educators of a higher order. They need to empower citizens to become skilled coproducers of such public goods and services, to mobilize the assets of their communities to solve problems, to bring their local knowledge to bear and work to meld it with the best professional and scientific expertise available, and to develop collaborative relationships with a broad and sometimes unlikely range of partners—in short, to incorporate a fuller and richer mixture of the policy design principles discussed in chapter 2 and present in various configurations in the case study chapters. Public safety, community development, public health, youth and family services, ecosystem restoration, urban education, climate change—these are all areas of policy and management that can benefit from this higher-order civic mission of federal agencies. The EPA has proceeded far enough along that one could now imagine a well-defined and robust civic mission statement to complement its substantive mission, though not without ongoing negotiation and clarification over program alignment, boundaries, resources, and the proper mix of governance tools from its entire toolbox.

Other federal agencies have some ready opportunities to begin to elaborate civic missions. The Department of Housing and Urban Development's community development programs provide many handles, along with community building in the HOPE VI public housing program, YouthBuild, and the Community Outreach Partnership Centers program in the Office of University Partnerships. In some cases, there already exist national intermediaries that make leadership development a central focus, such as Youth-Build USA and the Corps Network, which work with the department and a variety of other federal agencies.[16] Community, environmental, and public health programs at the Department of Health and Human Services and the Centers for Disease Control and Prevention also provide many handles for developing an explicit civic mission.[17] The U.S. Department of Agriculture sponsors programs on land conservation, environmental stewardship, and sustainable agriculture that could be developed further within a more robust civic framing, and cooperative extension services and 4-H provide a solid foundation for civic problem-solving approaches and network development. In 2001–02, through a series of local, county, and state conversations that engaged tens of thousands of youths and adults and culminated in a centennial congress with the secretary of agriculture, the "4-H movement" rededicated itself to a "common mission" whose central themes are "empowering youth as equal partners" and developing a "new generation of citizen leaders."[18]

Many less obvious opportunities for civic mission development also exist. In 2006, before the full-blown financial crisis hit, an interagency commission led by the Treasury Department Office of Financial Literacy, with representatives from twenty federal departments, agencies, and offices and authorized by congressional passage of the Financial Literacy and Education Improvement Act (2003), issued *Taking Ownership of the Future: The National Strategy for Financial Literacy*. The participating agencies ranged from the Departments of Agriculture, Defense, and Veterans Affairs, the Small Business Administration, and the Federal Reserve Board to the Social Security Administration and the Departments of Education, Labor, Health and Human Services, and Housing and Urban Development, in addition to more specialized agencies such as the Federal Deposit Insurance Corporation, the Office of Thrift Supervision, and the National Credit Union Administration. The premise of the strategy is that citizens, and especially those who are most vulnerable, have a growing need for financial literacy to navigate today's increasingly complex financial services market so that they—and their families, communities, and local businesses—can fully benefit from the new opportunities afforded while limiting serious risks. Subprime mortgages and predatory lending practices that have since burst into full public view further reinforce the importance of financial literacy for an informed and empowered citizenry—not quite Thomas Jefferson's paradigmatic citizen-farmers but seriously challenged nonetheless to maintain financial independence as a basis for self-governance.

The National Strategy for Financial Literacy covers much ground, some of which is fundamentally about civic education and community capacity building. It provides examples of a homeownership network in Montana, a housing association in California, a faith-based housing agency in Michigan, public-private partnerships of various sorts, and education in K–12 and postsecondary education settings and in various youth agencies that might reach poorer youth and high-school dropouts. This strategy challenges the public to become more responsible citizens through a shift of mindset from consumption to savings. Financial institutions, however, are also challenged to act as responsible corporate citizens and indeed as active partners with a broad range of community groups. The strategy links financial literacy to wealth-building and poverty-reducing approaches, and related research examines how such financial literacy education can become a key component of financial asset building and community development through community development corporations, community action agencies, and a range of other civic partners. Most important for our purposes here is the presence of an explicit civic frame informing the strategy: "Community involvement can greatly enhance the effectiveness of collaborative resource development and dissemination efforts."[19]

Although it now seems indisputable that more-effective regulatory tools, grassroots organizing and "choice architecture" are also needed in financial services to keep the burden of the costs and risks of financial information from falling disproportionately on vulnerable families and communities,[20] it is instructive that so many agencies now have a frame linking their substantive missions to financial literacy, broadly defined. If these agencies begin to design and adequately fund robust civic components of their strategy as they make other substantive reforms, financial literacy could provide an opportunity to reflect more deeply on still other potential elements of their civic missions.

Indeed, looking at the civic mission challenge from the bottom up illustrates this point. If citizens and local government innovators in Seattle, Hampton, and many other cities can undertake civic mission–driven work on an increasingly ambitious scale, should not the federal agencies working with them align their own missions and programs to enable such collaborative work? If various associations such as the National 4-H Council and the YMCA of the USA can begin to renew their civic missions, and various initiatives arising within educational institutions can also begin to renew the civic mission of K–12 schools and higher education, then ought not the major federal departments and programs that have purview in these and related areas develop civic missions that complement and reinforce such efforts? Consequential civic framing documents and calls to action over the past decade, such as *The Civic Mission of Schools* (2003) and the *Presidents' Fourth of July Declaration on the Civic Responsibility of Higher Education* (1999), as well as the Education Commission of the States' *Every Student a Citizen: Creating the Democratic Self* (2000) and the National League of Cities' *The Rise of Democratic Governance* (2006), stand as challenges—not just to local institutions and the professionals who ply their trade in them but also to federal agencies—to articulate their own civic missions, develop appropriate partnerships, and support the work of citizens, youth and adult alike.[21]

Expansion and Alignment of National Service

My third policy recommendation is to invest substantially more resources in the Corporation for National and Community Service in a way that strategically aligns its mission and programs with the civic missions of other federal agencies. There is much opportunity to accomplish this in an organizationally manageable fashion that enhances federal agency and civic network capacities all around. However, I would add my voice to those who caution against universal service mandates or rapidly escalating enrollment, not the least because mandates would cause unnecessary public backlash and because universal voluntary or overly ambitious enrollment targets would tend to jeopardize quality and drain federal dollars and political attention from other critical areas of federal civic investment. Like all investment, federal civic investment needs to be calculated in terms of marginal returns and opportunity costs. Each additional dollar for AmeriCorps or other national service programs is not, by definition, a wiser investment in democratic self-governance than an additional dollar for civic capacity building through the EPA, Housing and Urban Development, or Health and Human Services or, by extension, to the range of state and local government agencies, networks, and partnerships that might leverage such federal agency investments for collaborative public work. Nurturing a universal ethic of reciprocity through national service is neither the equivalent of nor a precondition for building robust institutional and network capacities for self-governance.[22]

Created in 1993 with the passage of the National and Community Service Trust Act, the Corporation for National and Community Service built upon the previous Commission on National and Community Service (1990–93) and incorporated several earlier federal service programs. Its signature program, AmeriCorps, has grown from approximately twenty thousand full-time members a year in 1994 to some seventy-five thousand today, with a variety of part-time options as well. Another office within the corporation, Learn and Serve America, has been charged with supporting service learning in K–12 schools, communities, and higher education and has responded energetically, though with a far smaller budget, to the burgeoning service learning movement. The Senior Corps, a third office, has brought together various existing elder volunteer programs. While the three main eras of national service innovation (1930s, 1960s, 1990s) have been quite different in terms of American political development, as University of Mississippi political scientist Melissa Bass shows in her important study "The Politics and Civics of National Service," the organizational capacity that has emerged across federal levels and civic sectors in the latest round has been substantial.[23]

The corporation has been effective by a variety of measures, as an increasing number of studies show, despite disruptive philosophical and political disputes during its early years and some management problems that required serious attention. It has helped build the field of service systematically by catalyzing the formation of state service commissions, responsible for developing service plans and priorities for their states, and has assisted these commissions in improving their organizational and network capacities through the formation of the American Association of State Service Commissions and other means. Support from the corporation

has also enabled considerable capacity building among national intermediaries, some of which (for example, City Year, Corps Network, Campus
Compact, and YouthBuild USA) have combined broad civic leadership
development goals with service.[24]

The 1993 act also made every state eligible for K–12 school- and
community-based service learning funds through state departments of education or state commissions on service. As a result, virtually all state departments of education have developed staff capacity for service learning. Seed
grants to local schools and districts have promoted growth, innovation,
and institutionalization. In addition, Learn and Serve has helped to build
the capacity of key national intermediaries, sponsored the development of
far-flung networks of practitioners and researchers through annual conferences, and supported the creation of a national clearinghouse for best practice. While various private foundations have provided strategic direction
and resources for the growth of service learning, "Learn and Serve has been
a critical engine in that growth and has played a major (if not the major)
role in the establishment of the field," as Brandeis University's Alan Melchior, one of the nation's leading evaluators of service learning programs,
has argued.[25]

The expansion of programs under the Corporation for National and
Community Service needs to be linked to the strategic planning of federal
agencies to build civic capacities in ways most appropriate to their agency
missions. The congressional ban on AmeriCorps grants to federal agencies,
which became effective during its third year, put a brake on the emergence
of creative, strategic linkages. Thus, for example, just as the EPA was developing its community-based environmental protection strategy in the mid-
1990s and had begun several pilot projects with AmeriCorps, it lost the
incentives and mechanisms to think strategically about how AmeriCorps
could contribute to the effort. Even as the EPA's watershed approach has
become increasingly coherent over the past decade and a half, there has been
no attempt to directly link EPA financial and technical support for watershed intermediaries (for example, the River Network and the Southeast
Watershed Forum) and their local partners with AmeriCorps grants, which
could bring much-needed assistance in building partnerships, allowing
them to use state-of-the art networking technologies and geographic information systems and leveraging volunteers for monitoring and restoration.

Some of this, of course, happens through state agencies or at the initiative of national intermediaries and local groups, but far less effectively and

strategically than needed for civic capacity building in the field as a whole. The EPA is not at all exceptional in this regard. One finds suboptimal strategic linkages with AmeriCorps in the healthy communities and public health programs of Health and Human Services and in the Centers for Disease Control and Prevention, community policing and community justice programs of the U.S. Department of Justice, and community development programs of Housing and Urban Development, even though much local deployment of AmeriCorps is in exactly these areas of work.

Various bills currently before Congress, especially the Kennedy-Hatch Service America Act, as well as proposals by Service Nation, Voices for National Service, and other such organizations, would expand national service programs considerably.[26] These proposals contain a variety of potential opportunities to link national service more strategically with the civic mission of other federal agencies. A new Clean Energy Corps, for instance, could link the expansion of national service to strategic goals of various federal agencies and leverage the bottom-up partnership experience of national associations like the Corps Network and its hundred and twenty or so service and conservation corps across the nation with federal, state, and local conservation agencies. A Clean Energy Corps could contribute to civic capacity building in substantial ways and link new federal strategies with those of governors and mayors (and their civic and business partners) on energy conservation and climate change while also providing job training for disadvantaged youth and career opportunities in the new green economy.[27]

To engage people effectively, however—not only for service today but for a lifetime of civic work and shared governance—necessitates broader collaborative governance and policy designs. For instance, a substantially expanded Community Health Corps, another promising proposal, would optimally require that local health departments be willing and able to engage citizens and stakeholders broadly in the coproduction of public health and that federal and state health agencies be willing and able to provide appropriate policy supports. Opportunities to share in governance in these and other areas must be available upon completion of service in a Health Corps or Energy Corps; and public health, urban, and environmental agencies will need to be much more robust partners during such service. National service alone cannot revitalize democracy in America, and those who would put too many eggs in that basket will likely fall seriously short. Combined with other forms of collaborative governance and linked strategically to broad civic capacity building by government agencies at all levels, however, national service can be a powerful engine of change.

The United States cannot effectively address many of the public challenges we face today without increasingly turning to collaborative forms of governance and civic problem solving. Society has simply become too complex and diverse for us not to bring every available source of civic intelligence and stakeholder contribution to the table or for us to imagine that clear and decisive victory by one interest group or political party over another will yield sustainable progress.

True, many political battles are worth waging, and conflict can be democratizing as well as productive. Complexity entails conflict, even as it elicits collaboration. Power generates conflict, even as we transform it from "power over" to "power with." Shared power, though by no means an easy accomplishment given deep sources of inequality of all sorts, has proved possible and productive, as this study and others demonstrate. Citizens are capable of foregrounding common interests and values and working pragmatically across many dividing lines to produce public goods of genuine value. Government at every level of our federal system has also found ways to become a genuine partner in such efforts. We should expect no less.

Indeed, we can no longer imagine that our crisis of democracy will somehow be reversed without government as a robust partner. Hence the focus of this book on policy design, administrative practice, and strategic government investment. The administrative state is clearly here to stay, and any relevant philosophy of self-governance for our democratic republic in today's world needs to find increasingly effective ways to harness the authority, capacity, and resources of the administrative state to enable the public work of citizens. A democratic republic—if only we can keep it.

The strategy sketched here cannot succeed without strong and dynamic presidential leadership that reiterates continually the importance of civic engagement and collaborative governance. As several former White House and agency officials in both Democratic and Republican administrations have confided, if high-sounding rhetoric in the State of the Union or other presidential speeches is not matched by resolute and attentive leadership, civic engagement programs tend to lag, as other executive staff push them to the periphery and signal that there is a low price paid for agency foot-dragging and resistance. A president truly committed to bottom-up change and engaged problem solving by everyday citizens would require cabinet secretaries and administrators to report regularly on their progress in transforming their agencies into genuine civic partners and catalysts—and would hold them clearly accountable. Inspiring citizens to roll up their sleeves to help solve the nation's enormously difficult and complex problems without also inspiring and instructing his top executive leadership and holding it accountable for providing the tools that citizens need to be effective would be a fool's errand, or worse. To recall Hampton youth leader Kathryn Price, "We don't want to be set up for failure."[28]

Our new president, in short, must ensure that federal agencies enable the collaborative "we" in "Yes we can."

Notes

Chapter One

1. Stephen Macedo and others, *Democracy at Risk: How Political Choices Undermine Citizen Participation, and What We Can Do about It* (Brookings, 2005), pp. 1, 4.

2. On the impacts of excessive partisanship on the capacity of our national legislature to function effectively, see Thomas E. Mann and Norman J. Ornstein, *The Broken Branch: How Congress Is Failing America and How to Get It Back on Track* (Oxford University Press, 2006).

3. For fresh interpretations of the role of participatory practices in twentieth-century American social movements, see Francesca Polletta, *Freedom Is an Endless Meeting: Democracy in American Social Movements* (University of Chicago Press, 2002); and Marshall Ganz, *Why David Sometimes Wins: Strategy, Leadership, and the California Agricultural Movement* (Oxford University Press, 2009).

4. For a spirited defense of the importance and effectiveness of citizen lobbies, see Jeffrey M. Berry, *The New Liberalism: The Rising Power of Citizen Groups* (Brookings, 1999).

5. See Marion Orr, ed., *Transforming the City: Community Organizing and the Challenge of Political Change* (University Press of Kansas, 2007); and Heidi J. Swarts, *Organizing Urban America: Secular and Faith-Based Progressive Movements* (University of Minnesota Press, 2008).

6. Carmen Sirianni and Lewis A. Friedland, "Civic Innovation, Conflict, and Politics," *Good Society* 12, no. 1 (2003): 74–82.

7. See Sean Wilentz, *The Rise of American Democracy: Jefferson to Lincoln* (New York: Norton, 2005); Michael Schudson, *The Good Citizen: A History of American Civic Life* (New York: Free Press, 1998); and James A. Morone, *The Democratic Wish: Popular Participation and the Limits of American Government* (New York: Basic Books, 1990).

8. Robert Putnam, *Bowling Alone: The Collapse and Revival of American Community* (Simon and Schuster, 2000), chapters 2–3.

9. Ibid., p. 60; Amy Caiazza and Robert D. Putnam, "Women's Status and Social Capital in the United States," *Journal of Women, Politics, and Policy* 27, nos. 1–2 (2005): 69–84.

10. Theda Skocpol, *Diminished Democracy: From Membership to Management in American Civic Life* (University of Oklahoma Press, 2002); Theda Skocpol, "Civic Transformation and Inequality in the Contemporary United States," in *Social Inequality,* edited by Kathryn M. Neckerman (New York: Russell Sage Foundation, 2004), pp. 729–67.

11. Robert Wuthnow, "United States: Bridging the Privileged and the Marginalized," in *Democracies in Flux: The Evolution of Social Capital in Contemporary Society,* edited by Robert Putnam (Oxford University Press, 2002), pp. 59–102.

12. J. Eric Oliver, *Democracy in Suburbia* (Princeton University Press, 2001).

13. Dora L. Costa and Matthew E. Kahn, "Understanding the Decline in Social Capital, 1952–1998," *Kyklos* 56, no. 1 (2003): 17–46; Dora L. Costa and Matthew E. Kahn, "Civic Engagement and Community Heterogeneity: An Economist's Perspective," *Perspectives on Politics* 1, no. 1 (2003): 103–11.

14. Robert D. Putnam, "*E Pluribus Unum:* Diversity and Community in the Twenty-First Century," *Scandinavian Political Studies* 30, no. 2 (2007): 137–74.

15. Wendy M. Rahn and John E. Transue, "Social Trust and Value Change: The Decline of Social Capital in American Youth, 1976–1995," *Political Psychology* 19, no. 3 (1998): 545–65.

16. Cliff Zukin and others, *A New Civic Engagement: Political Participation, Civic Life, and the Changing American Citizen* (Oxford University Press, 2007).

17. See, for instance, Pamela Paxton, "Is Social Capital Declining in the United States? A Multiple Indicator Assessment," *American Journal of Sociology* 105, no. 1 (1999): 88–127; Pamela Paxton, "Social Capital and Democracy: An Interdependent Relationship," *American Sociological Review* 67, no. 2 (2002): 254–77; Roger V. Patulny and Gunnar Lind Haase Svendsen, "Exploring the Social Capital Grid: Bonding, Bridging, Qualitative, Quantitative," *International Journal of Sociology and Social Policy* 27, nos. 1–2 (2007): 32–51.

18. See Carmen Sirianni, "The Self-Management of Time in Postindustrial Society," in *Working Time in Transition: The Political Economy of Working Hours in Industrial Nations,* edited by Karl Hinrichs, William Roche, and Carmen Sirianni (Temple University Press, 1991), pp. 231–74. I would emphasize, more than I did in the original essay, that civic justifications can and should be a major part of the overall mix of workplace governance, gender equity, and life-planning rationales for expanded working-time options.

19. See Robert Wuthnow, *Loose Connections: Joining Together in America's Fragmented Communities* (Harvard University Press, 1998); Robert Wuthnow, "United States," in *Democracies in Flux,* edited by Putnam, pp. 59–102. Wuthnow's emphasis on culture in "Democratic Renewal and Cultural Inertia: Why Our Best Efforts Fall Short," *Sociological Forum* 20, no. 3 (2005): 343–67, is one I broadly share. However, I would place more emphasis on a pragmatic problem-solving culture in the United States, how policy design can provide opportunities for culture change at the level of everyday coproductive and collaborative work, and potential changes in agency and professional cultures that interact with deep cultural meanings and popular narratives. On problem-solving public culture in the American tradition, see especially Harry C. Boyte and Nancy N. Kari, *Building America: The Democratic Promise of Public Work* (Temple University Press, 1996). Also see Robert Putnam, "Conclusion," in *Democracies in Flux,* edited by Putnam, pp. 393–416.

20. Cass R. Sunstein, *Republic.com 2.0* (Princeton University Press, 2007), pp. 85–86. See also Matt Bai, *The Argument: Billionaires, Bloggers, and the Battle to Remake Democratic Politics* (New York: Penguin, 2007).

21. Carmen Sirianni and Lewis A. Friedland, *Civic Innovation in America* (University of California Press, 2001); Robert D. Putnam and Lewis M. Feldstein, *Better Together: Restoring the American Community* (Simon and Schuster, 2003). See also the citywide evidence, based on very different methodologies, for forms of problem solving in Chicago and Portland, Oregon, in Robert J. Sampson and others, "Civil Society Reconsidered: The Durable Nature and Community Structure of Collective Civic Action," *American Journal of Sociology* 111, no. 3 (2005): 673–714; and Steven Reed Johnson, "The Transformation of Civic Institutions and Practices in Portland, Oregon, 1960–1999," Ph.D. dissertation, Portland State University, 2002.

22. Zukin and others, *A New Civic Engagement,* p. 204; and Peter Levine, *The Future of Democracy: Developing the Next Generation of American Citizens* (Tufts University Press, 2007).

23. See Michael Lipsky's classic, *Street Level Bureaucracy: Dilemmas of the Individual in Public Services* (New York: Russell Sage Foundation, 1980); as well as John McKnight, *The Careless Society* (New York: Basic Books, 1995); Lisbeth Schorr, *Common Purpose: Strengthening Families and Neighborhoods to Rebuild America* (New York: Doubleday, 1997), chapters 3–4.

24. See Daniel J. Fiorino, *The New Environmental Regulation* (MIT Press, 2006); and DeWitt John, *Civic Environmentalism: Alternatives to Regulation in States and Communities* (Washington: CQ Press, 1994).

25. Lester M. Salamon, "The New Governance and the Tools of Public Action: An Introduction," in *The Tools of Government: A Guide to the New Governance,* edited by Lester M. Salamon (Oxford University Press, 2002), pp. 1–47, quotations 2–3; italics in original. See also Donald F. Kettl, *The Transformation of Governance: Public Administration for the Twenty-First Century* (Johns Hopkins University Press, 2002); Stephen Goldsmith and William D. Eggers, *Governing by Network: The New Shape of the Public Sector* (Brookings, 2004); Kenneth J. Meier and Laurence J. O'Toole Jr., *Bureaucracy in a Democratic State: A Governance Perspective* (Johns Hopkins University Press, 2006).

26. Steven Rathgeb Smith and Michael Lipsky, *Nonprofits for Hire: The Welfare State in the Age of Contracting* (Harvard University Press, 1993), pp. 115–19; Lipsky, *Street Level Bureaucracy.*

27. See Steven Rathgeb Smith and Helen Ingram, "Policy Tools and Democracy," in *The Tools of Government,* edited by Salamon, pp. 565–84; Smith and Lipsky, *Nonprofits for Hire,* chapter 10.

28. Bo Rothstein, "Sweden: Social Capital in the Social Democratic State," in *Democracies in Flux,* edited by Putnam, pp. 289–331, quotation 317; Staffan Kumlin and Bo Rothstein, "Making and Breaking Social Capital: The Impact of Welfare State Institutions," *Comparative Political Studies* 38, no. 4 (May 2005): 339–65. See also Wim van Oorschot and Wil Arts, "The Social Capital of European Welfare States: The Crowding-Out Hypothesis Revisited," *Journal of European Social Policy* 15, no. 1 (2005): 5–26; Juha Kääriäinen and Heikki Lehtonen, "The Variety of Social Capital in Welfare State Regimes: A Comparative Study of 21 Countries," *European Societies* 8, no. 1 (2006): 27–57.

29. Calculating relative costs of civic investment would also entail classifying various kinds of civic activities, such as community problem solving as distinct from national advocacy,

which would lead back to the issue of long-term shifts discussed above. It would also entail even trickier questions, such as how much human capital investment (education, job training) also represents an investment in relevant civic skills.

30. Stephen Holmes and Cass R. Sunstein, *The Cost of Rights: Why Liberty Depends on Taxes* (New York: Norton, 1999), pp. 15, 53.

31. Ibid., p. 31.

32. See Wesley G. Skogan, *Police and Community in Chicago: A Tale of Three Cities* (Oxford University Press, 2006); Wesley G. Skogan and others, *On the Beat: Police and Community Problem Solving* (Boulder: Westview, 1999); Wesley Skogan and Susan Hartnett, *Community Policing, Chicago Style* (Oxford University Press, 1997); Archon Fung, *Empowered Participation: Reinventing Urban Democracy* (Princeton University Press, 2004); Tracey L. Meares and Dan M. Kahan, "Law and (Norms of) Order in the Inner City," *Law and Society Review* 32, no. 4 (1998): 805–38, especially the discussion of the partnership of police and Black churches on the West Side of Chicago and the critical role of police sponsorship amid denominational fragmentation and competition. George L. Kelling and Catherine M. Coles, *Fixing Broken Windows: Restoring Order and Reducing Crime in Our Communities* (New York: Free Press, 1996).

33. Budget figures are, to be sure, incomplete, and overall costs also depend on how one calculates net staffing impacts. I have drawn from the studies cited above, as well as from the annual and other periodic reports of the Chicago Community Policing Evaluation Consortium.

34. See Kelling and Coles, *Fixing Broken Windows*; and Robert J. Sampson, "Crime and Public Safety: Insights from Community-Level Perspectives on Social Capital," in *Social Capital and Poor Communities,* edited by Susan Saegert, J. Phillip Thompson, and Mark R. Warren (New York: Russell Sage Foundation, 2001).

35. National Research Council, *New Strategies for America's Watersheds* (Washington: National Academies Press, 1999).

36. National Academy of Public Administration, *Taking Environmental Protection to the Next Level: An Assessment of the U.S. Environmental Services Delivery System: A Report to the U.S. EPA* (Washington, April 2007), pp. 160–61. I borrow the academy's wording almost completely here, though avoid its bulleted format.

37. N. LeRoy Poff, Mark M. Brinson, and John W. Day Jr., *Aquatic Ecosystems and Global Climate Change: Potential Impacts on Inland Freshwater and Coastal Wetland Ecosystems in the United States* (Arlington, Va.: Pew Center on Global Climate Change, 2002); Susan Kadera and Don Elder, *Water, Energy, and Climate Change: Webcast* (Washington: U.S. Environmental Protection Agency, Watershed Academy, October 3, 2007).

38. See, for instance, Edward P. Weber and Ann M. Khademian, "Wicked Problems, Knowledge Challenges, and Collaborative Capacity Builders in Network Settings," *Public Administration Review* 68, no. 2 (2008): 334–49; Bobby Milstein, *Hygeia's Constellation: Navigating Health Futures in a Dynamic and Democratic World* (Atlanta, Ga.: Centers for Disease Control and Prevention, 2008); Schorr, *Common Purpose;* Judith E. Innes and David Booher, "Consensus Building and Complex Adaptive Systems: A Framework for Evaluating Collaborative Planning," *Journal of the American Planning Association* 65, no. 4 (1999): 412–23.

39. Clarence N. Stone and others, *Building Civic Capacity: The Politics of Reforming Urban Schools* (University Press of Kansas, 2001), p. 50. See also Paul Thomas Hill and others, *It Takes a City: Getting Serious about Urban School Reform* (Brookings, 2000).

40. See especially Iris Marion Young, *Inclusion and Democracy* (Oxford University Press, 2000).

41. See, for instance, James Bohman, *Public Deliberation: Pluralism, Complexity, and Democracy* (MIT Press, 1996).

42. Robert Agranoff, *Managing within Networks: Adding Value to Public Organizations* (Georgetown University Press, 2007), p. 85. Agranoff nicely delineates several major types of public management networks based on grounded theory and case studies.

43. Edward P. Weber, *Bringing Society Back In: Grassroots Ecosystem Management, Accountability, and Sustainable Communities* (MIT Press, 2003).

44. Johnson, "The Transformation of Civic Institutions and Practices in Portland," chapter 8.

45. See, for instance, Lawrence Susskind, Sarah McKearnan, and Jennifer Thomas-Larmer, eds., *The Consensus Building Handbook* (Thousand Oaks, Calif.: Sage, 1999).

46. See Ronald Ingelhart, "Postmodernization Erodes Respect for Authority, but Increases Support for Democracy," in *Critical Citizens: Global Support for Democratic Governance,* edited by Pippa Norris (Oxford University Press, 1999), pp. 236–56; Ronald Ingelhart, "Postmaterialist Values and the Erosion of Institutional Authority," in *Why People Don't Trust Government,* edited by Joseph Nye, Philip Zelikov, and David King (Harvard University Press, 1997).

47. See Mark R. Warren, *Dry Bones Rattling: Community Building to Revitalize American Democracy* (Princeton University Press, 2001); Richard L. Wood, *Faith in Action: Religion, Race, and Democratic Organizing in America* (University of Chicago Press, 2002); Dennis Shirley, *Community Organizing for Urban School Reform* (University of Texas Press, 1997).

48. See Sidney Verba, Kay Schlozman, and Henry Brady, *Voice and Equality: Civic Voluntarism in American Politics* (Harvard University Press, 1995); Stephen L. Elkin and Karol Edward Soltan, eds., *Citizen Competence and Democratic Institutions* (Pennsylvania State University Press, 1999).

49. See William Galston, "Political Knowledge, Political Engagement, and Civic Education," *Annual Review of Political Science* 4 (2001): 217–34; Peter Frumkin and JoAnn Jastrzab, *Volunteering in America: Who Benefits from National Service* (Harvard University Press, 2009, forthcoming).

50. Holmes and Sunstein, *The Cost of Rights.* Of course, there are important theoretical and practical issues at stake in debates over how to invest. Faith-based and other community organizing coalitions might claim they are better positioned to exert independent power and thus often resist government funding for neighborhood-based models, whereas citywide systems of neighborhood representation might claim that they are more broadly representative and more capable of engaging citizens on a wider range of neighborhood planning and improvement issues. In any given city, the interplay might be quite dynamic and complex.

51. See Melissa Bass, "The Politics and Civics of National Service: Lessons from the Civilian Conservation Corps, VISTA, and AmeriCorps," Ph.D. dissertation, Brandeis University, 2004.

52. Robert D. Putnam, with Robert Leonardi and Raffaella Y. Nanetti, *Making Democracy Work: Civic Traditions in Modern Italy* (Princeton University Press, 1993), p. 170. See also Levine, *The Future of Democracy*, pp. 99–105, on civic education as a public good; and Elinor Ostrom, *Crafting Institutions for Self-Governing Irrigation Systems* (San Francisco: Institute for Contemporary Studies Press, 1992), p. 38, on underinvestment.

53. Sirianni and Friedland, *Civic Innovation in America*, stresses shifts from contentious to collaborative forms of participatory democracy, as well as organizational and policy learning, from the 1960s through the 1990s as a part of biographical pathways.

54. Andrea Louise Campbell, *How Policies Make Citizens: Senior Political Activism and the Welfare State* (Princeton University Press, 2003); Paul Pierson, "When Effect Becomes Cause: Policy Feedback and Political Change," *World Politics* 45, no. 4 (1993): 595–628.

55. See Alan Melchior and others, "Evaluation of the W. K. Kellogg Foundation's Learning in Deed Initiative: Policy and Practice Demonstration," final report (Waltham, Mass.: Center for Youth and Communities, Brandeis University, July 2003); Alan Melchior and others, "Evaluation of the W. K. Kellogg Foundation's Learning in Deed Initiative: Assessing LID's National Strategies," final report (Waltham, Mass.: Center for Youth and Communities, Brandeis University, January 2004).

56. Steven M. Born, with Kenneth Genskow, *Exploring the Watershed Approach: Critical Dimensions of State-Local Partnerships*, final report of the Four Corners Watershed Innovators Initiative (Portland, Ore.: River Network, September 1999).

57. See Bruce Sievers, "Can Philanthropy Solve the Problems of Civil Society?" *Kettering Review* (December 1997): 62–70; Patrick Scully and Richard Harwood, *Strategies for Civil Investing: Foundations and Community Building* (Dayton, Ohio: Harwood Group for the Kettering Foundation, January 1997). I also draw upon my discussions with various foundation presidents, executive directors, boards, and program officers over the past decade.

58. See Cynthia Gibson and Peter Levine, *The Civic Mission of Schools* (New York and College Park, Md.: Carnegie Corporation and the Center for Information and Research on Civic Learning and Engagement, 2003); Zukin and others, *A New Civic Engagement*, pp. 203–10.

59. See R. Mark Mussell, *Understanding Government Budgets* (New York: Routledge, 2008).

60. Questions such as these are not peculiar to the kinds of civic policy design that I examine in this book, nor even to the public sector. For instance, Campbell, in *How Policies Make Citizens*, demonstrates how the policy design of Social Security helped to empower both high-income and low-income seniors—in effect, transforming them into actively mobilized citizens. But she also admits that this policy design, on its own, does not enable civic education and robust public discourse about generational equity or spending on children as both consumption and investment, which is in tension with spending on seniors as consumption. This problem of structured policy asymmetry in claims making and public investment represents a policy design deficit of serious proportions.

61. Alexander L. George and Andrew Bennett, *Case Studies and Theory Development in the Social Sciences* (MIT Press, 2005), defines typological theorizing as "the development of contingent generalizations or configurations of variables that constitute theoretical types" (p. 233), which is part of a methodological tradition in the social sciences going back to Max Weber's ideal types. My use of typological theory is somewhat different from that of George and Bennett, since normative democratic theory plays a direct role in my approach, as does the selection of cases from different levels of the federal system that are not designed to be directly comparable but are potentially complementary.

62. My approach builds upon some of the foundational contributions of Helen Ingram and Steven Rathgeb Smith, eds., *Public Policy for Democracy* (Brookings, 1993); and Anne

Larason Schneider and Helen Ingram, *Policy Design for Democracy* (University Press of Kansas, 1997).

63. George and Bennett, *Case Studies and Theory Development*, p. 19. See also John Gerring, *Case Study Research: Principles and Practices* (Cambridge University Press, 2006).

64. In this vein, see also Peter Bogason and Mette Zølner, eds., *Methods in Democratic Network Governance* (New York: Palgrave Macmillan, 2007); and David Collier and Steven Levitsky, "Democracy with Adjectives: Conceptual Innovation in Comparative Research," *World Politics* 49, no. 3 (1997): 430–51.

65. Charles C. Ragin, "Turning the Tables: How Case-Oriented Research Challenges Variable-Oriented Research," in *Rethinking Social Inquiry: Diverse Tools, Shared Standards,* edited by Henry E. Brady and David Collier (New York: Rowman and Littlefield, 2004), pp. 123–38; George and Bennett, *Case Studies and Theory Development*, chapter 10. Process tracing, in George and Bennett's summary description, "attempts to trace the links between possible causes and observed outcomes. In process tracing, the researcher examines histories, archival documents, interview transcripts, and other sources to see whether the causal process a theory hypothesizes or implies is is in fact evident in the sequence and values of the intervening variables in that case" (p. 6).

66. Ragin, "Turning the Tables," pp. 133–36, quotation 133.

67. Carmen Sirianni and Diana Schor, "City Government as Enabler of Youth Civic Engagement: Policy Designs and Implementation," in *Policies for Youth Civic Engagement,* edited by James Youniss and Peter Levine (Vanderbilt University Press, 2009, forthcoming).

68. Jeffrey M. Berry, Kent E. Portney, and Ken Thomson, *The Rebirth of Urban Democracy* (Brookings, 1993).

69. For the National River Restoration Science Synthesis database see the website www.restoringrivers.org (December 8, 2008), as well as related websites at partner universities. Published articles from this study are cited in chapter 5.

70. See Paul A. Sabatier and others, *Swimming Upstream: Collaborative Approaches to Watershed Management* (MIT Press, 2005), pp. 11–17, as well as other published studies from this and related databases, cited in chapter 5 of this volume.

71. Charles C. Ragin, *Fuzzy-Set Social Science* (University of Chicago Press, 2000), p. 5.

72. See Freeman House, *Totem Salmon: Life Lessons from Another Species* (Boston: Beacon Press, 1999); and National Research Council, Committee on Assessing and Valuing the Services of Aquatic and Related Terrestrial Ecosystems, *Valuing Ecosystem Services: Toward Better Environmental Decision-Making* (Washington: National Academies Press, 2005).

73. Martin Marcussen and Hans Peter Olsen, "Transcending Analytical Cliquishness with Second-Generation Governance Network Analysis," in *Democratic Network Governance in Europe,* edited by Martin Marcussen and Jacob Torfing (New York: Palgrave Macmillan, 2007), pp. 273–313. See also Mario Diani and Doug McAdam, eds., *Social Movements and Networks: Relational Approaches to Collective Action* (Oxford University Press, 2003); Silke Adam and Hanspeter Kriesi, "The Network Approach," in *Theories of the Policy Process,* edited by Paul A. Sabatier, 2d ed. (Boulder, Colo.: Westview, 2007), pp. 129–54; David Knoke and Song Yang, *Social Network Analysis,* 2d ed. (Thousand Oaks, Calif.: Sage, 2007); and Mustafa Emirbayer and Jeff Goodwin, "Network Analysis, Culture, and Agency," *American Journal of Sociology* 99, no. 6 (1994): 1411–53.

74. On the uses of narrative in social science research, see Catherine Kohler Riessman, *Narrative Methods for the Human Sciences* (Thousand Oaks, Calif.: Sage, 2007); Joseph E.

Davis, ed., *Stories of Change: Narrative and Social Movements* (State University of New York Press, 2002).

75. See Robert K. Lin, *Case Study Research: Design and Methods,* 3d ed. (Thousand Oaks, Calif.: Sage, 2003), pp. 97–101, on various types of triangulation (data, investigator, theory, methodological), of which I used several, depending on availability for the case or episode under consideration.

76. On the role of engaged scholarship in helping to revitalize democracy, see Timothy K. Stanton and others, *New Times Demand New Scholarship: Research Universities and Civic Engagement: Opportunities and Challenges* (Center for Community Partnerships, University of California at Los Angeles, 2007). While sometimes playing the role of an engaged scholar, or what the American Sociological Association refers to as a "public sociologist," I did not attempt a participatory action research design at any stage of the research process. On the multiplicity of public sociologies, see Michael Burawoy, "For Public Sociology: 2004 Presidential Address," *American Sociological Review* 70 (2005): 4–28.

77. Carmen Sirianni, "Can a Federal Regulator Become a Civic Enabler? Watersheds at the U.S. Environmental Protection Agency," *National Civic Review* 95, no. 3 (2006): 17–34.

78. Needless to say, because *the Journal of the American Planning Association* is a prominent journal among planning scholars and practitioners, forthcoming publication of the article provided strategic opportunities and risks for various players in the debate. I made every effort to remain conscious of these throughout the process and not to let them distort my data gathering or perspective.

79. In the interests of length, however, I limit the citations in the concluding chapter, especially to the additional interviews.

80. See, for example, Bruce Ackerman and James S. Fishkin, *Deliberation Day* (Yale University Press, 2004); Ethan J. Leib, *Deliberative Democracy in America: A Proposal for a Popular Branch of Government* (Pennsylvania State University Press, 2004); Kevin O'Leary, *Saving Democracy: A Plan for Real Representation in America* (Palo Alto, Calif.: Stanford Law and Politics, 2006).

Chapter Two

1. Marc Landy, "Public Policy and Citizenship," in *Public Policy for Democracy,* edited by Helen Ingram and Steven Rathgeb Smith (Brookings, 1993), pp. 19–44, quotation 26. See also Camilla Stivers, "The Public Agency as Polis: Active Citizenship in the Administrative State," *Administration and Society* 22, no. 1 (1990): 86–105.

2. Steven Rathgeb Smith and Helen Ingram, "Public Policy and Democracy," in *Public Policy for Democracy*, edited by Ingram and Smith, p. 1.

3. Terry L. Cooper, *An Ethic of Citizenship for Public Administration* (Upper Saddle River, N.J.: Prentice Hall, 1991); Terry L. Cooper, *The Responsible Administrator: An Approach to Ethics for the Administrative Role,* 5th ed. (San Francisco: Jossey-Bass, 2006). See also Camilla Stivers, "Citizenship Ethics in Public Administration," in *Handbook of Administrative Ethics,* edited by Terry Cooper (New York: Marcel Dekker, 1994), pp. 583–602. Alexis De Tocqueville, *Democracy in America,* translated by Arthur Goldhammer (New York: Library of America, 2004).

4. William Doyle Ruckelshaus, "Restoring Public Trust in Government: A Prescription for Restoration" (Webb Lecture, National Academy of Public Administration, Washington, D.C., November 15, 2006). Ruckelshaus began his tenure as first EPA administrator with an incipient civic frame, though this frame was largely submerged by a law enforcement strategy designed to allay environmentalists' suspicions of a Republican administration. Upon his return to the agency in 1983, he became convinced that a civic strategy was essential to the Chesapeake Bay Program, as well as to contentious public disputes on toxics, such as the ASARCO smelter in Tacoma, Washington. See William Doyle Ruckelshaus, "The Citizen and the Environmental Regulatory Process," *Indiana Law Journal* 47 (1971–72): 634–44, quotation p. 638; Sheldon Krimsky and Alonzo Plough, *Environmental Hazards: Communicating Risks as a Social Process* (Dover, Mass.: Auburn House, 1988), chapter 5.

5. Archon Fung, "Democratic Theory and Political Science: A Pragmatic Method of Constructive Engagement," *American Political Science Review* 101, no. 3 (2007): 443–58; Archon Fung, "Varieties of Participation in Complex Governance," special issue, *Public Administration Review* 66, no. s1 (2006): 66–75.

6. Some important early contributions on this more expansive conception are Elaine B. Sharp, "Toward a New Understanding of Urban Services and Citizen Participation: The Coproduction Concept," *Midwest Review of Public Administration* 14 (June 1980): 105–18; and Charles Levine, "Citizenship and Service Delivery: The Promise of Coproduction," *Public Administration Review* 44 (March 1984): 178–89.

7. Harry C. Boyte and Nancy N. Kari, *Building America: The Democratic Promise of Public Work* (Temple University Press, 1996).

8. See especially Wesley G. Skogan and Susan Hartnett, *Community Policing, Chicago Style* (Oxford University Press, 1997), pp. 8–9. Public safety was the first policy arena in which coproduction emerged as a relatively robust concept.

9. Institute of Medicine, *Improving Health in the Community: A Role for Performance Monitoring* (Washington: National Academies Press, 1997), pp. 11, vi.

10. On the core philosophy behind healthy communities, see "Focus on Healthy Communities," edited by Leonard J. Duhl and Peter R. Lee, special issue, *Public Health Reports* 115, nos. 2–3 (2000). On Healthy Boston, see Roberta Miller, Marsha Morris, and Mary Skelton, "Healthy Boston Evaluation," final report (Office of Community Partnerships, Boston, May 15, 1996).

11. See the references in chapter 5.

12. For elaboration on some of the terms used here, see Carmen Sirianni and Lewis A. Friedland, *Civic Innovation in America* (University of California Press, 2001), pp. 2–5, and chapter 3. For the governance frameworks, see chapter 5.

13. Deliberative democracy theorists, whose insights I incorporate as essential in the fourth design principle, might argue for pride of place, and I would not contest this on grounds of overall philosophical justification. After all, deliberation is about giving reasons. But too often, deliberative theorists narrow their frames to democratic reasoning and policy decisions and tend to forget that a whole range of productive civic roles that citizens play before and beyond deliberation anchor the possibilities of rational democratic discourse in ongoing coproduction and relationship building.

14. John McKnight, telephone interview, April 27, 2007. See also John McKnight, *The Careless Society* (New York: Basic Books, 1995), p. 106.

15. Edward P. Weber, *Bringing Society Back In: Grassroots Ecosystem Management, Accountability, and Sustainable Communities* (MIT Press, 2003), p. 217. See also Mark Baker and Jonathan Kusel, *Community Forestry in the United States: Learning from the Past, Creating the Future* (Washington: Island Press, 2004).

16. Dr. Stephanie Bailey, chief, Office of Public Health Practice, Centers for Disease Control and Prevention, personal and panel discussions, Decatur, Ga., January 11, 2008; National Association of County and City Health Officials, *Protocol for Assessing Community Excellence in Environmental Health: A Guidebook for Local Health Officials* (Washington, May 2000).

17. McKnight, telephone interview; and John Kretzmann, telephone interview, May 8, 2007. See John P. Kretzmann and John L. McKnight, *Building Communities from the Inside Out* (Chicago: ACTA Publications, 1996); Mike Green, with Henry Moore and John O'Brien, *When People Care Enough to Act* (Toronto: Inclusion Press, 2006).

18. See Sydney Cresswell, Jordan Wishy, and Terrence Maxwell, *Fostering Social Equity and Economic Opportunity through Citizen Participation* (Albany, N.Y.: Rockefeller College of Public Affairs and Policy, June 2003); Paul D. Epstein, Paul M. Coates, and Lyle D. Wray, with David Swain, *Results That Matter: Improving Communities by Engaging Citizens, Measuring Performance, and Getting Things Done* (San Francisco: Jossey-Bass, 2006), pp. 155–64; and *Neighbors Building Neighborhoods: Sector Action Plans,* CD-ROM (Rochester, N.Y.: Department of Community Development, Bureau of Planning, 2005).

19. Charles E. Lindblom and David K. Cohen, *Usable Knowledge: Social Science and Social Problem Solving* (Yale University Press, 1979), p. 12. See also Frank Fischer, *Citizens, Experts, and the Environment: The Politics of Local Knowledge* (Duke University Press, 2000); Clifford Geertz, *Local Knowledge: Further Essays in Interpretive Anthropology* (New York: Basic Books, 1983).

20. Phil Brown and Edward J. Mikkelsen, *No Safe Place: Toxic Waste, Leukemia, and Community Action* (University of California Press, 1990), p. 2.

21. See chapter 5.

22. Jason Corburn, *Street Science: Community Knowledge and Environmental Health Justice* (MIT Press, 2005), p. 8.

23. Richard K. Brail and Richard E. Klosterman, eds., *Planning Support Systems: Integrating Geographic Information Systems, Models, and Visualization Tools* (New York: ESRI Press, 2001), especially chapters 1, 10.

24. See Michael Kwartler and Robert N. Bernhard, "CommunityViz: An Integrated Planning Support System," in *Planning Support Systems,* edited by Brail and Klosterman, chapter 11; and the CommunityViz website (www.communityviz.com [December 8, 2008]). See also Robert Scally, *GIS for Environmental Management* (Redlands, Calif.: ESRI Press, 2006).

25. Archon Fung, Mary Graham, and David Weil, *Full Disclosure: The Perils and Promise of Transparency* (Cambridge University Press, 2007), p. 152.

26. See Sirianni and Friedland, *Civic Innovation in America,* p. 160. See also Amy Gutmann and Dennis Thompson, *Why Deliberative Democracy?* (Princeton University Press, 2004); and Jane Mansbridge, *Beyond Adversary Democracy* (New York: Basic Books, 1980), the classic study that set the original terms of the debate on citizen capacities to revise, switch, and combine a variety of forms of democracy.

27. See especially Gutmann and Thompson, *Why Deliberative Democracy?* See also the excellent overviews by Michael X. Delli Carpini, Fay Lomax Cook, and Lawrence R. Jacobs,

"Public Deliberation, Discursive Participation, and Citizen Engagement: A Review of the Empirical Literature," *Annual Review of Political Science* 7 (2004): 315–44; and Simone Chambers, "Deliberative Democratic Theory," *Annual Review of Political Science* 6 (2003): 307–26, which also reviews some of the major criticisms and limits of deliberative democracy.

28. Delli Carpini, Cook, and Jacobs, "Public Deliberation, Discursive Participation, and Citizen Engagement," p. 328.

29. See National Civic League, *Community Visioning and Strategic Planning Handbook* (Denver, 2000); National Civic League, *Civic Index: Measuring Your Community's Civic Health* (Denver, 1999); Lawrence Susskind, Sarah McKearnan, and Jennifer Thomas-Larmer, eds., *The Consensus Building Handbook* (Thousand Oaks, Calif.: Sage, 1999).

30. For good critical overviews of various deliberative models, see John Gastil, *Political Communication and Deliberation* (Thousand Oaks, Calif.: Sage, 2008); and John Gastil and Peter Levine, eds., *The Deliberative Democracy Handbook: Strategies for Effective Civic Engagement in the 21st Century* (San Francisco: Jossey-Bass, 2005). See Matt Leighninger, *The Next Form of Democracy* (Vanderbilt University Press, 2006), on how deliberation and relational organizing can be melded through study circle and other processes; and Katherine Cramer Walsh, *Talking about Race: Community Dialogues and the Politics of Difference* (University of Chicago Press, 2007), on issues of power and identity, as well as the role of public officials, in civic dialogues on race. See also Beth Simone Noveck, *Wiki Government: How Technology Can Make Government Better, Democracy Stronger, and Citizens More Powerful* (Brookings, 2009).

31. Gutmann and Thomson, *Why Deliberative Democracy?*

32. See Sirianni and Friedland, *Civic Innovation in America,* pp. 152–62, for an extended case study of the Oregon Health Plan, based on interviews with key innovators and policy entrepreneurs and extensive documentary evidence of the grassroots deliberative and relationship-building process over a decade. We also review the national controversy and scholarly debate surrounding the Oregon Health Plan.

33. Henry S. Richardson, *Democratic Autonomy: Public Reasoning about the Ends of Policy* (Oxford University Press, 2002), p. 132. See also James Bohman, *Public Deliberation: Pluralism, Complexity, and Democracy* (MIT Press, 1996), chapter 4; and Robert Reich, "Policy Making in a Democracy," in *The Power of Public Ideas,* edited by Robert Reich (Harvard University Press, 1988), pp. 123–56.

34. See, for instance, Lawrence R. Jacobs and Robert Y. Shapiro, *Politicians Don't Pander: Political Manipulation and the Loss of Democratic Responsiveness* (University of Chicago Press, 2000); and Daniel Yankelovich, *Coming to Public Judgment: Making Democracy Work in a Complex World* (Syracuse University Press, 1991).

35. See Joan C. Tonn, *Mary Parker Follett: Creating Democracy, Transforming Management* (Yale University Press, 2003). For natural resource management, see, for instance, Julia M. Wondolleck and Steven L. Yaffee, *Making Collaboration Work: Lessons from Innovation in Natural Resource Management* (Washington: Island Press, 2000). For urban and regional planning, see Patsy Healey, *Collaborative Planning: Shaping Places in Fragmented Societies,* 2d ed. (New York: Palgrave Macmillan, 2006); and David E. Booher, "Civic Engagement as Collaborative Complex Adaptive Networks," in *Civic Engagement in a Network Society,* edited by Kaifeng Yang and Erik Bergrud (Charlotte, N.C.: Information Age Publishing, 2008), pp. 111–48. On healthcare, see Roz D. Lasker and Elisa S. White, "Broadening Participation in Community Problem Solving: A Multidisciplinary Model to

Support Collaborative Practice and Research," *Journal of Urban Health* 80, no. 1 (2003): 14–49. For related analyses in business settings, see Charles Hecksher and Paul S. Adler, eds., *The Firm as Collaborative Community: Reconstructing Trust in the Knowledge Economy* (Oxford University Press, 2006); and Jody Hoffer Gittell, *The Southwest Airlines Way: Using the Power of Relationships to Achieve High Performance* (McGraw-Hill, 2003).

36. See Mark R. Warren, *Dry Bones Rattling: Community Building to Revitalize American Democracy* (Princeton University Press, 2001), chapter 6; Paul Osterman, *Gathering Power: The Future of Progressive Politics in America* (Boston: Beacon, 2002), chapter 5.

37. On communicative ethics, see especially those planning theorists who draw upon the communicative ethics of Jürgen Habermas, such as John Forester, *Planning in the Face of Power* (University of California Press, 1989); John Forester, *The Deliberative Practitioner: Encouraging Participatory Planning Processes* (MIT Press, 1999); and Judith E. Innes, "Planning Theory's Emerging Paradigm: Communicative Action and Interactive Practice," *Journal of Planning Education and Research* 14, no. 3 (1995): 183–89.

38. See Elena Fagotto and Archon Fung, "Sustaining Public Engagement: Embedding Deliberation in Local Communities," in *Varieties of Civic Innovation,* edited by Jennifer Girouard and Carmen Sirianni (Vanderbilt University Press, 2009); and Caroline E. Lee, "Is There a Place for Private Conversation in Public Dialogue? Comparing Stakeholder Assessments of Informal Communication in Collaborative Regional Planning," *American Journal of Sociology* 113, no. 1 (2007): 41–96.

39. For an excellent overview of the community development field that gives an indication of the types of civic and institutional actors one might find in many fields, and the issues of power, trust, and capacity that arise among them, see Ronald F. Ferguson and Sara E. Stoutland, "Reconsidering the Community Development Field," in *Urban Problems and Community Development,* edited by Ronald F. Ferguson and William T. Dickens (Brookings, 1999), pp. 33–75.

40. Stephen Goldsmith and William D. Eggers, *Governing by Network: The New Shape of the Public Sector* (Brookings, 2004), p. 70.

41. Although new institutionalism and organizational ecology provide a variety of analytic tools for field building, these frameworks have generally been underused in mapping the challenges of field building from the normative perspective of democratic theory. For a variety of formative studies from these analytic frameworks, see Walter M. Powell and Paul J. DiMaggio, eds., *The New Institutionalism in Organizational Analysis* (University of Chicago Press, 1991); and Joel Baum, "Organizational Ecology," in *Handbook of Organization Studies,* edited by Stewart Clegg, Cynthia Hardy, and Walter Nord (London: Sage, 1996), pp. 77–114.

42. See Eva Sørensen and Jacob Torfing, "The Democratic Anchorage of Governance Networks," *Scandinavian Political Studies* 28, no. 3 (2005): 195–218; Eva Sørensen and Jacob Torfing, eds., *Theories of Democratic Network Governance* (Basingstoke, U.K.: Palgrave Macmillan, 2007); and Jon Pierre, ed., *Debating Governance: Authority, Steering, and Democracy* (Oxford University Press, 2000).

43. Paul C. Light, *Sustaining Innovation: Creating Nonprofit and Government Organizations That Innovate Naturally* (San Francisco: Jossey-Bass, 1998), pp. 92–93.

44. On Portland State University, I draw upon a week of interviews and field observations with faculty, administrators, student leaders, and community and watershed activists in June 2005, subsequent telephone interviews, and a review of curricular and partnership

tools, as well as discussions with the city's Bureau of Environmental Services watershed staff several years earlier. The university has also served as a catalyst for the national grassroots movement to restore urban watersheds through its seven Country in the City symposiums. On the movement to renew the civic mission of higher education, see Anne Colby and others, *Educating Citizens: Preparing America's Undergraduates for Lives of Moral and Civic Responsibility* (San Francisco: Jossey-Bass 2003); Thomas Ehrlich and Elizabeth Hollander, "Presidents' Fourth of July Declaration on the Civic Responsibility of Higher Education" (paper prepared for the Presidential Leadership Colloquium, Campus Compact, Providence, R.I., 1999); and Carmen Sirianni and Lewis A. Friedland, "The New Student Politics: Sustainable Action for Democracy," *Journal of Public Affairs* 7, no. 1 (2004): 101–23.

45. See Anne M. Khademian, *Working with Culture: The Way the Job Gets Done in Public Programs* (Washington: CQ Press, 2002).

46. National Advisory Council for Environmental Policy and Technology, *Everyone's Business: Working Towards Sustainability through Environmental Stewardship and Collaboration* (EPA, March 2008); Innovation Action Council, *Everyday Choices: Opportunities for Environmental Stewardship*, technical report prepared by the EPA Environmental Stewardship Staff Committee (EPA, November 2005).

47. Lester M. Salamon, "The New Governance and the Tools of Public Action: An Introduction," in *The Tools of Government: A Guide to the New Governance*, edited by Lester M. Salamon (Oxford University Press, 2002), pp. 1–47, especially 16–18; italics in original. See also Robert Agranoff, *Managing within Networks: Adding Value to Public Organizations* (Georgetown University Press, 2007); and Goldsmith and Eggers, *Governing by Network*.

48. See Paul C. Light, *The New Public Service* (Brookings, 1999), p. 3; Paul C. Light, *A Government Ill Executed: The Decline of the Federal Service and How to Reverse It* (Harvard University Press, 2008); and Janet V. Denhardt and Robert V. Denhardt, *The New Public Service: Serving, Not Steering* (Armonk, N.Y.: M. E. Sharpe, 2003).

49. See Skogan and Hartnett, *Community Policing, Chicago Style,* chapter 4; and Susan L. Miller, *Gender and Community Policing: Walking the Talk* (Northeastern University Press, 1999).

50. See Albert W. Dzur, *Democratic Professionalism: Citizen Participation and the Reconstruction of Professional Ethics, Identity, and Practice* (Penn State University Press, 2008); Frank Fischer, *Democracy and Expertise: Policy Inquiry for Public Deliberation* (Oxford University Press, 2009); William J. Doherty and J. A. Carroll, "The Citizen Therapist and Family-Centered Community Building," *Family Process* 41 (2002): 561–68.

51. See especially James G. March and Johan P. Olsen, *Democratic Governance* (New York: Free Press, 1995), chapter 3, on identity formation as a key challenge of governance.

52. Robert D. Behn, *Rethinking Democratic Accountability* (Brookings, 2001), p. 198.

53. Ibid.; Donald F. Kettl, *The Transformation of Governance: Public Administration for the Twenty-First Century* (Johns Hopkins University Press, 2002).

54. March and Olsen, *Democratic Governance*, chapter 5, p. 153.

55. See Archon Fung, *Empowered Participation: Reinventing Urban Democracy* (Princeton University Press, 2004), for a discussion that responds convincingly to the most important theoretical objections to deliberative democracy. Of course, there is a large literature on the hazards of citizen participation in these kinds of settings, some of which I cite along the way.

56. Ibid., p. 82.

57. Weber, *Bringing Society Back In.* See also Edward P. Weber, Nicholas Lovrich, and Michael Gaffney, "Assessing Collaborative Capacity in a Multi-Dimensional World," *Administration and Society* 39, no. 2 (2007): 194–220.

58. See Anders Esmark, "Democratic Accountability and Network Governance: Problems and Potentials," in *Theories of Democratic Network Governance,* edited by Sørensen and Torfing, 274–96; Community Indicators Consortium, *Creating Stronger Linkages between Community Indicator Projects and Government Performance Measurement Efforts.* Report funded by the Alfred P. Sloane Foundation, April 30, 2007 (www.communityindicators. net/documents/Linkages%20Final%20Report.pdf [February 14, 2008]); Beryl A. Radin, *Challenging the Performance Movement: Accountability, Complexity, and Democratic Values* (Georgetown University Press, 2006); David G. Frederickson and George Frederickson, *Measuring the Performance of the Hollow State* (Georgetown University Press, 2006); Laurence J. O'Toole Jr., "Implications for Democracy of a Networked Bureaucratic World," *Journal of Public Administration Research and Theory* 7, no. 3 (1997): 443–59; Goldsmith and Eggers, *Governing by Network,* chapter 6.

59. March and Olsen, *Democratic Governance,* p. 28.

Chapter Three

All interviews were conducted by the author.

1. Margaret Gordon and others, "Seattle: Grassroots Politics Shaping the Environment," in *Big City Politics in Transition,* edited by H. V. Savitch and John Clayton Thomas (Newbury Park, Calif.: Sage, 1991), pp. 216–34, quotation 223. See also Barrett A. Lee and others, "Testing the Decline-of-Community Thesis: Neighborhood Organizations in Seattle, 1929–1979," *American Journal of Sociology* 89, no. 5 (1984): 1161–88; Carl Abbott, "Regional City and Network City: Portland and Seattle in the Twentieth Century," *Western Historical Quarterly* 23, no. 3 (1992): 293–319.

2. Rebecca Sadinsky, personal interview, Seattle, Wash., June 6, 2005; John Eskelin, personal interview, Seattle, Wash., June 8, 2005. Sadinsky was a VISTA volunteer and low-income housing organizer in Pike's Place during the mid-1980s; Eskelin was a housing planner in downtown during these and later years. See also Mark R. Bello, "Urban Regimes and Downtown Planning in Portland, Oregon, and Seattle, Washington, 1972–1992," Ph.D. dissertation, Portland State University, 1993.

3. Jim Street, personal interview, Seattle, Wash., June 9, 2005; Norm Rice, telephone interview, March 18, 2008. Rice was city councilor at the time the Department of Neighborhoods was created. See also Seattle Planning Commission, *Recommendations on Neighborhood Planning and Assistance* (Seattle, Wash., July 1987); and Jim Diers, *Neighbor Power: Building Community the Seattle Way* (University of Washington Press, 2004), chapter 1.

4. Jim Diers, personal interview, Seattle, Wash., June 10, 2005; Jim Diers, telephone interview, February 10, 2005. On faith-based or relational organizing, see Mark R. Warren, *Dry Bones Rattling: Community Building to Revitalize American Democracy* (Princeton University Press, 2001); and Richard L. Wood, *Faith in Action: Religion, Race, and Democratic Organizing in America* (University of Chicago Press, 2002).

5. Ezekiel Emanuel and Linda Emanuel, "Preserving Community in Health Care," *Journal of Health Politics, Policy, and Law* 22, no. 2 (1997): 147–84, especially 158–62; Robert Thompson, "What Have HMOs Learned about Clinical Prevention Services? An

Examination of the Experience at Group Health Cooperative of Puget Sound," *Milbank Quarterly* 74, no. 4 (1996): 469–509.

6. On the early staffing of the Department of Neighborhoods, I draw on a number of interviews: Diers, personal interview; Diers, telephone interview; Sadinsky, interview; Bernie Matsuno, telephone interview, June 10, 2005. Matsuno was director of the department's community-building division at the time of the interview.

7. Field notes, Seattle, Wash., June 6–10, 2005; *Seattle Neighborhood News,* vols. 1–17 (1990–2007), which contain reports on a broad range of projects over the years; Sadinsky, interview; Shireen Deboo, telephone interviews, October 4, 1999, and January 23, 2005; Diers, *Neighbor Power,* chapter 4. Sadinsky later left the Neighborhood Matching Fund program to become director of Powerful Schools. Deboo is a former project manager in the matching fund. See also the comprehensive set of brief project descriptions on the Department of Neighborhoods website (www.cityofseattle.net/neighborhoods [December 8, 2008]).

8. Sadinsky, interview.

9. Dawne Brevig, telephone interview, January 4, 2002; Dawne Brevig, personal interview, Boston, March 3, 2002; David Kelly-Hedrich, telephone interview, December 4, 2001; Lucia Ramirez and Jessica Levy, presentations at YMCA of the USA, Civic Engagement Symposium, Rosemont, Ill., October 9, 2002. Dawne Brevig was previously national director of the YMCA's Earth Service Corps, housed at Seattle Metrocenter; Ramirez, Kelly-Hedrich, and Levy were members of the Seattle Metrocenter staff. See also Laurie Dunlap, *Environmental Projects: Help Yourself! How to Use the Neighborhood Matching Fund to Build Community* (Seattle, Wash.: Department of Neighborhoods, 1993); *Seattle Neighborhood News* 6, no. 2 (1996): 5. AmeriCorps provided as many as ten staff a year for the national YMCA Earth Service Corps office in its early phase of development.

10. See Living Cities: The National Community Development Initiative, *Seattle in Focus: A Profile from Census 2000* (Brookings, 2003). Seattle has a relatively low level of residential segregation compared with other large cities.

11. Sadinsky, interview; Chris Leman, telephone interview, June 28, 2007. Leman was chair of the city neighborhood council and a longtime neighborhood activist who, with others on the councils, pushed for diversity as a core value of the neighborhood matching fund. See also Andrew Gordon, Hubert Locke, and Cy Ulberg, "Ethnic Diversity in Southeast Seattle," *Cityscape* 4, no. 2 (1998): 197–219. To lower the entry costs for poorer neighborhoods, the fund reduced the match from 50 percent to 25 percent.

12. Matsuno, interview.

13. Anne Takekawa, personal interview, Seattle, Wash., June 7, 2005; Martha Goodlett, personal interview, Seattle, Wash., June 9, 2005; Yvonne Sanchez, personal interview, Seattle, Wash., June 6, 2005. At the time of the interviews, Goodlett was director of the Department of Neighborhoods' Cultivating Communities program, and Sanchez was the department's second director. See also City of Seattle, *Immigrant and Refugee Report and Action Plan* (Office of the Mayor, June 2007), p. 9. For a parallel on "having tea" as part of relationship building in community-based health work with Vietnamese through Public Health–Seattle and King County, see James Krieger and others, "What's with the Wheezing? Methods Used by Seattle–King County Healthy Homes Project to Assess Exposure to Indoor Asthma Triggers," in *Methods in Community-Based Participatory Research for Health,* edited by Barbara A. Israel and others (San Francisco: Jossey-Bass, 2005), pp. 230–50.

14. Sadinsky, interview.

15. On the history of this tradition, see Laura J. Lawson, *City Bountiful: A Century of Community Gardening in America* (University of California Press, 2005).

16. Field notes at Bradner Gardens Park, Belltown P-Patch, and Interbay P-Patch, Seattle, Wash., June 8–11, 2005; discussion with youth from Marra Farms and the Seattle Youth Garden Works at the Columbia City Farmers Market, June 8, 2005; Joyce Moty, personal interview, Seattle, Wash., June 8, 2005; Richard Macdonald, personal interview, Seattle, Wash., June 8, 2005. Macdonald was director of the P-Patch Program. See also Diers, *Neighbor Power,* chapter 5, and the P-Patch website (www.seattle.gov/neighborhoods/ ppatch/ [December 8, 2008]), which contains data from the P-Patch survey on participation among various ethnic and income groups.

17. Goodlett, interview; discussion with Seattle public housing resident leaders at the panel on the Department of Housing and Urban Development's HOPE VI program, National Community Building Network Conference, Kansas City, Missouri, May 16, 1997. See also Arthur Naparstek, Dennis Dooley, and Robin Smith, *Community Building in Public Housing: Ties That Bind People and Their Communities* (U.S. Department of Housing and Urban Development, April 1997).

18. Moty, interview; Macdonald, interview.

19. For a classic Lockean analysis of the contentiousness of neighborhood politics that nonetheless enhances the governability of the city as a whole, see Matthew A. Crenson, *Neighborhood Politics* (Harvard University Press, 1983).

20. Rob Mattson, personal interview, Seattle, Wash., June 7, 2005.

21. Gary Johnson, telephone interview, July 29, 2005.

22. Diers, *Neighbor Power,* p. 47; Brent Crook, telephone interview, July 28, 2005. As head of the community-building division at the Department of Neighborhoods, Crook hired and supervised neighborhood service center coordinators from 1995 to 2005.

23. Gary Johnson, interview. See Jane Mansbridge, *Beyond Adversary Democracy* (New York: Basic Books, 1980). To be sure, the director of the development association may have had other situated motives, shaped by the accountability of publicity, on the one hand, and the educative opportunity to teach his staff a democratic lesson, on the other. Most likely, it was a mix, and a more microfocused research program would explore such mixes as part of the "situated actions and vocabularies of motive" that are the everyday stuff of developing a collaborative governance culture, as well as specifying how it is that participatory democracy can be educative but is not automatically so. See C. Wright Mills, "Situated Actions and Vocabularies of Motive," *American Sociological Review* 5, no. 6 (1940): 904–13; and Carole Pateman, *Participation and Democratic Theory* (Cambridge University Press, 1970).

24. Ron Angeles, personal interview, Seattle, Wash., June 7, 2005.

25. For discussions of participation biases in cities, see Jeffrey M. Berry, Kent E. Portney, and Ken Thomson, *The Rebirth of Urban Democracy* (Brookings, 1993), chapter 4; Edward Goetz and Mara Sidney, "Revenge of the Property Owners: Community Development and the Politics of Property," *Journal of Urban Affairs* 16, no. 4 (1994): 319–34; and Crenson, *Neighborhood Politics,* who notes correctly, however, that more-privileged participants often bring resources to the process that are directly beneficial to the less well off in the neighborhood.

26. John Leonard, telephone interview, July 28, 2005; Christa Dumpys, telephone interview, October 10, 2007; Matsuno, interview. Matsuno was director of the Department of Neighborhoods' community-building division at the time of the interview; Dumpys suc-

ceeded Leonard as district coordinator. For the relatively robust expansion of the number of organizations in the district councils citywide, see Bernie Matsuno and Hazel Bhang Barnett, "Department of Neighborhoods 2007–08 Budget Presentation to Seattle City Council," October 2, 2006, p. 2 (www.seattle.gov/neighborhoods/Presentation%20to%20Council %20Oct%202006_final.pdf [October 11, 2007]). The Queen Anne–Magnolia district council has more or less maintained this number and has admitted its new member groups with little controversy compared with some other districts. Both Democrats and Republicans of the 36th District also have seats on the district council and sponsor candidate forums and play other roles as individuals in various civic and advisory groups. This design would seem to hold much promise for cross-fertilizing partisan and nonpartisan civic politics at the local level, though in the absence of further study this must remain speculative.

27. Crook, interview.

28. Ibid. Many Department of Neighborhoods' staff spoke about the importance of asset-based community development training.

29. Neil R. Peirce, "Recapturing Paradise Lost," *Seattle Times,* October 1–8, 1989.

30. Street, interview. Street still believes this view correct, and I suspect he was right, though he paid a price for it in the next election. See also Bello, "Urban Regimes and Downtown Planning," especially chapters 4, 6, and 8 on the evolving formation of civic coalitions. For a critical examination of some of the battles over downtown revitalization in these years, though one that ignores neighborhood planning and public discourse on sustainability, see Timothy A. Gibson, *Securing the Spectacular City: The Politics of Revitalization and Homelessness in Downtown Seattle* (Lanham, Md.: Lexington Books, 2004).

31. See City of Seattle, *Toward a Sustainable Seattle* (Department of Planning and Development, 1994); Alan AtKisson, "Developing Indicators of Sustainable Community: Lessons from Sustainable Seattle," *Environmental Impact Assessment Review* 16, nos. 4–6 (1996): 337–50, quotations pp. 337, 339; Kent E. Portney, *Taking Sustainable Cities Seriously: Economic Development, the Environment, and Quality of Life in American Cities* (MIT Press, 2003), pp. 193–97; Peter Calthorpe and William Fulton, *The Regional City* (Washington: Island Press, 2001), pp. 159–71. See also Jane Jacobs, *The Death and Life of Great American Cities* (New York: Random House, 2002 [1961]).

32. Rice, interview. For background on Rice in Seattle politics, see Mylon Winn and Errol G. Palmer, "The Election of Norman B. Rice as Mayor of Seattle," in *Race, Politics, and Governance in the United States,* edited by Hugh L. Perry (University Press of Florida, 1996), pp. 82–95.

33. Seattle Planning Commission, *Seattle's Neighborhood Planning Program, 1995–1999: Documenting the Process* (Seattle, Wash., November 2001), p. 10.

34. Street, interview; Diers, personal interview; Karma Ruder, personal interview, Seattle, Wash., June 7, 2005. Ruder is a former director of the Neighborhood Planning Office. See also Cy Ulberg, Laura Pierce, and Julie Salvi, *Neighborhood Planning Program Evaluation: Draft Final Report* (Seattle, Wash.: Office of Management and Planning, October 22, 1996), p. 44, which covers the first twenty-one months; Seattle Planning Commission, *Seattle's Neighborhood Planning Program, 1995–1999,* p. 36.

35. Kaifeng Yang, "Trust and Citizen Involvement Decisions: Trust in Citizens, Trust in Institutions, and Propensity to Trust," *Administration and Society* 38, no. 5 (2006): 573–95.

36. Ruder, interview. Ruder's perspective on building relationships for self-organizing models was influenced by her previous experience as assistant and acting city manager in

several other cities, where she had learned that "everything is relational," as well as by her reading of the best-selling management guide by Margaret J. Wheatley, *Leadership and the New Science: Discovering Order in a Chaotic World* (San Francisco: Berrett-Koehler, 1992).

37. Ruder, interview.

38. Eskelin, interview.

39. Tom Hauger, telephone interview, March 13, 2008; and Hauger's presentations at the Neighborhood Planning Forum, Seattle, Wash., March 1, 2008. Hauger serves as lead staff for neighborhood planning at the city's Department of Planning and Development and was involved throughout the original round of neighborhood planning, as well as in the planning update process analyzed later in the chapter. See also Ulberg, Pierce, and Salvi, *Neighborhood Planning Program Evaluation*, pp. 12–13, and appendix C.

40. Tom Veith, telephone interview, July 3, 2007.

41. Ulberg, Pierce, and Salvi, *Neighborhood Planning Program Evaluation*, p. 5, provides a graphic illustration of the unevenness of start-up rates. Moreover, Seattle did not set aside funding for citywide publicity of neighborhood planning, as Chicago had for its community policing (see chapter 1 in this volume). As a result, general public awareness, at least in the early phases, was low, and this no doubt hindered outreach.

42. Angeles, interview; and field observations at Delridge's neighborhood service center; Daniel B. Abramson, Lynn C. Manzo, and Jeffrey Hou, "From Ethnic Enclave to Multi-ethnic Community: Contested Identities and Urban Design in Seattle's Chinatown-International District," *Journal of Architectural and Planning Research* 23, no. 4 (2006): 341–60. At the time of the interview, Angeles was Delridge district coordinator. On the use of stakeholder analyses in planning, see Philip P. Berke, David R. Godschalk, and Edward J. Kaiser, with Daniel A. Rodriguez, *Urban Land Use Planning*, 5th ed. (University of Illinois Press, 2006), pp. 275–76.

43. Ruder, interview.

44. Rice, interview. See Amy Gutmann and Dennis Thompson, *Democracy and Disagreement* (Harvard University Press, 1996), pp. 144–64. In stories of their relational work with immigrants, refugees, and other communities of color, Neighborhood Planning Office and Department of Neighborhoods staff were quite sensitive to the kinds of problems with deliberative forums that some political theorists have identified. See, for instance, Iris Marion Young, *Inclusion and Democracy* (Oxford University Press, 2000).

45. Eskelin, interview. See also the article by the former chair of Seattle's planning commission, Roger K. Wagoner, "Planning Downtown Seattle: Neighborhoods and Urban Center" (paper presented at the American Planning Association National Planning Conference, Seattle, Wash., 1999) (www.design.asu.edu/apa/proceedings99/WAGONR/WAGONR. HTM [March 31, 2007]).

46. Ruder, interview; Gary Johnson, interview. Johnson is a former district coordinator of Queen Anne–Magnolia, as well as the downtown. Citizen leaders in other neighborhoods, such as Wallingford and Morgan, described similarly contentious struggles. Veith, interview; Cindi Barker, telephone interview, July 5, 2007.

47. Richard K. Brail and Richard E. Klosterman, eds., *Planning Support Systems: Integrating Geographic Information Systems, Models, and Visualization Tools* (New York: ESRI Press, 2001). See also City of Seattle, *Design Review Program Evaluation* (Seattle, Wash.: Department of Planning and Development, 2002); City of Seattle, *Seattle's Design Review Program: Successes and Opportunities* (Seattle, Wash.: Office of the City Auditor, December 5, 2006).

48. Field notes, Seattle, Wash., June 8, 2005; Eskelin, interview; Leman, telephone interview; Chris Leman, e-mail communication, June 20, 2007. See Ulberg, Pierce, and Salvi, *Neighborhood Planning Program Evaluation,* pp. 13–14.

49. Seattle Planning Commission, *Seattle's Neighborhood Planning Program.*

50. Jody Grage Haug, telephone interview, July 28, 2005; David Woods, consultant, personal discussion, Boston, February 23, 2006. See also the account by the other member of the visioning consultant team, Judith M. Green, *Deep Democracy: Community, Diversity, and Transformation* (Lanham, Md.: Rowman and Littlefield, 1999), pp. 210–12. Haug continues to chair the Ballard district council's planning committee, the stewardship group for the plan.

51. Haug, interview. See the *Crown Hill/Ballard Neighborhood Plan,* prepared by the Crown Hill–Ballard Neighborhood Planning Association; and the interdepartmental review and response team's *Crown Hill/Ballard Approval and Adoption Matrix,* amended by the city council central staff, August 10, 1998.

52. Leman, telephone interview; Veith, interview. The city neighborhood council, with broad and iterative consultation among district councilors across the city, also published ten recommendations on neighborhood planning in 1996 that highlighted such principles as priority setting within each neighborhood (in view of limited funds), the right of all neighborhoods to plan (not just the thirty-seven designated for growth), and "that each neighborhood plan contributes to the common good." See Jay Estie, chair of the city neighborhood council, "Neighborhood Planning Recommendations," *Neighborhood News,* May 1996, p. 7.

53. Richard Conlin, personal interview, Seattle, Wash., June 6, 2005; Sally Clark, personal interview, Seattle, Wash., June 8, 2005; Leman, telephone interview. Clark was lead staff person of the city council's work group on approval and adoption of the neighborhood plans while councilor Tina Podlodowskij chaired the neighborhoods committee. Seattle's nine city councilors are elected at large on a nonpartisan basis.

54. Clark, interview. See also Seattle Planning Commission, *Seattle's Neighborhood Planning Program,* pp. 29–31. For all the neighborhood plans, matrixes, and priority reports, see the Department of Neighborhoods website (www.cityofseattle.net/neighborhoods/npi [December 8, 2008]). For the ten-year update, see City of Seattle, *Comprehensive Plan: Toward a Sustainable Seattle; A Plan for Managing Growth, 2004–2024* (Seattle, Wash.: Department of Planning and Development, January 2005), Neighborhood Planning Element, sec. 8. For the percentages of lead agencies identified for plan implementation, see City of Seattle, *Neighborhood Plan Implementation* (Seattle Wash.: Office of the City Auditor, September 20, 2007), p. 8.

55. Clark, interview.

56. Russell Hardin, *Trust and Trustworthiness* (New York: Russell Sage Foundation, 2002), pp. 140–42; Robert D. Behn, *Rethinking Democratic Accountability* (Brookings, 2001), pp. 198–217; see also the discussion in chapter 2 of this volume. The role of government staff as intermediaries of trust in Seattle adds an indispensable conceptual ingredient to expanding the complementarities and managing the tensions between trust and deliberative challenge that are inherent in democracy, especially complex democratic problem solving. On these issues, see Mark E. Warren, "Democratic Theory and Trust," in *Democracy and Trust,* edited by Mark E. Warren (Cambridge University Press, 1999), pp. 310–45.

57. Rice, interview.

58. Ruder, interview.

59. Ibid. See Albert O. Hirschman, *Exit, Voice, and Loyalty* (Harvard University Press, 1970).

60. Eskelin, interview; Clark, interview; Conlin, interview; Ruder, interview.

61. See John Forester, *Planning in the Face of Power* (University of California Press, 1989); John Forester, *The Deliberative Practitioner: Encouraging Participatory Planning Processes* (MIT Press, 1999); and Judith E. Innes, "Planning Theory's Emerging Paradigm: Communicative Action and Interactive Practice," *Journal of Planning Education and Research* 14, no. 3 (1995): 183–89.

62. Ulberg, Pierce, and Salvi, *Neighborhood Planning Program Evaluation,* pp. 27–29, highlights the uncertainty in the minds of neighborhood planning groups in the early period. Rice's major regret on neighborhood planning is that he was not able to get the budgets aligned with the emerging plans while in office. Rice, interview.

63. Conlin, interview; Diers, *Neighbor Power,* 139–40. For a comprehensive year-by-year inventory of city fund sources available for implementation from 1999 to 2007, see City of Seattle, *Neighborhood Plan Implementation,* pp. 24–25.

64. See Seattle Planning Commission, *Neighborhood Plan Stewardship Survey: A Snapshot of Plan Stewardship in Seattle* (Seattle, Wash., May 2001).

65. For the role of brokers in networks, see Ronald S. Burt, *Brokerage and Closure: An Introduction to Social Capital* (Oxford University Press, 2005).

66. Haug, interview.

67. Quotes from Eskelin, interview; Clark, interview; Brent Crook, telephone interview, July 28, 2005. Crook worked closely with all six neighborhood development managers before becoming the director of neighborhood planning at the Department of Neighborhoods. Eskelin and Clark are former development managers.

68. Crook, interview, July 28, 2005. See also Seattle Planning Commission, *Neighborhood Plan Stewardship Survey;* and City of Seattle, *Neighborhood Plan Implementation,* pp. 10–11, 15–17. As with Neighborhood Planning Office project managers, of course, some neighborhood development managers were perceived to be more dexterous than others as relational linchpins in this collaborative decentralized design, and some neighborhood leaders complained that at times some development managers colluded with department staff without fully engaging all neighborhood stakeholders in a timely fashion.

69. City of Seattle, *Neighborhood Plan Implementation,* pp. 10–11, 21–23, quotation 10. On the emergence of a new public norm for planning, see Carmen Sirianni, "Comments on the City Auditor's Draft Report," September 5, 2007, *Neighborhood Plan Implementation,* appendix XIV.

70. Seattle Public Library, "Public Outreach and Discussions: Libraries for All, Proposed 1998 Capital Plan," March 13, 1998; field notes, Seattle, Wash., June 7–9, 2005; Conlin, interview; Angeles, interview; and Paul Fischburg, personal interview, Seattle, Wash., June 9, 2005. Fischburg was executive director of the Delridge Neighborhood Development Association at the time of the interview. See also Seattle Planning Commission, *Citizen Participation Evaluation: Final Report* (Seattle, Wash., March 2000), pp. 18–19.

71. Veith, interview.

72. Pamela Green, telephone interview, July 29, 2005; Gary Johnson, interview; Clark, interview; Eskelin, interview. See also Andrew Garber, "Light-Rail Suit Cut Down: Judge Tosses Out Most Claims Made by Rainier Valley Group," *Seattle Times,* July 17, 2001 (http:

//community.seattletimes.nwsource.com/archive/?date=20010717&slug=rail17m [November 13, 2008]); Karen Ceraso, "Seattle Neighborhood Planning: Citizen Empowerment or Collective Daydreaming?" *Shelterforce Online,* no. 108 (1999) (www.nhi.org/online/issues/108/seattle.html [March 31, 2007]). On broader issues of transportation and social justice in Seattle, see Anne F. Peterson and others, "Bringing the Spatial In: The Case of the 2002 Seattle Monorail Referendum," *Urban Affairs Review* 43, no. 3 (2008): 403–29.

73. Conlin, interview.

74. James Johnson, telephone interview, July 11, 2005. See also James N. Levitt and Lydia K. Bergen, "Using Nature's Plumbing to Restore Aquatic Ecosystems: The City of Seattle's Natural Drainage System," in Harvard University Program on Conservation Innovation, *The Report on Conservation Innovation* (Petersham, Mass.: Harvard Forest, Fall 2004), pp. 8–13. For a broader view (and widely used guide) of emerging civic action for urban stream restoration in these years, see Ann L. Riley, *Restoring Streams in Cities: A Guide for Planners, Policymakers, and Citizens* (Washington: Island Press, 1998); for the National River Restoration Science Synthesis study of spatial distribution, levels of financial investment, and timeline of river restoration project emergence, see Stephen L. Katz and others, "Freshwater Habitat Restoration Actions in the Pacific Northwest: A Decade's Investment in Habitat Improvement," *Restoration Ecology* 15, no. 3 (2007): 494–505.

75. Denise Andrews, telephone interview, July 20, 2005; James Johnson, interview.

76. Carmen Sirianni, "Neighborhood Planning as Collaborative Democratic Design: The Case of Seattle," *Journal of the American Planning Association* 73, no. 4 (2007): 373–87; City of Seattle, *Neighborhood Plan Implementation,* pp. 16–18. The auditor's office used the prepublication version of my article in preparing its draft and then appended my further detailed comments of September 5, 2007, to the final report submitted to the city council. The auditor's office, needless to say, did extensive original and independent research to reach its conclusions and offered much new insight on the dynamics of implementation. Its report represents—and recommends—forms of accountability in implementation that should be built into the process on a regular basis.

77. Irene Wall, telephone interview, July 12, 2007; Veith, interview; Barker, interview; City of Seattle, *Neighborhood Plan Implementation,* pp. 28–29. At the time of the interview, Irene Wall was chair of the neighborhood planning committee of the city neighborhood council. Kaifeng Yang and Kathe Callahan, "Citizen Involvement Efforts and Bureaucratic Responsiveness: Participatory Values, Stakeholder Pressures, and Administrative Practicality," *Public Administration Review* 67, no. 2 (2007): 249–64, demonstrates the importance of staff time as a determinant of meaningful citizen participation. Indeed, lack of staff time devoted to participation is, in their national survey of 823 city and county administrators, a bigger impediment than lack of citizen time or citizen skills.

78. City of Seattle, *Neighborhood Plan Implementation,* pp. 27, 30, 31, and appendix VI; Barker, interview; Leman, telephone interview; Veith, interview. See also Jim Diers's "Comment" on the city auditor's draft, City of Seattle, *Neighborhood Plan Implementation,* appendix XV, where he argues that cuts to the Department of Neighborhoods were even greater than recognized because the already existing Office of Education and its budget were added to the department, thereby disguising other losses, and because staff costs for the neighborhood matching fund were shifted to the fund's main grant budget.

79. In addition to the works cited above, see the general analyses by Sidney Verba, Kay Schlozman, and Henry Brady, *Voice and Equality: Civic Voluntarism in American Politics*

(Harvard University Press, 1995); and Lawrence R. Jacobs and Theda Skocpol, eds., *Inequality and American Democracy* (New York: Russell Sage Foundation, 2005).

80. See Wesley G. Skogan, *Police and Community in Chicago: A Tale of Three Cities* (Oxford University Press, 2006); and Archon Fung, *Empowered Participation: Reinventing Urban Democracy* (Princeton University Press, 2004). Citywide systems of neighborhood representation in general do a better job at inclusive participation and issue responsiveness than other forms, as Berry, Portney, and Thomson demonstrate in *The Rebirth of Urban Democracy*, chapter 6. As they conclude, "The higher community participation cities are more responsive to everyone, not just those who are traditionally well represented" (154–55).

81. Robert Dahl, *After the Revolution* (Yale University Press, 1970), pp. 59–63; italics in original.

82. See Carmen Sirianni, "Participation and Democratic Theory" (paper presented at the Yale University Law School and Department of Political Science, Political Theory Colloquium, New Haven, Conn., April 9, 1991), which presents this as but one of the many "dilemmas of participatory pluralism" in a highly differentiated society with a broad array of potential venues for citizen engagement. See also Dahl, *After the Revolution*, p. 59; and James Bohman, *Public Deliberation: Pluralism, Complexity, and Democracy* (MIT Press, 1996), chapter 4.

83. John McKnight, *The Careless Society* (New York: Basic Books, 1995).

84. Tea with Stella Chao, Seattle, Wash., March 1, 2008, and field notes from the citywide Neighborhood Planning Forum earlier on the same day. See also Stella Chao and Diane Sugimura, "Memorandum to Councilmember Sally Clark, Chair, Planning, Land Use, and Neighborhoods Committee, Councilmember Tim Burgess, and Councilmember Tom Rasmussen," Seattle, Wash., February 11, 2008; and City of Seattle, Department of Neighborhoods, *Community Feedback Report on Process for Neighborhood Plan Updates* (Seattle, Wash., April 2008).

85. Field notes, Neighborhood Planning Forum, Seattle, Wash., March 1, 2008, breakout session.

86. Ibid.; formal written summaries of break-out discussions provided by designated facilitators at Neighborhood Planning Forum, Seattle, Wash., March 7, 2008; Wall, interview; Leman, telephone interview; Chris Leman, personal interview, Seattle, Wash., February 28, 2008; and various planning documents, webcasts, and minutes of city neighborhood council meetings and city council committee hearings in 2007–08. See also Phuong Cat Le and Kathy Mulady, "Nickels' Style in His First Year Surprises Some Supporters," *Seattle Post-Intelligencer,* December 21, 2002 (http://seattlepi.nwsource.com/local/101019_nickels21.shtml [February 16, 2007]).

87. Sally Clark, "Seattle View: Special Edition," September 2008 E-News (www.seattle.gov/council/clark/news/news0806.htm [November 13, 2008]); Hauger, interview; field notes, Neighborhood Planning Forum, Seattle, Wash., March 1, 2008, and discussion materials provided for the forum.

88. Patsy Healey, *Collaborative Planning: Shaping Places in Fragmented Societies* (New York: Palgrave Macmillan, 2006), pp. 324–36.

89. Deborah Kuznitz, personal interview, Seattle, Wash., November 16, 2006. Kuznitz was program coordinator of the Sustainable Urban Neighborhoods Initiative at the time of the interview. See also Sustainable Seattle, *Sustainable Urban Neighborhoods Initiative* (Seat-

tle, Wash., June 30, 2006); Greg Nickels, *Restore Our Waters Strategy* (Seattle, Wash., September 13, 2004); Clare M. Ryan and Jacqueline S. Klug, "Collaborative Watershed Planning in Washington State," *Journal of Environmental Planning and Management* 48, no. 4 (2005): 491–506. See also the interviews cited for the Puget Sound Partnership in chapter 5. Compare Freeman House, *Totem Salmon: Life Lessons from Another Species* (Boston: Beacon Press, 1999).

90. For several important typologies of urban regimes, see Clarence Stone, "Urban Regimes and the Capacity to Govern: A Political Economy Approach," *Journal of Urban Affairs* 15, no. 1 (1993): 1–28; Margaret Weir, "Power, Money, and Politics in Community Development," in *Urban Problems and Community Development,* edited by Ronald F. Ferguson and William T. Dickens (Brookings, 1999), pp. 139–92.

Chapter Four

1. Cindy Carlson and Richard Goll, personal interviews, Hampton, Va., April 22, 2002. Carlson was director of the Hampton Coalition for Youth; Goll is founding director of Alternatives Inc. and served as one of the nonprofit stakeholders on the city task force on economic development and quality of the workforce.

2. Quotations from Cindy Carlson and Richard Goll, personal interviews, Hampton, Va., April 22, 2002, and discussions, April 21–24, 2007; and David Osborne and Peter Plastrik, *Beyond Bureaucracy: Five Strategies for Reinventing Government* (Reading, Mass.: Addison-Wesley, 1997), pp. 241–55, quotation 248. See also Clarence Stone and Donn Worgs, "Community-Building and a Human Capital Agenda in Hampton, Va.: A Case Analysis of the Policy Process in a Medium-Sized City," University of Maryland, July 30, 2004. Bob O'Neill is the executive director of the International City/County Management Association and past president of the National Academy of Public Administration.

3. Mike Montieth, personal interview, Hampton, Va., April 24, 2002; Terry O'Neill, personal interview, Hampton, Va., April 24, 2002; Bill Potapchuk, personal discussion, Washington, D.C., July 29, 2008. At the time of the interviews, Montieth was the assistant city manager of the City of Hampton and O'Neill the city's director of planning; Bill Potapchuk is the consultant who trained Montieth.

4. Cindy Carlson, personal interview, Hampton, Va., April 23, 2002.

5. Goll, interview, April 22, 2002.

6. Ibid.; Richard Goll, presentation at Civic Engagement Summit, YMCA of the USA, Rosemont, Ill., October 9, 2002.

7. Sean O'Keefe and Christie Burgos, personal discussions, Hampton, Va., April 24, 2002; Richard Goll, telephone interviews, January 9, April 22, and April 24, 2002; Kathryn Johnson, telephone interview, January 31 and April 22, 2002; Linda Hansen, telephone interview, April 22, 2002; Della Hughes, personal interview, Waltham, Mass., March 21 and May 8, 2001; Cindy Carlson, "The Hampton Experience: Creating a Model and a Context for Youth Civic Engagement," in *Youth Participation and Community Change,* edited by Barry N. Checkoway and Lorraine M. Gutierrez (New York: Haworth Press, 2006), pp. 98–99. O'Keefe and Burgos were youth involved in the early efforts and subsequently served on the staff of Alternatives; Johnson was director of Alternatives; Hansen was director of the Creativity Center at Alternatives; and Hughes is a former director of the National Network for Youth.

8. Paul C. Light, *Sustaining Innovation: Creating Nonprofit and Government Organizations That Innovate Naturally* (San Francisco: Jossey-Bass, 1998), pp. 34–36, 93; Goll, interview, April 24, 2002.

9. Kathryn Johnson, presentation to the national meeting Seeing and Believing: Lessons Learned on the Power of Youth to Improve Communities, Hampton Coalition for Youth and Alternatives Inc., Hampton, Va., April 23, 2007.

10. Carlson, interview, April 22, 2002; Hampton Coalition for Youth, *2 Commit 2 the Future 4 Youth: Proposed Plan of Action* (Hampton, Va., 1993).

11. Hampton Coalition for Youth, *2 Commit 2 the Future 4 Youth,* pp. i, 2, 6.

12. Ibid., p. iii; italics in original.

13. On designing pathways for youth engagement that are diverse and developmentally appropriate, see Merita Irby, Thaddeus Ferber, and Karen Pittman, with Joel Tolman and Nicole Yohalem, *Youth Action: Youth Contributing to Communities, Communities Supporting Youth,* Community and Youth Development 6 (Takoma Park, Md.: International Youth Foundation, Forum for Youth Investment, 2001).

14. Kathryn Price, presentation at the national strategy conference Youth Development and Civic Engagement: Leveraging Innovation, Building a Movement, Boston, February 1–3, 2002.

15. See Hampton Coalition for Youth, *2 Commit 2 the Future 4 Youth,* pp. 16–17.

16. Jennifer L. O'Donaghue, "'Taking Their Own Power': Urban Youth, Community-Based Youth Organizations, and Public Efficacy," in *Beyond Resistance: Youth Activism and Community Change,* edited by Shawn Ginwright, Pedro Noguera, and Julio Cammarota (New York: Routledge, 2006), pp. 229–45.

17. Michael Bock, personal interview, Hampton, Va., April 21, 2007; Bock was Hampton youth commissioner at the time of the interview. On the development and use of a common language of youth civic engagement across the city, I draw from various documents, field observations, and interviews, especially with the Alternatives leadership team of Kathryn Johnson, Allyson Graul, and Linda Hansen, telephone interview, May 10, 2007. For the assets and community approach to youth development, see Della M. Hughes and Susan P. Curnan, "Community Youth Development: A Framework for Action," *CYD Journal* 1, no. 1 (2000): 7–13; and Melvin Delgado, *New Arenas for Community Social Work Practice* (Columbia University Press, 2000), chapter 3.

18. Two of the private high schools are located in neighboring Newport News.

19. Remarks by a group of youth commissioners, Innovations in American Government meeting at City Hall, Hampton, Va., April 23, 2007, as well as observations and interviews cited throughout this chapter. Of course, this does not imply that there are not class, race, and gender differences in civic skills or participation rates among youth in the city as a whole, only that these seem relatively negligible among those whose leadership skills have been nurtured through the Youth Commission and, indeed, through the various other youth planner and advisory groups studied.

20. Gregory Harrison, personal interview, Hampton, Va., April 21, 2007, and his comments at the Innovations in American Government meeting with a group of youth commissioners, Hampton, Va., April 23, 2007; and interviews with youth commissioners serving between the years 2001 and 2007. See also Cindy Carlson and Elizabeth Sykes, *Shaping the Future: Working Together, Changing Communities; A Manual on How to Start or Improve Your Own Youth Commission* (Hampton, Va.: Hampton Coalition for Youth, 2001, and

2007 update). Harrison was the chair of the Hampton Youth Commission at the time of his interview. Sykes served as chair of the Youth Commission while she and Carlson were writing the manual.

21. Youth commissioner and staff presentations at the Innovations in American Government meeting in City Hall, Hampton, Va., April 23, 2007; Quelonda Bruer, Hampton Coalition for Youth, telephone interview, May 9, 2007; interviews with the various senior and junior staff in the mentoring network, as well as youth commissioners themselves, cited throughout this chapter. Bruer was program manager and youth commission coordinator at the time of the interview.

22. Tamara Whitaker, remarks presented at the national strategy conference Youth Development and Civic Engagement: Leveraging Innovation, Building a Movement, Boston, February 1–3, 2002; Allyson Graul, telephone interview, August 2, 2002. Graul was director of the Youth Civic Engagement Center, Alternatives Inc., at the time. To be sure, various adults also become close personal mentors and family friends of some of the youth leaders.

23. Field notes from the Hampton Youth Commission meeting, April 22, 2002. Katherine Cramer Walsh, *Talking about Race: Community Dialogues and the Politics of Difference* (University of Chicago Press, 2007), finds some different dynamics in her analysis of study circle dialogues on race among adults in other communities, which were similarly fruitful, though with more contentious assertiveness about issues of identity and justice. I suspect that the difference derives from two factors: changing norms on race and interracial friendships among youth, and a relative familiarity in Hampton with various forms of interracial deliberation and leadership development in schools and other venues.

24. John Johnson, personal interview, Hampton, Va., April 24, 2002; Cindy Carlson, telephone interview, February 7, 2005; Allyson Graul, telephone interview, March 9, 2005; John Landesman, personal conversations, Study Circles Resource Center staff retreat, Pomfret, Conn., November 9, 2004. Johnson was director of the Citizens Unity Commission and Landesman the study circles facilitator in Hampton at the time of these interviews. See also William Potapchuk, Cindy Carlson, and Joan Kennedy, "Growing Governance Deliberatively: Lessons and Inspiration from Hampton," in *The Deliberative Democracy Handbook: Strategies for Effective Civic Engagement in the 21st Century,* edited by John Gastil and Peter Levine (San Francisco: Jossey-Bass, 2005), pp. 260–61. The Study Circles Resource Center, it should be noted, fully welcomes such adaptation to the specific dynamics of different communities.

25. Jaron Scott, personal interview, Hampton, Va., April 21, 2007; Harrison, interview; Bock, interview; Patrick Russo and Terry O'Neill, personal conversations, Hampton, Va., April 24, 2007; Bruer, interview. Scott, Harrison, and Bock were Hampton youth commissioners; Russo was superintendent of schools; and O'Neill was planning director.

26. Group discussion with youth commission leaders and staff, Hampton, Va., April 23, 2007; Harrison, interview; Scott, interview; Bruer, interview. Bruer provides consultation to youth groups on the request-for-proposal process as well as financial oversight and logistical support to the commissioners for site visits. On the increasing practice of "youth philanthropy," in which young people themselves determine which projects to fund, see Pam Garza and Pam Stevens, *Best Practices in Youth Philanthropy* (Austin, Tex.: Coalition of Community Foundations for Youth, 2002); and Youth Leadership Institute, *Changing the Face of Giving: An Assessment of Youth Philanthropy* (San Francisco: James Irvine Foundation, 2001).

27. O'Neill, interview; Terry O'Neill, presentation and discussions at the national meeting Seeing and Believing: Lessons Learned on the Power of Youth to Improve Communities, Hampton Coalition for Youth and Alternatives Inc., Hampton, Va., April 24, 2007.

28. Shellae Blackwell, personal interview, Neighborhood Office, Hampton, Va., April 23, 2002.

29. Kathryn Price, personal interview, Boston, February 1–3, 2002; Rashida Costley, personal interview, Rosemont, Ill., October 8, 2002; Alicia Tundidor, telephone interview, May 16, 2005; Ivey Hawkins, personal interview, Hampton, Va., April 23, 2007; Will Bane, personal discussions, Hampton, Va., April 23, 2007; Will Bane, telephone interview, May 11, 2007; O'Neill, interview; Donald Whipple, telephone interview, May 11, 2007. Whipple was Hampton city planner; Price, Costley, Tundidor, Hawkins, and Bane were all youth planners.

30. Hampton Planning Department, *Youth Component of the 2010 Comprehensive Plan: City Planning from a "New" Perspective* (Hampton, Va., 1999), pp. 4–14.

31. Will Bane, interview, May 11, 2007; Whipple, interview.

32. Tundidor, interview.

33. Ibid.; Bradford Knight, personal interview, Hampton, Va., April 21, 2007; Will Bane, interview, May 11, 2007. On consumer action as a form of youth civic engagement, see Cliff Zukin and others, *A New Civic Engagement: Political Participation, Civic Life, and the Changing American Citizen* (Oxford University Press, 2007), pp. 77–81.

34. Whipple, interview. See also Hampton Planning Department, *Youth Component of the 2010 Comprehensive Plan;* and Cindy Carlson, "Youth with Influence: The Youth Planner Initiative in Hampton, Va.," *Children, Youth, and Environments* 15, no. 2 (2005): 213–26.

35. Tundidor, interview; Whipple, interview; Will Bane, interview, May 11, 2007. See City of Hampton, *Youth Component of the Community Plan,* Hampton, Va., February 8, 2006; City of Hampton, *Community Plan,* Hampton, Va., February 8, 2006. Bane organized the youth commission's summer retreat in 2006.

36. O'Neill, interview.

37. In addition to the interviews and documents cited below, I draw from my field notes of the principal's advisory group at Hampton High School, April 23, 2002.

38. Arnold Baker, telephone interview, April 15, 2005; Graul, interview, August 2, 2002; Cindy Carlson, personal discussion, Rosemont, Ill., October 8, 2002. Baker was principal of Kecoughtan High School at the time; Graul and Carlson initially facilitated the Kecoughtan advisory group when it shifted from dialogue-and-gripe sessions to structured partnerships and projects.

39. Baker, interview; Leah Dixon, telephone interview, April 25, 2005; Mary Patterson, telephone interview, May 16, 2007. As part of her job as youth and community development director at Alternatives, Patterson oversaw the Kecoughtan principal's advisory and consulting team, as well as Phoebus and Bethel high school advisory groups. See Principal's Advisory and Consulting Team, *Safe Schools Handbook* (Hampton, Va., n.d.)

40. Patterson, interview; Baker, interview; Dixon, interview.

41. Dixon, interview; Baker, interview; Keisha Ashe, telephone interview, May 24, 2005; Patterson, interview. Dixon and Ashe were both vice chairs of the Improving Student Achievement committee. See Principal's Advisory and Consulting Team, *Kecoughtan High*

School Idea Book (Hampton, Va., 2003; revised edition, 2007); and PACT Idea Book presentation at faculty meetings (outline, May 7 and May 8, 2007).

42. Shauna Adams, Imani Adams, and Lydia Huey, telephone interview, June 11, 2007; Patterson, interview. See Alternatives Inc., *RELATE Project: Trainers Manual, 2007–08* (Hampton, Va., 2007). Adams, Adams, and Huey were RELATE youth trainers.

43. Adams, Adams, and Huey, interview. For a broad range of related practice in youth and community organizations, see P. Caitlin Fullwood, *The New Girls' Movement: Implications for Youth Programs* (New York: Ms Foundation for Women, 2001). On issues of gender and citizenship, especially the impact of sexual harassment and violence, see Carole Pateman, *The Disorder of Women: Democracy, Feminism, and Political Theory* (Stanford University Press, 1990), chapter 4; and Virginia Sapiro, "'Private' Coercion and Democratic Theory: The Case of Gender-Based Violence," in *Reconsidering the Democratic Public,* edited by George E. Marcus and Russell L. Hanson (Penn State University Press, 1993), pp. 427–49.

44. Michael Cromartie, as quoted by Patterson, interview.

45. Field observations, Superintendent's Youth Advisory Group, Hampton, Va., April 23, 2002; Tamara Whitaker, personal interview, Boston, Mass., February 1–3, 2002; Ashe, interview; Eliott Clark, personal interview, Hampton, Va., April 21, 2007; Andrea Sealey, telephone interview, May 2, 2007; Graul, interviews, August 2, 2002, and March 9, 2005. Whitaker and Clark were youth advisory group members. Graul oversaw youth leadership training, and Sealey was youth development director, at Alternatives Inc. Beginning in the eighth grade, Ashe served on the youth advisory group under two superintendents and an acting superintendent.

46. Field observations, Superintendent's Youth Advisory Group, Hampton, Va., April 23, 2002; Allen Davis III and Johnny Pauls, follow-up conversations, Hampton, Va., April 23, 2002. Davis was superintendent of Hampton schools, and Pauls director of secondary education.

47. Donna Woods, telephone interview, May 2, 2007; Ann Bane, telephone interview, May 2, 2007; Sealey, interview. Woods was director of secondary education and Bane the director of community and legislative relations of Hampton City Schools.

48. Graul, interviews, August 2, 2002, and March 9, 2005.

49. Sealey, interview; Graul, interviews, August 2, 2002, and March 9, 2005; Kim Borton, telephone interview, March 9, 2005. Borton was the Alternatives staff person initially in charge of implementing the Kellogg grant. See Center for Civic Education, *We the People: Project Citizen* (Calabasas, Calif., n.d.).

50. Sealey, interview.

51. Clark, interview; Carmen Hills, personal interview, Hampton, Va., April 21, 2007; Woods, interview; Sealey, interview; Ann Bane, interview. Clark and Hills were members of the superintendent's youth advisory group.

52. Woods, interview; Ann Bane, interview; Clark, interview.

53. Russo, interview; and Davis, follow-up conversation.

54. Ann Bane, interview and follow-up e-mail, May 2, 2007. See also the Hampton City Schools award application, "Community Visioning: HCS Community Priorities Workshop," Hampton, Va., n.d.

55. See Melvin Delgado and Lee Staples, *Youth-Led Community Organizing: Theory and Action* (Oxford University Press, 2008); Ginwright, Noguera, and Cammarota, eds., *Beyond*

Resistance; and Social Policy Research Associates, *Extending the Reach of Youth Development through Civic Activism: Research Results from the Youth Leadership Development Initiative,* 2 vols. (Takoma Park, Md.: Innovation Center for Community and Youth Development, 2003). See also the various reports on the website of the Funders Collaborative for Youth Organizing (www.fcyo.org [December 8, 2008]).

56. Borton, interview; Graul, interview, March 9, 2005; Will Bane, interview, May 11, 2007. Bane, a youth planner in 2005–07, first became involved as a ninth-grader through these activities.

57. Zacchary Ferguson, personal interview, Hampton, Va., April 21, 2007; Will Bane, interview, May 11, 2007; field observations, Power of Youth Rally, Hampton, Va., April 21, 2007. See also Ethan Enz, "UthACT: Youth Activists of Today," *WORD!* 1, no. 3 (2007): 7–8.

58. Carlson, interview, April 22, 2002; Goll, interview, April 22, 2002. See also presentations by Mayor Mamie Locke, youth planner Kathryn Price, and Cindy Carlson at the federal interagency Youth Summit, Washington, D.C., June 2002.

59. Montieth, interview.

60. Blackwell, interview, April 23, 2002; Shellae Blackwell, personal interview, Hampton, Va., April 24, 2007; field notes from Neighborhood Youth Advisory Board meeting, Hampton, Va., April 22, 2002; Michael Canty, presentation, Seeing and Believing: Lessons Learned on the Power of Youth to Improve Communities, Hampton Coalition for Youth and Alternatives Inc., Hampton, Va., April 23, 2007. At the time of the presentation, Canty was director of In-SYNC Partnerships. See also Michael Bayer and William Potapchuk, *Learning from Neighborhoods: The Story of the Hampton Neighborhood Initiative, 1993–2003* (Hampton, Va.: Hampton Neighborhood Office, 2004); and Potapchuk, Carlson, and Kennedy, "Growing Governance Deliberatively," pp. 262–65. Kennedy had been a VISTA volunteer with deep commitments to citizen participation.

61. Field notes, Public Safety Forum, sponsored by the Neighborhood Youth Advisory Board and the Hampton Youth Commission, Hampton, Va., April 23, 2007.

62. Blackwell, interview, April 24, 2007.

63. Laurine Press, personal interview, Hampton, Va., April 23, 2002; Art Thatcher, presentation, Seeing and Believing: Lessons Learned on the Power of Youth to Improve Communities, Hampton Coalition for Youth and Alternatives Inc., Hampton, Va., April 23, 2007; field observations and presentations, Hampton–Newport News BEST (Building Exemplary Systems of Training for Youth Workers) Initiative, Three-Year Anniversary: The Best Is Yet to Come, Hampton, Va., April 24, 2002. Some three hundred youth workers from fifty youth agencies in Hampton and Newport News had completed the core course as of 2002. See also Center for School and Community Services, Academy for Educational Development, *BEST Strengthens Youth Worker Practice: An Evaluation of Building Exemplary Systems of Training for Youth Workers* (Washington: Academy for Educational Development, 2002).

64. Thomas Townshend, personal interview, Hampton, Va., April 24, 2002; Jeffrey Davis, personal interview, Hampton, Va., April 24, 2002; field observations at the Newtown Leadership Group/Y-COPE meeting, with Captain William Davis, Tony Perkins, Alvin Hunter, president of the Newtown Leadership Group, and other members of the community, Hampton, Va., April 23, 2002. Townsend was police chief, Jeffrey Davis a sergeant, and Captain Davis and Perkins detectives with the Hampton police. Hunter was president of the Newtown Leadership Group.

65. Townsend, interview; Jeffrey Davis, interview; see also the membership lists of the original youth council of 1992 and the superintendent's advisory group for 2001–02.

Chapter Five

1. On the opportunities and conundrums of citizen participation in environmental regulation in the 1970s, as well as the changing "organizational ecology" of environmental groups over the past four decades, see Carmen Sirianni, "Environmental Organizations," in *The State of Nonprofit America,* edited by Lester M. Salamon, 2d ed. (Brookings, 2009, forthcoming). See also Richard Harris and Sidney Milkis, *The Politics of Regulatory Change: A Tale of Two Agencies,* 2d ed. (Oxford University Press, 1996), chapter 3; Walter Rosenbaum, "Slaying Beautiful Hypotheses with Ugly Facts: EPA and the Limits of Public Participation," *Journal of Voluntary Action Research* 6, no. 6 (1978): 161–73; and Paul Sabatier, "Social Movements and Regulatory Agencies: Towards a More Adequate—and Less Pessimistic—Theory of 'Clientele Capture,'" *Policy Sciences* 6, no. 3 (1975): 301–42. "Maximum feasible participation" is the term most famously used in reference to federally sponsored community action agencies in the War on Poverty, but its sentiment was included in various other programs, though with varying nomenclature.

2. Marc Landy, Marc Roberts, and Stephen Thomas, *The Environmental Protection Agency: Asking the Wrong Questions* (Oxford University Press, 1990), p. 300.

3. Rebecca Hanmer, telephone interview, February 2, 2006. Hanmer has since retired. For the legal framework in which collaborative watershed strategies began to emerge, as well as the broad ecological intent of the 1972 Clean Water Act amendments, see especially Robert W. Adler, "Addressing Barriers to Watershed Protection," *Environmental Law* 25, no. 4 (1995): 973–1106. For the scientific underpinnings, see Luna B. Leopold, *A View of the River* (Harvard University Press, 1994); Leopold is the former chief hydrologist for the U.S. Geological Survey and professor of geology at the University of California at Berkeley. See also Paul A. Sabatier, Chris Weible, and Jared Ficker, "Eras of Water Management in the United States: Implications for Collaborative Watershed Approaches," in *Swimming Upstream: Collaborative Approaches to Watershed Management,* edited by Paul A. Sabatier and others (MIT Press, 2005), pp. 23–52; and Bob Doppelt and others, *Entering the Watershed: A New Approach to Save America's River Ecosystems* (Washington: Island Press, 1993). As Doppelt and colleagues noted in the early 1990s, "Despite expenditures of at least $473 billion to build, operate, and administer water pollution control facilities since 1970, the nation's water resources continue to decline in both quality and quantity" (Doppelt and others, *Entering the Watershed,* p. xxii).

4. On these early participatory programs in water planning, see David Godschalk and Bruce Stiftel, "Making Waves: Public Participation in State Water Planning," *Journal of Applied Behavioral Science* 17, no. 4 (1981): 597–614; Stephen A. Cohen, "Citizen Participation in Bureaucratic Decision Making: With Special Emphasis on Environmental Policy," Ph.D. dissertation, State University of New York at Buffalo, 1979; Michael Jungman, "Areawide Planning under the Federal Water Pollution Control Act Amendments of 1972: Intergovernmental and Land Use Implications," *Texas Law Review* 54 (1976): 1047–80; Conservation Foundation, *Water Quality Training Institute Handbook* (Washington: Conservation Foundation, 1974).

5. For an influential analysis of the scientific and management components of the watershed approach, see the National Research Council, *New Strategies for America's Watersheds* (Washington: National Academies Press, 1999), and John Randolph's more recent comprehensive textbook, *Environmental Land Use Planning and Management* (Washington: Island Press, 2004). For a good summary of the approach in cross-agency perspective, see the report by the interagency team, U.S. Environmental Protection Agency (EPA), *Protecting and Restoring America's Watersheds: Status, Trends, and Initiatives in Watershed Management* (2001), and EPA, Office of Wetlands, Oceans, and Watersheds, *A Watershed Decade* (2001).

6. For a most important early civic analysis, see Kim Herman Goslant, "Citizen Participation and Administrative Discretion in the Cleanup of Narragansett Bay," *Harvard Environmental Law Review* 12, no. 3 (1988): 521–68.

7. Hanmer, interview. See also John Wesley Powell, "Institutions for Arid Lands," *Century Magazine,* June 1890, pp. 111–16; sections of this work have been reprinted in various reports and mentioned in several staff interviews.

8. Peter Lavigne, telephone interview, May 7, 2007; Karen Firehock, telephone interview, October 11, 2005; Andrew Moore, telephone interview, February 15, 2002. At the time of the interview Moore was the vice president of the National Association of Service and Conservation Corps (now the Corps Network). See also Peter M. Lavigne, *The Watershed Innovators Workshop: Proceedings* (Portland, Ore.: River Network, 1995); "Watershed Councils East and West: Advocacy, Consensus, and Environmental Progress," *UCLA Journal of Environmental Law and Policy* 22, no. 2 (2004): 301–10; Michael Houck, "Bankside Citizens," in *Rivertown: Rethinking Urban Rivers,* edited by Paul Stanton Kibel (MIT Press, 2007), pp. 179–96. See also Ann L. Riley, *Restoring Streams in Cities: A Guide for Planners, Policymakers, and Citizens* (Washington: Island Press, 1998). Riley, with Luna Leopold, catalyzed the Berkeley network node of the movement, and Houck the Portland, Oregon, one. On the importance of reframing in both policy analysis and social movements, see Donald A. Schön and Martin Rein, *Frame Reflection: Toward the Resolution of Intractable Policy Controversies* (New York: Basic Books, 1994); and Robert D. Benford and Donald A. Snow, "Framing Processes and Social Movements: An Overview and Assessment," *Annual Review of Sociology* 26 (2000): 611–39. This reciprocal process of reframing within both organizationally and culturally constituted networks warrants a far richer analysis than can be provided here. For a taste of the cultural richness, see Freeman House, *Totem Salmon: Life Lessons from Another Species* (Boston: Beacon Press, 1999); and Blaine Anton Vogt, "Border Fish: Salmon Crises, Environmental Imaginaries, and the Politics of Sustainability," Ph.D. dissertation, Brandeis University, 1999.

9. See EPA, Office of Wetlands, Oceans, and Watersheds, *Community-Based Watershed Management: Lessons from the National Estuary Program* (2005); National Academy of Public Administration (NAPA), *environment.gov: Transforming Environmental Protection for the 21st Century* (Washington, 2000), chapter 4; Mark T. Imperial and Timothy Hennessey, *Environmental Governance in Watersheds: The Importance of Collaboration to Institutional Performance* (Washington: NAPA, October 2000); EPA, Office of Wetlands, Oceans, and Watersheds, *The National Estuary Program: A Network Protecting and Restoring Coastal Ecosystems* (2007). See also the methodologies for estimating the economic value supplied by aquatic ecosystems in National Research Council, Committee on Assessing and Valuing the Services of Aquatic and Related Terrestrial Ecosystems, *Valuing Ecosystem Services: Toward Better Environmental Decision-Making* (Washington: National Academies Press, 2005). The

acronym *NEP* is commonly used for both the national program and the individual programs on particular estuaries; NEPs in the plural thus refers to multiple local programs.

10. See Mark Lubell, "Do Watershed Partnerships Enhance Beliefs Conducive to Collective Action?" in *Swimming Upstream,* edited by Sabatier and others, pp. 201–32; Mark Lubell, "Resolving Conflict and Building Cooperation in the National Estuary Program," *Environmental Management* 33, no. 5 (2004): 677–91; Katrin Smith Korfmacher, "Invisible Successes, Visible Failures: Paradoxes of Ecosystem Management in the Albemarle-Pamlico Estuarine Study," *Coastal Management* 26, no. 3 (1998): 191–212; Mark Lubell and others, "Building Consensual Institutions: Networks and the National Estuary Program," *American Journal of Political Science* 47, no. 1 (2003): 143–58.

11. EPA staff, telephone interview, March 3, 2006. I have also examined the Watershed Academy course schedules and resource materials and have viewed a wide variety of webcast courses. See also Watershed Academy, *Watershed Protection: A Statewide Approach* (EPA, 1996).

12. For the contributions of local and statewide watershed associations to the development of state watershed management and a national network of "shedheads," see the reports of the Four Corners Watershed Innovators Initiative, especially Stephen M. Born, with Kenneth Genskow, *Exploring the Watershed Approach: Critical Dimensions of State-Local Partnerships,* final report of the Four Corners Watershed Innovators Initiative (Portland, Ore.: River Network, September 1999); Mark Smith and others, *Four Corners Watershed Innovators Workshop: Massachusetts Background Report* (Portland, Ore.: River Network, October 5, 1998); Ken Slattery, Joy Huber, and Phil Shelton, *Four Corners Watershed Innovators Initiative: Washington Background Report* (Portland, Ore.: River Network, September 19, 1997); Fran Vitulli and others, *Four Corners Watershed Innovators Workshop: California Background Report* (Portland, Ore.: River Network, March 18, 1998). Also see Oregon Watershed Enhancement Board, *A Strategy for Achieving Healthy Watersheds in Oregon* (Salem, Ore., January 2001); Ryan Bidwell and Clare Ryan, "Collaborative Partnership Design: Organizational Affiliation for Watershed Partnerships," *Society and Natural Resources* 19, no. 9 (Oct. 2006): 827–43; and William D. Leach and Paul A. Sabatier, "Are Trust and Social Capital the Keys to Success? Watershed Partnerships in California and Washington," in *Swimming Upstream*, edited by Sabatier and others, pp. 233–58.

13. Firehock, interview; EPA staff, telephone interviews, November 15 and December 12, 2005; field notes from Community Culture and Environment workshop at the CARE [Community Action for a Renewed Environment] National Training Workshop, Denver, November 16, 2005. Firehock was with the Institute for Environmental Negotiation at the time of the interview. See EPA, *Community Culture and the Environment* (2002); Tom Schueler and Anne Kitchell, *Methods to Develop Restoration Plans for Small Urban Watersheds* (Ellicott City, Md.: Center for Watershed Protection, 2005); Karen Firehock, Fran Flanigan, and Pat Devlin, *Community Watershed Forums: A Planners Guide* (Baltimore: Alliance for Chesapeake Bay, 2002); and EPA, Office of Water, *Handbook for Developing Watershed Plans to Restore and Protect Our Waters* (March 2008). For an overview of related manuals in the broader community-building field, see Carmen Sirianni and Lewis A. Friedland, *The Civic Renewal Movement* (Dayton, Ohio: Kettering Foundation, 2005), part 4.

14. Shelley H. Metzenbaum, "Measurement That Matters: Cleaning Up the Charles River," in *Environmental Governance: A Report on the Next Generation of Environmental Policy,* edited by Donald F. Kettl (Brookings, 2002), pp. 58–117.

15. EPA staff, telephone interview, March 17, 2006. See Paul A. DeBarry, *Watersheds: Processes, Assessment, and Management* (Hoboken, N.J.: Wiley and Sons, 2004), especially chapters 10 and 17; Dale Manty and others, "Bringing High-Tech GIS Tools to Community Decisionmaking" (paper prepared for EPA Community Involvement Conference and Training, Buffalo, N.Y., July 14, 2005); EPA, Office of Water, Watershed Plan Builder (http://iaspub.epa.gov/watershedplan/planBuilder.do?pageId=51&navId=39 [November 12, 2007]); and Water Quality Exchange (www.epa.gov/storet/wqx.html [November 12, 2007]). These tools were preceded by Surf Your Watershed and EnviroMapper for Water. The National Oceanic and Atmospheric Administration's PIVOT (Performance Indicators Visualization and Outreach Tool) is designed to enable local programs under the National Estuary Program to use interactive graphics and maps to illustrate problems and visually track progress in restoring habitat, and is also available through the EPA website (www.epa.gov/owow/estuaries/pivot/overview/intro.htm [November 20, 2008]). Such performance reporting is required by the Estuaries and Clean Water Act of 2000 (as well as other laws), which establishes a multiagency Estuary Habitat Restoration Council responsible for developing a national restoration strategy to ensure a comprehensive and integrated restoration approach and to foster coordination of federal and nonfederal restoration activities. The goal of the strategy is to restore a million acres of habitat by 2010. For a still broader range of geographic information system tools, see Robert Scally, *GIS for Environmental Management* (Redlands, Calif.: ESRI Press, 2006).

16. Field observations, informal discussions, and public forum, Puget Sound Partnership: Building the Action Agenda workshop, Bremerton, Wash., February 28, 2008; Betsy Peabody, telephone interview, March 11, 2008; Martha Neuman, telephone interview, March 20, 2008; Scott Redman, telephone interview, March 26, 2008; John Williams, telephone interview, March 11, 2008; Hilary Franz, personal interview, Washington, D.C., March 18, 2008. At the time of the interviews, Neuman was director of the Puget Sound Partnership Action Agenda, Redman was a team member of the Action Agenda and a former science coordinator for the Puget Sound Action Team; Williams was director of Still Hope Productions, which produces public educational videos on Puget Sound; and Franz, an environmental lawyer who has served on the Puget Sound Recovery Council, was Bainbridge Island city councilor. See also Puget Sound Action Team, *Serving Puget Sound with PIE: Success Stories from the Puget Sound Action Team's Public Involvement and Education Program, 1997–2003* (February 2004); U.S. Office of Management and Budget, *Ocean, Coastal, and Estuary Protection: Program Assessment* (Assessment year 2005); Puget Sound Partnership, *Public Awareness and Engagement Plan* (August 2006), for an initial iteration, which runs the gamut of regulatory tools, corporate reinvention, civic action, and individual behavior; and documents on the Puget Sound Partnership website (www.psp.wa.gov/ index.php [November 20, 2008]), especially the initial 2008 strategic priorities and action area profiles and maps. The full Action Agenda was scheduled for release in December 2008.

17. For the basic contours and regional diversity of this movement, as well as estimates of its size from various national and state directories, see Carmen Sirianni and Lewis A. Friedland, *Civic Innovation in America* (University of California Press, 2001), pp. 102–07 and 305 n. 34; Peter M. Lavigne, "Watershed Councils East and West: Advocacy, Consensus, and Environmental Progress," *UCLA Journal of Environmental Law and Policy* 22, no. 2 (2004): 301–10; John T. Woolley and Michael Vincent McGinnis, with Julie Kellner, "The California Watershed Movement: Science and the Politics of Place," *Natural Resources Journal* 42,

no. 1 (2002): 133–83; Elizabeth A. Moore and Tomas M. Koontz, "A Typology of Collaborative Watershed Groups: Citizen-Based, Agency-Based, and Mixed Partnerships," *Society and Natural Resources* 16, no. 5 (2003): 451–60. For comparative analysis of community-level networks, as well as processes of bridging multiple "ways of knowing" among their key participants, see Anne Taufen Wessels, "Constructing Watershed Parks: Actor-Networks and Collaborative Governance in Four U.S. Metropolitan Areas," Ph.D. dissertation, University of California at Irvine, 2007. On the importance of monetary resources and intergovernmental transfers for reducing transaction costs and building organizational capacity, see the quantitative analysis of 958 watershed partnerships by Mark Lubell and others in "Watershed Partnerships and the Emergence of Collective Action Institutions," *American Journal of Political Science* 46, no. 1 (2002): 148–63. Social movement theorists have long recognized the importance of outside supporters to movement resource mobilization but have been less cognizant of government's role in helping to facilitate movement network formation and growth. Of course, the latter makes more sense for civic movements attempting to develop capacities for collaboration with government and other partners. For new directions in research, see Mario Diani and Doug McAdam, eds., *Social Movements and Networks: Relational Approaches to Collective Action* (Oxford University Press, 2003).

18. For overall data and project descriptions on the Chesapeake Bay Small Watershed grants program, see Ken Jones and others, *A Review of Planning and Implementation of Protection and Restoration Activities in Small Chesapeake Bay Watersheds* (National Fish and Wildlife Foundation, February 2004, draft), and the websites of the Chesapeake Bay Program (www.chesapeakebay.net), the National Fish and Wildlife Foundation (www.nfwf.org [December 8, 2008]), and the Chesapeake Bay Funders Network (www.chesbayfunders.org [December 8, 2008]). Also see Chesapeake Bay Program, *Small Watershed Grants Program: FY 98 Final Report* (EPA, 1998); and National Fish and Wildlife Foundation, *2005 Annual Report* (2006). For the most comprehensive recent analyses of the Chesapeake Bay Program overall, see NAPA, *Taking Environmental Protection to the Next Level: An Assessment of the U.S. Environmental Services Delivery System; A Report to the U.S. EPA* (April 2007), especially chapters 3–5; and Mary Doyle and Cynthia A. Drew, eds., *Large-Scale Ecosystem Restoration: Five Case Studies from the United States* (Washington: Island Press, 2008), part 4.

19. For National Estuary Program small-grants programs and project descriptions, see the websites of the each of the estuary programs, accessible through the Office of Wetlands, Oceans, and Watersheds' website (www.epa.gov/owow/estuaries [November 20, 2008]); Long Island Sound Study, *Comprehensive Conservation and Management Plan* (March 1994), section IX, and the study's website (www.longislandsoundstudy.net/futuresfund/ffprojects_lg_07.htm [November 20, 2008]). See also the jointly developed strategy document, Restore America's Estuaries and National Oceanographic and Atmospheric Administration, *A National Strategy to Restore Coastal and Estuarine Habitat* (Arlington, Va.: Restore America's Estuaries, April 2002). The National Oceanographic and Atmospheric Administration (NOAA) Restoration Center, it should be noted, has had nearly two dozen other partners besides Restore America's Estuaries and has some grants that go through the National Estuary Program. The administration's Community-Based Restoration Program provided $10 million for projects in 2002, for instance, as well as technical assistance, and leveraged this amount several times with matching funds and in-kind services, bringing the estimated value of funded projects to more than $40 million. From 2000 to 2005, Restore America's Estuaries received $8,717,249 from the Restoration Center, to be regranted to

local groups, which leveraged $9,136,416 directly and a further $8,404,916 through the partnership. These amounts do not, of course, count the dollar value of the several million hours of work by an estimated two hundred fifty-six thousand volunteers over this period. See Restore America's Estuaries, *Annual Report 2005* (Arlington, Va., 2006), p. 5; and the Restore America's Estuaries and NOAA Restoration Center websites (www.estuaries.org and www.nmfs.noaa.gov/habitat/restoration/ [November 20, 2008]).

20. The term *watershed democracy,* which appeared in the official watershed innovators report of 1995, has since been watered down in official organizational mission statements but still enjoys currency among many activists. Lavigne, interview; Kathy Luscher, telephone interview, September 19, 1997; field notes, River Rally, Bretton Woods, N.H., May 5–9, 2006. Luscher is currently partnership program director for the River Network. See also Lavigne, *The Watershed Innovators Workshop,* as well as the companion state reports and proceedings (cited in note 12). The Rivers, Trails, and Conservation Assistance program of the National Park Service initially sponsored the River Network's development of the national directory of river and watershed conservation groups. The River Network collaborates with a variety of other national organizations, such as American Rivers, but delineates its role within the watershed movement thus: "We do not take positions on national or state legislative or regulatory issues, become directly involved in local or state affairs, endorse political candidates at any level, or litigate. These are roles better filled by others— including the local, state and regional groups we serve, other national organizations, and coalitions that form within our network to address specific issues." River Network, *2005–2008 Strategic Plan* (Portland, Ore., 2005), p. 9.

21. See Suzanne Easton, *Watershed Assistance Grants: Building Capacity of Community-Based Watershed Partnerships; An Evaluation* (Portland, Ore.: River Network, March 2001). While the percentage of contributions from government grants has varied from year to year, the River Network's *Annual Reports* and audited financial statements show substantial government transfers (with EPA programs providing the lion's share), ranging in recent years from one-fifth to one-third of overall yearly outlays, and in some years even more.

22. Richard Fox, telephone interview, March 3, 2006; Fox is cofounder and current treasurer of the Colorado Watershed Assembly, cofounder of Trees, Water, and People (a targeted watershed grants intermediary chosen in the second round), and former executive director of the Potomac Conservancy; EPA staff, interview, March 17, 2006; EPA, *EPA's Targeted Watershed Grants: 2005 Annual Report* (December 2005), pp. 56–61. The River Network website (www.rivernetwork.org/wsn.php# [November 20, 2008]) provides the most current data on new state networks preparing to join.

23. EPA staff, interview, March 17, 2006; Wendy Wilson and Pat Muñoz, *Sustainable Financing for Watershed Groups,* Watershed Academy live webcast, March 22, 2006 (www.cluin.org/conf/tio/owsusfund_032206/ [November 22, 2007]); Bill Jarocki, Amy Williams, and Lee Napier, *Plan2Fund: A Tool to Organize Your Watershed Funding,* Watershed Academy live webcast, February 15, 2006 (www.clu-in.org/conf/tio/owplan2fund_021506/ [November 22, 2007]). Jarocki and Williams are with the Environmental Finance Center at Boise State University; Napier is deputy director of community development, Grays Harbor County (Wash.) Department of Public Services. See also Tim Jones and Dan Nees, "Watershed Financing: Moving beyond Grants," Watershed Academy live webcast, October 17, 2007 (www.clu-in.org/conf/tio/owwtrfin_101707/ [November 22, 2007]). Jones is with the EPA, and Nees, the World Resources Institute.

24. Fox, interview.

25. Ibid.; Firehock, interview; EPA staff, interview, March 17, 2006. Firehock also attended the headquarters meeting.

26. DeWitt John, *Civic Environmentalism: Alternatives to Regulation in States and Communities* (Washington: CQ Press, 1994).

27. Firehock, interview; Firehock is a former director (1985–97) of Save Our Streams program of the Izaak Walton League of America.

28. Hanmer, interview; EPA staff, telephone interview, December 7, 2005; Firehock, interview. On the relative importance of EPA and other federal agency funding for building the field of volunteer monitoring, see Eleanor Ely, "Where Funding for Volunteer Monitoring Comes From," *Volunteer Monitor* 5, no. 2 (1993) (www.epa.gov/volunteer/news letter/volmon05no2.pdf [December 8, 2008]); and Alice Mayio, "Current Clean Water Act Funding for Volunteer Monitoring," in the same issue, both available at the Office of Wetlands, Oceans, and Watersheds website (www.epa.gov/owow/monitoring/volunteer/ newsletter/volmon05no2.pdf [November 20, 2008]). Funds from the EPA have been provided through the Clean Water Act, sections 314 (Clean Lakes Program), 319 (nonpoint-source grant program), 320 (National Estuary Program), and several other sections. The national weather service also served as a long-standing model of citizen monitoring.

29. Seba Sheavly, telephone interview, September 21, 2005; Firehock, interview; EPA staff, interview, December 7, 2005. I have also examined conference proceedings and participant lists of the EPA-sponsored national volunteer monitoring conferences. See, for instance, the one facilitated by the Izaak Walton League, *Building Partnerships in the Year of Clean Water: Proceedings of the Third National Citizen's Volunteer Water Quality Monitoring Conference* (EPA, Office of Water, September 1992). See also the National Water Quality Monitoring Council website (http://acwi.gov/monitoring [November 20, 2008]) for its conference proceedings.

30. EPA staff, interview, December 7, 2005. Over time, the growth of volunteer monitoring outpaced the EPA's capacity to track numbers and activities accurately. For the National Directory of Volunteer Environmental Monitoring Programs, as well as a selection of citizen monitoring guides published in conjunction with the EPA, see the Office of Wetlands, Oceans, and Watersheds website (www.epa.gov/owow/monitoring/volunteer/ [November 20, 2008]).

31. Eleanor Ely, telephone interview, December 12, 2005, and follow-up e-mail, December 30, 2005. Ely was the editor of *Volunteer Monitor* at the time. I have examined issues from the *Volunteer Monitor* dating back to its inception. On the general concept of "street science" that melds local community and professional scientific knowledge, see Jason Corburn, *Street Science: Community Knowledge and Environmental Health Justice* (MIT Press, 2005), discussed in chapter 2.

32. Sheavly, interview; EPA staff, interview, December 7, 2005. See Ronald L. Ohrel Jr. and Kathleen M. Register, *Volunteer Estuary Monitoring: A Methods Manual*, 2d ed. (Washington: Ocean Conservancy, 2002). This manual builds upon the 1993 edition developed by Nina A. Fisher. Independent evaluations by internationally recognized oceanographic institutions in several estuaries have shown that water quality data collected through volunteer monitoring and shared through networked arrangements are of equal quality to that collected by state agencies.

33. EPA staff, interview, December 7, 2005. See also EPA, Office of Wetlands, Oceans, and Watersheds, Assessment and Watershed Protection Division, *Elements of a State Water*

Monitoring and Assessment Program (March 2003); EPA, *The Volunteer Monitor's Guide to Quality Assurance Project Plans* (1996); and Elizabeth Herron and others, *Building Credibility: Quality Assurance and Quality Control for Volunteer Monitoring Programs,* National Facilitation Project, Factsheet VI (U.S. Department of Agriculture, Cooperative State Research Education Extension Service, Volunteer Water Quality Monitoring, December 2004).

34. Danielle Donkersloot, telephone interview, December 13, 2005. Donkersloot was volunteer monitoring coordinator with the New Jersey Department of Environmental Protection at the time of the interview. See also Eleanor Ely, "Using Volunteer Data at NJDEP: A Tiered Approach," *Volunteer Monitor* 16, no. 1 (2004): 1–6; and the New Jersey program's website (www.state.nj.us/dep/wms/bfbm/vm/index.html [November 20, 2008]).

35. See Ruth Anne Hanahan and Caitlin Cottrill, *A Comparative Analysis of Water Quality Monitoring Programs in the Southeast: Lessons for Tennessee* (Knoxville: Tennessee Waters Resources Research Center, University of Tennessee, 2004); Julia Frost Nerbonne, "Volunteer Macroinvertebrate Monitoring as a Tool for Citizen Empowerment," Ph.D. dissertation, University of Minnesota at St. Paul, 2003; Julia Frost Nerbonne and Kristen Nelson, "Volunteer Macroinvertebrate Monitoring: Resource Mobilization and Comparative State Structures" (paper prepared for Panel on State-Managed Volunteer Monitoring Programs, National Water Quality Monitoring Council, National Monitoring Conference, Chattanooga, May 17–20, 2004).

36. Elaine Andrews, presentation to Engaging Youth in Environmental Action and Restoration, National Research and Strategy Conference, organized by Brandeis University and the University of Wisconsin at Madison, Boston, Mass., March 2, 2002; Elaine Andrews, telephone interview, February 21, 2002. Telephone interviews with Tom Martin, January 18 and February 21, 2002; Kristin Johnstad, January 17, 2002; Dawne Brevig, January 4, 2002; Sally Prouty, February 14, 2002; Lisa LaRocque, February 15, 2002; Atziri Ibanez, February 13, 2002; Bahrat Venkat, January 18, 2002; Scott Richardson, February 19, 2002; and Susan Seacrest, December 5, 2001. See also Elaine Andrews, Mark Stevens, and Greg Wise, "A Model of Community-Based Environmental Education," in *New Tools for Environmental Protection: Education, Information, and Voluntary Measures,* edited by Thomas Dietz and Paul C. Stern (Washington: National Academies Press, 2002), pp. 161–82; National Environmental Education Advisory Council, *Report Assessing Environmental Education in the United States and Implementation of the National Environmental Education Act of 1990,* report prepared for Congress (EPA, December 1996). At the time of the interviews, Martin was executive director of Earth Force (which absorbed the Global Rivers Environmental Education Network); Brevig was national director of YMCA Earth Service Corps; Prouty was president of the National Association of Service and Conservation Corps (now Corps Network); and LaRocque, executive director of Project del Rio; Ibanez was with the Academy for Educational Development; Venkat was a member of the Earth Force Youth Advisory Board; and Seacrest was president of the Groundwater Foundation. Johnstad is a former national director of YMCA Earth Service Corps, and Richardson a former curriculum chair of the National Council for Social Studies and director of curriculum development at Earth Force. I also draw upon their collective contributions, as well as those of others, to understanding environmental education networks at our national strategy conference.

37. Sheavly, interview. See the website of the Volunteer Water Quality Monitoring National Facilitation Project (www.usawaterquality.org/volunteer [November 21, 2008]), a

partnership of the U.S. Department of Agriculture's Cooperative State Research Education Extension Service and various land-grant colleges and universities. See also Hanahan and Cottrill, *A Comparative Analysis of Water Quality Monitoring Programs in the Southeast.* As of November 2007, the cooperative extension service sponsored some forty-nine volunteer monitoring programs, including several widely reputed to be among the most robust in the nation. Its project website also contains substantial research on the quality of volunteer monitoring.

38. See Steven A. Cohen, Thomas Ingersoll, and James Janis, "Institutional Learning in a Bureaucracy: The Superfund Community Relations Program," *National Conference on Uncontrolled Hazardous Waste Sites: Proceedings* (Washington: Hazardous Materials Control Research Institute, 1981), pp. 405–10; and ICF Incorporated, *Analysis of Community Involvement in Hazardous Waste Site Problems* (EPA, Office of Emergency and Remedial Response, 1981).

39. Robert T. Nakamura and Thomas W. Church, *Cleaning Up the Mess: Implementation Strategies in Superfund* (Brookings, 1993). On the flaws in the Superfund program design and administrative process from the point of view of citizen deliberation, see Ellison Folk, "Public Participation in the Superfund Cleanup Process," *Ecology Law Quarterly* 18 (1991): 173–221; and Marc Landy and Mary Hague, "The Coalition for Waste: Private Interest and Superfund," in *Environmental Politics: Public Costs and Private Rewards,* edited by Michael Greve and Fred Smith (New York: Praeger, 1992), pp. 67–87. More generally, see Landy, Roberts and Thomas, *The Environmental Protection Agency,* chapter 5; John Hird, *Superfund: The Political Economy of Environmental Risk* (Johns Hopkins University Press, 1994); and Daniel A. Mazmanian and David Morell, *Beyond Superfailure* (Boulder, Colo.: Westview, 1992).

40. Sonya Pennock, telephone interview, May 8, 2006. Pennock was regional community involvement coordinator for the EPA's Region 8.

41. Bruce Engelbert, telephone interview, September 14, 2005. See also EPA, Office of Emergency and Remedial Response, *Community Relations in Superfund: A Handbook* (Interim version 1988; final version 1992).

42. Robert T. Nakamura and Thomas W. Church, *Taming Regulation: Superfund and the Challenge of Regulatory Reform* (Brookings, 2003). See also Robert Hersh and Kris Wernstedt, "Land Use, Risk, and Superfund Cleanups: At the Nexus of Policy and Practice," *Public Works Management and Policy* 4, no. 1 (1999): 31–40. Round 1 of the reforms actually began in 1993, concurrently with legislative initiatives in Congress, and built upon recommendations of several task forces over the previous four years. The full-blown Round 2 reforms began in February 1995.

43. Folk, "Public Participation in the Superfund Cleanup Process," p. 217.

44. Pennock, interview; Suzanne Wells, telephone interview, September 14, 2005; Engelbert, interview. See EPA, Office of Solid Waste and Emergency Response, *Community Advisory Group Toolkit: For the Community* (September 1998), as well as the general *Superfund Community Involvement Toolkit* (www.epa.gov/superfund/community/toolkit.htm [November 21, 2008]). Both Wells and Engelbert were with the EPA Superfund Community Involvement and Outreach Branch at the time of the interviews; Wells was its chief.

45. John DeVillars, quoted in Jodi Perras, *Reinventing EPA New England: An EPA Office Tests Innovative Approaches to Environmental Protection* (Washington: NAPA, 2000), p. 14; Metzenbaum, "Measurement that Matters." Reinvention proceeded on many fronts at Region 1, including compliance assistance and targeted and flexible enforcement. It also

elicited a good deal of resistance internally, especially on enforcement, though environmental and business leaders alike proved generally enthusiastic.

46. Jim Murphy, personal interview, Boston, May 9, 2006. See also EPA, Office of the Regional Administrator, Region 1, *Evaluation Report on the Pine Street Barge Canal Coordinating Council, Burlington, VT: Lessons Learned from This Region 1 Community Advisory Group* (Boston, Mass.: EPA, Region 1, July 2000); and EPA, Office of the Regional Administrator, Region 1, *Community Update: Pine Street Barge Canal Superfund Site, Burlington, VT* (Boston Mass.: EPA, Region 1, January 2007).

47. For a comparative case study analysis that includes the relatively successful Industri-Plex site in Woburn, Mass., in Region 1, see Kris Wernstedt, "Devolving Superfund to Main Street: Avenues for Local Community Involvement," *Journal of the American Planning Association* 67, no. 3 (2001): 293–313.

48. The mission statement can be found on the TOSC website (www.toscprogram.org [November 20, 2008]), which also provides links to the regional centers and ongoing projects. See also Saradhi Balla, "Bringing High-Tech GIS Tools to Community Decisionmaking" (paper prepared for the EPA's 2005 Community Involvement Conference and Training, Buffalo, N.Y., July 14, 2005). Technical assistance grants are less restricted in terms of advocacy but cannot go to local groups that are affiliates of national organizations that may directly or indirectly predefine their agendas or decisions.

49. Murphy, interview; Pennock, interview; Wells, interview; Engelbert, interview; field observations at the 1998 (Boston), 2004 (Denver), and 2005 (Buffalo) EPA national community involvement conferences. See also Suzanne Wells, "Superfund's Community Involvement Program: Building on Our Past" (paper prepared for ECO-INFORMA 2001 conference, Public Policy and Due Process: Involving Stakeholders in Developing Environmental Solutions panel, Argonne, Ill. May 14–18, 2001); and the course brochure for Community Involvement University.

50. For background on the rise of the environmental justice movement, see Charles Lee, ed., *Proceedings of the First National People of Color Environmental Leadership Summit* (New York: United Church of Christ Commission for Racial Justice, 1992); Phil Brown, *Toxic Exposures: Contested Illnesses and the Environmental Health Movement* (Columbia University Press, 2007); Luke W. Cole and Sheila R. Foster, *From the Ground Up: Environmental Racism and the Rise of the Environmental Justice Movement* (New York University Press, 2000).

51. Environmental Law Institute, *Opportunities for Advancing Environmental Justice: An Analysis of U.S. EPA Statutory Authorities* (Washington, 2001); Environmental Law Institute, *A Citizen's Guide to Using Federal Environmental Laws to Secure Environmental Justice* (Washington, 2002), and its companion video, *Communities and Environmental Laws*. The development of these resources was funded by the EPA. See also Nicholas Targ, "The States' Comprehensive Approach to Environmental Justice," in *Power, Justice, and the Environment: A Critical Appraisal of the Environmental Justice Movement*, edited by David Naguid Pellow and Robert J. Brulle (MIT Press, 2005), pp. 171–84; NAPA, *Models for Change: Efforts by Four Sates to Address Environmental Justice* (Washington, June 2002), which includes among its recommendations building upon the experience of Superfund and brownfields programs in trust building through community involvement coordinators, full information sharing, and other mechanisms. See also the comprehensive

collection by Michael B. Gerrard and Sheila R. Foster, eds., *The Law of Environmental Justice: Theories and Procedures to Address Disproportionate Risk,* 2d ed. (Chicago: American Bar Association, 2008).

52. See Holly D. Gordon and Keith I. Harley, "Environmental Justice and the Legal System," in *Power, Justice, and the Environment,* edited by Pellow and Brulle, pp. 153–70; Lisa Schweitzer and Max Stephenson Jr., "Right Answers, Wrong Questions: Environmental Justice as Urban Research," *Urban Studies* 44, no. 2 (2007): 319–37; Christopher H. Foreman Jr., "The Civic Sustainability of Reform," in *Environmental Governance,* edited by Kettl, pp. 146–76; Evan J. Ringquist, "Environmental Justice: Normative Concerns, Empirical Evidence, and Government Action," in *Environmental Policy: New Directions for the Twenty-First Century,* edited by Norman J. Vig and Michael E. Kraft, 6th ed. (Washington: CQ Press, 2006), pp. 239–63; Cole and Foster, *From the Ground Up.*

53. National Environmental Justice Advisory Council (NEJAC), *Ensuring Risk Reduction in Communities with Multiple Stressors: Environmental Justice and Cumulative Risks/Impacts* (EPA, 2004). This report builds upon the EPA's far more technical *Framework for Cumulative Risk Assessment* (EPA, May 2003), as well as the Centers for Disease Control and Prevention's Racial and Ethnic Approaches to Community Health (REACH) 2010 program. See Centers for Disease Control and Prevention, *REACHing across the Divide: Finding Solutions to Health Disparities* (Atlanta, Ga.: U.S. Department of Health and Human Services, Centers for Disease Control and Prevention, 2007), as well as the REACH website (www. cdc.gov/reach/ [November 21, 2008]). See also the International City/County Management Association, *Righting the Wrong: A Model Plan for Environmental Justice in Brownfields Redevelopment* (Washington, 2002).

54. NEJAC, *Advancing Environmental Justice through Pollution Prevention* (EPA, 2003). Working within the multistakeholder policy forum of the advisory council, of course, has alerted movement leaders to some of the concerns of industry about how environmental justice is framed. See, for instance, Marasco Newton Group and others, *Moving towards Collaborative Problem Solving: Business and Industry Perspectives on Environmental Justice* (EPA, 2003).

55. Interviews, workgroup meetings, and panel discussions with Charles Lee, Denver, June 16, 2004; Washington, D.C., March 14, 2005; and Washington, D.C., May 23, 2006. See NEJAC, Waste and Facility Siting Subcommittee, *Environmental Justice, Urban Revitalization, and Brownfields: The Search for Authentic Signs of Hope; A Report on the Public Dialogues* (EPA, 1996); Federal Interagency Working Group on Environmental Justice, *Environmental Justice Collaborative Model: A Framework to Ensure Local Problem Solving* (EPA, 2002). See also K. A. Dixon, "Reclaiming Brownfields from Corporate Liability to Community Asset," in *Natural Assets: Democratizing Environmental Ownership,* edited by James K. Boyce and Barry G. Shelly (Washington: Island Press, 2003), pp. 57–76. For Lee's original report, see United Church of Christ Commission for Racial Justice, *Toxic Waste and Race in the United States* (New York, 1987). For a twenty-year update, see Robert D. Bullard and others, *Toxics Wastes and Race at Twenty: 1987–2007* (New York: United Church of Christ Justice and Witness Ministries, March 2007).

56. On the role of these environmental justice movement leadership networks, I draw upon the membership lists of the various NEJAC subcommittees; full and partial proceedings of NEJAC meetings; and interviews, presentations, and trainings by various environmental

justice leaders and community health practitioners and scholars: Mary Nelson, personal discussion and presentation, Denver, June 16, 2004, and presentation, Denver, November 16, 2005; Wilma Subra, Boston, Region 1 office (training via teleconference), May 12, 2005; Patricia Hynes, personal and group discussion and training, Boston, May 12, 2005; Swati Prakash, Boston (training via teleconference), May 12, 2005; Vernice Miller-Travis, Boston (training via teleconference), April 7, 2005; and Sue Briggum, Boston (training via teleconference), May 12, 2005. Nelson was with Bethel New Life, Subra was cochair of the NEJAC pollution prevention workgroup, Hynes was professor of environmental health at Boston University and a member of the Cumulative Risk/Impact Working Group of NEJAC; Prakash and Miller-Travis were with the West Harlem Environmental Action. Briggum, an industry representative on NEJAC, is with Waste Management Inc. See also Christopher Foreman Jr., *The Promise and Peril of Environmental Justice* (Brookings, 1999). For two analyses of environmental justice framing that would take it in more radical directions, see Robert Benford, "The Half-Life of the Environmental Justice Frame: Innovation, Diffusion, and Stagnation," in *Power, Justice, and the Environment*, edited by Pellow and Brulle, pp. 37–53; and Robert D. Bullard, "Environmental Justice in the Twenty-First Century," in *The Quest for Environmental Justice: Human Rights and the Politics of Pollution*, edited by Robert D. Bullard (San Francisco: Sierra Club Books, 2005), pp. 19–42.

57. EPA, Office of Environmental Justice, *Environmental Justice Small Grants Program: Emerging Tools for Local Problem Solving*, 2d ed. (2005). I have also examined the descriptions of all the small grants since their inception in 1994 and have benefited greatly from conversations with Marva King, who previously administered the program at the Office of Environmental Justice. See also EPA, Office of Environmental Justice, *Summary of Previous Grant Awards for Environmental Justice through Pollution Prevention* (1997); and Eastern Research Group, *Assessment of the U.S. EPA EJP2 Grant Program* (Arlington, Va.: August 2000).

58. Presentation and personal discussions with Mary Nelson, Denver, June 16, 2004. See Charles Lee, "Collaborative Models to Achieve Environmental Justice and Healthy Communities," in *Power, Justice, and the Environment*, edited by Pellow and Brulle, pp. 219–49. See also Cory Fleming and Katrena Hanks, *Not Business as Usual: Using Collaborative Partnerships to Address Environmental Justice Issues* (Washington: International City/County Management Association, 2004); Marva King, "Collaborative Program Effectiveness: Comparing Two Community Partnership Programs," Ph.D. dissertation, George Mason University, 2009, forthcoming; William Shutkin, *The Land That Could Be: Environmentalism and Democracy in the Twenty-First Century* (MIT Press, 2000), chapters 4–5; and William Shutkin, "Environmental Justice: Democracy, Public Health, and Community Development," Brandeis University, March 30, 2005, which examines the innovative role that community development corporations can play in environmental justice.

59. Jason Corburn, *Street Science: Community Knowledge and Environmental Health Justice* (MIT Press, 2005). The Office of Prevention, Pesticides, and Toxic Substances also funded the training of more than one thousand students from eight area schools in Greenpoint-Williamsburg to map polluting facilities, conduct environmental surveys, and engage the larger community in pollution prevention. See Eastern Research Group, *Assessment of the U.S. EPA EJP2 Grant Program*, pp. 46–47.

60. See EPA, Ecosystem Protection Workgroup, "Toward a Place-Driven Approach: The Edgewater Consensus on an EPA Strategy for Ecosystem Protection," March 1994;

and EPA, Office of Sustainable Ecosystems and Communities (OSEC), Policy and Coordination Division, "An Annotated Chronology of CBEP-Related Policy Milestones," November 1998. For the evolution of the ecosystem approach more broadly, see Hanna J. Cortner and Margaret A. Moote, *The Politics of Ecosystem Management* (Washington: Island Press, 1999), especially chapter 2, on the various scientific and professional streams leading up to this critical point of innovation at various agencies; and Richard O. Brooks, Ross Jones, and Ross A. Virginia, *Law and Ecology: The Rise of the Ecosystem Regime* (Burlington, Vt.: Ashgate, 2002), especially chapter 8.

61. DeWitt John, telephone interview, October 31, 2005. See DeWitt John, *Civic Environmentalism: Alternatives to Regulation in States and Communities* (Washington: CQ Press, 1994); NAPA, *Setting Priorities, Getting Results: A New Direction for the Environmental Protection Agency; A National Academy of Public Administration Report to Congress* (Washington, 1995); NAPA, *Resolving the Paradox of Environmental Protection: An Agenda for Congress, EPA, and the States* (Washington, September 1997); Landy, Roberts, and Thomas, *The Environmental Protection Agency,* chapter 10. On the National Civic League's extensive networks in the community-building field during these years, see Sirianni and Friedland, *Civic Innovation in America,* pp. 252–56.

62. Enterprise for the Environment, *The Environmental Protection System in Transition: Toward a More Desirable Future* (Washington: Center for Strategic and International Studies, 1997), which was published in collaboration with NAPA and the Keystone Center; President's Council on Sustainable Development, *Sustainable America: A New Consensus for Prosperity, Opportunity and a Healthy Environment for the Future* (February 1996); Debra Knopman, *Second Generation: A New Strategy for Environmental Protection* (Washington: Progressive Foundation, April 1996); Aspen Institute, *The Alternative Path: A Cleaner, Cheaper Way to Protect and Enhance the Environment* (Washington, 1996); Marian R. Chertow and Daniel C. Esty, *Thinking Ecologically: The Next Generation of Environmental Policy* (Yale University Press, 1997).

63. EPA, Ecosystem Protection Workgroup, "Toward a Place-Driven Approach," p. 3.

64. Gerald Filbin, telephone interview, September 12, 2005. Filbin was director of the Innovative Pilots Division at the Office of Policy, Economics, and Innovation, former director of OSEC, and OSEC team leader on the resource book. See EPA, Office of Policy, Planning, and Evaluation, *Community-Based Environmental Protection: A Resource Book for Protecting Ecosystems and Communities* (September 1997); EPA, Office of Policy, Economics, and Innovation, *Evaluation of Community-Based Environmental Protection Projects: Accomplishments and Lessons Learned* (March 2003), prepared under contract by Industrial Economics Inc.; Steven L. Yaffee and others, *Ecosystem Management in the United States: An Assessment of Current Experience* (Washington: Island Press, 1996).

65. Karen Hamilton, telephone interview, November 9, 2005; Ayn Schmit, telephone interview, November 9, 2005; Filbin, interview. Hamilton and Schmit were EPA Region 8's Ecosystem Protection Program staff members: Hamilton was chief of the Water Quality Unit, and Schmit was chief of the Resource Protection and Stewardship Unit. While at OSEC, Filbin oversaw (and provided me with a comprehensive list of) the national network of community-based environmental protection regional coordinators. See also Marc Alston, "Dispatches," *Grist Magazine,* January 19–23, 2004; Robbie Roberts, Region 8 administrator, Welcoming Remarks to the CARE National Training Workshop, Denver, November 15, 2005. I have also reviewed all issues of *Natural News* from fall 2000 to fall 2007.

66. Fox, interview; Richard Fox, "The Road Ahead for the Colorado Watershed Assembly: Protecting and Improving the Water Resources of Colorado," Colorado Watershed Assembly, 2005. I also reviewed the Colorado Watershed Assembly's *State of Colorado Watersheds* reports from 2004 to 2007. For an overview of the network, training, tools, and watershed plans, see the proceedings of the October 2007 Breckenridge conference (www. coloradowater.org/2007%20Conference [December 16, 2007]). Fox is also cofounder of Trees, Water, and People (a group based in Fort Collins but engaged more broadly in the American West, Mexico, and Latin America), which enabled the watershed assembly to work effectively at the state level within a relatively short period of time.

67. Amanda Tipton Bassow, telephone interview, September 21, 2005. See EPA, Office of Policy, Economics, and Innovation, *EPA's Framework for Community-Based Environmental Protection* (February 1999). Bassow was with the National Center for Environmental Innovation and a team member for the community-based environmental protection framework at OSEC. Hansen initially requested that OSEC develop a comprehensive community-based environmental protection framework in January 1997.

68. EPA, *EPA's Framework for Community-Based Environmental Protection,* pp. 18–19; italics in original. See DeWitt John and Marian Mlay, "Community-Based Environmental Protection: Encouraging Civic Environmentalism," in *Better Environmental Decisions: Strategies for Government, Businesses, and Communities,* edited by Ken Sexton and others (Washington: Island Press, 1999), pp. 353–76.

69. Filbin, interview; Bassow, interview; Engelbert, interview; quotation from Filbin, interview. See also OSEC, Policy and Coordination Division, "An Annotated Chronology of CBEP-Related Policy Milestones." The community-based environmental protection fund called for a $1 million set aside of regional geographic initiative funds to be supplemented by $500,000 from each of the four main national program offices: Air and Radiation; Water; Solid Wastes and Emergency Response; and Prevention, Pesticides, and Toxic Substances.

70. John, interview.

71. Patricia Bonner, telephone interview, October 10, 2005; Bonner was with the Office of Policy, Economics and Innovation. See also EPA, Office of Policy, Economics, and Innovation, Public Participation Policy Review Workgroup, *Engaging the American People: A Review of EPA's Public Participation Policy and Regulations with Recommendations for Action* (December 2000); and Rosemary O'Leary and Lisa B. Bingham, eds., *The Promise and Performance of Environmental Conflict Resolution* (Washington: Resources for the Future, 2003). San Diego became an early innovator on the environment partly because citizens had established a highly participatory process through their Health Systems Agency (mandated by the National Health Planning Act of 1974), and the National Science Foundation provided them with a Science for Citizens grant to conduct training workshops across the county. See Sirianni and Friedland, *Civic Innovation in America,* p. 147.

72. Bonner, interview; EPA, Public Participation Policy Review Workgroup, *Engaging the American People,* p. iv.

73. EPA, Office of Policy, Economics, and Innovation, *Public Involvement Policy of the U.S. Environmental Protection Agency* (May 2003), p. 4. The permanent administrators were Christine Todd Whitman (January 31, 2001, to June 27, 2003), Michael Leavitt (November 6, 2003, to January 25, 2005), and Stephen Johnson (beginning May 2, 2005). Johnson served as acting administrator for four months after Leavitt resigned to take over

the Department of Health and Human Services, and two other acting administrators served in the interim between Whitman and Leavitt.

74. Daniel Kemmis, *This Sovereign Land: A New Vision for Governing the West* (Washington: Island Press, 2001). See also Matthew McKinney and William Harmon, *The Western Confluence: A Guide to Governing Natural Resources* (Washington: Island Press, 2004).

75. Linda Kimble, personal discussion, Denver, November 16, 2005, and her formal presentation to the CARE National Training Workshop on that date; William Long, discussions, Buffalo and Niagara Falls, N.Y., July 13, 2005, as well as his workshop on large leadership campaigns in communities, Denver, November 16, 2005; Dennis O'Connor, discussion, Buffalo and Niagara Falls, N.Y., July 13, 2005. Kimble was director of the Cleveland Clean Air Century Campaign; Long, who specializes in community leadership development, served as director of the EPA's Center for Radon and Air Toxics, in the Indoor Environments Division, and as EPA program officer for the Cleveland project. O'Connor was with the EPA's indoor air office. See EPA team, *Cleveland Air Toxics Pilot Project,* cover memorandum, February 2003; Juliana E. Birkhoff, *Cleveland Air Toxics Pilot Project: Final Evaluation Report* (Washington: RESOLVE, 2008); EPA, "National Air Toxics Program: The Integrated Urban Strategy: Notices," *Federal Register* 64, no. 137 (Monday, July 19, 1999): 38706–740. See Sirianni and Friedland, *Civic Innovation in America,* pp. 120–22, on the South Baltimore partnership and Design for Environment industry network strategies.

76. Hank Topper, e-mail communications, July 29, 2006, and February 4, 2008; Larry Weinstock, discussions, various occasions throughout 2005–07, including the all-day CARE staff meeting that preceded the Second National CARE Training Workshop, Seattle, November 15, 2006. In that meeting, Weinstock characterized CARE as a form of "mass customization at the retail level," in contrast to wholesale environmental regulation. Topper was cochair of the CARE action team. See EPA, *Framework for Cumulative Risk Assessment* (May 2003); and NEJAC, *Ensuring Risk Reduction in Communities with Multiple Stressors.* Both documents build further upon the prestigious study by Paul C. Stern and Harvey V. Fineberg, eds., *Understanding Risk: Informing Decisions in a Democratic Society,* Report of the Committee on Risk Characterization, National Research Council (Washington: National Academies Press, 1996), which includes an important role for public deliberation in risk assessment.

77. Robert Brenner, "Telling the CARE Story," plenary address to the CARE National Training Workshop, Denver, November 15, 2005; personal discussions with Brenner before and after our joint panel (with Dan Kemmis, Charles Lee, and Mary Nelson of Bethel New Life and organized by Hank Topper), The New Role of Communities in Environmental Protection, EPA National Community Involvement Conference, Denver, June 16, 2004.

78. Field notes, Second Annual National CARE Training Workshop, Seattle, November 15–17, 2006. On the broad communities movement, see Sirianni and Friedland, *The Civic Renewal Movement.*

79. Charles Chase, telephone interview, June 7, 2008; personal conversations with Deldi Reyes, on leave from Region 8 to cochair CARE, Washington, D.C., May 19, 2008; neighborhood tour and roundtable discussions with HAND workgroup (Fernando Piñeda-Reyes, Charles Chase, and Lisa Bardwell, executive director of Front Range Earth Force), and Deldi Reyes and Diane Sanelli from Region 8; personal conversation with Dennis Creamer, CARE National Training Workshop, Denver, November 15, 2005, and his presentation to the Second Annual CARE National Training Workshop, Seattle, November 15, 2006.

80. Joyce Pisnanont, discussion, Denver, November 16, 2005, and her presentation, "Computerized Neighborhood Tracking (ComNET)," CARE National Training Workshop, Denver, November 16, 2005; Michael Davis, discussion, Denver, November 16, 2005, and his presentation to the Second Annual CARE National Training Workshop, Seattle, November 16, 2006; field notes at the WILD annual community meeting and one-on-one meetings with youth leaders, Seattle, November 14, 2006. Pisnanont was program manager for WILD (Wilderness Inner-City Leadership Development), and Davis was community programs manager for Seattle Public Utilities. See also Daniel B. Abramson, Lynn C. Manzo, and Jeffrey Hou, "From Ethnic Enclave to Multi-ethnic Community: Contested Identities and Urban Design in Seattle's Chinatown-International District," *Journal of Architectural and Planning Research* 23, no. 4 (2006): 341–60.

81. I draw upon my field observations at the all-day CARE staff meeting, Seattle, November 14, 2006, which had a candid discussion of work responsibilities and commitments, as well as my interviews, discussions, and observations in many other formal and informal settings. It should be noted, however, that as OSEC, staffed with many from the Office of Water, showed a clear tilt toward ecosystems, CARE initially demonstrated a tilt toward human health and had some difficulty getting commensurate engagement from watershed staff. A better balance has emerged, however, and a CARE cochair from the water office is set to assume a full leadership position in 2009. On the issue of overwork, one might take some consolation in the analysis of Michael T. Imperial, who notes in "Using Collaboration as a Governance Strategy: Lessons from Six Watershed Management Programs," *Administration and Society* 37, no. 3 (2005): 281–320, that "one of the important functions of collaborative organizations is to absorb the transaction costs associated with organizing, supporting, or conducting collaborative activities at the operational or policy-making level among network members" (p. 304).

82. Field observations at CARE training conferences, including CARE: Building Partnerships Session, April 7, 2005 (Region 1 offices, teleconference); CARE Training, May 12, 2005 (Region 1 offices, teleconference); CARE National Training Workshop, Denver, November 14–17, 2005; Second Annual CARE National Training Workshop, Seattle, November 15–17, 2006; EPA, *Third Annual CARE National Training Workshop in Atlanta, October 30–November 2, 2007* (Washington: December 2007), CD-ROM made available to all participants. I also draw upon several dozen project planning telephone calls and conferences with CARE cochairs and team members in 2004–07, as well as field observations at CARE headquarters team meetings, including CARE Team meeting, Washington, D.C., March 14, 2005; CARE Team strategy sessions, EPA National Community Involvement Conference, Buffalo, July 12–14, 2005; and CARE staff meeting, Seattle, November 14, 2006. For a window into the array of resources provided by the program, see especially the *CARE Community Resource Guide* at the EPA's CARE website (www.epa.gov/CARE [November 21, 2008]). See also King, "Collaborative Program Effectiveness." King has been a central figure in both the Office of Environmental Justice and CARE.

83. Here I draw upon discussions with the Centers for Disease Control and Prevention's Behavioral and Social Science Working Group during my workshop, Organizing Public Action and Directing Social Change toward Healthier Conditions for All: What Is the Civic Mission of Federal Agencies? sponsored by the National Center for Environmental Health, Decatur, Ga., January 11, 2008, as well as formal exchanges and informal conversations in Decatur on January 10–11, 2008, with Dr. Stephanie Bailey, chief of Public Health Practice,

Office of the Director; Stan Meiburg, former EPA Region 4 administrator, who is leading the EPA–Centers for Disease Control and Prevention partnership; Roger Bernier, senior adviser for scientific strategy and innovation, National Center for Immunization and Respiratory Diseases; Marilyn Metzler, cocoordinator, Social Determinants of Health Working Group; Bobbie Millstein, outgoing chair of the Behavioral and Social Science Working Group; and Meredith Reynolds, incoming chair of the same working group. See also EPA and Centers for Disease Control and Prevention–Agency for Toxic Substances and Disease Registry, *Memorandum of Understanding* (July 18, 2007). For a selection of the vast literature on civic and collaborative approaches to health promotion and healthy communities, see Sirianni and Friedland, *Civic Innovation in America,* chapter 4; Meredith Minkler, ed., *Community Organizing and Community Building for Health,* 2d ed. (Rutgers University Press, 2004); Barbara A. Israel, Eugenia Eng, Amy J. Schulz, and Edith A. Parker, eds., *Methods in Community-Based Participatory Research for Health* (San Francisco: Jossey-Bass, 2005).

84. For an important recent contribution to this larger debate, see Daniel J. Fiorino, *The New Environmental Regulation* (MIT Press, 2006), which draws especially upon reflexive law, sociopolitical governance, and policy learning.

85. EPA staff, interviews, March 14 and March 17, 2006. See EPA, Office of Inspector General, *Sustained Commitment Needed to Further Advance Watershed Approach: Evaluation Report* (September 21, 2005), chapter 2; EPA, Office of Water, *A Review of Statewide Watershed Management Approaches: Final Report* (April 2002); EPA, Office of Water, *National Water Program Guidance: Fiscal Year 2008,* section 3 (2007).

86. See Tomas M. Koontz and others, *Collaborative Environmental Management: What Roles for Government?* (Washington: Resources for the Future, 2004); Edward P. Weber, Nicholas P. Lovrich, and Michael Gaffney, "Collaboration, Enforcement, and Endangered Species: A Framework for Assessing Collaborative Problem-Solving Capacity," *Society and Natural Resources* 18, no. 8 (2005): 677–98.

87. Imperial and Hennessey, *Environmental Governance in Watersheds,* pp. 32, 154–61; EPA staff, interviews, March 17, 2006, and June 20, 2006. Despite many recognized advantages of the watershed approach among states, some have voiced skepticism in terms of federal regulatory nonalignment (such as total maximum daily loads, fragmented rules, and asynchronous timetables) and inadequate resources for hiring basin coordinators and building the capacity of multistakeholder teams and local watershed groups. In addition, there are major challenges linking state watershed programs to local government planning, zoning, and land-use authorities. Furthermore, point-source projects still make up 93 percent of Clean Water State Revolving Fund spending. It should, of course, be noted that permitting issues at the state and local level are also controversial for robust watershed restoration, as the National River Restoration Science Synthesis studies (cited in following note) demonstrate. See EPA, Office of Water, *A Review of Statewide Watershed Management Approaches.* Some of these issues are being addressed. On regulatory and watershed alignment, see also EPA, Office of Inspector General, *Sustained Commitment Needed to Further Advance Watershed Approach,* chapter 2; NAPA, *Taking Environmental Protection to the Next Level,* pp. 164, 167; Meridian Institute, "Final Report of the National Watershed Forum," Arlington, Va., June 27–July 1, 2001, pp. 39–40. For the general challenges of building trust among state, region, and headquarters staff, see Denise Scheberle, *Federalism and Environmental Policy: Trust and the Politics of Implementation,* 2d ed. (Georgetown University Press, 2004).

88. Emily S. Bernhardt and others, "Restoring Rivers One Reach at a Time: Results from a Survey of U.S. River Restoration Practitioners," *Restoration Ecology* 15, no. 3 (2007): 482–93, 490; Margaret Palmer and others, "River Restoration in the Twenty-First Century: Data and Experiential Knowledge to Inform Future Efforts," *Restoration Ecology* 15, no. 3 (2007): 472–81, 478. For the National River Restoration Science Synthesis database, see the organization's website (www.restoringrivers.org [November 21, 2008]) and related websites at partner universities. For regional-level results, see the companion articles in *Restoration Ecology* 15, no. 3 (2007).

89. Wilson and Muñoz, *Sustainable Financing for Watershed Groups.* See also NAPA, *Taking Environmental Protection to the Next Level*, p. 133.

90. EPA staff, interviews, December 12, 2005, March 17, 2006, and March 13, 2006; Fox, interview; Christine Olsenius, telephone interview, April 4, 2006. See also EPA, Chesapeake Bay Program, *Chesapeake Bay Watershed Assistance Network: Access to Federal Funds* (Annapolis, Md.: March 2007); EPA, Office of Inspector General, *Sustained Commitment Needed to Further Advance Watershed Approach,* chapter 3; Margaret A. Palmer and others, "Climate Change and the World's River Basins: Anticipating Response Options," *Frontiers in Ecology and the Environment* 6 (www.palmerlab.umd.edu/docs/Palmer_et_al_2007_Frontiers_Environ_Climate_change_rivers.pdf [November 20, 2008]); Meridian Institute, "Final Report of the National Watershed Forum"; William D. Leach and Neil W. Pelkey, "Making Watershed Partnerships Work: A Review of the Empirical Literature," *Journal of Water Resources Planning and Management* 127, no. 6 (2001): 378–85; Imperial and Hennessey, *Environmental Governance in Watersheds,* pp. 29, 146–47, 167.

91. On funding sources within the environmental justice movement based on survey data from local groups, see Robert J. Brulle and Jonathan Essoka, "Whose Environmental Justice? An Analysis of the Governance Structure of Environmental Justice Organizations in the United States," in *Power, Justice, and the Environment,* edited by Pellow and Brulle, pp. 205–18; Jo Marie Rios, "Environmental Justice Groups: Grassroots Movement or NGO Networks? Some Policy Implications," *Policy Studies Review* 17, nos. 2–3 (2000): 179–211. See also EPA, Office of Inspector General, *EPA Needs to Consistently Implement the Intent of the Executive Order on Environmental Justice* (March 1, 2004), p. 4; EPA, *Environmental Justice Small Grant Program Fact Sheet,* March 2004; Targ, "The States' Comprehensive Approach to Environmental Justice."

92. National Environmental Education Advisory Council, *Report to Congress II* (EPA, September 29, 2000). The trend lines for environmental education grants show a nearly uninterrupted increase through fiscal year 1998 and then an erratic but substantial decline, with fiscal year 2007 standing at 43 percent of the peak year (www.epa.gov/enviroed/grants/index.html [December 15, 2007]).

93. NAPA, *Taking Environmental Protection to the Next Level,* pp. 163, 164; NAPA, *environment.gov,* p. 192. See also NAPA, *Principles for Federal Managers of Community-Based Programs* (Washington, 1997).

94. Patricia Bonner, telephone interviews, April 11, 2007, and November 5, 2008; field notes, Champions of Participation Conference, Strengthening Public Engagement and Knowledge Sharing within and across Federal Agencies, Queenstown, Maryland, June 20, 2006, which resulted in an informal network of practitioners (FedNet); field notes from FedNet conference calls, March 30, June 26, and November 2, 2007. See EPA, *Working Together: An Introduction to Collaborative Decision Making* (2008), and U.S. Government

Accountability Office, *Natural Resource Management: Opportunities Exist to Enhance Federal Participation in Collaborative Efforts to Reduce Conflicts and Improve Natural Resource Conditions* (February 2008). It should be noted, of course, that current budget cuts across the EPA tend to make regional and media offices far more cautious about providing staff for CARE and similar programs.

95. Walter A. Rosenbaum, "Improving Environmental Regulation at the EPA: The Challenge in Balancing Politics, Policy, and Science," in *Environmental Policy,* edited by Vig and Kraft, pp. 169–92, quotations 174–75. See also Christopher McGrory Klyza and David Sousa, *American Environmental Policy, 1990–2006: Beyond Gridlock* (MIT Press, 2008), chapters 6–7; Donald F. Kettl, "Conclusion: The Next Generation," in *Environmental Governance,* edited by Kettl, pp. 177–90; and NAPA, *environment.gov,* p. 185.

96. National Advisory Council for Environmental Policy and Technology, *Everyone's Business: Working towards Sustainability through Environmental Stewardship and Collaboration* (EPA, March 2008), p. 1 and cover letter to administrator Stephen Johnson; italics in original. See also EPA Environmental Stewardship Staff Committee, *Everyday Choices: Opportunities for Environmental Stewardship,* technical report prepared by the Innovation Action Council (Washington: EPA, November 2005); personal discussions on the Innovation Action Council and National Advisory Council for Environmental Policy and Technology reports with Dennis O'Connor and Chris Tirpak at EPA headquarters, Washington, D.C., May 20, 2008.

Chapter Six

1. Alexander L. George and Andrew Bennett, *Case Studies and Theory Development in the Social Sciences* (MIT Press, 2005), chapter 12, quotation p. 281.

2. For some important critical reflections, see Iris Marion Young, *Inclusion and Democracy* (Oxford University Press, 2000); and Ian Shapiro, *The State of Democratic Theory* (Princeton University Press, 2003).

3. See Elaine Fagotto and Archon Fung, "Empowered Participation in Urban Governance: The Minneapolis Neighborhood Revitalization Program," *International Journal of Urban and Regional Research* 30, no. 3 (2006): 638–55; Edward Goetz and Mara Sidney, "Local Policy Subsystems and Issue Definition: An Analysis of Community Development Policy Change," *Urban Affairs Review* 32, no. 4 (March 1997): 490–512; Connie P. Ozawa, ed., *The Portland Edge: Challenges and Successes in Growing Communities* (Washington: Island Press, 2004); Mark R. Bello, "Urban Regimes and Downtown Planning in Portland, Oregon, and Seattle, Washington, 1972–1992," Ph.D. dissertation, Portland State University, 1993; Pradeep Chandra Kathi and Terry L. Cooper, "Democratizing the Administrative State: Neighborhood Councils and City Agencies," *Public Administration Review* 65, no. 5 (2005): 559–67; Juliet A. Musso and others, "Neighborhood Governance Reform and Networks of Community Power in Los Angeles," *American Review of Public Administration* 36, no. 1 (March 2006): 79–97; and Stephen Goldsmith, with Ryan Streeter, *Putting Faith in Neighborhoods: Making Cities Work through Grassroots Citizenship* (Noblesville, Ind.: Hudson Institute, 2002).

4. See Carmen Sirianni and Diana Schor, "City Government as Enabler of Youth Civic Engagement: Policy Designs and Implementation," in *Policies for Youth Civic Engagement,* edited by James Youniss and Peter Levine (Vanderbilt University Press, 2009).

5. See Wesley G. Skogan, *Community Policing: Can It Work?* (Belmont, Calif.: Wadsworth, 2004); David Weisburd and Anthony A. Braga, eds., *Police Innovation: Contrasting Perspectives* (Cambridge University Press, 2006).

6. See Samuel D. Brody, David R. Godschalk, and Raymond J. Burby, "Mandating Citizen Participation in Plan Making: Six Strategic Planning Choices," *Journal of the American Planning Association* 69, no. 3 (2003): 245–65.

7. See Craig W. Thomas, *Bureaucratic Landscapes: Interagency Cooperation and the Preservation of Biodiversity* (MIT Press, 2003); Jeanne Nienaber Clarke and Daniel C. McCool, *Staking Out the Terrain: Power and Performance among Natural Resource Agencies,* 2d ed. (State University of New York Press, 1996).

8. See Carmen Sirianni, Kirk Emerson, and Lisa Blomgren Bingham, "Collaborative Governance: Strategy for a New Administration," Obama '08 Urban Policy Committee, October 13, 2008. In this memo, we present three complementary initiatives, the first of which is to work through the deputy director for management at the Office of Management and Budget, in conjunction with one designated assistant secretary within each federal department and independent agency, who would be responsible for initiatives of the sort that I propose here for the more ambitious Office of Collaborative Governance. The deputy director for management would report periodically to the cabinet, and the president would hold cabinet members accountable for progress, as he himself uses his powers of the bully pulpit to catalyze collaborative engagement and governance at all levels of the federal system. Should this arrangement prove productive, one could imagine the proposed functions of a collaborative governance office remaining here. Our two other proposals in this memo are a presidential commission on collaborative governance to help address the urgent issue of generational renewal of the public service, but on robust civic foundations, and an independent national campaign for leadership development that would help draw newly engaged activists from the 2008 presidential campaign, especially those with significant new relational and network organizing skills, to various nonpartisan associations involved in collaborative problem solving and shared governance. On the larger contours of the crisis in public service, see especially Paul C. Light, *The New Public Service* (Brookings, 1999); and Paul C. Light, *A Government Ill Executed: The Decline of the Federal Service and How to Reverse It* (Harvard University Press, 2008), chapter 5.

9. Specific agencies, of course, would aim to draw national advocacy organizations and other organized stakeholders into the architecture of collaborative governance. For instance, should the Sierra Club revitalize its volunteer leadership training in ways that build upon the Harvard–Sierra Club Leadership Development Project, which stressed moving to relational and collaborative team leadership and tapping significant moral resources, one can imagine a much more robust melding of effective advocacy and collaborative governance, two streams within the Sierra Club that typically do not converge. See Marshall Ganz and Ruth Wageman, *Sierra Club Leadership Development Project: Pilot Project Report and Recommendations* (Harvard University, May 2008); and Carmen Sirianni and Lewis A. Friedland, *Civic Innovation in America* (University of California Press, 2001), p. 134, on collaborative approaches to ecosystem restoration in many local chapters.

10. Beth Simone Noveck, *Wiki Government: How Technology Can Make Government Better, Democracy Stronger, and Citizens More Powerful* (Brookings, 2009), chapter 7. Noveck envisions the chief technology officer working with a corps of civic innovators and, of course, is not arguing that he or she function as the sole chief democracy officer. Her

analysis of deliberative stakeholder participation in regulatory rulemaking through new technologies can also be extended to the design process of the overall architecture of collaborative governance in any given agency.

11. Lisa Blomgren Bingham, "Collaborative Governance: Emerging Practices and the Incomplete Legal Framework for Citizen and Stakeholder Voice," *Hastings Annual Law Review* (SSRN-id1162409.pdf [November 23, 2008]). The National Academy of Public Administration has also expressed interest in a thorough review of federal regulations on public participation to help move toward a more productive framework for collaborative governance.

12. Social entrepreneurship can hardly be a substitute for transforming culture and capacity in public agencies, though it can be an important complement, especially those forms that engage people as active and productive citizens, as some clearly do. Unfortunately, much of the literature on social entrepreneurship does not specify how and whether citizens with capacities and powers for sustained democratic action are key to the much vaunted, yet often poorly demonstrated, "pattern-breaking change." Thus any planned government investment in establishing a network of social entrepreneurship funds or investment banks ought to be subject to the test of marginal returns and opportunity costs compared with investments in federal, state, and local government agency capacity to partner with citizens. Would $100 million of new federal spending, funneled through social investment banks and spread across youth development start-ups headed by recently minted Master of Business Administration degrees, yield a greater return than investing that same amount through Housing and Urban Development for emerging city-based systems of youth civic engagement, modeled on proven designs such as Hampton or San Francisco? Would the Office of Environmental Justice or the Community Action for a Renewed Environment program at the EPA (in partnership with the Centers for Disease Control and Prevention) not be able to empower more communities to address environmental health risks with $100 million for their collaborative grants than social entrepreneurship investment bankers with the same federal money? See Paul Light's parallel argument for "insourcing" versus "outsourcing" in *A Government Ill Executed,* p. 236; and Sirianni and Schor, "City Government as Enabler of Youth Civic Engagement: Policy Designs and Implementation." For more general analyses, see Paul C. Light, *The Search for Social Entrepreneurship* (Brookings, 2008); Alex Nichols, ed., *Social Entrepreneurship: New Models of Sustainable Social Change* (Oxford University Press, 2006); and Steven Rathgeb Smith and Michael Lipsky, *Nonprofits for Hire: The Welfare State in the Age of Contracting* (Harvard University Press, 1993).

13. Sirianni and Friedland, *Civic Innovation in America,* analyzes new models in the context of learning from and beyond 1960s "maximum feasible participation" fostered by the federal government.

14. See, for instance, Paul C. Light, *Sustaining Innovation: Creating Nonprofit and Government Organizations That Innovate Naturally* (San Francisco: Jossey-Bass, 1998); Jean Philippe Deschamps, "Innovation and Leadership," in *The International Handbook of Innovation,* edited by Larisa V. Shavinina (Amsterdam; Boston: Elsevier Science, 2003), pp. 815–34; and Rosabeth Moss Kanter, *The Change Masters: Innovation and Entrepreneurship in the American Corporation* (New York: Simon and Schuster, 1983).

15. See Marc Landy, "Public Policy and Citizenship," in *Public Policy for Democracy,* edited by Helen Ingram and Steven Rathgeb Smith (Brookings, 1993), pp. 19–44; and chapter 2 in this volume. Of course, public agencies cannot do this alone. Political elites,

public pollsters, and media institutions also need to alter their own forms of "crafted talk" for more robust public deliberation to flourish. See Lawrence R. Jacobs and Robert Y. Shapiro, *Politicians Don't Pander: Political Manipulation and the Loss of Democratic Responsiveness* (University of Chicago Press, 2000); Daniel Yankelovich, *Coming to Public Judgment: Making Democracy Work in a Complex World* (Syracuse University Press, 1991); and Sirianni and Friedland, *Civic Innovation in America,* chapter 5, on civic journalism, which retains its relevance, though in the current media environment requires a new business model.

16. See, for instance, Arthur J. Naparstek and others, *HOPE VI: Community Building Makes a Difference* (U.S. Department of Housing and Urban Development, February 2000); Avis Vidal and others, *Lessons from the Community Outreach Partnership Center Program* (Washington: Urban Institute, 2002); Office of Policy Development and Research, *Empowering Local Communities through Leadership Development and Capacity Building* (U.S. Department of Housing and Urban Development, October 2007); and YouthBuild USA, *Leadership Development at a YouthBuild Program* (Somerville, Mass., n.d.).

17. See Bobby Milstein, *Hygeia's Constellation: Navigating Health Futures in a Dynamic and Democratic World* (Atlanta, Ga.: Centers for Disease Control and Prevention, 2008); National Association of County and City Health Officials, *Protocol for Assessing Community Excellence in Environmental Health: A Guidebook for Local Health Officials* (Washington, May 2000); Sirianni and Friedland, *Civic Innovation in America,* chapter 4.

18. National 4-H Council, *The National Conversation on Youth Development in the 21st Century: Final Report* (Chevy Chase, Md., 2002), p. 9; National 4-H Council, *Creating the Future: The Story of 4-H's National Conversation on Youth Development in the 21st Century* (Chevy Chase, Md., 2003); Scott J. Peters and Margo Hittelman, eds., *We Grow People: Profiles of Extension Educators* (New York: Cornell University Cooperative Extension, 2003).

19. Financial Literacy and Education Commission, *Taking Ownership of the Future: The National Strategy for Financial Literacy* (Washington, 2006), p. xi. See also Elizabeth Johnson and Margaret S. Sherraden, "From Financial Literacy to Financial Capability among Youth," *Journal of Sociology and Social Welfare* 34, no. 3 (2007): 119–45; and Jonas Parker, "Financial Literacy Education as an Asset-Building Strategy: The Potential of Community Action Agencies," Ph.D. dissertation, Brandeis University, 2009, forthcoming.

20. See, for instance, Richard H. Thaler and Cass R. Sunstein, *Nudge: Improving Decisions about Health, Wealth, and Happiness* (Yale University Press, 2008); Mark Zandi, *Financial Shock: A 360-Degree Look at the Subprime Mortgage Implosion, and How to Avoid the Next Financial Crisis* (Upper Saddle River, N.J.: FT Press, 2009); and Gregory D. Squires, ed., *Organizing Access to Capital: Advocacy and the Democratization of Financial Institutions* (Temple University Press, 2003).

21. Field notes, Civic Engagement Symposium, YMCA of the USA, Rosemont, Ill., October 8–10, 2002. See Cynthia Gibson and Peter Levine, *The Civic Mission of Schools* (New York: Carnegie Corporation, 2003); Thomas Ehrlich and Elizabeth Hollander, *Presidents' Fourth of July Declaration on the Civic Responsibility of Higher Education* (Providence, R.I.: Campus Compact, 1999), endorsed by the Presidential Leadership Colloquium convened by Campus Compact and the American Council of Education; Education Commission of the States, *Every Student a Citizen: Creating the Democratic Self* (Denver: Education Commission of the States, 2000); National League of Cities, *The Rise of Democratic Gover-*

nance: How Local Leaders Are Reshaping Politics for the 21st Century (Washington, 2006); National League of Cities, *Changing the Way We Govern: Building Democratic Governance in Your Community* (Washington, November 2006).

22. Estimates of the cost of universal service, some $60 billion or more annually, clearly show how far removed such ideas are from realistic civic investment strategies based on marginal returns and opportunity costs. While there are important philosophical issues at stake in this debate, it is critical that the national service lobby not function as just any other lobby in attempting to expand its programmatic reach and federal funding, without also confronting broader issues of federal investments in civic infrastructure and collaborative governance, or indeed without engaging in a far richer discussion of civic democracy than the service frame permits. For exchanges on different sides of the debate on universal service, see E. J. Dionne, Kayla Meltzer Drogosz, and Robert E. Litan, eds., *United We Serve: National Service and the Future of Citizenship* (Brookings, 2003); Will Marshall and Marc Porter Magee, eds., *The AmeriCorps Experiment and the Future of National Service* (Washington: Progressive Policy Institute, 2005); and Verna Gehring, ed., *Community Matters* (Lanham, Md.: Rowman and Littlefield, 2005).

23. Melissa Bass, "The Politics and Civics of National Service: Lessons from the Civilian Conservation Corps, VISTA, and AmeriCorps," Ph.D. dissertation, Brandeis University, 2004.

24. Abt Associates, *Serving Country and Community: A Longitudinal Study of Service in AmeriCorps; Early Findings* (Washington: Corporation for National and Community Service, December 2004); Leslie M. Anderson and Lara Fabiano, *The City Year Experience: Putting Alumni on the Path to Life-Long Civic Engagement* (Washington: Policy Studies Associates, January 2007); Anne Colby and others, *Educating Citizens: Preparing America's Undergraduates for Lives of Moral and Civic Responsibility* (San Francisco: Jossey-Bass, 2003); and Carmen Sirianni and Lewis A. Friedland, "The New Student Politics: Sustainable Action for Democracy," *Journal of Public Affairs* 7, no. 1 (2004): 101–23. It should be noted, of course, that the intermediaries mentioned above have diverse sources of funding, including from various federal agencies, state and local agencies, foundations, and (in some cases) business partnerships.

25. Alan Melchior, "The Growth of Service Learning in America," *Generator: Journal for Service Learning and Youth Leadership* 23, no. 2 (2005): 18–20, quotation p. 20. See also Alan Melchior and others, *Growth and Institutionalization of Service-Learning among Learn and Serve America Grant Recipients* (Waltham, Mass.: Brandeis University, Center for Youth and Communities, January 2003). As this study shows, local grant recipients in schools, school districts, community-based organizations, and higher education institutions credit their initial Learn and Serve America grants, even when of quite modest amounts of $10,000 or less, with helping them institutionalize service learning by enabling them to hire critical staff, attract other funding, and provide legitimacy to their efforts. More than three-quarters of those surveyed seven years after the first round of Learn and Serve America funding in 1994–95 still had service learning programs, including two-thirds of those without current grants. More than one-third had developed institution-wide programs (for example, whole-school or district-wide), and nearly a third more had relatively comprehensive programs covering whole grades, disciplines, or organizational programs. Most had developed a substantial network of community partners—often several dozen—as well as

substantial stakeholder support (school boards, superintendents, trustees) and a diversified set of funding sources, including nearly two-thirds that drew upon general operating funds, a clear sign of institutional commitment.

26. See, for instance, John Bridgeland and Alan Khazei, eds., *Service Nation Agenda* (Washington: Civic Enterprises, 2008).

27. See Kirk Emerson and Peter Murchie, "Collaborative Governance and Climate Change: Opportunities for Public Administration" (paper prepared for the Minnowbrook III conference, Maxwell School of Public Administration, Lake Placid, N.Y., September 6, 2008).

28. Kathryn Price, presentation at the national strategy conference Youth Development and Civic Engagement: Leveraging Innovation, Building a Movement, Boston, February 1–3, 2002.

Index